The Seinfeld Talmud:
A Jewish Guide to a Show About Nothing

Jarrod Tanny

The Seinfeld Talmud:
A Jewish Guide to a Show About Nothing

Jarrod Tanny

Academica Press
Washington~London

Library of Congress Cataloging-in-Publication Data is available.

Names: Tanny, Jarrod (author)
Title: The seinfeld talmud : a jewish guide to a show about nothing |
Tanny, Jarrod.
Description: Washington : Academica Press, 2023. | Includes
bibliographical references and index.
Identifiers: LCCN 2023940845 | ISBN 9781680536232 (hardcover)
| 9781680536249 (ebook) | 9781680536256 (paperback)

Advance Praise for The Seinfeld Talmud

"The inane escapades of some delusional Jews in a messy yeshivah that may or may not contain a chicken"
- Mark Twain

"Who knew the early rabbis were so obsessed with their shlongs?"
- Sigmund Freud

"If you are wondering why statehood eluded the Jews for 2000 years in exile, look no further than this text"
- Theodor Herzl

"Not for Jews only, a joy for goys"
- Nicholas II, Tsar of all the Russias

"Helped me pass the time in prison"
- Dr. Hannibal Lecter

"This is as good as anything my Father has written"
- Jesus of Nazareth

Contents

Preface

Introducing The Seinfeld Talmud

Are there degrees of coincidence?

Is it permissible to parallel park headfirst?

Is it poor hygiene to "double dip" a chip?

How long must you keep a greeting card before you can throw it out?

Why does Jerry's new girlfriend wear the exact same dress on every date?

Is it appropriate to say "God bless you" to a woman who sneezes if her husband does not?

If you named a kid Rasputin do you think that would have a negative effect on his life?

Did they have roommates in the Middle Ages?

Who leaves a country packed with ponies to come to a non-pony country?

Why do these stories seem to be little more than a list of things in a messy apartment, which may or may not contain a chicken?

For nine seasons, the *Seinfeld* gang engaged in argument and debate over such weighty matters of etiquette, leaving no stone unturned, no double dipped chip ignored, no exposed nipple on a greeting card unexamined.

But Jerry, George, Elaine, and Kramer were hardly the first to do this. In fact, they built their comedy around the sort of discussions we can find in the greatest collection of texts in the Jewish religion: The Babylonian Talmud.* Like the eminent Rabbis of ancient Israel and Babylon (Persia), the Seinfeld gang spend their days poring over the excruciating minutiae of every single event imaginable. *Seinfeld* is the Jewish Talmud of a new generation.

So I bring you the *The Seinfeld Talmud – Seinfeld* as analyzed by the Sages of the Near East who gave us the illustrious Talmud, which, depending on whom you ask, is either the most comprehensive body of Jewish law ever produced or thousands of pages about nothing.

---

* Although most foreign terms in this text translate to "penis," we have nevertheless included a comprehensive glossary at the back of the book. All words that can be found in the glossary are marked with * upon their first usage.

Although repulsed at first, especially by Kramer's erratic behavior, George's obsession with toilets, and Elaine's maladroit dancing, the Rabbis ultimately came to recognize their kinship with the *Seinfeld* gang, four fellow sages who also lived in a fantasy world musing over the quotidian rather than working for a living. In the interest of posterity, the Rabbis decided to apply their wit and wisdom to painstakingly analyzing *Seinfeld*, episode by episode, from Bubble Boy to Babu Bhatt, architecture to marine biology, Jujyfruits to Junior Mints. The masters of Judaic Law were on a quest to master *Seinfeld*'s domain. And they left no stone unturned, no double dipped chip ignored, no exposed nipple on a greeting card unexamined.

Season 1

The Rabbis Discover They Have Embarrassing Relatives in New York

The Seinfeld Chronicles

Much like American audiences, the Rabbis of yore were slow to take to *Seinfeld*. Few in the Yeshivahs* of Yavneh* or Pumbedita* left the synagogue, the shvitz,* or the study hall to tune in to what was a rather mediocre show about four self-absorbed possibly Jewish New Yorkers who sat around discussing nothing all day. It is said that Rav Sheshet in the name of Rav Huna even accused Larry David and Jerry Seinfeld of cultural appropriation, because poring over the excruciating minutiae of daily life was the Talmud's greatest contribution to western civilization.

"They're stealing our material," kvetched* Rav Sheshet during the first episode, titled "The Seinfeld Chronicles," after hearing Jerry and George argue whether you can over-wash and over-dry clothing.

It's more like they are stealing our method of debate, not the content, mused Bar Kappara.

Moses received this method of debate – our Oral Torah* – at Sinai from the Lord, said Resh Lakish. The method is the content, and the content is the method, and it is all Torah.* *Seinfeld* is guilty of plagiarizing God.

Is "Thou shalt not plagiarize God" among the Commandments? asked Rabbah.

Irrelevant, said Resh Lakish. On such matters we defer to *The Elements of Style* by Strunk and White, and *How to Talk Jewish* by Jackie Mason.

Plagiarism, plagiarism, plagiarism! said the Sages in unison.

Besides, everyone knows you can't over-dry clothing, said Rav Pappa. Dry is dry. Otherwise the Israelites would have been over-dried in the scorching heat of the Sinai Desert, leaving discharge from their bleeding noses all over the landscape. And we would be over-drying our bodies during our daily shvitz.

Yet we leave the dry-shvitz wet all over, not dry, noted Rav Kahana. Perhaps even over-wet since one should not become wet in a dry sauna in the first place.

What's the deal with wet dry saunas? chuckled Shimon ben Pazi, adopting the best Jewy Seinfeldesque intonation of a mediocre stand-up comedian he could muster. What's up with that? Are you with me fellow Yids?

It's because sweat is wet, said Abba the Surgeon, one of the few sages present who did not receive his diploma from a gaggle of non-accredited sweaty rabbis.

Oh boy, now it sounds as if we are stealing David and Seinfeld's material, said Rav Sheshet. Next thing we know Pazi will be feeding us jokes about airline peanuts and shopping carts with broken wheels.

So should we continue watching this show about nothing? asked Resh Lakish. It sounds like this David and this Seinfeld may be our progeny, or at the very least distant meshpuchah.*

Absolutely not, said Rav Huna. We have more important things to discuss. For instance, a plate: how do you know when it is time to throw it out? Do the Houses of Hillel and Shammai agree on it? Or, how about: would you rather go out with the blind or the deaf?

If I were deaf I'd rather go out with Shammai, said Shimon ben Pazi. That's a no-brainer; his aphorisms suck rocks.

Listening to Shammai drone on all day is certainly a nightmare, mused Resh Lakish.

The Rabbis thus abandoned Seinfeld, confident they would never look back and have no regrets.

But it is said that during Season 1 Episode 4, "Male Unbonding" the Sages of Babylon were aghast when they heard Jerry announce he was travelling to Persia because "Hezbollah has invited me to perform. You know, it's their annual terrorist luncheon. I'm gonna do it in Farsi." Accordingly, the Rabbis of Pumbedita convened an emergency meeting on the banks of the Euphrates, hoping to catch sight of said terrorist luncheon.

Male Unbonding

GEMARAH:*

Fellow Sages, said Rav Huna, the Dean of the Yeshivah at Pumbedita, how is it that Reb Seinfeld, a Member of the Tribe, agreed to do a show in Persia and did not invite any of us?

He should have at least alerted the Babylonian Exilarch, said Bar Kappara. This is just bad form. Some Jew.

We could have put him up for the night, said Rav Huna. Surely bunking with sweaty rabbis in a dilapidated Yeshivah is better than bunking with sweaty terrorists in a cave?

At the very least, I should have been invited, insisted Rav Pappa, who was a bit of a player, and because of his numerous trysts with the fair maidens of Persia had acquired fluency in Farsi. I should have been the goodwill rabbinic ambassador.

Keep it in your pants, admonished Resh Lakish. Hezbollah's luncheons are gender segregated. You are far more likely to meet Salman Rushdie than get a date.

Still, said Rav Sheshet. Where are our invitations?

Perhaps Postal Employee Newman lost our invitations in the mail, suggested Resh Lakish.

The Sages adjourned, vowing never to miss a *Seinfeld* episode again.

The Stock Tip

GEMARAH:

Fellow Sages, said Rav Huna convening the meeting. This episode raises some perplexing questions.

I'll say, replied Resh Lakish. George "I'm Disturbed, I'm Depressed, I'm Inadequate" Costanza investing in the stock market? Did he not just last week in "Male Unbonding" bring a jar of pennies to the bank to convert into bills, which was rejected by the teller? George would never invest in the stock market, neither in New York, nor in Babylon. Not even his 50,000 pennies.

I disagree, said Rav Pappa. Maybe he took out a loan. And the Babylonian real estate market is booming. The Rabbis fleeing the Roman Empire are building all those dachas along the Euphrates. George is in real estate. He would know how to profit.

Then why does he not invest in Kramerica's revolving tie startup? Surely that is a sounder investment, insisted Rav Sheshet.

And once again, I disagree, said Rav Pappa. Kramer hangs out with anarchists whom he met at a rock concert. They don't wear ties. Not much of a business, if you ask me.

Abba the Surgeon, known for his elephant infirmary, curtly interrupted: are we not missing the elephant in the room? Did Elaine not try to hire Jerry, a second-rate Jewish comedian to poison her lover's cats? And you Rav Pappa, have the temerity to talk about anarchists in ties? We should be discussing their callous disregard for our feline friends.

Sorry, but I find anarchists far more topical, than a couple of dead cats, replied Rav Pappa. And Kramerica industries has great promise, even if George thought otherwise.

You're cruel Pappa, replied Abba the Surgeon. Was there not recently an ox in your house with a toothache, which "went inside, and broke the lid of a utensil, and drank the liquor inside and was cured?" (Bava Kamma 35a:5). You Pappa are a lover of oxen, but you're a hater of cats. How can you be so pitiless? You are a very very bad man.

Pappa is a very very bad man, said the Sages in unison.

A new student, citing Rabbi Yehudah added "any animal whose stones are bruised, or crushed, or torn, or cut you shall not sacrifice to the Lord" (Leviticus 22:24). "All of these blemishes are referring to the animal's testicles; this is the statement of Rabbi Yehudah." (Kiddushin 25b)

The Rabbis concurred that Rav Pappa must have cured his stricken ox of testicular torsion, not of a toothache and were now convinced that he was fantasizing about hiring Kramer and his band of anarchists to liquidate the lover's cats. But they were unaware that this was just the first of many "altercations" Elaine Marie Benes would have with members of the animal kingdom.

The class subsequently adjourned, admittedly perplexed as to why their discussion about investing in Petramco Corp, alleged inventor of "the robot butcher," degenerated into a quarrel over blemished testicles. Zutra the Mohel* offered a sheepish smile and slunk out of the room, suspecting that Jewish genitalia would be a contentious topic at many future meetings. And he also knew it would be good for his circumcision business.

Season 2

The Rabbis Discover Poland and Learn of its Celebrated Ponies

The Ex-Girlfriend

GEMARAH:

Before the Rabbis even finished their morning shvitz, with the melodic sound of Adon Olam* still echoing in the Yeshivah halls, Rav Huna threw himself into a debate that had yet to happen.

Rav Huna (in his best Seinfeldesque voice) exclaimed: What's the deal with all these books? Why do people want them all around their house? Are these trophies of some kind? And why does George want them back after reading them?

The New Student (see "The Stock Tip," s1e5) added (allegedly) in the name of Rabbi Yehudah (who denied all involvement): doesn't George only read comic books and the sports page? how can George have read *Moby-Dick*? Didn't the great Vilna Gaon* admit to not having finished it, even with his peyos* tied to the ceiling, his feet soaking in ice cold water, and a chastity belt enveloping his beytzim?*

Hillel, son of Gamaliel III immediately interjected, commanding his Yichus,* his grandfather Judah the Prince: Again with the testicles. What's with you and beytzim? Every shiur* you bring them up. Who is this new student? Please stick to the subject at hand. It is George and Moby Dick. I do not see how you drift from Moby Dick to testicles.

What is a Mobydick? asked the probing Shimon ben Pazi. I've heard of Pesachdick* and Shabbosdick,* but not Mobydick.

The sages left the question hanging as someone asked SIRI, and learned that "Moby" in fact means "large."

Ah, the Sages nodded in unison.

Rav Sheshet took advantage of this rare moment of silence to show off his wisdom and added: Torah was given to Moses at Sinai, *Moby-Dick* was given to

Melville in New York. There were as many Israelites in the Big Apple as there were at Sinai, perhaps the texts are related?

If only the Moby Dick ate the Golden Calf who ate the goat who ate the dog that bit the cat that ate the goat at Sinai, lamented Rav Pappa.

That ate the old lady who swallowed the fly, added the New Student.

Not so, interjected Resh Lakish: Moby Dick swallowed George because he refused his mission from the Lord to break up with his shiksa* girlfriend from Nineveh, Mississippi. She was wicked, having meditated with Moby Dick in the mikvah.* God sent the great beast into New York Harbor to swallow George.

And, he hurt his back, in the belly of the great fish, added Rabbah, the sea being angry that day my friends. Is that not why he had to visit the doctor?

But a chiropractor is not a real doctor, insisted the New Student, George should not have even paid him the $35. Restitution! There's a principle at stake. "Yeah, doctor!"

And you are not a real rabbi, Mar* New Student, shrieked Rav Huna, who rarely lost his temper. Who even let you in the building?

I'm hear for the jokes, the new student replied. Am I not funny? I also have material about changing lanes in traffic, waiting rooms, and supermarket cantaloupe. You know what they say, "Lucky in love, unlucky with fruit."

Your act is just so much fluff, Hillel Son of Gamliel III replied. We took a gamble with you, and you are what Jerry Seinfeld called unreturnable fruit. We neither want to shvitz nor daven* with you. Please take your cantaloupe and your beytzim and leave the building.

Having purged the academy of the troublemaker, the Amoraim* disbanded, headed to Yossel's fruit store for some fresh cantaloupe, and geared up for "The Pony Remark," the Pride of Krakow.

The Pony Remark

MISHNAH:*

Rabban Gamliel: So was Manya telling the truth?
Rabbi Tarfon: No she was a liar, like the old lady in *Titanic*.
Rabbi Akivah: That was the boat that got rammed by Noah's Ark.
Yohanan ben Zakkai: Yes, the two ponies perished, leaving Manya and Rose to float to America on a piece of wood.
Jose the Galilean: That's a shame.

GEMARAH:

Chevreh,* said Bar Kappara in the name of Rav Huna convening the meeting, now that we've ejected Mar New Student the Comedian for his ill-timed testicle jokes we can get back to business and discuss what's important. No more shlongs* and beytzim.*

I agree, said Abba the Surgeon, we need to talk about ponies.

What is a pony? asked Shimon ben Pazi

It is a kind of compact car, suggested Rav Ashi, as Jerry explained it.

No, It is a small horse, replied Abba the Surgeon, who had treated many in his elephant infirmary after the ponies had been trampled by the elephants. Apparently these ponies are the pride and joy of Poland.

What is a Poland? asked Shimon ben Pazi.

It is a place, said Rabbah, filled with plenty of living space, ponies, and inhabitants who do not know how to change a light bulb.

Or hang a picture on the wall without moving the wall, added Rav Pappa who had inherited his father's wit and a tattered joke book.

Please refrain from ethnic jokes, Pappa, said Bar Kappara. The question at hand is whether Jerry is guilty of homicide. Did Jerry kill Manya from Poland?

I think he did, said Resh Lakish. He spoke lashon harah* about her pony. Has Jerry even been to Poland? What kind of sicko does that to an immigrant?

I agree, said Rav Pappa. When Avraham Avinu* went to the Hittites and said, "I am a stranger in a strange land" (Genesis 23:4) did they reply with "we hate you because you have a horse?" Abraham would have expired on the spot, having barely recovered from his self-inflicted circumcision, when the Lord provided him nothing but a cleaver, a bandage, and a poorly drawn anatomical chart. The Hittites welcomed him, notwithstanding Abraham's significant shrinkage.

Yes, it is remarkable Abraham was even able to ride a horse after that, lamented Resh Lakish, who then turned and gave Zutra the Mohel the crook-eye.

I disagree, said Hanina ben Pappa in the name of Rav Azrael ben Gargamel. Jerry made every effort to appease Manya, even while being smothered by Uncle Leo. He humiliated himself, revealing that sugar makes his ankles swell up, leaving him unable to dance. Manya had the chutzpah* to ask if that was a joke.

And if it was a joke, she didn't even laugh, conceded Resh Lakish. First the shiksa from Mississippi, and now a Pole tells Jerry his comedy stinks.

Manya is clearly not a nice person, concluded Rav Huna.

Perhaps this is why she was chased out of Poland without her pony, offered Abba the Surgeon. Why else would she leave a country packed with ponies to come to a non-pony country?

Either that or she didn't know how to change a lightbulb, offered Rabbah.

Thus it was written: the Sages exculpated Jerry of the homicide charge and indicted Poland and its formerly pony owning immigrants.

The Jacket

GEMARAH:

Hillel II, grandson of Gamliel IV and creator of the Hebrew calendar convened the shiur, claiming rank because he was the only one who remembered to switch his clock from Daylight Savings Time to Jewish Wholesale Time.

Chevreh, said Hillel II, finally an episode we can relate to. It is all about The Master of the House doling out the charm and ready with a handshake.

But why is Costanza, Lord of the Idiots, the Master of the House? Asked Resh Lakish. He's clearly a coward, afraid of Alton Benes, an admittedly burly Goy but one with a Yiddishe kop.* Benes calls him "chorus boy" and Costanza is ready to flee, like Sir Robin in *Monty Python and the Holy Grail*.

No, Resh Lakish continued. Alton Benes is the Ba'al Habait, the Master of the House, for as Rabbi Meir said, "even a goy who engages in Torah study is considered like a High Priest." (Avodah Zarah, 3a:2). Benes is a writer of sacred texts. And what is Costanza? Costanza is a stocky slow-witted bald man, soon to be unemployed and living with his parents. No beytzim, on this Costanza, not master of the house, not even master of his domain.

Precisely, offered Rav Sheshet. A coward, just like Jonah, which is why George was previously swallowed by the Moby Dick for fleeing the shiksa of Nineveh, Mississippi. We should move on. Chorus Boy is not worth our time.

I agree, said Rav Shmuel bar Yehudah. It is said that Reb Seinfeld is a comedian. I do not understand why he is a comedian. Nobody finds him funny.

Why don't cows get ruined in the rain? said Abba the Surgeon, whose elephant infirmary treated more than its share of cows gored by oxen, crushed by elephants, fallen into ditches on the Sabbath, but never ruined by the rain or the snows of Mount Ararat. And he's supposed to be the funny guy?

Perhaps that's why, said Rav Huna, Reb Benes's comedian tail gunner friend got his beytzim blown-up all-over Korea. Nobody laughed at his jokes.

I have noticed, interjected Abba the Surgeon, that Reb Seinfeld is an animal hater. He despises ponies and has knocked off at least one of their "immigrant" owners; he ostentatiously wears pricey cow and then lets the poor beast of burden get ruined in the snow; and I have no doubt he would have killed Kramer's pigeons if given the chance, even though we have a deal with the pigeons. Had he been in Egypt he would not have been redeemed.

Yes, a very very bad man, rejoined Bar Kappara, his mother was wrong. I think the Moby Dick should have also swallowed Jerry.

Oh he'll get what's coming to him, said Zutra the Mohel, who deviously glanced at his scalpel and clamp.

Well that settles it, said Rav Sheshet in the name of Rabbah. Let's call the SPCA and call it a day. He needs to be watched. I think we're done here. Let's go back to Schnitzer's. All this talk of cows and ponies and Moby Dicks has left me hungry.

The Phone Message

MISHNAH:

It is told that in the days of the Mishnah the early sages gathered amidst the carnage of the Second Temple to discuss "The Phone Message," because they knew the future Sages of Babylon were going to struggle with it.

Yohanan ben Zakkai: Fellow Sages, I am giving you each one of these strange devices. Please study it.

Rabbi Tarfon: What is it?

Yohanan ben Zakkai: They call it an answering machine because the current *Seinfeld* episode revolves around it. It records messages. From the future.

Jose the Galilean: Messages from the future? Like the Lord Our God telling Abraham Our Father that the Israelites will be enslaved in Egypt for 400 years and face the wrath of Pharaoh?

Rabban Gamaliel: No, no it's like Michael J. Fox telling Christopher Lloyd he needs 1.21 gigawatts to get *Back to the Future* or he will face the wrath of the Libyans.

Shimon bar Yochai: No, no it's like the higher levels, the emanations in the Zohar* telling Bruce Willis that a virus will destroy humanity and face the wrath of the *12 Monkeys*.

Rabbi Tarfon: This all sounds very complicated.

Rabbi Akivah: Doesn't it, though? I don't get it. We'll let those yolds* at the academy in Pumbedita in the future sort it out. Not our problem.

GEMARAH:

The Sages of Babylon gathered at the academy in Pumbedita and marveled at "the answering machine" with a "phone message" bequeathed to them by Yavneh.

What do we do with this thing? asked Rav Huna reading the rather cryptic Mishnah debate between Akivah, Tarfon, Jose the Galilean, and others.

It has something to do with the Exodus, the Zohar, 1.21 gigawatts, and 12 monkeys, offered Resh Lakish.

Perhaps the 12 monkeys have something to do with the Moby Dick that swallowed Costanza near Nineveh, said Shimon ben Pazi.

Or maybe Jerry had a jacket made from 12 monkeys, replied Resh Lakish. Unlike cow, monkeys don't get ruined in the snow.

Here's an idea! Perhaps we should hit the button that says "Play" suggested Rav Sheshet.

…

Having listened to Costanza's message on the answering machine tape, Bar Kappara said, ok friends, the question at hand is whether coffee means coffee or whether coffee means sex.

Coffee's coffee in the morning, it's not coffee at twelve o clock at night, insisted Hillel, son of Gamaliel III.

But what about those who work at NORAD, rejoined Rabbi Abbahu.

What is a NORAD, asked Shimon ben Pazi?

NORAD was the Son of Cush and the great ruler of Babel (Genesis 10:8-10) who constructed the Tower of Babel (Avodah Zarah 53b:13), said Rav Sheshet pulling out a Torah, flaunting his erudition, yet oblivious to the fact that his library book, much like his copy of *Tropic of Cancer*, was 17 years overdue.

Yes. Obviously anyone who worked for King Norad had to drink coffee late at night, said Rabbah. That Tower of Babel was some building. George must have designed it before he did the addition to the Guggenheim ("The Race," s6e10). He always wanted to pretend to be an architect.

What is a Guggenheim? asked Shimon ben Pazi.

It is a Temple in the Big Apple named for an "immigrant" who went down on the Titanic after it was rammed by Noah's Ark, killing all the ponies on board, said Rav Kahana. He probably knew Manya. Maybe even killed her pony, a makher* like Guggenheim surely hated anyone who owned a pony.

So then coffee is coffee, concluded Bar Kappara. That was easy, I think we're done here.

Rav Pappa, however, the stud of Sassanid* Persia, who daily boasted of his big beytzim to Babylonian women, was having none of this.

Coffee means sex, said Rav Pappa the Player. I casually roam the streets of Pumbedita in my cotton dockers, eating my big apple and the "coffee invitations" flow until my cup runneth over. And I've never worked for King Norad or Meyer Guggenheim. I don't even drink coffee.

Ah, assented the Sages in unison, more than a little impressed and envious.

Well that settles it, concluded Bar Kappara, coffee means sex. George Costanza is Lord of the Idiots after all. He is not a take-charge guy – he is not a colonel, a kaiser, or a tsar.

What is the proper blessing for the Tsar? asked the pious and usually reticent Rami bar Hama.

That, my friends, added Bar Kappara, is a discussion for another day. It's getting late, who's up for coffee?

The Apartment

MISHNAH (For I am Tarfon Lord of the Idiots):

Rabbi Akivah: I am such an idiot.

Rabban Gamliel: Why do you say such things, Akivah Rabbeinu?*

Rabbi Akivah: Remember those answering machines we got? I left an inappropriate hot and heavy message on Bari Weiss's answering machine after we met for coffee. She promised to show me the "promised land" and "to thrust me into the messianic age."

Jose the Galilean: Yo-Yo Ma!

Rabban Gamliel: Boutros Boutros-Ghali!

Rabbi Eliezer ben Hurcanus: Sounds like she considered you sponge worthy!

Rabbi Akivah: Yeah so I went ahead, lent her 5000 shekels to rent her a chamber in my cave.

Rabban Gamliel: Nu? This all sounds great. You are a latter-day Samson. You're truly the Wiz Akivah, and nobody beats you. Did you get to know her, biblically speaking?

Rabbi Akivah: No. It turned out she was soliciting me to join Bar Kochbah's rebellion* against the Romans. Coffee meant coffee. The promised land meant Jerusalem, and well, thrusting into the messianic age, suffice it to say, did not involve treating anyone's body like an amusement park. She's a political Zealot this Weiss. Now the Romans are trying to cancel me. I am such an idiot.

Shimon bar Yochai: You idiot. That's why I say stick to Torah and Kabbalah. Who needs this?

Jose the Galilean: With all due respect, Akivah, I am a much bigger idiot than you are. I traded my answering machine for thirty pieces of silver and a bowl of lentil soup. But I forgot to erase the tape on which I said, "Romans go home." Now the Romans are trying to cancel me. I am such an idiot.

Shimon bar Yochai: Yes you are clearly an idiot.

Rabbi Tarfon: Don't insult me, my friend. Remember who you're talking to. No one's a bigger idiot than me. I decided to leave a message on my kosher butcher's answering machine placing an order for a trimmed shank bone, but I called my mohel by mistake. And he came over to fulfill the order and fulfill it he did. This is the most public yet of my many humiliations.

Shimon bar Yochai: Yes you are clearly an idiot. At the very least, I hope you called Dr. Byson, and he told you to put the balm on. Are the Romans trying to cancel you?

Does it even matter, replied Rabbi Tarfon, retreating like a frightened turtle. Lest there be any doubt, I am Tarfon. Lord of the Idiots.

GEMARAH (the day the Rabbis were at a loss for words):

It is told that when the third star appeared in the skies of Pumbedita Bar Kappara, Rav Huna, Resh Lakish, and Rav Sheshet gathered to discuss the Mishnah, on "The Apartment."

The Sages sat around the table, sipping their coffee with a look of horror and bemusement on their faces.

This is a problem, offered Rav Huna. It's outrageous, egregious, preposterous.

I agree said Resh Lakish, it's deplorable, unfathomable, improbable.

It's lewd, lascivious, salacious, outrageous. I think we should Passover this text and move on, said Rav Sheshet.

Yeah, I am shocked and chagrined, mortified and stupefied. I'm out of here, concluded Bar Kappara. Let's go home and never speak of this again.

The Statue

GEMARAH:

Hillel the Unhilly convened the shiur and said: Rabbis, "The Statue" has revealed a great many truths, but most disturbingly, that we have an impostor in this Yeshivah.

Rav Huna immediately jumped in: Yes, you mean Reb Ray Thomas that new student. He's clearly a fraud. I called the Yeshivah's registrar. There's nobody here with that name. I never trusted him.

No, said Bar Kappara, that's Ray Thomas Wochinski. He's kosher. Grad student transfer from the Jewish Theological Seminary.

Wochinski? Said Hillel son of Gamliel III. It sounds like he's from Poland.

What is a Poland? asked Shimon ben Pazi seemingly oblivious to earlier discussions.

Remember, said Yontl the Librarian who usually skipped these meetings but knew his knowledge was needed today, it is the place with the ponies where they can't change lightbulbs. Epicenter of Manya's criminal den of iniquity.

Maybe he's in cahoots with Manya, offered Resh Lakish. Jerry should have done away with both of them. He could have hired Elaine's cat hitman. $28 would have sufficed to take out both of them.

But look how clean Jerry's apartment is, noted Bar Kappara. Ray even windexed the peephole.

And Ray considers Jerry, Lord of the Manor, to be the King of Comedy, added Resh Lakish. Nobody finds Jerry funny.

No you yolds, interjected Hillel the Unhilly. We are not discussing Polish Ray and the polished peephole. This is about his companion: Rava

All eyes immediately turned to Rava, alleged disciple of Rabbi Yohanan and fourth generation Amora at Pumbedita.

Do you have anything to say for yourself Rava? said Hillel the Unhilly accusingly. You are hereby charged with being from Finland and writing a major novel without the Yeshivah's blessing.

And, added an envious Rav Pappa, of making love with Ray on the floor like two animals. You are insatiable.

What is a Finland? Asked the evidently slow-witted Shimon ben Pazi.

I Know Finland, said Rami bar Hama. They're neutral!

Look, said Rav Yehudah, as Reb Kramer put it, "We don't take impostors to People's Court." What say you Rava?

Rava said, defiantly, my mother left us when I was six years old. All seven of us and our pony. We never heard from her again. It's like Ray said: you Rabbis are jealous of our love. Isn't that right Rav Pappa.

[Rav Pappa hid his head in shame]

Hey Rava, said Bar Kappara, shouldn't you be out on a ledge somewhere?

The Sages immediately ejected Rava from the academy and started deportation proceedings to neutral Finland, a land devoid of Jews but replete with ponies.

I think we're done here, said Hillel the Unhilly.

This experience has changed me, lamented Bar Kappara. It's made me more cynical, more bitter, more jaded, more Jewish.

Really? Asked Resh Lakish.

Sure, why not? said Bar Kappara.

The Revenge

MISHNAH:

Hillel: If I am not for myself, who will be?

Shammai: Not me. You won't let me use your private bathroom. I have to pee with Pace Electronics. It's disgusting

Hillel: If I am only for myself, what am I?

Shammai: A laughingstock, a joke, a nothing, no brains, no ability, nothing. And you look like a blowfish.

Hillel: If not now, when?

Shammai: Right now, I need to use the bathroom. Your bathroom. Your only bathroom that you loveth.

Hillel: Is it a number 1 or a number 2? My "guys" don't know your "guys" and I want to keep it that way.

Hananiah ben Hezekiah ben Garon: You two and your petty squabbling. It's adorable, but I think we need to open up the academy to more members.

GEMARAH:

Bar Kappara in the name of Adda bar Ahavah convened the group, and said: Chevreh, we have a resume sitting here, from a George Costanza. He wants to join our team.

Why should we let him in? replied Resh Lakish. Isn't he the one known as Lord of the Idiots?

Because according to the Mishnah we cannot only be for ourselves, admonished Bar Kappara, citing Hillel the Elder. Otherwise what are we? It's all about Tikkun Olam. And now that we deported Rava to Finland and Ray to Poland we have an opening.

Does he have any skills? asked Rav Pappa.

Well he likes horses and wants to be a stable boy, replied Bar Kappara.

Then maybe he should go to Poland and work for Manya, offered Shimon ben Pazi, proud of himself for finally remembering what Poland is. She likes horses. He can become the pride of Krakow.

He likes talk shows, movies, and makes interesting comments during sporting events, said Bar Kappara.

It says here he likes history, the Civil War, and wants to be a professor, noted Resh Lakish.

But he tried to poison his previous employer, added Rav Huna.

Then he really should go to Poland, said Resh Lakish. He could get in cahoots with Manya and Ray Thomas Wochinski, running their east European pony Ponzi scheme.

I'm really not feeling this, said Hillel, son of Gamliel III. Why is this shmendrik* our problem?

And I don't want him using our private bathroom, said Resh Lakish. As Hillel the Elder put it in the Mishnah, we don't want our beytzim mixing with his beytzim. Let some other yolds deal with him and his beytzim.

Plus he might poison us, added Hamnuna. The Persian mickey industry is booming now.

You're right relented Bar Kappara. I'm not feeling this. Tikkun Olam my tokhes.

Let's move on, said Rav Sheshet. We need to talk about laundry.

Yes! Said Resh Lakish. We need to discuss whether it is effeminate for a man to put clothes on the gentle cycle.

Totally, said Rav Pappa the Player, the stud of Sassanid Persia. Only stone washing for me. Not that there's anything wrong with it.

The Heart Attack

GEMARAH:

Why hasn't George ever had a normal, medium orgasm? asked Rav Pappa the Player, who always put his virility first.

Why hasn't Jerry ever had a really good pickle, replied Resh Lakish who held shares in Wickles Pickles of Pumbedita, and always put his pickles before his petzl.*

Maybe George's petzl got pickled during his treatment at Dr. Tor Eckman's? Asked Rav Kahana.

Perhaps this is connected to George's "outside cucumber" which he brought into the coffee shop and brazenly sliced in public, mused Bar Kappara.

Cosmic justice from HaShem* offered Rabbah bar Rav Huna who was now a mohel in training under Zutra and was getting ready to practice on, if you will, his first "outside cucumber."

Well let this be a lesson to all of us, stated Hillel the Unhilly.

The Deal

GEMARAH:

Chevreh, In light of "The Deal" I have a question for the group, said Rav Huna, convening the meeting.

Please speak, replied Hillel the Unhilly.

We are a rather intimate group of rabbis said Rav Huna.

More than just talmudic colleagues added Resh Lakish.

Muchachos, if you will, affirmed Bar Kappara.

We not only know about each other's deep dark secrets, but we sit here debating them, said Rav Huna.

True, said Bar Kappara. I can tell you more about the hemorrhoids and boils that plague the beytzim and buttocks of Hanan bar Rava than I can tell you about my own wife's cycles.

Yes, and if it were not for our discussions, I wouldn't know what blessing to recite over my boils, agreed Hanan bar Rava.

And all those roundtables on seminal emissions, said Samuel ben Nahman.

Ahh, yes, the emissions, nodded the Sages in agreement.

I can literally set my clock to Rav Pappa's emissions, said Resh Lakish.

Rav Pappa assented with a slight smile on his face, soaking up the envy of his muchachos.

See, we are so much like the "Seinfeld Four" said Rav Huna, which brings me to my question: we have "THIS," and "THIS" is wonderful.

Yes "THIS" is wonderful: boils, canker sores, semen, and hemorrhoids said Shimon Ben Pazi, these are the building blocks of the Oral Torah revealed at Sinai.

And we've been within four cubits* of each other naked, added Rav Pappa, knowing full well that rumors of his Nephilim*-sized beytzim had spread far beyond the yeshivah walls.

So then if we can have "THIS," can't we have "THAT" as well? Can we take "THIS" and add "THAT"? Entreated Rav Huna.

We would need ground rules, said Resh Lakish.

No sharing each others tefillin!* said Bar Kappara.

No nibbling on each others peyos, that's just gross, said Rav Kahana.

No ménage à trois, said Resh Lakish.

We don't want to become orgy guys said Bar Kappara. Isn't that right Rav Pappa? I've seen your lotions, thick carpeting, and weirdo lighting.

I think you may be onto something, said Rav Yehudah.

It's go time! Exclaimed Rav Huna.

Not so fast, interjected Rav Yehudah. This requires far more extensive debate and regulations. We are the Sages of Babylon, the Jews who made answering a question with a question a stereotype. Grab a Snapple, we've got a long night ahead of us.

The Baby Shower

GEMARAH:

Isn't this wonderful, said Bar Kappara, we got a shoutout on "The Baby Shower"!

Oh, because we the great Rabbis of Babylon are like the Kennedys of pre-modern Jewry? said Resh Lakish. I've always felt that way.

Ask not what your mohel can snip for you, but what you can snip for your mohel! Exclaimed Rav Kahana.

Ich bin ein Sufganiyah!* shouted Rav Sheshet.

No you shmendriks, interrupted Bar Kappara. Our shoutout was in Reb Seinfeld's opening monolog. Allow me to quote it:

> "Before there was flipping around, before there was television, kings and emperors and pharaohs and such had story-tellers that would tell them stories 'cause that was their entertainment. I always wonder, in that era, if they would get, like, thirty storytellers together so they could still flip around. Just go, 'Alright start telling me a story, what's happening? I don't want to hear anymore. Shut up. Go to the next guy. What are you talking about? Is there a girl in that story? ..No? Shut up. Go to the next guy. What do you got? I don't want to hear that either. Shut up. No, go ahead, what are you talking about?.. I don't want to hear that. No, the all of you, get out of here. I'm going to bed.'"

I don't get it, said Resh Lakish.

Did Pharaoh have 30 storytellers, asked Raba bar Rav Huna? Is that why the Israelites were enslaved in the Egyptian Gulag?

That's why they sent Sakharov the Cable Guy to the Gulag: he was quite the storyteller, said Rav Sheshet. But he escaped with his stories to tell.

Which reminds me, how does a storyteller cook dinner for God? asked Resh Lakish.

And is it not wrong to hold a grudge like Khomeini? Does it not say in Leviticus "You shall not take vengeance or bear a grudge against your countrymen or the Lord" (Leviticus 19:18) even if God dumps chocolate sauce all over your red shirt and flies and maggots congregate on your hair?

I want to know if storytellers perform "Hair" in grassy knolls, with all that nudity, risking Epstein-Barr and Lyme Disease, asked Hillel the Unhilly.

What is an Epstein-Barr? asked Shimon ben Pazi.

I think Bar Epstein is that yold we didn't let into the Yeshivah. Yes, Khomeini Bar Epstein. Not the sharpest knife in the drawer, added Zutra the Mohel, but he holds grudges.

So this is why we don't have cable? This is why we don't get the naked station? lamented Rav Pappa.

If we had the naked channel we'd never misjudge fetal girth, insisted Resh Lakish. Sometimes I think this "four cubits" rule we use for everything is rather arbitrary.

I'm tired of having Sears cater our affairs, the refreshments suck, complained Rav Pappa, even though he allegedly "had a belly like the baskets made in

Harpanya." (Bava Metzia, 84a:6)

So maybe we should get illegal Roman cable installed, suggested Resh Lakish. Gladiators. And orgies, eh Pappa? We might have an easier time sticking to the topic at hand.

What was the topic at hand, asked Raba bar Rav Huna?

I think it was: "why our lessons are like a Seinfeld episode" said Rav Sheshet.

I still don't get it, said Shimon ben Pazi.

The Chinese Restaurant

GEMARAH:

Chevreh, this "Chinese Restaurant" episode presents us with a bit of a conundrum, said Rav Huna, convening the meeting.

I know, it makes no sense, said Hanan bar Rava.

That's right. Absolutely nothing happened. Nothing at all, interjected Resh Lakish. These 23 minutes of TV had less substance than even the most tiresome rabbinical debate over how many times Rav Pappa should cleanse himself after one of his seminal emissions before putting on his tefillin.

Three times, said Hanan bar Rava. Isn't that right Pappa, you need to immerse yourself in the mikvah three times after one of your nocturnal escapades.

Rav Pappa lowered his head in shame, albeit with a smile on his face.

No you yolds, retorted Rav Huna, that's not the issue. The problem is clear – why are a bunch of Jews eating Chinese food when it's not Christmas?

Yes the Mishnah is very explicit on this added Bar Kappara, citing Rabbi Tarfon who quoted Leviticus: "on Nitl Nakht and Nitl Tog[*] one may indulge in won ton and kung pao, on all other days it is kreplach,[*] gefilte fish and bagels. I am the Lord."

So maybe we were wrong, said Rav Pappa. Maybe the "Seinfeld Four" aren't Jewish?

We've established that Elaine is a shiksa, said Resh Lakish. Have you ever seen a bigger goy than her father, Alton Benes?

Is George a Jew? Inquired Rav Sheshet.

Cartwright? What kind of name is Cartwright for a Jew? replied Rabbah.

But George said, "For 50 bucks, I'd put my face in the soup and blow" and then he only offered six dollars for the proposed bribe. He's a bit, how shall I put this, parsimonious, said Rav Pappa.

Cheap, cheap, cheap, said the Sages in unison.

And he has so many "intestinal" issues, added Resh Lakish.

You're right, Cartwright is definitely one of us, conceded Hanan bar Rava.

Bowel ailments are discussed fifty times in the Mishnah.

And seminal emissions are discussed 41 times, added Rav Pappa. You'd be surprised how many times I've had to look this up.

Cartwright must have changed his name to disguise his identity, said Hanan bar Rava.

Just like Batman, added Shimon ben Pazi.

So when George said that he was Batman and had seen the Bat-Signal, hypothesized Rav Huna, he wasn't making a joke – he was making a profound observation on the tragic assimilation of American Jewry.

Failed assimilation, interjected Bar Kappara. He may have changed his name, he may boast of having intercourse with shiksas, he may eat kung pao shrimp when it's not Christmas, but nobody but a Member of Our Tribe has such recurrent bowel and ejaculatory problems. Bat-Signal is code for bathroom.

Poor Cartwright, lamented Shimon ben Pazi. Oh wretchedness of our exile!

Poor Cartwright, echoed Rav Kahana, trapped in the Hellenized bowels of American Jewry.

I think we're done here, concluded Hillel the Unhilly. Now let's go grab a bite to eat. And it's not my turn to pick up the check.

The Busboy

GEMARAH:

Bar Kappara said in the name of Rav Huna, OK "The Busboy" is not the greatest of episodes, but we do need to discuss one matter.

Yes, replied Resh Lakish: who is responsible for getting the busboy fired?

An important question, interjected Adda bar Ahavah. Was it the busboy, George, or Elaine? Each one was integral in the process.

I think it was Reb Kramer's fault, said Hanan bar Rava.

How was it Kramer's fault? asked Resh Lakish. He wasn't even there.

Because he left the Busboy's door open and Pequita the cat ran away, replied Hanan bar Rava.

Yes Kramer keeps leaving doors open, said Rav Sheshet. Had he been at the restaurant, he would have clearly been responsible. It's his fault.

This is absurd, said Resh Lakish. Why don't you blame Manya the Horse Thief once you're at it? She was a liar like the old lady on the *Titanic*.

No you yolds, said Bar Kappara in the name of Rav Huna. This is not what we are here to discuss. We are here to offer Reb Costanza/Cartwright a position in the academy.

Oy Gevalt, why? said Resh Lakish.

You do realize the Romans fed Rabbi Akivah to the lions, said Bar Kappara. Was a shtupp* in the hay worth it? Eh Rav Pappa, always thinking with your petzl. … Again, I ask, was that worth it?

I'm thinking about the question, replied Rav Pappa.

OK I think we're done here, concluded Rav Huna. Let's not speak of this again and move on to Season 3. Rumor has it George will get a massage from a man, and he will think it moved. Sounds like it's right up your alley, Pappa.

Season 3

The Rabbis Measure Their Noses and Debate Jewish Law on Sleeping with a Nazi

The Note

MISHNAH:

Hillel: If a Jew enters a Temple of Zeus and he feels it move, he has committed idolatry.

Shammai: No, it only counts as having moved if one is at a Greek bathhouse sitting within four cubits of a Hellenizer, and if it moves a distance of at least 3 cubits.

Hillel: Woe unto the Hebrew who loosens his pants in a Greek bathhouse within four cubits of a Hellenizer.

Shammai: Praise unto the Hebrew who possesses the girth to feel it move 3 cubits.

Rabbi Tarfon: Without discharge that travels a distance of at least 3 cubits it is not idolatry.

Rabbi Akivah: And where is this written, Tarfon?

Rabbi Tarfon: a gym teacher once told me.

GEMARAH:

I think we need to discuss George and Raymond: We need to determine whether it moved or not, said Rav Pappa.

Again with the petzls, Pappa, retorted Resh Lakish, why is it always about your privates?

They are not "my" privates, snapped Rav Pappa. Do you know that "Penis" is mentioned 95 times in the Talmud and "seminal emissions" are mentioned 177 times?

[All eyes turned with raised eyebrows to Rav Pappa]

Or so I've heard, sheepishly added Rav Pappa.

No it is an important question, agreed Bar Kappara. George Bar Costanza-Cartwright wants a position in our academy. We are considering him because of his knowledge of toilets and his intestinal insights. But as a Rav Azrael in the name of Bar Gargamel once said, "Man cannot live by bowels alone." (Talmud Boweli, Seder Intestinim 3:2)

Even a Jew cannot, added Rabbi Abbahu.

So then did it move? asked Rabbah.

Raymond is a strapping dude of Philistine proportions, admitted Rav Sheshet. A Roman Gladiator towering over the rather dainty Costanza, who is a bit of a "Mary" that one if you ask me.

And Raymond got about two tenths of a cubit from … there, added Bar Kappara. Not that there's anything wrong with it.

So then why wouldn't it move, asked Abba the Surgeon. These things move on my examination table all the time.

Thumb-breadths or hand-breadths? Inquired Rav Pappa, perking up.

Cubits and Parasangs, replied Abba the Surgeon. That's why I moved to a larger office.

But George also disclosed his solitary "hobby" ("I'll be in the middle"), said Resh Lakish. Is that not a problem?

Treating one's body like an amusement park is only mentioned nine times in the Talmud, said Rav Pappa.

"It has been taught," quoted Rav Huna, that "proselytes and those who masturbate delay the advent of the Messiah" (Tractate Kallah Rabbati, 2:4). Eh Rav Pappa, isn't that right?

As it is written, added Rav Yehudah "an emission a day will keep the Messiah away" (Tractate Shmekl Rabbati, 3:5). Do you know that one, Rav Pappa?

Why are you looking at me? snapped Rav Pappa. You think something's wrong? Am I different?

Let's just say, added Rav Huna, if this were a court of law, I would advise you to plead "no contest." [To be continued in Season 4]

The Truth

GEMARAH:

So, should Costanza have told Patrice the truth or not? asked Bar Kappara.

She was awfully pretentious, replied Rav Sheshet. Pretentiousness is a terrible quality. The cowardly Costanza is finally developing some beytzim.

That's true, added Resh Lakish. But the Mishnah states that during the Bar Kochbah revolt, Bari Weiss called Rabbi Akivah pretentious. When he asked why, she said it is because he referred to everyone by their full names: "Rabban Gamli-El," "Rav Garga-Mel," "Bar Azra-El," "Rabbi Yishma-El."

So what happened? asked Hanan Bar Rava.

Rabbi Akivah lost his composure and smeared Bari as a harpy, a grifter, and a Zionist troll, replied Resh Lakish. She became so distraught that she cancelled herself and checked into a Roman mental institution.

Just like Bob Sacamano, but without the enlarged synapses, added Shimon ben Pazi.

She clearly wanted pity, said Rav Kahana.

Pity is very underrated, said Shimon ben Pazi. I should be in a place like that. Would you all come visit me?

Even I've never driven a woman to a mental institution, interjected Rav Pappa. Lesbianism yes, but never a mental institution.

Yes you are an exemplary rabbi and a gentleman, Pappa, said Resh Lakish. A nice Jewish boy. Every Yiddishe-mama's dream son-in-law.

Look, retorted Rav Pappa, I didn't want to bring this up, but I was in fact the first in my neighborhood to donate precious shekels to a relief fund for the victims of Pompeii's eruption three years ago. Admittedly I did it to impress a Persian lady friend, but still, it was a nice gesture.

I don't recall Pompeii erupting three years ago, said Abba the Surgeon.

It didn't, replied Pappa. Hence the subsequent audit from the Sassanid Revenue Service. They even wanted receipts for the posh Persian public toilets I had frequented.

I hear those are the financial equivalent of a complete rectal examination. Isn't the right Pappa? Said Resh Lakish.

Do You mean the audit or sitting on the toilets? I respectfully ask my colleagues to cease discussing my petzl, my rectum, and my beytzim, not to mention my finances, replied Rav Pappa.

Motion denied, replied Resh Lakish. As you yourself recently pointed out, penises and toilets are mentioned close to 200 times in the Talmud.

I think we've established, interrupted Rav Huna, that honesty is not always the best policy. As Rabbi Yehudah HaNasi once said, "Donkey-drivers are mostly wicked, and camel-drivers are mostly honest, sailors are mostly pious. The best of doctors go to Hell, and the most honest butchers are the partner of Amalek." (Mishnah Kiddushin 4:14).

What in the name of Gehenna does that mean? interjected Resh Lakish.

Beats me. But it sounds apropos, said Rav Huna. Let us forget about it. We should put on our slippers instead and play some word association:

"Hellenism"
  -"Tuberculosis"

"Bob Sacamano"
 -"Synapses"
"Answering machine"
 -"Tuberculosis"
"Poland"
 -"Ponies"
"Rav Pappa"
 -"The Clap"
"Invisible Coffee Table"
 -"Tuberculosis"
"Lesbianism"
 -"Bari Weiss"
"The Truth"
 -"Tuberculosis"

The Sages played word association all that night until their students came at dawn and told them: "Our Masters! The time has come for reciting the morning Shema!* They left for morning prayers completely unprepared for Morty Seinfeld's upcoming retirement from the presidency of Phase Two of the Pines of Mar Gables Condo Association.

The Pen

MISHNAH:

Shimon bar Yochai: Let's settle up for last night's Chinese food, and remember nobody needs to know we had kung pao when it wasn't Christmas.
    Rabbi Tarfon: Hey what kind of pen is that?
    Shimon bar Yochai: This pen? This is the pen The Lord used to inscribe the Ten Commandments on top of Mount Sinai. He then gifted it to Moses before telling him his people would wander the scorching desert heat for 40 years and he would die amidst the desolation of Moab before reaching the Promised Land.
    Jose the Galilean: Still a nice gesture. HaShem could be vindictive, but he was never cheap with the gifting. How did you get it?
    Shimon bar Yochai: It was passed down to Joshua and then the Prophets and then the Pharisees eventually finding its way to Hillel the Elder and then me. I used it to write our sacred Zohar; The Fiery Chariot of Elijah burned through my nostrils as I etched the Lord's mystical incantations onto sacred parchment. Now I use it to highlight the menu from "Yavneh Oriental Express."
    Rabbi Akivah: You know I often times try to write my notes while sitting in the shvitz – the steam clears the fog from my goyishe kop* – but the heat always melts my pen. I'd love to get a pen like that.
    Shimon bar Yochai: Take the pen.

Rabbi Akivah: I couldn't.

Shimon bar Yochai: Do me a personal favor and take the pen.

Rabbi Akivah: I couldn't.

Shimon bar Yochai: Come on, Moses would be down with it, take the pen.

Rabbi Akivah: OK, I'll take it! Now allow me to write the check for dinner using the pen!

Rabbi Tarfon: OK so we had lo mein, egg fu young, won ton soup, and kung pao chicken.

Shimon bar Yochai: Someone had a Coke.

Rabbi Akivah: That wasn't me. Here I owe you 19.45 Dinars.

Shimon bar Yochai: OK so let's make it 20 Dinars even.

Rabbi Akivah: No, that would be 19.45 Dinars.

GEMARAH:

This is the first I am hearing of this pen, said Rav Huna, convening the emergency meeting.

What do you suppose happened to it, asked Rav Sheshet?

Maybe it was stolen along with the Ark of the Covenant, suggested Resh Lakish. We need to form an expedition.

Impossible, interjected Rav Kahana. Indiana Jones would have found it in the Canyon of the Crescent Moon.

No that was the Holy Grail, interjected Rabbah. FFS please get your filmography straight.

And we do not talk about Yoshke* the Nazarene* at the academy, admonished Rav Huna. He's been blacklisted, like Manya the "immigrant" Horse Thief.

Boy, Rabbi Akivah really had some nerve taking that pen, said Ravina.

Why? Bar Yochai offered it to him, Akivah never asked for it. All he said was he liked the pen, retorted Rav Pappa. And Akivah had such brilliant thoughts while in the shvitz:

-"A fence to wisdom is silence." I bet you he wrote that with the pen.

-"The paper burns, but the words fly away." Again, with the pen in the shvitz.

I don't understand what any of those sayings even mean, sheepishly said Hamnuna.

Nobody does, added Shimon Ben Pazi.

I just had an alarming thought, said Resh Lakish. What if Akivah gave the pen to Bari Weiss during the Bar Kochbah revolt? They were shvitzing up the sukkah together, there was all this lulav shaking and etrog fondling going on. As

Rabbi Meir says, "Whoever gives a virgin less than 200 dinar, or a widow less than a maneh, this is [considered] unchaste intercourse." (Mishnah Ketubot 5:1)

This will be a disaster, lamented Rav Huna. If word gets out, we will be accused of Zionist colonialism and of plundering the treasures of the Palestinians.

What is a Palestinian? Asked Shimon Ben Pazi.

The Sages sat silently perplexed.

My sources tell me you will need to wait and look that up in about 1600 years, said Yontl the Librarian.

The Dog

GEMARAH:

Bar Kappara convened the meeting in the name of Rav Huna who was absent on this day because he thought this episode sucked.

So, comrades, said Bar Kappara, what is the Halakhah* on Jerry's obligation to take in and care for this dog, especially in light of its inebriated owner's disappearance?

As a Jew he has a commitment to his fellow humans and fellow mammals, replied Abba the Surgeon, whose elephant clinic was famous throughout Babylon for taking in stray possums, snakes, oxen, jackals, and even the occasional unemployed rabbi.

I disagree, said Rav Sheshet, and I quote Chagigah 14b: "They asked ben Zoma: What is the Halakhah with regard to castrating a dog? The prohibition against castration appears alongside the sacrificial blemishes, which may imply that it is permitted to castrate an animal that cannot be sacrificed as an offering." (Chagigah 14b, 10).

Yes, replied Resh Lakish. If one may castrate a dog then Jerry was at liberty to neutralize the mutt.

But you are missing the point: Jerry need not have taken in the dog in the first place, insisted Rami bar Hama. He already had a barely domesticated beast in his care. As it was spoken, when Gavin asked, "do you have any pets," Jerry replied, "just my next-door neighbor."

Is Kramer a pet, asked Rav Pappa?

The Sages sat in silence pondering this conundrum.

This is precisely what Caesar the Chimp asked James Franco in *Rise of the Planet of the Apes*, noted Hanina ben Pappa.

Caesar and Kramer both know sign language, added Hamnuna.

But Caesar was able to feed himself and could actually shut a door, even as a baby Simian, whereas Kramer roams the building in search of luncheon meat leaving doors open, said Resh Lakish. He's a helpless primate.

And a helpless primate who felled himself on the very invisible coffee table he built out of garbage, noted Hanan bar Rav.

OK so that settles it, said Rabbi Assi, Kramer should be considered Jerry's pet.

And as Gavin said to Kramer, added Rav Pappa, "I'll wager... [Farfel's] parents are more pure than yours."

So then why doesn't poor Jerry take Kramer to the pound? It's almost as if some shmendrik dropped Kramer off at the building and never retrieved him, asked Shimon ben Pazi.

Gee Pazi, rebuked Abba the Surgeon in anger. Why don't you just ask Ben Zoma to castrate him? Or let Zutra the Mohel take a stab at him. No, there will always be room for Reb Kramer in my elephant clinic.

Once you feed him he will never leave, predicted Rav Sheshet.

Our session is now adjourned, declared Bar Kappara, and we shall expand upon the Mishnah where it is written, "one may not raise pigs anywhere, and a person may not raise a dog unless it is tied with chains" (Mishnah Bava Kamma 7:7), but a Kramer may be domesticated at Abba the Surgeon's clinic. The Kehilla* shall not be held responsible for feeding him.

The Library

MISHNAH:

Shimon bar Yochai: Akivah, what are you doing?

Rabbi Akivah: Just reading this copy of your illustrious Zohar, which I took out of the Yavneh public library.

Shimon bar Yochai: But you are writing in the library book! And is that the sacred pen bequeathed to us by The Lord at Sinai that I gifted you!?

Rabbi Akivah: Chill. Nobody has to know. Bari asked me to highlight the good parts. I'm off to see Bar Kochbah and get this rebellion a rocking and a rolling, TTYL.

Rabbi Tarfon: Famous last words.

GEMARAH:

Sorry to interrupt the shiur but there is a Mar Buchman here, said Rabbi Abbahu. He claims to be a library cop, here on a case that pertains to the Yeshivah.

Yes, Mar Buchman, what can we do for you? said Rav Huna.

Our records indicate that someone checked out a book in the yeshivah's name in 135 CE and never returned it, said Buchman.

Is this a joke? said Bar Kappara. 300 years ago? Very funny.

The Yavneh Public Library's sole copy of the Zohar was checked out in 135 CE. Here is the signature of a Rabbi Akivah on the card, said Buchman.

Rabbi Akivah's been dead for centuries, fed to the lions by the Romans, said Rav Huna. May his memory be a blessing.

A blessing for libraries. They undoubtedly executed him for his delinquency, said Buchman. 135 CE was a bad year for libraries, bad year for the Empire. Zealots burning library cards, Bar Kochbah telling everyone to steal books and cast them into the Dead Sea to precipitate the messianic age, Emperor Hadrian saving precious manuscripts and storing them in his personal latrine. I don't judge a man by the fluff of his beard or the length of his tzitzit,* but you better respect the library.

Look this has nothing to do with us, retorted Hillel the Unhilly. Our Rabbis are not collectively responsible for the sins of our forefathers.

Allow me to quote your Torah, said Buchman, "I am a jealous librarian, punishing the children for the delinquency of the parents unto the third and fourth generation of those who abuse their library privileges." (Exodus 20:5). Yes, I may be a Goy, but I have read your law book, and guess what, I didn't steal my copy of it from the public library.

Right, you probably swiped it from the nightstand of a hotel room, snapped Rav Pappa.

You think this is all a big joke, don't you? said Buchman. Are you a comedian?

I've performed at a bris or two, retorted Rav Pappa.

Chevreh, interrupted Yontl the Librarian, it appears we actually do have this copy of the Zohar; I found it in the stacks. Somehow it made its way to Babylon. Here you go Mar Buchman. Our apologies; have an Everything Bagel, on the House.

What did you do to this book? howled Buchman. Someone made drawings of pee-pees and wee-wees all over the pages.

The Zohar is a pretty erotic text, said Bar Kappara. One might say it is the *Tropic of Cancer* of Rabbinic Judaism.

Yes, pee-pees and wee-wees are discussed in Kabbalah hundreds of times, added Rav Pappa with a countenance that spoke of erudition and perhaps an uncontrollable erection.

And what does this inscription in the margins say? asked Mar Buchman.

Uh, replied Resh Lakish, it says, "Akivah and Bari sitting in a Zionist tree. K-I-S-S-I-N-G."

Is this how you people get your kicks? said Buchman. You and your good-time Rabbi buddies? Or maybe this turns you on?

It admittedly sounds more poetic in the original Aramaic, said Rav Huna, lowering his head in embarrassment.

It kinda turns me on, admitted Rav Pappa, who kept a copy of the Zohar on his nightstand and was known to highlight the smutty parts.

Party time is over. Your people are permanently exiled from all public libraries in Palestine. If anyone shows up I will be all over you like a pit bull on a poodle.

The Parking Garage

GEMARAH:

Rav Huna convened the meeting and asked, so Chevreh what shall we discuss from "The Parking Garage"?

We need to discuss the proper halakhic arrangement of parking spots, replied Rav Sheshet. I've misplaced my camel three times in Pumbedita's Wal-Mart Supercenter. And I know I'm not alone here.

No, replied Bar Kappara, we need to discuss public urination, this is the major halakhic issue raised in the episode.

Agreed, said Rav Pappa. "Urine" is mentioned 76 times in the Mishnah and 189 times in the Talmud.

So then we've exhausted the topic, retorted Rav Sheshet, allow me to quote merely one passage – Shabbat 110 – to suggest why we are tapped out: "Ravina said to Rava: What is the ruling with regard to drinking urine on Shabbat? Rava said to him: We already learned in the Mishnah: One may drink all drinks, and people do not drink urine and [it] is not considered a drink. It is only consumed for medical purposes and is therefore prohibited." (Shabbat 110a:5)

Yeah, that seems a bit much, added Resh Lakish. We wasted an hour discussing whether urine was a beverage or not?

I disagree, said Rav Pappa. That was a memorable debate and the reference to "medical purposes" feeds directly into the "Parking Garage." Jerry had to pee in the garage for health reasons. One may interpret "drinking urine" as "making urine" in this context. Uromycitisis poisoning should not be taken lightly, and if he did in fact have a public urination pass issued by the city, he should not have been arrested.

But the passage you cited, interjected Resh Lakish, also mentions a prohibition against "drinking urine" on Shabbat. The Seinfeld Four were in New Jersey on Shabbat, because, as Jerry pointed out, "everybody's doing something better than me on a Saturday afternoon... cooking burgers ... making out on blankets.," i.e. not urinating in a parking garage.

But they were imprisoned in that parking lot against their will, said Rav Pappa, and accordingly-

And accordingly, interrupted Rav Sheshet, we need to discuss how to better arrange our parking garages, so people don't lose their camels. Allow me to quote Jerry himself:

> "The problem with the mall garage is that everything looks the same. They try to differentiate between levels. They put up different colors, different numbers, different letters. What they need to do is name the levels, like, 'Your mother's a whore.' You would remember that."

I think we need to follow Reb Seinfeld's advice. Our Yeshivah Camel Lot alone has six levels. We need names for the levels.

OK we are now accepting proposals for level names, said Rav Huna, but please leave our mothers out of it.

-"Pappa the Petzl."
-"Sheshet the Shmekl"
-"Hillel the Unhilly and His Willy"
-"The Dong of Babylon"
-"The Shlong of Babylon"

Wait a minute, interrupted Bar Kappara. These names are too similar. And people are going to confuse Dong and Shlong. They will end up on the wrong level. We will be back to square one: Purple 23, Red 6, etc.

"I was wrong all along to have been in the Dong and not the Shlong of Babylon," mused Rabbah. I can see how this would be a problem.

But it makes for a lovely song, added Rav Sheshet.

This is harder than it looks, lamented Rav Huna. I say we go back to discussing public urination on the Sabbath.

Agreed, said the Sages in unison.

The Cafe

MISHNAH:

Rabbi Akivah: My fellow sages, you wanted to see me?

Yohanan ben Zakkai: We've become concerned about your erratic behavior of late, Akivah: consorting with a Zionist of ill-repute, partaking in a messianic rebellion, defacing library books with pee-pees and wee-wees.

Rabbi Akivah: Those pictures were supposed to be private.

Rabban Gamliel: We've concluded something drastic needs to be done.

Rabbi Akivah: "Merriment and frivolity accustom one to sexual licentiousness; Tradition is a fence to the Torah; Tithes a fence to wealth, Vows a fence to abstinence; A fence to wisdom is silence." (Pirkei Avot 3:13)

Rabbi Tarfon: Who said that?

Rabbi Akivah: Actually, I did.

Yohanan ben Zakkai: And we have absolutely no idea what it means. So we would like you to take this IQ test. Don't worry. You'll do fine, you're smart.

Rabbi Tarfon: Well, people think he's smart. Yet his SAT scores seem to fluctuate.

GEMARAH:

Rav Huna convened the emergency meeting and said, some troubling documents have come to light.

I'm completely innocent, said Rav Pappa, as the Mishnah states: "Once she is twelve years and one day old and has grown two pubic hairs, which is a sign of adulthood, even without examination her vows are in effect." (Niddah 45b:2)

The Sages stared at Rav Pappa in silence.

No you yold, this is not about you, at least not yet, replied Rav Huna. This is about Rabbi Akivah, our venerated ancestor.

Well what is it, asked Resh Lakish, impatiently. I thought we were done with this entire Bari Weiss affair.

It seems, Rav Huna continued, Rabbi Akivah took an IQ test and only scored an 85.

85! cried Rav Sheshet. Caesar the Chimp in *Rise of the Planet of the Apes* scored considerably higher. And he, like Kramer, was a pet. Was Rabbi Akivah a pet? Who scores 85?

Even Shmerl, our local ventriloquist here in Pumbedita and known for being a shmegegge* on the best of days, scored higher than 85, added Resh Lakish.

So did Maurice, his wooden dummy, score higher than 85, added Bar Kappara.

How can a wooden dummy take an IQ test, asked Shimon Ben Pazi?

"Rava created a man, a golem, using forces of sanctity. Rava sent his creation before Rabbi Zeira. Rabbi Zeira would speak to him but he would not reply," said Anani ben Sason the mystic, quoting from Sanhedrin 65b. It stands to reason if one can create a golem out of clay one can breathe life into a dummy out of wood, and, it follows, both can take an IQ test.

We may need to expunge Rabbi Akivah's adages from our texts, suggested Rabbah. He is cited 759 times in the Mishnah. Maybe this is why his sayings make little sense.

Maybe it's not his fault, reasoned Bar Kappara. This was a standardized Hellenistic Roman test. Maybe it had an anti-Jewish bias, with questions about gladiators, hunting, and foreskins.

And this was 300 years ago, added Rav Pappa. Surely there is a statue of limitations on this.

"Statute;" "statute of limitations" you shnook,* said Rav Huna.

Maybe we should make Rav Pappa take the IQ test, suggested Resh Lakish. At least we know he will get the questions about testicles correct.

"Why must I always be the focal point of attention? Why can't I just be?" said Rav Pappa in annoyance.

And if Pappa scores an 85, said Rav Sheshet, he can always become our Yeshiva's resident ventriloquist.

Or the dummy, added Resh Lakish, and we can then use Maurice for firewood.

The Tape

GEMARAH:

So Chevreh, said Rav Huna, convening the meeting. Was it wrong for Elaine to leave that smutty message on Jerry's tape?

Of course it was, said Rav Sheshet. How can she toy with Jerry and George's emotions like that?

I disagree, said Rav Pappa. My female love newtons leave me dirty messages all the time. And for this I am a better Jew, a tzaddik* if you will, perhaps even a Lomed Vovnik.*

How exactly is that so? interjected Resh Lakish, you are the horniest Israelite in Babylonian Exile. The Alexander Portnoy of the Levant.

Technically speaking Persia isn't in the Levant, this is Mesopotamia, interjected Abba the Surgeon. whose Babylonian elephant clinic was presently in a trademark dispute with a Levantine elephant clinic.

My muchachas have shown me my inner beauty, I have no need to pursue vanity, replied Rav Pappa. "For the LORD sees not as man sees: man looks on the outward appearance, but the LORD looks on the heart." (1 Samuel 16:7)

The Sages stared at Rav Pappa, mouths agape.

Is that so? replied Rav Sheshet, well then how about: "Like a gold ring in a pig's snout is a beautiful woman who shows no discretion." (Proverbs 11:22)

Pappa, interjected Bar Kappara, I think you tied your tzitzit a bit to tight and you have cut off circulation to your tokhes. Wasn't it you who just last week ordered that new Chinese cure for baldness?

Only because a free coupon came with my kung pao chicken. As it is written, "And if his neighbor gives it to him as a gift, even on condition that he return it, it is a bona fide gift, and he takes it and fulfills his obligation with it and then returns it." (Mishnah Sukkah 3:13)

That passage pertains to the lulav,* not to Chinese hair, replied Resh Lakish.

Yes but it also says, retorted Rav Pappa, "A bald-headed person is unfit [for the priesthood]. What is considered bald-headed? One who does not have a line of hair from ear to ear. If he has one, then he is fit." (Mishnah Bekhorot 7:2). I need to be fit and pure for the priesthood for when the Messiah comes.

The Sages stared at Rav Pappa, mouths agape.

Nu, so what happened? asked Bar Kappara, I see no budding follicles bursting through your yarmulke.

The cream just arrived, said Rav Pappa. The instructions say, "Gym a gun sen tokomo. Chin che. You grow hair, Look a like Stalin."

What is a Stalin? asked Shimon Ben Pazi.

I think it means "Man of Steel," replied Rabbah. He's a superhero.

Like the Batman, agreed Shimon Ben Pazi.

But hadn't we determined in an earlier tractate that Reb Costanza-Cartwright was in fact the Batman? Why then, in "The Tape" is George trying to be "the Man of Steel from Krypton?

Maybe he believes he deserves a superhero promotion? offered Bar Kappara. Is Superman not superior to Batman? And think about Superman's nemesis: Lex Luthor. Bald as a Babylonian baby's bottom. Man of Steel hair is the negation of Costanza's bald exilic condition.

I think, concluded Rav Huna, the question of "the Tape" stands. There is hair-Halakhah at stake, and we should not be hasty. We will do weekly checks on Rav Pappa's cranium. And good luck with that whole priestly thing Pappa. Your Stalinist hair will surely be an asset with the Temple in the messianic age. And with the ladies. And with the ladies who will surely be soliciting outside the Temple during the messianic age.

I'm counting on it, said Rav Pappa, gazing off in the direction of Zion.

The Nose Job

GEMARAH:

Let's get right to the point, said Rav Huna.

LOL, Huna, LOL, retorted Rav Pappa.

It is clear that Kramer should have not told Audrey to get a nose job, said Rav Huna, convening the meeting.

But it is written, interjected Resh Lakish: "The Mishna taught that if one's nose is disproportionately large relative to his limbs or disproportionately small relative to his limbs, he is blemished. The Sages taught in a baraita: The measure of disproportion is the size of one's small finger." (Bekhorot 44a:17)

Yet it is still cruel to point out one's blemishes, responded Bar Kappara.

But is also written, interjected Rav Sheshet: "The Mishnah lists additional blemishes that disqualify a priest from performing the Temple service: If a priest's eyes are large like those of a calf or small like those of a goose; ... if his nose is disproportionately large relative to his limbs or disproportionately small relative to his limbs, he is disqualified." (Mishnah Bekhorot 7:4)

But Audrey is not a priest, insisted Rabbi Assi, she's not even from Long Island, so this entire debate is irrelevant.

But if it applies to priests, asked Rav Pappa, does it not also apply to rabbis? We are in many respects the post-Temple priesthood of Judaism, and, to quote Reb Cosmo Kramer, "my face is my livelihood, my allure... my twinkle! Everything I have I owe to this face." ("The Abstinence," s8e9). Our Talmud clearly states our faces should be unblemished.

A tough question, mused the Sages in unison.

Maybe we should measure each other's noses, proposed Rav Huna.

Isn't that getting a bit too personal? said Rav Sheshet.

Why? asked Rav Hama. We know the location of all of Resh Lakish's boils. And we can literally set our clocks to Rav Pappa's nocturnal emissions.

Word, replied Rav Pappa.

Also, added Rav Hama, I heard some chatter around the markets of Babylon about "Jew noses." What do you suppose that means?

It can't be good, said Bar Kappara.

Alright let's line up alphabetically, said Rav Huna. Zutra the Mohel will take measurements.

I object, said Rav Pappa. Zutra will likely, if you will, get a little trigger happy with his utensils. He has yet to handle an appendage he does not prune.

Fine, said Rav Huna, then Abba the Surgeon will take the measurements.

…

And it appears, announced Abba the Surgeon, the longest nose in the academy goes to Rav Pappa. One third of a cubit in length with capacious nostrils from which could gush the waters of the Euphrates and drown us all in a sea of shnot and shmutz.

Oh poor Pappa, so much for your dreams of the Priesthood, said Resh Lakish. Even your recently sprouted hair of Stalin is not sufficient to render you pure.

Fair enough, replied Rav Pappa. But it has also been said that a large shnoz* connotes a majestic shmekl.* It's all about my snout giving me clout, as it is written.

Where exactly does it say that in the Mishnah? asked Resh Lakish.

No not the Mishnah, replied Rav Pappa. It is said among Zoroastrian witch doctors. I have been consulting them of late. Zoroaster himself banned rhinoplasty after operating on Peter Jennings, and it is why they consider circumcision such a cultural affront.

Every cubit counts, said Rav Sheshet. If only poor Audrey hadn't been misled by Reb Costanza.

"The LORD is a passionate, avenging God" (Nahum 1:2), quoted Rav Ashi. For he who shrunk his girlfriend's shnoz will himself suffer significant shrinkage in Season 5.

Just retribution, the Sages nodded in unison.

Hey Pappa, who do you think would win if your nose faced off with your penis in a chess game? asked Rav Sheshet.

Why speculate? Interjected Resh Lakish. I'll grab the board.

Well that settles it, concluded Rav Huna. I declare that we, Israelites, will embrace the "Jewish Nose." It's not as if the Messiah is coming anytime soon. I predict our noses will be the envy of the nations. What could go wrong?

The Stranded

GEMARAH:

What a lame ass party, said Resh Lakish. I can't believe they went all the way to Long Island for that!

We are not supposed to use the word "lame" in that manner as it implies someone with a disability, said Abba the Surgeon, whose renowned elephant infirmary had treated many a lame elephant.

While I have reservations with you policing my speech, said Resh Lakish, I will concede. That party really blew. No pun intended.

Is the pun a reference to George shtupping Ava? Asked Rav Pappa. Because that's also grossly inaccurate. She asked George "to make love to her." There is nuance here for us on the Babylonian swingers circuit and there is clearly nuance on Long Island. Maybe you rabbis need to get out more. Even a party on Long Island would be a step up for you.

If this is another lecture about your Jewish nose's sex appeal, Pappa, we're not interested, said Rav Sheshet. We respect your shnoz and your beytzim, but please, save it for your dames in the marketplace.

Let's discuss how Jerry gets his comedic material from a German voice in his head, said Bar Kappara. Has anyone ever heard a German tell a funny joke? Has anyone ever heard a funny German joke?

How about, "Why did Hitler commit suicide?" offered Rabbah.

Because he was stuck at a party on Long Island with a woman named Ava, said Resh Lakish.

This joke is not only lame – sorry I mean lousy – but it is offensive, said Rav Huna. Committing suicide is a sin in Judaism.

Agreed, said Rav Pappa. We need to focus on how Jerry is an honorable man, German or not. He followed the male code: "All plans between men are tentative. If one man should suddenly have an opportunity to pursue a woman, it's like these two guys never met each other ever in life. This is the male code."

Again with the shtupping, chided Resh Lakish. But you are correct, honor is important. And we need to point out that Jerry quoted Hillel the Elder in "The Stranded." He turned to George and said: "If not now, when?" Not only are we analyzing *Seinfeld*, but the Seinfeld Four are analyzing us. I think this marks our television debut.

Big deal, said Abba the Surgeon, everyone knows "If not now, when." I've gotten it in fortune cookies. And I think we are avoiding the elephant in the room: what is the Halakhah around dingo baby-eating? What do you do if the dingo eats your baby?

What do you do if the dingo eats your baby? repeated the Sages in unison.

What exactly is a dingo? asked Shimon Ben Pazi.

I think dingo is a kind of pastry, replied Rabbah.

No, dingo is one of the few non-Yiddish words for penis, said Rav Pappa.

I fail to understand how a penis can eat a baby, said Shimon Ben Pazi.

No it's actually a dog, said Rabbi Abbahu. You know from the song: "there was a farmer who had a dog and Dingo was his name-o, D-I-N-G-O."

No that was BINGO, not Dingo, replied Bar Kappara. Dingo is actually the drummer for The Beatles.

Of course, said Rav Sheshet. Did you not see the cover art for the notorious Beatles "Butcher Album"? Paul, John, George, and Dingo are drenched in blood and holding dead babies. It was withdrawn from circulation in infamy.

Dingo Starr has a rather Jewish nose, pointed out Rav Pappa. Now it makes sense why his name sounds like penis. Are we sure he's not one of us? If he is in fact a Yid, there is no way he would eat a baby, "ye shall eat no manner of blood in any of your dwellings" (Leviticus 7:26).

Then this is worse than slander, said Bar Kappara. This constitutes blood libel, a charge of ritual murder against a Jew at a party on Long Island. Antisemitism!

Antisemitism, repeated the sages in unison.

Chevreh, concluded Rav Huna. This party not only blew, but I will suggest that it was an antisemitic gathering: Jerry is brainwashed by a German voice, yet he still pulls out a quote from Hillel the Elder to make his claim as a proud diasporic Jew; jokes about Hitler circulate while George is led away by a woman aptly named Ava; and a charge of ritual murder is impugned against Dingo.

The longest hatred; oh wretchedness of our exile! lamented Rav Sheshet.

Nevertheless, added Rav Pappa, In spite of everything, I still believe that Long Islanders are really good at heart.

The Alternate Side

MISHNAH:

Yohanan ben Zakkai: I called this meeting because we need to work on our enunciation. It has been brought to my attention that our flock of Semites thinks we Rabbi-Shepherds endlessly drone on, and in a rather whiny voice with a nasal Jewy intonation.

Rabbi Tarfon: About us they said this? May all their teeth fall out but one and in that one may they get a toothache.

Rabbi Shimon bar Yochai: Respect, Tarfon, respect.

Rabbi Tarfon: A pox on their house.

Yohanan ben Zakkai: OK Tarfon, now that you've proved their point, here is what I propose: We practice one of Hillel the elder's adages in our best mellifluous yet commanding voices: "The more flesh, the more worms; the more possessions, the more worry. The more Pretzels, the more they are making me thirsty."

Rabban Gamliel: "The MORE flesh, the MORE worms; the MORE possessions, the MORE worry. The MORE Pretzels, the MORE they are making me thirsty."

Jose the Galilean: "The more FLESH, the more worms; the more POSSESSIONS, the more worry. The more PRETZELS, the more they are making me thirsty."

Rabbi Tarfon: "What, the more flesh, the more I should have WORMS? the more possessions, the more I should have WORRY-oy vey? The more I have pretzels, the more they should be making ME thirsty?"

Rabbi Akivah: "The more flesh, THE MORE WORMS! the more possessions, THE MORE WORRY! The more Pretzels, the more THESE

PRETZELS ARE MAKING ME THIRSTY!"

Shimon bar Yochai: Is something amiss, Akivah?

Rabbi Akivah: "What was wrong with that? I had a different interpretation! Do you know anything about Hillel's imagined pretzel guy?! Maybe he has been hiding in a cave a really long time and he's really depressed because he has lost Bari his woman and his pen from Sinai disappeared in the shvitz and he is out of work because he partook in a failed messianic rebellion and he only scored 85 on his IQ test."

Yohanan ben Zakkai: I hate to bring this up, Akivah, but who puts your pants on?

The Red Dot

MISHNAH:

Rabbi Tarfon: I am the bearer of bad news. I caught Rabbi Akivah on the wagon.

Yohanan ben Zakkai: The expression is "off the wagon." Oh no he's started drinking? Akivah's become a shicker?* Maybe we've been a bit too hard on him.

Rabbi Tarfon: No I caught him on the wagon, literally. I caught him rolling in the hay, if you will, on your wagon, Master Zakkai, with a Samaritan woman.

Yohanan ben Zakkai: On my wagon? In my hay? What did he have to say for himself?

Rabbi Tarfon: Unclear because he was also drunk.

Jose the Galilean: So he was off the wagon on the wagon?

Rabbi Tarfon: He rambled on about a good Samaritan. How he was lying on the wagon, off the wagon, naked and in tears, all the Yeshivah students walking by and laughing at him, until this Samaritan lady came by, climbed in to console him, poured him some wine, and then dipped his bald head in oil and rubbed it all over her body.

Rabban Gamliel: Akivah needs to be punished. "The person driving [the two different animals yoked together] receives the forty [lashes]. And the person sitting in the wagon receives the forty [lashes]." (Mishnah Kilayim 8:3)

Shimon bar Yochai: That passage refers to two beasts of burden of different species yoked together, not two people of different genders yoked together.

Yohanan ben Zakkai: But Akivah and the Samaritan "yoked together" on my wagon!

Shimon bar Yochai: As it is written, "you anoint my head with oil; my cup overflows." (Psalms 23:5)

Yohanan ben Zakkai: Again, I don't want his cup overflowing on my wagon. The hay is fresh.

Jose the Galilean: Someone go fetch Akivah, just for a little chat.

……

Rabbi Akivah: You wanted to see me, Master?

Yohanan ben Zakkai: Akivah It has been brought to my attention that you and a Samaritan woman engaged in sexual intercourse on Yeshiva grounds on my wagon. Is that correct?

Rabbi Akivah: Was that wrong? Should I not have done that? I tell you I gotta plead ignorance on this thing because if anyone had said anything to me at all when I first started here at the Yeshivah that that sort of thing was frowned upon, you know, cause I've preached at a lot of Yeshivahs, and I tell you people do that all the time.

Yohanan ben Zakkai: And you are still drunk. Akivah you need to get back on the wagon.

Rabbi Akivah: But I just got off your wagon. And TBH it's a bit soiled; the Samaritan anointed my bald head with oil and my cup overflowed.

Yohanan ben Zakkai: I mean you need to get sober. Check into the local Batya Ford clinic.

Rabbi Akivah: But I'm a minor celebrity. Everyone will recognize me in my shame.

Yohanan ben Zakkai: Attach your IQ test to your garments. Nobody will believe you are the Great Sage Akivah, having scored 85. Oh, and that reminds me, bar Yochai would like his Mosaic pen back.

Rabbi Akivah: Funny thing – about that pen…

GEMARAH:

Chevreh, said Rav Huna, convening the emergency meeting, the disturbing evidence against Akivah keeps mounting. What is to be done?

For starters, I think we need to add "These Pretzels are making me thirsty" to his list of sayings, suggested Bar Kappara alluding to yesterday's shiur on "The Alternate Side."

Easy peasy, interjected Rav Zeira: "Before I taste anything, I recite a blessing, because these pretzels are making me thirsty."

But what about his roll in the hay on the wagon off the wagon with the Good Samaritan? Asked Resh Lakish. The entire escapade, is, how shall I put it, a bit too goyish.

We have a conundrum, insisted Resh Lakish. What is worse for our image, our future yichus? That Akivah be remembered for a drunken roll in the hay with a shiksa? Or for a raunchy Zionist fling of messianic proportions with Bari Weiss?

We can probably bury one of the incidents, but not both. Hey Pappa, you are the expert in whitewashing debauchery. Which is worse?

I'm afraid there is an easy answer, but one without a solution, said Pappa enigmatically, demonstrating that despite his dissipation he possessed wisdom: among the goyish Christian soldiers, Akivah and the Good Samaritan will not play well. It will be branded blasphemy and a mockery of Yeshu the Hanged One.* As for Akivah and the Zionist of ill-repute, it will be a disaster if word gets out on college campuses.

You're right, said Rav Sheshet. Either the Nazarenes will massacre us, or the Woke anti-Zionist Twerps will cancel us; we'll be dropped from the Jewish studies curriculum.

Oh who cares, said Bar Kappara. Nobody listens to Jewish studies professors. Everyone knows it is the rabbis who carry weight among our flock. Let's stick with Akivah and Bari; it's a Hollywood tale worthy of Paul Newman and Gal Gadot.

The Subway

MISHNAH:

Rabbi Tarfon: Fellow, sages, I return from the mountains, where the shepherds at the water well speak of a fallen Rabbi who while searching for work was conned by an Amalekite dungeon mistress and ended up naked and handcuffed to a bed at a Red Roof Inn.

Yohanan ben Zakkai: Oh no, I'm afraid to ask, is it Akivah?

Rabbi Tarfon: I received no confirmation, but it was also said he identified himself as Biff Loman and whistled the entire way down the elevator.

Shimon bar Yochai: Shackled in a house of bondage, Akivah did whistle for liberation.

Yohanan ben Zakkai: That's not bad Shimon; you should write it down.

Shimon bar Yochai: I can't; Akivah absconded with my pen.

GEMARAH:

Chevreh, said Rav Huna convening the shiur, while it may seem not much happened on "The Subway," it turns out the Mishnah speaks directly to it: "One who humiliates a naked person, or one who humiliates a blind person, or one who humiliates a sleeping person is liable, but a sleeping person who humiliates another is exempt." (Mishnah Bava Kamma 8:1)

Indeed, said Resh Lakish. George humiliated a blind musician by not offering him tzedakah.* He later paid for it himself by ending up naked and handcuffed to a hotel bed, much like Rabbi Akivah after his drunken roll in the hay on the wagon. How humiliating.

First off, the musician wasn't really blind, countered Rav Sheshet, second those charges against Akivah were never proven, and, finally, the expression is "off the wagon."

Yes, but George had no way of knowing any of that, replied Resh Lakish. More importantly, Jerry went to great lengths to humiliate a portly naked subway rider and suffered no punishment. In fact he was rewarded profusely with Coney Island hot dogs.

I agree, said Rav Sheshet, but I see your Mishnah and I raise you an Isaiah: "When you see the naked…you cover him" (Isaiah 58:7). Jerry should have robed him up, much as Shem and Japheth covered up Noah's nakedness. (Genesis 9)

I disagree, said Rav Pappa. Jerry owed the zhlob on the subway nothing. To compare him to Noah, "a righteous man, blameless among the people of his time… [walking] faithfully with God" (Genesis 6:9) is blasphemy.

But Noah had gotten completely plastered and fell asleep naked; some role model, retorted Bar Kappara.

The poor shmuck* was forced to live at sea for 40 days on a cramped boat replete with the revolting stench of two of every animal. I think he deserved an afternoon on the wagon naked, said Rav Pappa.

Again, the expression is off the wagon, replied Rav Sheshet.

And really, big frickin deal! Interjected Rav Kahana. Have you been on the New York subway? Two of every animal is nothing compared to the riffraff of Manhattan. To quote Elaine: "God, it's so crowded. How can there be so many people? This guy really smells, doesn't anyone use deodorant in the city? What is so hard, you take the cap off, you roll it on. What's that? I feel something rubbing against me. Disgusting animals, these people should be in a cage. We are in a cage."

I agree, said Bar Kappara; Noah got himself free passage on a cruise, like Jack Dawson in *Titanic*, except Noah's female companion didn't sink him to the bottom of the sea.

At least Rose could have left Jack's handcuffs attached to something dry. Both Akivah and Constanza survived their humiliating bondage to tell the tale, said Resh Lakish.

I think we have concluded, said Rav Huna, that the New York subway system is an abomination, worse than a leper colony, where the rats converge and the sewage of our exile flows. The Seinfeld Four endured a great tribulation of biblical proportions, one that puts Noah's Ark and the Titanic to shame.

The Pez Dispenser

GEMARAH:

Chevreh, said Rav Huna, convening the meeting, we have so much to discuss with "The Pez Dispenser."

I agree said Rav Kahana. We need to discuss why Postum isn't a more popular drink.

No, you shmegegge, countered Rav Pappa, we need to discuss how one gets hand in a relationship.

No, said Bar Kappara, we need to discuss why these Pez dispensers are so difficult to load.

No, said Resh Lakish, we need to discuss who was at fault for ruining Noel's piano recital. Pez dispensers are dangerous, and I don't think they're kosher. Jews aren't supposed to mess with machinery like that.

Then why does Jerry have one? asked Rav Sheshet, and, to quote Costanza, What kind of a sick impulse led Jerry to put it on Elaine's leg? He's a genuine mental defective.

I disagree, responded Resh Lakish. Elaine is at fault. To quote Jerry, "Anyone who would laugh at a recital is probably some sort of lunatic anyway. I mean only a sick twisted mind could be that rude and ignorant."

No George is at fault, countered Rav Kahana. He should have come clean and told Noel that her friends are jerks.

But he had no hand, said Rav Pappa. SHE…would have broken up…with HIM. A man without hand is not a man.

And Biff is not a man, added Rav Kahana. What kind of idiot thinks they have fleas at the flea market?

Costanza does, said Bar Kappara. And not without reason. Remember in "The Stranded" he actually contracted fleas and Jerry told him to get a flea collar? That's probably why he has never been to a flea market.

No the entire debacle is Kramer's fault, said Raba bar Rav Huna. He's the one who gave Jerry that lethal Pez dispenser in the first place. "Just as it is prohibited to sell [a weapon] to a gentile, it is prohibited to sell [a weapon] to an armed bandit who is a Jew." (Avodah Zarah 15b:13)

A Pez dispenser is not a weapon, said Bar Kappara.

Not true, said Resh Lakish. During the intervention, Richie relates how his father crashed his car into a high school cafeteria while trying to load a Pez dispenser, sparking the admittedly short-lived "Don't Load Pez and Drive" campaign and the "Mothers Against Pezzed Driving" movement. Maybe that traumatic incident laid the foundations for Richie's later drug problem.

For which Kramer was also responsible! Added Shimon ben Pazi.

I don't trust this Kramer, said Rabbi Abbahu. Always interfering and never intervening.

Yes, said Abba the Surgeon, and I think we are ignoring the elephant in the room: why does Reb Kramer go swimming in frigid waters with a bunch of old Jewish men? Is this Polar Bear Club a Jewish organization?

Polar Bear Club is mentioned zero times in the Mishnah, noted Yontl the Librarian. Zero.

Maybe they are remnants of the Dead Sea Qumran Sect who fled the Romans into icy depths like the survivors of the Titanic and Noah's Ark? suggested Rav Sheshet.

What makes you so sure they're Jewish? asked Rav Pappa.

"What??? You don't want to be a POLAR BEAR Anymore??? It's too COLD for you? … I have POUCH envy!!! At least give me a POCKet?" quoted Abba the Surgeon.

Oy, he could be my mother-in-law, admitted Rav Huna.

Jews, agreed Rav Sheshet.

Jews, Jews, Jews, Jews, repeated the Sages in unison.

I think, concluded Rav Huna, we need to work on our intonation, lest we bequeath "the Jewish Voice" to history alongside our Jewish noses (Sander Gilman, *The Jewish Body*).

Not that there's anything wrong with it, added Rav Pappa.

The Suicide

MISHNAH:

Rabbi Tarfon: I've got news. Akivah is in a coma.

Jose the Galilean: He fell off the wagon again?

Rabbi Tarfon: Literally, while riding on his wagon – actually your wagon, Zakkai – he deliberately collided with a pony and fell off the wagon. A suicide attempt.

Shimon bar Yochai: I am going to ransack his cave and find my pen. He never gave it back.

Rabbi Tarfon: I'm going to hit up Bari Weiss for a date; she's useless to Akivah now.

Jose the Galilean: I loaned him my vacuum cleaner. He never returned it. And you Zakkai, you can go over to Akivah's and get your wagon back.

Yohanan ben Zakkai: We will do no such things. That would be terrible coma etiquette.

Rabbi Tarfon: What kind of a man are you?

Yohanan ben Zakkai: A man who respects a good coma.

Rabban Gamliel: You're just a coward, Zakkai. Akivah is under that thug Bar Kochbah's protection. The violent messianics will slice off our beytzim and parade them around Mount Moriah. Hence your so-called coma etiquette.

Jose the Galilean: And you Tarfon, what will you do if he wakes up. Run away like a mouse?

Yohanan ben Zakkai: No, Tarfon will run like the Three Stooges at the end of every performance.

Rabbi Tarfon: Who are these Stooges you speak of?

Yohanan ben Zakkai: You don't know the Stooges, Tarfon?

Jose the Galilean: Neither do I. Tell us about the Stooges. Everything.

Yohanan ben Zakkai: They're three kind of funny looking rabbis who hit each other a lot in the Yavneh marketplace.

Rabbi Tarfon: You will show me the Stooges?

Yohanan ben Zakkai: I will show you the stooges. But you are not calling Bari Weiss.

GEMARAH:

Fellow sages, said Rav Huna, calling the emergency meeting, for the first time ever I am genuinely disgusted with our predecessors.

I know, I have never seen such terrible coma etiquette, said Resh Lakish.

There is no coma etiquette, insisted Adda bar Ahavah. You see that's the beauty of the coma, man. It doesn't matter what you do around it.

So you're saying, his wagon, his pen, his vacuum cleaner, Bari Weiss, it's all up for grabs? Asked Resh Lakish. You can just loot the coma victim?

Rabbah, promise me something, implored Rav Pappa. If I'm ever in a coma. In the first 24 hours get everything out of my apartment and put it in storage.

Not a chance, said Rabbah. I don't want to be seen around Babylon with your orgy stuff, your lotions, and robes, and weirdo lighting. No way, Pappa. Get some of your swinger friends like Spector or Bob Sacamano to help you out.

No you yolds, interjected, Rav Huna. This has nothing to do with coma etiquette. This is about the Sages of Yavneh not knowing the Three Stooges.

I don't know these Stooges you speak of, admitted Resh Lakish.

Me neither, said Rav Pappa. Huna, Will you show me the Stooges?

I will show you the Stooges, Pappa, promised Rav Huna. But I will not go near your orgy stuff, even if you are in a coma.

The Fix-Up

GEMARAH:

Chevreh, began Rav Huna, convening the meeting, I think we need to discuss some of the finer points of Reb Costanza-Cartwright's adventures in intimacy.

Finally, a topic I can get with, replied Rav Pappa the Player, whose sexual escapades were infamous all across Babylon, although the jury was still out as to whether his notoriety was good for the Jews or bad for the Jews.

I knew you'd be enthusiastic Pappa, replied Rav Huna, but please keep your pants on, this is a serious matter.

Costanza, Lord of the Idiots, is a yold, a shmegegge, a shmendrik, and quite possibly as big a shnorrer* as Kramer, insisted Resh Lakish.

And he prefers sexual intercourse in the kitchen, apparently on the stove, added Rav Sheshet. He's what Archie Bunker would call a "preevert."

I enjoy sexual intercourse in the kitchen, interjected Rav Pappa.

Q.E.D. retorted Rav Sheshet. Not kosher, to put it mildly.

I think it depends on whether the seminal emission occurs in propinquity to the milchig or fleishig dishes,* and what they had consumed for dinner, suggested Shimon ben Pazi.

"The Sages taught: Five food items bring a man to a state of impurity due to emission. And these are: garlic, cress, purslane, eggs, and arugula." (Yoma 18a-b), quoted Rav Kahana.

We do not know whether food caused George to ejaculate in the kitchen, countered Rav Pappa.

Yet we do know that ejaculation occurred, and the emission traveled a number of cubits because he used one of Bob Sacamano's defective free condoms. We have already established that George is a bit parsimonious, said Rabbah, hence his use of a defective condom because it was free. His stinginess may have rendered the kitchen impure.

Cheap, cheap, cheap, cheap, said the Sages in unison.

Ah, but his breakthrough emission and Cynthia's near pregnancy demonstrated Costanza's menshlichkeit,* said Rav Pappa. A nice Jewish boy, prepared to commit in full to Cynthia's decision. And he will have progeny, because, as he put it, "my boys can swim!" A major accomplishment since he had previously kvetched that "I've never had a normal, medium orgasm." ("The Heart Attack," s2e8).

And his virility is all the more remarkable, given that Costanza is one of the few documented survivors of an atomic wedgie, noted Hillel the Unhilly. The Lord had mercy on his beytzim, and we must see him as a man of God.

"His power is in his loins and his strength is in the navel of his belly. His tail is hard as a cedar; the sinews of his testicles are knit together," (Job: 16-17), quoted Zutra the Mohel, in wonder, contemplating what it would be like to get Costanza on his operating table.

May I add, interjected Resh Lakish, that his resume also includes: the attempted poisoning of his boss, sexual intercourse on the desk of his office – which presumably included having "a normal medium orgasm," – an inability to hold down a job, cheating on an IQ test, compelling a woman to get a nose job because Peter Jennings had one, and thinking he has lupus.

And he's cheap, added Rav Sheshet.

Cheap, cheap, cheap, cheap, said the Sages in unison.

But he's read *Moby-Dick* and knows the best public bathroom in every corner of New York, countered Rav Pappa.

He can also lift a hundred pounds over his head and bait a hook, added Shimon ben Pazi.

Sure, baiting a hook must really come in handy in Manhattan, retorted Resh Lakish.

As Hillel the Elder said, "In a place where there are no fish to catch, one must strive to catch a marble rye," offered Yontl the Librarian.

It appears we are at an impasse, concluded Rav Huna. I suspect we are only beginning to unravel the enigma of Costanza. But let us agree – for the sake of our health – to never set foot in Rav Pappa's kitchen.

The Limo

GEMARAH:

Fellow sages, began Rav Huna, "The Limo" is a rather disturbing episode. There is so much to discuss.

This is the Seinfeld Four's second encounter with antisemitism, said Bar Kappara, and it is far worse than the notorious Dingo Starr Long Island Blood Libel in "The Stranded."

And George's yearning to sleep with Eva the Nazi is rather unbecoming for a Jew, said Resh Lakish.

She did say she was ready to die for him, pointed out Rav Sheshet, and did you see the way she looked at him?

But she's a Nazi, Sheshet, a Nazi, screamed Resh Lakish.

I know, I know. Kind of a cute Nazi though, replied Rav Sheshet.

I don't even think a philanderer like Rav Pappa would shtupp a Nazi, said Resh Lakish. Would you Pappa?

Of course not, how can you even ask me that? replied Rav Pappa. OK maybe I would. Rav Huna, what is the Halakhah on sexual intercourse with an antisemite?

The law is clear, replied Rav Huna. It is impermissible to shtupp a Nazi.

What if shtupping a Nazi could prevent a pogrom? asked Bar Kappara. Did Queen Esther's betrothal to Ahasuerus not prevent Haman from exterminating the Jews of Persia?

But Queen Esther did not know he would assent to the extermination of the Jews until after they had hooked up and exchanged nocturnal emissions, countered Rav Kahana.

Yes, but she knew Ahasuerus was a misogynist; he had treated Vashti like a camel and chose his next bride through a beauty pageant, said Resh Lakish. Even a philanderer like Rav Pappa wouldn't behave so egregiously. Would you Pappa?

Of course not, how can you even ask me that? replied Rav Pappa. OK maybe I would. Rav Huna, what is the Halakhah on sexual intercourse with an antisemite if it could avert a pogrom?

Well Esther does have much in common with George, aside from the baldness, replied Rav Huna. They are both closeted Jews, and they both turned out to be heroes to our people.

George was going to be a Queen Esther, a Queen Esther! said Rav Pappa.

Yeah well, Queen Esther did not live in Queens with Frank and Estelle Costanza, replied Rav Sheshet. Mother Costanza won't even buy a German car or let George have sexual intercourse in their bed. He should not have phoned Estelle from the Limo. How exactly would he get away with shtupping a Nazi?

And how exactly was George a hero to the Jews? There was zero evidence in "The Limo" that he was prepared to fight the Nazis, countered Resh Lakish. In fact he was trying to weasel his way out of it, as usual.

Much as he lied about seeing the Bat-Signal in "The Chinese Restaurant," in order to make a number two in private, lamented Shimon ben Pazi.

He even blamed the Jews for AstroTurf, in "The Limo" added Rav Sheshet. Feh!

What are AstroTurfs? Asked Shimon ben Pazi.

They are transphobes who believe hermaphrodites, tumtums, and eunuchs come from outer space, specifically celestial objects between Mars and Jupiter, said Bar Kappara.

No you are thinking of Astro-TERFS, not AstroTurfs, replied Abba the Surgeon, whose clinic had seen its fair share of hermaphrodites, tumtums, and eunuchs back when Zutra the Mohel first set up his private practice and occasionally went overboard practicing on privates.

But what does this have to do with the Jews? asked Shimon ben Pazi. We are not from outer space.

Tell that to Dave Chappelle, concluded Rav Huna.

The Good Samaritan

MISHNAH:

Hillel: Do not judge a man until you stand in his place.
Shammai: But If I say "God bless you" to another man's wife?
Hillel: You are no Good Samaritan; you are a disgrace.
Shammai: And what if I sleep with his wife?
Hillel: Then he will sew your ass to your face.

GEMARAH:

Fellow sages, began Rav Huna, today's lesson is about whether George deserves to have his ass sewn to his face.

I don't think it's possible to sew someone's ass to their face, said a confused Shimon ben Pazi.

Actually, you'd be surprised, replied Abba the Surgeon. Individuals burdened with such, if you will, rectum transplants, show up at my clinic all the time. It is a common form of punishment for adulterers among the mountain people of Persia.

What does someone with their ass sewn to their face look like? asked a still perplexed Shimon ben Pazi.

That depends on what they looked like beforehand, said Abba the Surgeon. With a short stocky slow witted bald man like George, pretty much the same. In fact if he puts his glasses on his ass-face, the difference is negligible.

Still, interjected Rav Pappa, this would have been a cruel and unjust punishment for George, who did nothing wrong. George is a Good Samaritan, whose ass should remain where his ass belongs. And he is a documented survivor of an atomic wedgie.

I disagree, insisted Resh Lakish, he committed adultery.

No he didn't, replied Rav Pappa. The law is clear, Robin is the adulterer. And as she said, "If I didn't do it with you, I would have done it with someone else."

And probably with someone who doesn't say "God bless you," added Shimon ben Pazi.

Yes it is obvious that Robin is the sinner and should be punished, said Rav Pappa. I would also seize her husband, Michael, and sew his ass to his face. Who doesn't say "God bless you" to their own wife? George is a Good Samaritan.

Do not blame Robin, interjected Bar Kappara; she was lonely and all juiced up, because of Elaine's invented affair with Eduardo Carochio, the bullfighter. She pulled a Hemingway. And did anyone sew Hemingway's ass to his face?

Where does one even meet a matador in Babylon? asked Rav Sheshet.

Actually, you'd be surprised, replied Abba the Surgeon. Gored matadors show up at my clinic all the time. The Mishnah has quite a bit of Halakhah on oxen that gore men, including bullfighters.

Which is worse? To be gored by an ox or to have your ass sewn to your face? asked Shimon ben Pazi.

I would say it depends on the ox and it depends on the face, suggested Rav Kahana.

I would say gored by an ox is worse, replied Rav Pappa. To have your ass sewn to your face in Babylon implies that intercourse has transpired, so at the very least your butt goes out with a bang. Conversely, having your beytzim bludgeoned by a bull is not for me.

I disagree, said Resh Lakish. Everyone loves a matador. Nobody loves a short stocky slow-witted bald man in glasses who looks the same with or without his ass sewn to his face.

There is actually Halakhah on such matters, interjected Yontl the Librarian. None other than Rabbi Yehudah HaNasi distinguishes between one who is "sneezing from above, his nose" and one who is "sneezing from below, flatulence … One who sneezes in the midst of prayer, it is a good omen for him. Just as the sneeze soothes his irritation, giving him pleasure below, it is a sign that they are similarly giving him pleasure above." (Berakhot 24b:5).

So then does one say "God bless you" if one sneezes from below? asked Bar Kappara.

A very good question, said the Sages in unison.

I would say no, replied Resh Lakish. "Blessed are the fart makers" is from the Gospels, a text which we Jews do not recognize.

But what if the fart maker has his ass sewn to his face? asked Bar Kappara. His sneeze from below is now coming from above. Can one even tell what type of sneeze it is if they all come from above?

Perhaps this is why Michael wanted to sew George's ass to his face. It would be a lesson in God bless yous. With every sneeze-fart George would be reminded of Robin.

Well it looks like we have made headway on this unexpectedly complex topic, concluded Rav Huna. I say we take a field trip to Abba the Surgeon's clinic before we discuss ass-to-face sewing any further. We need to engage in some empirical observation, lest we lose credibility among our flock.

The Letter

GEMARAH:

Wow what an episode, said Rav Huna, convening the meeting. I think I know what everyone wants to discuss today.

Of course, replied Rav Pappa, yet another episode that centers shlongs and the hazards we Jews face walking around with these things.

Your obsession with Mr. Johnson is rather tiring and so predictable, Pappa, yet I admit I am intrigued, said Rav Huna. How exactly is this episode about the penis?

First off, I call him "Rabbi Johnson," not "Mr. Johnson," insisted Rav Pappa. Second, "The Letter" raises two important penile debates, and both pertain to Judaic ritual.

Sorry, please tell us about "Rabbi Johnson's" presence in "The Letter," said Rav Huna.

George and Jerry debate whether it is better to have buttons or a zipper as the fly on your pants, said Rav Pappa.

A weighty question! said Bar Kappara. I admit that I have had multiple mishaps with my fly. George is correct: those buttons are cumbersome, and I once spent 20 harrowing minutes trapped in the latrine on a Friday trying to button up and I missed sundown. One is not allowed to usher in the Sabbath in a latrine with one's hands down one's pants. I have been a zipper guy ever since.

I disagree, countered Resh Lakish. Jerry is correct in saying that "that is one place on my wardrobe I do not need sharp interlocking metal teeth."

Agreed, interjected Zutra the Mohel. Do you know how bad jagged metal teeth in the crotch is for my business? My work is an art and mishaps below the equator taint my artwork. If a prospective client sees a petzl mutilated by an overzealous zipper they may mistake it for my craftsmanship.

Much as Kramer desecrated George's painting with his shnot, said Shimon ben Pazi. People would assume Kramer's boogers were part of Nina's artistic expression. The zipper is your nemesis, Zutra.

Exactly, replied Zutra the Mohel. The Bris is part performance and part product, and I am an Artiste.

Yet it's a performance nobody wants to witness, said Rav Pappa, which brings us to the second debate from the episode. As Elaine said regarding Mr. Lipman's son's bris, "What makes you think anyone would want to go to a circumcision?"

Yes, like George, "I'd rather go to a hanging," said Rav Sheshet.

Agreed, said Resh Lakish. More people attended Haman's execution than Abraham's bris.

And we commemorate the hanging with festive merriment and abundant liquor every Purim, added Rav Pappa, whereas the goys mocked Abraham for taking a cleaver to his own privates.

Hey, I distribute vodka shots at all my circumcisions, insisted Zutra the Mohel.

But your audience drinks to forget, not to celebrate, countered Resh Lakish.

I am very attached to my artwork, insisted Zutra the Mohel, and you are tarnishing my reputation as a professional.

You are essentially an overpaid zipper, replied Rav Pappa.

Maybe we should replace Zutra with a zipper? suggested Resh Lakish.

Or at the very least, rename him "Zutra the Zipper," suggested Rav Sheshet. People should know what they are paying for.

I think, resolved Rav Huna, we need to attend a bris and a hanging this week, and then decide which is a more gratifying experience.

But what about the zipper? asked Resh Lakish.

I think, resolved Rav Huna, we also need to accompany Bar Kappara to the latrine twice this week and watch him do up his pants with buttons and then do up his pants with a zipper, and then decide which is a more gratifying experience.

The Parking Space

GEMARAH:

Fellow Sages, we have an unexpected attendee today, Rav Chisda, who almost never shows up for our shiurs, said Rav Huna, launching the meeting.

Yes, where have you been Chisda? interjected Resh Lakish. Let me guess, you were stuck in the latrine trying to button up your fly.

Or perhaps you ran out of underwear and couldn't leave the house? added Rav Sheshet.

Maybe he has zippers on all his pants? Which means zipping up would have been particularly dangerous, if he ran out of underwear, added Rav Pappa.

Rav Pappa, Rav Sheshet, and Resh Lakish laughed in unison, a rare moment of bonding over privates among three otherwise quarrelsome colleagues.

I am here today, replied Rav Chisda, to make a case for front-first parking.

This is such an important issue for you that you leave the house without underwear risking your Rabbi Johnson on your razor-sharp zipper? asked Rav Pappa.

Drop it Pappa, said Resh Lakish. That joke has been played out. So, so played. And I'm still not your friend.

I demand the right to parallel park my camel headfirst in the Yeshivah district, said Rav Chisda.

Chisda, I don't think this is a problem. Has anyone prevented you from front-first camel parking? Asked Rav Huna.

Uh no, not really, replied Rav Chisda.

Does anyone here have a problem with front-first parking? asked Rav Huna.

The Sages remained silent.

Well that was easy, said Rav Sheshet. What shall we talk about now?

We should discuss whether or not George is correct: that paying for parking is like going to a prostitute. "Why should I pay, when if I apply myself, maybe I could get it for free?" asked Rav Pappa.

How often do you have to pay for it Pappa? asked Bar Kappara.

I know how to apply myself, thank you, insisted Rav Pappa, and I can get it for free.

Front-first and back-first, added Resh Lakish.

Touché, replied Rav Pappa.

I think we are all missing the principal lesson from "The Parking Space," interjected Abba the Surgeon: the hat George purchased at the flea market.

Why is that? asked Bar Kappara.

I know, I know, said Shimon ben Pazi jumping from his seat: because we are living in a bald paradise; we Jews of Babylon wear hats all the time. And so do the goyim.

Shimon is correct for once, said Resh Lakish. Jew-Pattern Baldness is not a disability here in Pumbedita.

But why do we wear the same hats all the time? Asked Shimon ben Pazi. Can't we mix it up a bit?

Agreed, said Rav Pappa. I would like an Orioles cap like Elaine wore in "The Letter." It was a bold statement on her part.

Always the transgressor, Pappa, mumbled Resh Lakish.

Then that settles it, concluded Rav Huna. To the flea market! But be mindful of their parking lot. They do not allow front-first camel parking.

The Keys

MISHNAH:

Shammai: My whole life has been a fantasy world. Everything is better by you. Better food, better view, better TV, better women. Nobody listens to my judgments, whereas yours become canonical. Take your keys back, I don't deserve entry into the House of Hillel.

Hillel: Take care of yourself – you never know when the world will need you.

Shammai: You see, always a snappy quote at the ready. Whereas I sit here like a yold, and I yearn. Do you ever yearn?

Hillel: I don't yearn, I learn. He who refuses to learn deserves extinction.

Shammai: Again with a zippy quote that will be sacralized by the Rabbis, whereas I am living in twilight, living in the shadows, living in darkness.

Hillel: If you are not for yourself who will be for you, Shammai?

Shammai: Stop it already, this is infuriating. Fine, I'm not going waste my life anymore, I'm going to do something for myself.

Hillel: But if you're only for yourself, what are you, Shammai?

Shammai: Obviously a shmegegge. I can't listen to this anymore. I've got the bug. I think I'm going to pack up and go to Babylon.

Hillel: Do not separate yourself from the community, Do not trust in yourself until the day of your death, Do not judge your fellow man until you have reached his place.

Shammai: This is exactly why I am leaving the community. I've got no money, no woman, no prospects, nothing on the horizon, no action at all. That's it, I have to get out of here soon.

Hillel: If not now, when?

Shammai (Pointing to his head): Up here, I'm already gone.

Season 4

The Rabbis Debate Nose Picking and Nipple Exposure on Jewish Holidays

The Trip – Part I

GEMARAH:

This episode got me thinking about reviving my acting career, said Rav Pappa.
What acting career? asked a skeptical Resh Lakish.

I used to perform with the Three Stooges in the marketplace, said Rav Pappa.
We were almost the Four Stooges. But my mother made me quit to become a rabbi.

How lucky for us, retorted Rav Sheshet.

Come on, said Rav Pappa, look at the K-Man, frolicking with Candace
Bergen and Fred Savage, George chatting up Corbin Bernsen and George Wendt.
Plus Kramer found himself a beautiful girlfriend.

Some catch, replied Bar Kappara. Her ambition was to play Eva Braun in a
mini-series, premised around what it would be like to have sex with Adolf Hitler.

And that's an important topic we've broached before, said Rav Pappa.

Yes, we are aware of your lack of inhibitions about sleeping with Nazis, said
Rav Sheshet.

We've ruled it is halakhically permissible to shtupp a Nazi in order to avert a
pogrom against the Jews, said Rav Pappa. Does it not follow that it is permissible
to play the girlfriend of a Nazi who has the power to avert a pogrom against the
Jews?

There is zero evidence to suggest Eva Braun was shtupping Hitler to save the
Jews, interjected Rav Huna. She was a Nazi, much like Eva in "The Limo." And
there's zero evidence Kramer's girlfriend wanted to portray Eva Braun as
anything other than a Nazi to experience what it was like to have sex with Adolf
Hitler.

And to learn what her parents thought of Hitler as a potential son-in-law,
added Bar Kappara.

Having sex with Adolf Hitler, couldn't be a pleasant experience, said Rav

Kahana, with the missing beytzah and all. And that bunker must have been a real shvitz.

Far less shvitzier with one testicle than with two! Added Shimon ben Pazi, doing the math.

She would have made a cute Nazi though, replied Rav Pappa.

Lupe was far cuter, insisted Resh Lakish.

Oh come on, replied Rav Pappa. She threw out Jerry's comedic material and can't keep her yes-tucks and no-tucks straight.

What is the Halakhah on sheet and blanket tucking? asked Bar Kappara.

That's easy, replied Rav Huna: "And Rabbi Yossei said: In all my days, the walls of my house never saw the seams of my robe due to modesty, as he would only undress under his bed sheets." (Shabbat 118b:11) It stands to reason Rabbi Yossei was a no-tuck, surmised Rav Huna. One can't get dressed with the sheets all tucked in. Lupe had no business giving Jerry and George the option. It should have been two no-tucks, not one tuck and one no-tuck.

Yet the Smog Strangler killed Chelsea, not Lupe, said Bar Kappara. Kramer's decision to get involved with a would-be Nazi was a far worse choice than Lupe's one tuck and one no-tuck. And bad choices have consequences.

Poor Kramer, said Shimon ben Pazi. All he wanted to do was work with color, imagine color, then find the emotional vibrational mood connected to the color. And then he was accused of being a serial killer.

I think we need to continue this discussion later, said Rav Huna.

The Trip – Part II

MISHNAH:

Hillel: Kramer possesses great vulnerability, a Pharisee child crying out for love, an innocent primate in the post-modern world.

Shammai: He is a parasite, a sexually depraved Hellenizer, who is seeking only to gratify his basest and most immediate urges.

Hillel: His struggle is Israel's struggle. He lifts my spirit.

Shammai: He is a loathsome, offensive bulvan, yet I can't look away.

Hillel: He transcends time and space.

Shammai: He sickens me.

Hillel: I love The Kramer.

Shammai: Me too.

GEMARAH:

Fellow Sages, began Rav Huna convening the meeting, today we continue our discussion about "The Trip." We Rabbis are a court of law and need to adjudicate the halakhic infractions committed by these depraved Hellenizers in La La Land.

The evidence against Kramer is pretty damning, said Resh Lakish. He traveled with a cult and boasted of killing a man, dated his subsequently murdered girlfriend who aspired to simulate sex with Adolf Hitler on West German TV, and flirted with an unemployed octogenarian in his building who quite possibly helped the Three Stooges hide a dead baby.

But he was innocent, insisted Rav Pappa.

Not quite, said Rav Sheshet. He did break the Covenant of the Keys. He turned Jerry's apartment into a house of ill repute with his lady friends and bubble baths.

Very minor infractions, replied Rav Pappa. Jerry overreacted, and should have not taken his keys back. And Kramer had the decency to towel up after the bubble bath.

With Jerry's towel! Interjected Bar Kappara.

Have you ever wondered, Pappa, why you do not have keys to any of our houses? asked Resh Lakish.

Or keys to the Yeshivah? added Rav Huna.

Or keys to the supply closet? added bar Kappara.

Or keys to the latrine? added Resh Lakish.

I'm an innocent primate, like Kramer. And he was acquitted of all charges, much as I was when I visited the Aramean woman who concealed a dead baby in her bed sheets (Berakhot 8b:10), and I only got off BECAUSE I made her untuck what should have been a no-tuck in her bedroom.

Well played Pappa, well played, said Resh Lakish – switching the conversation back to Lupe and the tucked bedsheets – though I still wonder what you were doing in an Aramean woman's bedroom in the first place.

I was going to hire her as my maid and I wanted to check to see if she was a tuck or a no-tuck, replied Rav Pappa.

Lupe was guilty, as Jerry predicted, said Bar Kappara. She failed in her one tuck and one no-tuck and ended up tucking George's covers in.

And I bet you she steals the little bars of soap from the hotel rooms, said Rav Sheshet.

Tuck or no-tuck, she's entitled to some bars of soap at the end of the week to supplement her paycheck, said Rav Pappa. She should be allowed to take a Bible or two as well.

Have you ever wondered, Pappa, why you do not have keys to any of our houses? asked Resh Lakish.

Or keys to the Yeshivah? added Rav Huna.

Or keys to the supply closet? added bar Kappara.

Or keys to the latrine? added Resh Lakish.

This is the most public yet of my many humiliations, lamented Rav Pappa.

And Season 4 has just begun, Pappa, concluded Rav Huna. You will never survive "The Contest." You'll be out before your Rabbi Johnson manages to get through the interlocking metal teeth.

The Pitch / The Ticket

MISHNAH:

Yohanan ben Zakkai: It's time we start writing our conversations down. It will serve as the basis for a sacred text, or at the very least a sitcom.

Rabban Gamliel: Good God why? Why would anyone want to read this stuff?

Yohanan ben Zakkai: Because we Sages, living in a time of turmoil yet low Nielsen Ratings, are guardians of a complex Oral Law and we possess insight. Look at Hillel the Elder and all he has contributed. His pearls of wisdom cannot be lost to history.

Jose the Galilean: You mean like "If Not Now, When?" Do we really need to write that down?

Yohanan ben Zakkai: It's a profound statement. It will spawn mass movements to end injustice on college campuses.

Rabbi Tarfon: He also said "What you yourself hate, don't do to your neighbor. This is the whole law; the rest is commentary. Go and study." If THAT is the whole law then this sounds like a rather short book. There's nothing left to say.

Eleazar ben Azariah: Our sacred sitcom will be devoid of plot. It will be called a book about nothing containing nothing.

Jose the Galilean: Then maybe we should manufacture fortune cookies instead.

Rabbi Tarfon: I like that idea. But we are not Chinese. We will be accused of cultural appropriation and of violating Yavneh's diversity, equity, and inclusion policy.

Jose the Galilean: No problem, let's do an Ellis Island and change some of our sagely Jewy names to sagely Chinese names. We will pull a Donna Changstein.

Rabbi Tarfon: That still sounds like cultural appropriation.

Jose the Galilean: No it's not. My name is "Jose" FFS. My parents pulled a Juan Epstein on me. But nobody questions my wisdom as a Puerto Rican Jew. And the upshot is the Puerto Ricans consider me a sage as well. They call me

"Jose Pendejo El Galileo."

Rabbi Tarfon: What does that mean?

Jose the Galilean: How the hell should I know? I'm not really Puerto Rican.

Rabbi Tarfon: Good point, Jose. OK then I officially proclaim that our master Yohanan ben Zakkai will henceforth be known as "Yo-Hunan Chen Zakkai."

All hail Yo-Hunan Chen Zakkai, said the Sages in unison.

Jose the Galilean: Yes! And we can use this opportunity to finally give poor Shammai his due. All our fortune cookies will be labeled "From The House of Shumai."

Let us bow before the House of Shumai, the Sages said in unison.

Rabban Gamliel: I dunno, this sounds like cultural appropriation, or at best the lyrics to an Allan Sherman song.

Jose the Galilean: What say you, Chen Zakkai, Master Shifu?

Yo-Hunan Chen Zakkai: Allow me to share a bit of wisdom from Confucius: "Real knowledge is to know the extent of one's ignorance."

Rabbi Tarfon: You're right, you're right. We are sitting here procrastinating, making up excuses, when in fact we should be coming up with ideas for our text.

Jose the Galilean: OK how about this –Yo-Hunan Chen Zakkai manages a Chinese circus…

GEMARAH:

It seems, said Rav Huna, convening the meeting, that our predecessors were procrastinators and took this idea of writing "a book about nothing" a bit too seriously, leaving us with a mess.

And to think, said Rav Pappa, we could have inherited a Chinese circus.

And this is why, added Rav Sheshet, Ted Danson makes so much more money than us.

I'm sorry, lamented Rav Pappa, I can't live knowing Ted Danson makes that much more than me. Who is he?

He's somebody, replied Resh Lakish.

And what about me? replied Rav Pappa.

You're a nobody whose life ambition is to manage a circus, said Resh Lakish.

You're also somebody, added Bar Kappara, who really needs help. A regular psychiatrist couldn't even help you. You need to go to Vienna, at the university level. A team of psychiatrists working round the clock thinking about you, having conferences, observing you, like the way they did with the Elephant Man.

But wasn't the Elephant Man in the circus? asked Shimon ben Pazi. Maybe the Elephant Man is the key to transcending the halakhic impasse we have reached?

Hey Pazi, interjected Resh Lakish, go back to your Batman comic, you're not helping.

The only solution, said Bar Kappara, is to pick up from where they left off. What have we got?

Let's see, said Rav Sheshet. George wants to know what they used for toilet paper in the Civil War. And later George and Jerry debate whether or not vomiting on someone is a deal breaker.

"Vomit" is mentioned 31 times in the Bible and 4 times in the Mishnah, noted Yontl the Librarian.

And it's go time! said a cheerful Rav Huna, we have our debate: is vomit a deal breaker? But first let's grab a bite to eat. Who's up for Chinese? Door Dash now delivers The House of Shumai in Babylon. No fortune cookies though.

The Wallet

GEMARAH:

I think we need to discuss Morty Seinfeld's aversion to Velcro, said Rav Huna convening the meeting.

If you ask me, replied Resh Lakish, Morty is a lunatic. Velcro is a perfectly logical way to conjoin things that need to be conjoined.

Like the fly of one's pants! Added Bar Kappara. Wouldn't it be wonderful if they had Velcro on our barn doors instead of buttons? No more getting stuck in the latrine before Shabbos with your mouse creeping out of the house.

"'Twas the night before Shabbos, when all through the house, my dingdong was stirring, it crept through like a mouse," crooned Rabbah, who was – admittedly by default – the resident Yeshivah Bard.

Yes! Exclaimed Rav Pappa. There is no good reason to risk Rabbi Johnson on interlocking metal teeth. Velcro can't decapitate. I see a bright future for my pants and their inimitable contents.

Not true, not true, chimed in Zutra the Mohel, also known as Zutra the Zipper. In an effort to put a more humane face on our operations and to salvage my floundering reputation, we have been experimenting with new circumcision techniques. We think using industrial strength Velcro might be the answer. One quick rip and you have entered into the Covenant with HaShem.

That sounds incredibly painful and most likely illegal, said Rav Sheshet. I think YOU are the lunatic Zutra, not Morty Seinfeld. Zutra the Zipper? I say you are Zutra the Ripper!

Zutra the Ripper, the Beytzim Butcher of Babylon, said the Sages in unison.

Perhaps Morty Seinfeld was circumcised as a child by a deranged mohel who used the Velcro Technique, suggested Resh Lakish. That would explain a lot. "I can't stand Velcro. It's that t-e-a-r-i-n-g sound. I used to be in raincoats. I refused to put that in any of my lines."

Poor Morty, lamented Shimon ben Pazi. Traumatized on his eighth day by Velcro, and he took it out on his raincoats for 38 years.

Fellow, Sages, asked Hanina ben Pappa, why do our discussions keep returning to the penises, and mangled ones at that?

To quote Jerry Seinfeld at the 23-minute mark, "Can we continue this another time?" said Rav Huna.

The Watch

GEMARAH

So where did we leave off? asked Rav Huna, convening the meeting.

I think we were talking about penises, when you abruptly ended the meeting, said Rav Pappa.

No we were talking about why it is that we are always talking about penises, said Resh Lakish.

Do you think there's something wrong with us? asked Rav Kahana, or does the subject matter keep leading us in the direction of penises?

"Penis" is mentioned 130 times in the Talmud, noted Rav Pappa. And that's not including numerous synonyms and euphemisms.

Does that mean the text is the problem, or that we are the problem? asked Rav Sheshet.

We are the text, and the text is us, said Bar Kappara.

Then I say we make a list of what else this Seinfeld episode has to offer, said Rav Huna. Shout out the topics as they come to mind:

-How can anyone not like Jerry?
-What were Russell and Cynthia eating for dinner?
-What happened to Morty's wallet?
-Should Naomi have asked out Uncle Leo?
-Who is Bobo?
-Why doesn't Dr. Reston serve decaf cappuccino?
-What night of the week was Blossom on TV?

These debates are unsustainable, complained Rav Pappa. This show really is about nothing.

Not necessarily, said Yontl the Librarian. I consulted the archives, and it turns out that Major Dad and Blossom were both on TV on Monday night at 8:30pm during the 1992-93 television season. Russell Dalrymple does not know the TV schedule and apparently doesn't even own a *TV Guide.*

I really like that Blossom, said Rav Pappa. You know, she's Jewish. Smart too, like a computer. Knows her Torah. A scientist. And she has some body on her. I should drop dead if she's not beautiful. I say we invite her into the academy, even though she is a woman. Maybe her nerdy scientist friends as well. What do you think?

We think Pappa wants to slip his Rabbi Johnson out of his new Velcro pants and get laid, said Resh Lakish.

So you noticed the new pants, did you? said Rav Pappa in satisfaction.

Why don't we just invite Major Dad into the academy? said Rav Sheshet.

Or how about Bobo? offered Shimon ben Pazi.

Because Pappa has no interest in shtupping either of them, said Resh Lakish.

I dunno that Major Dad has some body on him. I should drop dead if he's not beautiful, said Rami bar Hama.

Major Dad? You want to invite a Prime-Time military man into the academy? Why not just invite a Cossack? We can see if Bogdan Khmelnitsky* is available, said Resh Lakish in exasperation.

Isn't it Bobo Khmelnitsky? asked Shimon ben Pazi. Is Dr. Reston's friend Bobo Khmelnitsky the antisemite?

Go back to your comic book Pazi, said Bar Kappara. Let's invite Major Dad Just to see how Pappa responds.

OK all in favor of inviting Major Dad into the academy, cast your votes.

Let's bring Major Dad Khmelnitsky into the academy, said the Sages in unison.

Sorry Pappa, no Mayim Bialik or her nerdy scientist friends, chortled Resh Lakish. You'll have to test out your big bang theory on a towering Cossack.

Not that there's anything wrong with it, added Bar Kappara.

The Bubble Boy

MISHNAH:

Hillel: Moors
Shammai: Moops
Hillel: Moors
Shammai: Moops
Hillel: Moors
Shammai: Moops

Hillel: Moors
Shammai: Architecture
Hillel: City Planner
Shammai: Architecture
Hillel: Marine Biologist
Shammai: Moops
Hillel: You're ugly!
Shammai: You are!
Hillel: You are!
Shammai: That's what you think
Hillel: That's what I know

GEMARAH:

Fellow Sages, said Rav Huna convening the meeting, we need to start a fund to save the Bubble Boy; he's out of hemoglobin and Costanza irreparably damaged his bubble when he tried to kill him. We should buy the boy a new bubble for his birthday.

This would never have happened had they put him in an igloo, rather than sealing him in that thin dry-cleaning plastic, said Resh Lakish. It's his family's fault.

And the Bubble Boy tried to kill George. He's a lying little snot and a cheater, that little twerp, added Rav Sheshet.

Not so, retorted Rav Pappa, the Bubble Boy knew the correct answer to the Trivial Pursuit question. Costanza denied him his victory.

And Costanza, added Bar Kappara, ironically predicted he would engender the Bubble Boy's demise: "I can't go in there. I can't face the Bubble Boy," he told Susan, citing his role in his grandmother's untimely death.

Wait a second: George was correct, not the Bubble Boy, insisted Resh Lakish. The answer was Moops, not Moors, according to the written word, the Trivial Pursuit card. The pursuit of the written word is not trivial, it is the Law, as given to Moses at Sinai.

Moops, Moops, Moops, said the Sages in unison.

Oh stop being such a literalist, Lakish, said Bar Kappara. This is why Moses also received the Oral Torah at Sinai. "The Sadducees do not accept the Oral Torah, and they interpret the Written Torah literally." (Horayot 4a:12). And we in Pumbedita do not side with the Sadducees.

If the Sadducees say "Moops" then we must say "Moors," said Rav Sheshet.

Moors, Moors, Moors, said the Sages in unison.

We must defer to the Oral Torah, said Bar Kappara, which is precisely what Susan was doing in consulting the guidelines of the Trivial Pursuit set. Such guidelines were given orally at Sinai for this very reason.

But we must not defer to Susan, said Rav Pappa. Why, you ask? Because she refused to take her top off for the Bubble Boy.

First off, nobody asked. But OK, I'll bite: Why should Susan have taken her top off? asked Rabbah.

Because it was the Bubble Boy's birthday, said Rav Pappa. The poor yold lives in dry-cleaning plastic, he has probably never seen a naked woman, Seinfeld didn't show up, and his father is out on the road six days a week haulin' Yoo-Hoo. Give the Bubble Boy bosom for his birthday. He'd get some street cred, and the locals would likely start honoring him as the Booby Boy.

Booby Boy, Booby Boy, Booby Boy, said the Sages in unison.

And it's certainly a fine product, added Shimon ben Pazi.

Settle down Rabbis, chided Rav Huna. And please Pazi, you meat head, a little respect: do not refer to Susan's bosom as a "fine product."

I was talking about Yoo-Hoo, said Shimon ben Pazi. I love Yoo-Hoo.

Our time is up, said Rav Huna.

So what's the verdict, asked Rav Pappa, are we not starting a fund to buy the Bubble Boy boobies for his birthday?

Screw him, said Rav Huna. We are not even going to buy him a new Trivial Pursuit game. As far we are concerned, the Moops will have invaded Spain in the eighth century.

Moops, Moops, Moops, said the Sages in unison.

The Cheever Letters

MISHNAH:

Rabbi Tarfon: I found this letter in the archive, not sure what to make of it.
Rabban Gamliel: Well read it, Tarfon.
Rabbi Tarfon: "Dear Akivah, last night with you was bliss. I fear my… orgasm has left me a cripple. I don't know how I shall ever get back to work. I-"
Yohanan ben Zakkai: Tarfon, enough with this Bari Weiss already. So Akivah sneaked off to nibble on a Zionist love newton. Who among us hasn't done that?
Rabbi Tarfon: Wait you didn't let me finish. "I don't know how I shall ever get back to work, as my scepter no longer rises. I love you madly. Signed, Bar Kochbah. P.S. I loved your wagon."
Rabban Gamliel: Jesus Christ.

GEMARAH:

What a wonderful subject, said Rav Huna, convening the meeting. There are just so many layers of irony to discuss.

I know, said Rav Pappa, who would have thought Rabbi Akivah could evoke such passion, such craving, such utter ejaculatory ruin in another man. We had him pegged all wrong.

And not just any man, added Bar Kappara. This was the mighty Bar Kochbah, who may very well have been the Messiah, whose Rod could have ushered in the age of Zion and ended Roman persecution.

Yet instead, said Rav Kahuna, his Rod was crippled by one of our own.

Perfect irony, said the Sages in unison.

Maybe we should proclaim Rabbi Akivah the Messiah. As it is written, "He who cures can cripple through orgasm."

No you yolds, interjected Rav Huna. We are talking about the *Seinfeld* episode, "The Cheever Letters," not the Bar Kochbah revolt.

As Archie Bunker would say, this is very much German to the discussion, said Shimon Ben Pazi, who had taken to *All in the Family* of late because of his new nickname, "Pazi, The Meat Head."

The Meat Head is correct, said Resh Lakish. There is great irony is Susan's family finding out their father is a gay man – and one who can produce crippling orgasms at that – because her boyfriend's friend burned down his cherished cabin with the very cigars he had given him.

Much as our revolt against the Romans ended in failure, because Rabbi Akivah left the would-be Messiah a cripple, said Rav Sheshet.

How is it possible for an orgasm to leave someone a cripple? asked Rav Pappa, who was frantically taking notes, evidently planning his weekend in the mountains. I do not believe it.

Shmendrik, It's obviously metaphorical, said Rabbah.

Not necessarily, said Abba the Surgeon. I have seen the fallout of crippling orgasms from time to time at my clinic, commonly among Zoroastrians. It's not a pretty site to behold, although the patients tend to come in with smiles on their faces.

Zoroastrians, you say, repeated Rav Pappa, still frantically taking notes.

This is exactly why my services are needed, said Zutra the Mohel. Our Glatt Kosher Velcro Bris™ is the best prophylactic against crippling orgasms. Had John Cheever paid us a visit this could have been averted.

Seriously? said Abba the Surgeon. I can assure you that Bar Kochbah had a bris.

Yes, but not a Velcro Bris™, corrected Zutra the Mohel.

You're a butcher, Zutra, said Rav Huna, and this is all beside the point: had John Cheever had a Velcro Bris™, and was not rendered a cripple by Henry

Ross's ejaculatory talents, the cabin would still have burned down. The two have nothing to do with each other. This is about George, Kramer, and the cigars.

And Naomi, added Bar Kappara. The chain of events leading to the cabin's burning would have not commenced had she not laughed like Elmer Fudd sitting on a juicer.

I never did like that Elmer Fudd, said Abba the Surgeon, shaking his head. He and his goyish big-game hunting ilk are responsible for most of the crippled rabbits that show up at my clinic.

Wow, I did not know that Elmer Fudd was responsible for all those crippling orgasms you spoke of earlier, said Pazi the Meat Head in wonder.

Hey Pappa – where are you going? said a surprised Rav Huna, we aren't done here.

I'm going to find someone who hates "wittle gway wabbits!" yelled Rav Pappa as he sprinted off into the Babylonian sunset.

What a preevert, said Pazi the Meat Head.

The Opera

MISHNAH:

Yohanan ben Zakkai: So where is Akivah?

Jose The Galilean: Or as they now call him, "The Orgasm Crippler"

Rabbi Tarfon: We hear that the Romans have threatened to put the kibosh on him. They are sending out their toughest centurion to undertake the kibosh.

Rabban Gamliel: Oh no, not the kibosh! I assume they're deploying Biggus Dickus. His kiboshes are eminently brutal.

Rabbi Tarfon: No, actually Biggus Dickus chose to rendezvous with Akivah for, if you will, some private tutoring, as he heard about Akivah's aptitude for dispensing crippling orgasms while on the wagon off the wagon.

Yohanan ben Zakkai: And that would still be my wagon.

Rabbi Tarfon: Yes your wagon. I told you – you should have reclaimed your wagon while Akivah was in a coma. But no, you are "a man who respects a good coma"

Rabban Gamliel: Then who? Who is going to put the kibosh on him?

Rabbi Tarfon: None other than Crazy Josephus Davolus. Also known as the Tragic Clown.

GEMARAH:

Friends, said Rav Huna convening the meeting, "The Opera" was a very revealing episode.

Wasn't it though? said Resh Lakish. Who would have thought Crazy Joe Davola was such a skilled photographer? Not to mention a genius with makeup.

No you yold, interjected Rav Huna, I mean Jerry Seinfeld. He turned out to be such a wuss.

We already knew he was a wuss, said Rav Sheshet, from "The Statue," when he was too cowardly to take on the charming yet verbose Ray.

And now he is scared of an opera-loving scriptwriter who likes to dress up as a clown, said Rabbah.

But Davola knows karate, said Bar Kappara. Look what he did to Kramer's helmet. Jerry made the right move in calling the cops.

It's pronounced "ka-ra-TE" interjected Pazi the Meat Head.

And yet the cops wouldn't help him, said Resh Lakish, even though he is "a comedian of the United States under just as much pressure as the President."

Jerry should have taken ka-ra-TE, said Pazi the Meat Head. We should all be taking ka-ra-TE.

It does make me wonder, mused Rav Kahana, what will happen to us should the goys come after us. Who will protect us? We Israelites are a spiritual nation in exile who have renounced collective violence, awaiting our messiah.

If only, lamented Rav Sheshet, Bar Kochbah had not been quashed through Akivah's crippling orgasm, we'd be securely ensconced in the nurturing bosom of Zion rather than Babylonian captivity.

And if only Rabbi Akivah, our protector, who left Bar Kochbah a cripple, had not been quashed by the Romans, said Resh Lakish.

Crazy Josephus Davolus, said the Sages in unison.

Jerry is the Light of our Exile, said Rabbah, and the Crusaders came after him.

In the guise of a clown at the opera, yet, said Rav Kahana. Dangerous times.

As it is written, continued Rabbah, "And no wonder, for even Satan disguises himself as an angel of light. So it is no surprise if his servants, also, disguise themselves as tragic clowns at the opera." (2 Corinthians 11:14-15).

Wrong script Rabbah! Said Rav Huna.

This is why Jerry got into a near physical altercation over a quarter at the opera, suggested Resh Lakish. To prove he can be intimidating.

To quote Jerry, "I kinda like this opera crowd, I feel tough... Anybody else got a problem?" said Rav Sheshet.

Well at least we diasporic Jews can stand up to the opera crowd, said Bar Kappara.

So basically we're screwed, said Resh Lakish. We have nobody to protect us, except for Zutra the Mohel and his Velcro circumcision technique.

Boruch HaShem,* I knew you Rabbis would come around, said Zutra the

Mohel, smiling. I offer classes on Thursday evenings. Bring your own weedwhacker.

That wasn't an endorsement, retorted Resh Lakish.

I'm sorry but Jerry got what he deserved, said Rav Sheshet. It's as Rabbi Akivah famously said, "Jesting and levity lead a man to lewdness," and apparently cowardice as well. If only Jerry had studied Torah instead of becoming a "Comedian of the United States." He is the tragic clown. And a wuss.

Given the circumstances, interjected Rav Huna, I don't think we should be quoting Rabbi Akivah today.

Why not? asked Rav Sheshet. Rabbi Akivah could have crippled Davola. Without Velcro. Without Binaca. He was a serious scholar. And rumor has it an opera buff.

I will add that Jerry has never crippled anyone through orgasm, said Resh Lakish. Elaine admitted she faked every last orgasm with him. Jerry couldn't even make it with Marla the Virgin who fled into the arms of a Kennedy.

I bet you Jerry couldn't have even satiated the "I'll Have What She's Having" Lady from *When Harry Met Sally*, added Pazi the Meat Head.

It is fair to say, concluded Bar Kappara, that Jerry is neither an orgasm crippler nor a serious scholar. His entire knowledge of high culture comes from Bugs Bunny cartoons.

That reminds me, asked Rav Huna, where is Rav Pappa today?

The Virgin

MISHNAH:

Hillel: You see that fair maiden, Shammai? I went out with her once. She's a virgin.

Shammai: She's a virgin? Wow! I don't think I could do it. You know, they always remember the first time. I don't want to be remembered. I wanna be forgotten.

Hillel: Oh, she'll remember all right. Some wise men in the marketplace have announced that she, if you will, is pregnant, with the Holy Spirit.

Shammai: Jesus Christ.

Hillel: That's what she said.

The Contest

GEMARAH:

Fellow Sages, let's get started, said Rav Huna convening the meeting. The reason I sent out an advanced notice to prepare for our shiur is because our subject for today, "The Contest," is rather delicate.

Sorry I'm late, said Rav Pappa, breathlessly bursting into the room. Here, he continued, putting one hundred dinars on the table.

What's that for? asked Rav Huna.

I'm out! exclaimed Rav Pappa.

Out of what? asked Shimon ben Pazi the Meat Head.

I'm out of the contest! Exclaimed Rav Pappa.

What contest? Asked Resh Lakish.

The contest to see who can be Master of their Domain the longest, replied Rav Pappa.

What are you meshugeneh?* There is no contest! said Rav Sheshet.

Yesterday Rav Huna sent us a note, stating: "Fellow Sages, start 'the Contest' and we will compare notes tomorrow," replied Rav Pappa. Look I gave it a shot, but once Rabbi Johnson found his way through my Velcro fly I caved. And trust me, you'll all be next to cave!

Dude, said Resh Lakish, Rav Huna meant you should start watching "The Contest." He wasn't announcing the start of a contest.

Why would he send an advanced note to start watching "The Contest"? asked Rav Pappa. We all have copies of the *Seinfeld* schedule.

Because of the delicate subject matter, replied Rav Sheshet. He didn't want anyone to be triggered.

Triggered? We talk about shlongs, shmekls, dingdongs, and beytzim at every meeting, said an astounded Rav Pappa.

No, YOU talk about shlongs, shmekls, dingdongs, and beytzim at every meeting. You and Zutra the Mohel, said Resh Lakish. But at least Zutra makes a living off of them. Do you make a living off of treating your body like an amusement park, Pappa?

Maybe he does, said Rav Sheshet. He's probably very good at it. Maybe he sells out Sassanid Square Garden with thousands of people watching him. He could be a big star.

Maybe Pappa is making porn, added Bar Kappara.

Yeah, I'm Buck Naked, replied Pappa. And now I'm out of the damn contest.

People – treating one's body like an amusement park is strictly prohibited in Halakhah, said Rav Huna: "When a man has an emission of semen, he must bathe his whole body with water, and he will be unclean till evening." (Leviticus 15:16).

I had my nightly sponge bath before coming here, said Rav Pappa. Is that all you got against me?

He has a point, said Bar Kappara. Where is there a prohibition against a tickle of one's pickle in the Torah?

"If a man who had a seminal emission immersed himself but did not first pass urine, he again becomes unclean when he passes urine." (Mishnah Mikvaot 8:4), said Rav Kahana.

So then the question is, did Pappa make peepee before his sponge bath? Asked Bar Kappara.

Not only did I make a number one, but I also made a number two, said Rav Pappa. My emission has been halakhically purged into the Sassanid sewer system. So what else you got?

I know, I know! said Shimon ben Pazi: Did Jesus not throw the masturbators out of the Temple? "My house shall be a house of prayer, but you have made it a den of wankers." (Luke 19:46)

Pazi, you Meat Head, you are reading from the wrong script again; the Nazarene is not to be mentioned within these yeshivah walls, said Rav Huna.

Be that as it may, said Rav Pappa, I know with certainty the ejected ejaculators from the Temple immediately immersed themselves in the sacred waters of the Jordan. I believe this is how Christianity got launched.

"And now why tarriest thou? Arise and be baptized and wash away thy semen, calling on the name of the Lord," (Acts 22:16), quoted Shimon ben Pazi.

"John did baptize in the wilderness, and preach the baptism of repentance for the remission of emission," (Mark 1:4), quoted Zutra the Mohel. And trust me I know, added Zutra. Baptism is the main competition against my patented Velcro Bris™. And for some reason I appear to be losing.

Because you're a butcher Zutra, said Rav Huna, and one day you'll end up snipping the wrong shlong, and we will then deny knowing you. Having said that, joining the faith of Yoshke the Nazarene is still the greater sin. The Temple may have been corrupted by a sect of wankers, but the expelled ejaculators who followed Jesus into the Jordan ceased to be Jews.

Does this mean Rav Pappa is no longer a Jew, asked Resh Lakish?

I can assure you that I did not immerse myself with the masturbators, said Rav Pappa. I just watched. I enjoy watching. But I treat my body like an amusement park in solitude, and I ritually cleanse in solitude. Watching a sect of wankers flood the waters of the Jordan with their semen is no sin.

No, but it is admittedly abnormal, said Bar Kappara. Having said that, Pappa is still one of us. In dire need of psychiatric treatment, but still one of us.

Well we appear to be at an impasse, said Rabbah. Perhaps we should have a contest after all?

Works for me! Said Rav Pappa.

No, you're already out of the contest, Pappa, said Rav Huna. No second chances. And your one hundred dinars are staying in the pot. You must also turn over all your copies of *Glamor Magazine*. Moreover, we are reimposing the zipper on your fly as a safety precaution. The jagged metal teeth will keep your Rabbi Johnson out of all solitary mischief, and will likewise prevent you from becoming a Christian. Otherwise we are bringing in Zutra the Mohel to take drastic measures.

Five minutes, sire, that's all I need with him is five minutes, said Zutra feverishly.

And as for the rest of us, asked Rav Sheshet?

We will see who shall be proclaimed Master of their Domain, announced Rav Huna.

King of the County, said Rav Sheshet.

Lord of the Manor, said Resh Lakish.

Prince of Persia, said Bar Kappara.

Shah of the Yeshivah, said Rav Kahuna.

So let it be written, so let it be done, said the Sages in unison.

The Airport

GEMARAH:

Chevreh, said Rav Huna, convening the meeting, I do not think we have much to debate today. We do not have any airplanes in Babylon, and I am sure we are all pretty tapped out from "The Contest."

Yet none of us went blind from treating our bodies like amusement parks, said a vindicated Rav Pappa. My mother was wrong. And I'm not seeing a psychiatrist.

But Master, we would be betraying the Covenant should we leave an episode undiscussed, said Bar Kappara. This is also the 50th episode. A milestone!

Should we not discuss Elaine's contention that our goal should be a classless society? The oppression in coach is a clarion call for an uprising of exploited rabbis. How dare they get cookies in first class! said Rav Sheshet.

Should we not discuss how Kramer's quest to seek justice and compensation from Grossbard reveals the futility of retribution under capitalism? said Resh Lakish.

Should we not discuss how we learned yet again that George can't jump, and he runs like a girl? said Rav Kahuna. George is a blurb who does not deserve to be blurbed in *Time Magazine*.

Should we not discuss how charming and romantic it was when Jerry placed the slipper on Tia's foot, and it was a perfect fit? asked Rav Pappa. I will even admit to having shed a tear or two.

Maybe we should head to the market and sing "I like to stop at the duty-free shop" for the Sassanid public, suggested Shimon ben Pazi. Give the Three Stooges a run for their money. We can also pick up wine from the Tuscany region and even some cookies.

Hey Huna, said Rav Pappa, you never did tell us who won the contest.

Believe it or not, it was Zutra the Mohel, said Rav Huna.

I guess his work really got to him below the equator, said Resh Lakish. Where is he today?

He decided to go and watch a hanging to clear his mind, said Rav Huna.

The irony of treating everyone's body like an amusement park except one's own, mused Rav Pappa.

For someone like Zutra, said Abba the Surgeon, witnessing a decapitation is form of capitulation; every severed head represents a saved penis in his delusional mind. He is under the misconception that this will return him to a healthy relationship with Mr. Winky.

What should we do? said Bar Kappara.

Oh that's easy, said Abba the Surgeon. We change the locks on the Yeshivah, and pretend we've never heard of this sadistic mohel. And if that doesn't work, we'll slip him a mickey and stick him on a caravan of Gypsies to Byzantium.

A man of his "talents" will likely be conscripted into the Roman circus, said Rav Pappa.

Did he at least collect his contest winnings? asked Rabbah.

No he didn't, replied Rav Huna.

That's so unlike Zutra given how he has amassed so many tips, laughed Rav Pappa. Sorry I can never resist a foreskin joke.

LOL Pappa, LOL, said the Sages in unison.

The Pick

MISHNAH:

Rabbi Tarfon: Why isn't "Thou shalt not pick" one of the commandments?

Jose the Galilean: Indeed. It is a far worse an infraction than so many others: "Thou shalt not wear cloth woven of both wool and linen" (Deut. 22:11); "Thou shalt not pick your vineyard bare" (Leviticus 19:10). Surely thou shalt not pick your nose is a greater sin.

Rabban Gamliel: Maybe "vineyard" is a euphemism for nose. Picking your vineyard bare = cleaning your shnoz of shnot and shmutz in public.

Eleazar ben Azariah: So then why didn't the Lord simply say "nose"? "Thou shalt not pick your nose bare."

Rabbi Tarfon: Well it's kinda gross, perhaps either he or Moses was a bit squeamish?

Eleazar ben Azariah: Squeamish? Intercourse is mentioned 25 times in the Torah; semen is mentioned 26 times. And let's not even discuss Abraham's self-inflicted snip in Genesis 17. If the Lord can discuss that which brings forth semen, the Lord can discuss that which brings forth shnot. Moses should have descended from Sinai with a "Thou shalt not pick."

Rabbi Tarfon: I guarantee you Moses was a picker. You wander through the desert for forty years with that dry air. ... You telling me you're not going to have occasion to clean house a little bit?

Rabban Gamliel: Perhaps this was why the Lord punished Moses and denied him entry into Canaan. He cleaned his house and cast his boogers throughout the scorching Wilderness of Sin.

Eleazar ben Azariah: And the boogers fell like manna from heaven.

Jose the Galilean: "But now we have lost our appetite; we never see anything but this manna!" (Numbers 11:6).

Rabbi Tarfon: Poor Moses. Was he not human? If he picked did he not bleed?

Jose the Galilean: Let me ask you something, Tarfon. If you were going out with somebody and if she did that what would you do? Would you continue dating her?

Rabbi Tarfon: No. That's disgusting!

GEMARAH:

Fellow Sages, said Rav Huna convening the meeting, today's discussion is centered around a conundrum. Which is worse? Picking your nose in public or exposing your nipple on a holiday card?

I think the answer is clear, said Rav Sheshet: the Mishnah has established that "Thou Shalt Not Pick" was given at Sinai and that Moses was a picker. And the Lord punished Moses for his picking in the Wilderness of Sin.

Not so, said Bar Kappara. For even if Moses picked, the Torah speaks only of bare vineyards. God wanted to spare Moses the humiliation of being branded a picker and left it unmentioned. Moses was not an animal!

And the nipple, asked Rav Kahana?

Yes, I would think it would depend on which holiday the nipple is exposed, replied Resh Lakish. On Purim an exposed nipple is all in good fun. On Yom Kippur, it's a grave sin against the Lord at a time of atonement and fasting. The nipple will make one hunger for intercourse.

No, I would think it would depend on which holiday the shnot is expunged, replied Rav Pappa. On Purim some expunged shnot is all in good fun. On Yom

Kippur it's a grave sin against the Lord at a time of atonement and fasting. The boogers will make one hunger for food.

Well done Pappa, replied Resh Lakish. You have made a valiant effort to avoid discussing penises, and we commend you. But you have now raised the issue of shnot-eating Israelites.

Not quite, replied Pappa. I have raised the issue of how shnot-eating intersects with the Jewish calendar. This is about keeping Jewish time, not eating Jewish shnot. This conversation is well within the boundaries of halakhic discourse.

So what do we do now? asked Bar Kappara.

We discuss nose picking on and around biblical holidays, said Rav Huna. This is the logic of Talmud. We leave no stone unturned, no exposed nipple unexamined, no picked nose unexplored.

Es iz shver tsu zain a Yid, so so very hard to be a Jew, said Rav Pappa.

Yeah right, replied Rav Sheshet. Methinks the pervert doth protest too much.

True dat, said the Sages in unison.

The Movie

GEMARAH:

Friends, said Rav Huna, convening the meeting. Literally nothing happened in this episode. I fear there is nothing to discuss.

Actually, I'm more than a bit intrigued by "Rochelle, Rochelle," said Rav Pappa. Who wouldn't want to accompany a fair damsel on a strange erotic journey from Milan to Minsk?

You're a preevert, said Shimon ben Pazi the Meat Head.

And it also sounds way too goyish, added Bar Kappara.

Fine, then how about "Rokhl, Rokhl a Sheyneh Ponim* who Shlepped* from Minsk to Pinsk."

Isn't Minsk where all the ponies come from? asked Pazi the Meat Head.

Yes, Minsk is in Poland, replied Rabbah. At least it is some of the time.

Do you think Manya shlepped her horse on a strange erotic journey from Minsk to Pinsk? asked Rav Sheshet.

Or perhaps from Pinsk to Minsk, replied Resh Lakish.

It may explain why she was chased out of Poland and why she went from a country packed with ponies to a non-pony country.

Is it a mere coincidence that this is the very same episode where Jerry is described as having a "horse face, big teeth and flared nostrils?" asked Rav Pappa.

You may be onto something, Pappa. There is clearly an equine undercurrent to this episode, said Bar Kappara.

Being a horse face runs in Jerry's meshpuchah, noted Rav Kahana. His cousin Jeffrey looks like a horse as well.

Perhaps Manya did not actually have a pony in Poland, mused Rabbah. Perhaps she just had a brother or an uncle who looked like a horse.

"Manya, Manya: a Strange Erotic Journey with a Sheyneh Pony from Minsk to Pinsk," said Rav Pappa.

Now we're talking about a Jewish epic! said Bar Kappara.

Can you imagine? a horse-faced Jew being the pride of Krakow! mused Rav Kahana.

Poland, what a country! exclaimed Rabbah.

On behalf of my equine recovery center, said Abba the Surgeon, I would like to thank you, fellow Sages, for recognizing that horses are often culturally coded as Jewish.

I have no idea what that means, replied Bar Kappara.

Neither do I, interjected Rav Huna. But I do think our work here is done; we found a Jewish epic in 23 minutes of mediocre TV. We are still the greatest Sages of all time.

This is why it takes 7 1/2 years to read the Talmud, whereas the goys can breeze through their Gospels in an hour, concluded Bar Kappara.

Festivus Interlude

A FESTIVUS MIRACLE IN SASSANID PERSIA

Happy Festivus Everyone! Exclaimed Bar Kappara, entering the Yeshiva.

What are you talking about? it's not Festivus until April 8; I have our *Seinfeld* episode calendar right here, said Rav Sheshet.

No, Festivus is on December 23, and today is December 23, said Bar Kappara. It always falls around Hanukkah and the birthday of Yoshke Pandrek the Nazarene.

Yes I defer to Frank, said Resh Lakish. Nobody tells Frank Costanza what to do! Moreover, I already pulled my back getting the aluminum pole out of the crawl space.

It's most certainly on December 23, said Rav Huna. Look: I found a Festivus Card from Akivah to the Yeshivah sitting in the archive, clearly postmarked December.

A Festivus Miracle! exclaimed Shimon ben Pazi.

Nice pic, said Rav Pappa. His buttocks are sublime, though correct me if I'm wrong but I see his Mr. Winky opting for a no-tuck instead of a tuck. I can't believe nobody found the card all these years in the archive. It's probably worth a fortune in the wrong hands, the card that is, Lord knows his Rabbi Johnson ended up in the wrong hands plenty of times.

Another Festivus Miracle! exclaimed Shimon ben Pazi.

OK it's time for the Festivus Feats of Strength, said Bar Kappara. Until you pin me down, Pappa, Festivus is not over!

Let's rumble, Rabbi! screamed Rav Pappa, You wanna a piece of me?

Actually, interjected Rav Sheshet, Zutra the Mohel's already got a piece of you, Pappa, as well as the rest of us, and it's in in a jar in the crawl space by the Festivus Pole.

By the way, where is Zutra? asked Rav Huna, he never came back from the hanging.

They say he's traveling the Mediterranean, repenting, preaching conversion to Frank Costanza's belief system. "Beware of the Zipper fly, beware of the evil wankers, beware of the mutilation! These are my Grievances." (Philippians 3:2)

This is the best Festivus ever! exclaimed Shimon ben Pazi.

The Visa

MISHNAH:

Rabbi Tarfon: I bring news about Rabbi Akivah.

Jose the Galilean: Oy.

Rabbi Tarfon: He's at a messianic fantasy camp by the Dead Sea.

Eleazar ben Azariah: Akivah went to a fantasy camp? His whole life is a fantasy camp. He seduces hot Zionist babes without dating and induces crippling orgasms without mating.

Shimon bar Yochai: And he absconded with my sacred Mosaic pen from Sinai after giving me a check for only 19.45 dinars. Yeah right, he didn't have a coke with his Chinese food, ho ho ho!

Yohanan ben Zakkai: and he made time with a Good Samaritan after she rubbed his bald head in oil on my wagon and never returned it!

Rabban Gamliel: He's a shnorrer. Do you know how much food he's mooched off this Yeshivah? Anyone notice we've had no kreplach for years?

Rabbi Tarfon: People should plunk down two thousand dinars to live like Akivah for a week.

Jose the Galilean: He is a very very bad man.

Yohanan ben Zakkai: Perhaps it is our fault.

Rabbi Tarfon: How so, Master?

Yohanan ben Zakkai: Because of our open door Yeshivah policy.

Rabban Gamliel. Perhaps our sign by the entrance is a bit overboard: "Give us your tired, your poor, unhappy, sad, slow, ugly people who can't drive, can't merge or parallel park back-first, that have bad penmanship with stolen pens from Sinai, don't return calls about drinking coffee at night, have dandruff, food between their teeth, pick their noses, treat their bodies like amusement parks, have bad credit, have no credit, in other words any dysfunctional defective zhlob that you can somehow cattle prod onto a wagon, send them over, we want 'em."

Shimon bar Yochai: Wow that describes Akivah to a tee, right down to the dandruff and the wagon.

Eleazar ben Azariah: We should have passed that proposed Dandruff Exclusion Act when it was tabled in 82 CE.

Yohanan ben Zakkai: But it violated Rome's principle of diversity, equity, and inclusion. HR said no.

Jose the Galilean: I still say Akivah is a very very bad man.

Rabbi Tarfon: Perhaps we should have him deported to Pakistan.

Yohanan ben Zakkai: Anyone know what Pakistan's immigration policy is like?

Rabbi Tarfon: Based on the footage I've seen, they have an open-door dandruff policy.

The Shoes

GEMARAH:

Fellow Sages, said Rav Huna, convening the meeting, "The Shoes," brought home a sad reality about our Seinfeld Talmud: there are no women in it.

Perhaps George and Jerry are correct, suggested Bar Kappara: we don't know what women say.

I don't even know what women think, said Resh Lakish. That's why I'm never with any, but instead sit in this Yeshivah day after day poring over the excruciating minutiae of every single event with a gaggle of sweaty rabbis. No offense.

I know what some women think, said Zutra the Mohel. I see the look of horror and contempt on their faces when they bring me their child on the eighth day.

We men feel the exact same way about you Zutra, said Rav Sheshet, don't make this about women. And how did you get back into the building, Zutra? We changed the locks.

Picking a lock is not that different from snipping a shlong, replied Zutra, with more than a touch of pride.

Yes, don't make this about women, said Rav Kahana. We have no idea what Pazi's thinking, what meshugeneh narishkeit* is about to come out of his mouth, yet we write him into the script all the time.

Hey, I'm the resident expert on *Moby-Dick*, ponies, and Batman, retorted Pazi the Meathead. I'm also into architecture.

See, I knew Pazi was going to say that. This IS a female thing, said Rav Pappa, we ARE too inept to write women in. Enough of this. That said in think in light of "The Shoes" we do need to discuss a female matter – cleavage.

See, I knew Pappa was going to bring up cleavage, said Resh Lakish. See how easy it is to write perverted sweaty rabbis into the script compared to writing in women?

Thank you, said Rav Pappa. And now I would like to know if it's true that looking at cleavage is like looking at the sun. Can you go blind from it? Because my mother told me I'd go blind from treating my body like an amusement park, and that didn't happen. And trust me, I gave Rabbi Johnson quite the work out; I could have sold out Sassanid Square Garden.

Sure you could have. And I think it's just a metaphor Pappa, said Bar Kappara. You're probably safe. Just be sure the boobies you leer at are of age. We don't need anymore scandals!

Hey, I know the Law, countered Pappa. As the Mishnah states: "A girl twelve years and one day old who grew two pubic hairs is classified as a young woman. Six months later, she becomes a grown woman." (Mishnah Niddah 5:9)

You know the Law, we know the Law, but the Sassanid Persians do not care for our Law, so may I suggest you keep your leering within the Israelite community, cautioned Rav Huna, unless of course you want to see your severed beytzim on display at Sassanid Square Garden.

I actually wouldn't mind seeing that, chimed in Zutra the Mohel, you know, in the interest of my professional development.

Sounds good, I'm outta here you poor shlepps, said Rav Pappa, scrambling out the door.

OK now that Pappa the pervert is gone, said Bar Kappara, let's get back to our talmudic script. Why is it we can't bring in women? We are the greatest minds of Babylon; is the fairer sex really that much of a mystery to us?

Maybe we should try snubbing them, suggested Rav Kahana. Maybe it's as Kramer said, women love the snub.

I say we head to the marketplace and walk around snubbing every female we see, said Rav Sheshet. Maybe then they'll talk to us.

OK but if we run into Rav Pappa, pretend we don't know him, added Resh Lakish. Better safe that sorry. Better secure than snipped and severed in Sassanid Square Garden.

Giddy up, said the Sages in unison.

Hey Huna, I like those shoes! said Bar Kappara.

They're Botticelli's, replied Rav Huna.

Ooh, Botticelli's! Look at you! Fancy-shmancy Yeshivah bokher,* said Bar Kappara in awe.

That's why I'm the Chief Rabbi of Pumbedita, whose wisdom is sought out by every Jew in the Fertile Crescent, said Rav Huna with more than a touch of pride.

Yet you can't even write in a female character, said Resh Lakish shaking his head.

The Outing

MISHNAH:

Rabban Gamliel: I am a bit perplexed, by "The Outing." Is there something wrong with being out?

Rabbi Tarfon: No, no, of course not! People's personal sexual preferences are nobody's business but their own!

Jose the Galilean: And we see each other naked and even sneak a peak in the shvitz all the time.

Rabbi Tarfon: Who just sneaks a peak? I've complimented you all on your girth. And there's nothing wrong with it!

Eleazar ben Azariah: No there's nothing wrong with YOUR girth, Tarfon. [Azariah hides his head in shame.]

Rabban Gamliel: Well then we owe Akivah an apology. So what if he gave Bar Kochbah an orgasm. There's nothing wrong with that.

Rabbi Tarfon: But his orgasm left him a cripple. Is there nothing wrong with that?

Shimon bar Yochai: It's none of our business. And I dare say, some of us here may even be a bit envious of the crippling orgasm. I'm going to add a chapter on crippling orgasms in the Zohar.

Eleazar "I'm Inadequate" ben Azariah: Word. I'm with Shimon. And I'd even be with Akivah. Walking is overrated.

Yohanan ben Zakkai: For the last time, Akivah did this on MY WAGON. He turned MY WAGON into Bourbon Street. As it is written, "He that is without a wagon among you, let him cast the first stone."

Jose the Galilean: I told you to grab your wagon back while Akivah was in a coma.

Shimon bar Yochai: I ransacked his cave at the time, looking for my stolen pen from Sinai, to no avail.

Yohanan ben Zakkai: My wagon is filled with the bodily fluids of a Zionist, a Good Samaritan, a crippled messiah, and Lord knows who else. I do not want it back. I'm going to the market to snub wagon owners.

Shimon bar Yochai: Do not be too hard on Yohanan. "The Outing" has clearly evoked painful memories for him. His wagon was his Fortress of Solitude, built by his grandfather in 47. It was a '47 wagon. And now he's got nowhere to cogitate in peace. Or to treat his body like an amusement park.

Rabban Gamliel: Not that there's anything wrong with it.

GEMARAH:

Hey fellow Sages, I bring news, said Rav Pappa entering the meeting. We made the Pumbedita Post.

Let me see that, said Rav Huna grabbing the paper: "Although they maintain separate residences, the chief Rav and his long time rabbinical 'companions' are inseparable."

Let me see that, said Bar Kappara grabbing the paper: "Within the confines of their fastidious yeshivah, Resh Lakish and Rav Pappa bicker over petzls, shlongs, beytzim, and dingdongs like an old married couple."

Let me see that, said Rabbah grabbing the paper: "Their academy proudly displays a glamor shot of the legendary Rabbi Akivah with his weewee searching for daylight through a button fly. Akivah, of course, is famous for his numerous proverbs and for crippling the failed messiah Bar Kochbah through what is widely regarded as the most spectacular orgasm since Jesus threw the masturbators out of the Temple."

Let me see that, said Rav Sheshet grabbing the paper: "Meanwhile, Zutra the Mohel flaunts his jar of foreskins while passionately eyeballing the crotch of passing unclipped Gentiles in the marketplace, even as his fellow rabbis walk the streets snubbing every woman they encounter. Clearly, the Sages aren't interested in women and boast of not one in their gay academy."

I knew the snubbing was a bad idea, said Resh Lakish. I once snubbed every woman I saw for an entire year. Nothing.

Sadly, that information would have been helpful yesterday, lamented Rav Huna.

We've been "outed," said Bar Kappara, and we weren't even "in."

Not that there's anything wrong with it, said Shimon ben Pazi.

QUEER TALMUD YESHIVX, 2023:

This episode is so lame, and I can't believe it constitutes Sacred Torxh, said Rabba Jewliettx bat Ocasio-Cortezx. Gay Jewish pride worldwide! George should have embraced his high and whiny voice and eaten Jerry's forbidden unwashed fruit. And he clearly enjoyed the sponge bath in the hospital.

Agreed, said Rebbetzin Amirah "Cancel Student Debt" Mizrahi, but we are not supposed to use the word "lame" anymore; it constitutes ableist language.

When you graduate to being a Rabba, Rebbetzin Amirah, then you get to call the shots, until then I make the rules in the Yeshivah, retorted Rabba Jewliettx.

Agreed, but we aren't supposed to call it a "Yeshivah" anymore, said Rabba Maryam "Free Palestine" al-Yamun. Its history is too gendered; we need this to be a safe space. So please, everyone, say "Yeshivx."

Enough of this said Rabba Jewliettx. Are we going to discuss "The Outing"'s homophobia or not?

We will not, said the Rabbot, Rabbanx, and Rebbetzinx in unison.

Why not? asked Rabba Jewliettx.

Because, replied Rabbx Yehudis bnei Butler, the cismale in charge of The Seinfeld Talmud has no idea how to write in womyn, let alone queer people.

Agreed, this IS really lame, concluded Rabba Jewliettx. Smash the Patriarchy. We're cancelling The Seinfeld Talmud. Meeting adjourned.

The Old Man

MISHNAH:

Shammai: Something's missing Hillel, there's a void. There's gotta be more to life than this. What gives you pleasure?

Hillel: Listening to your eminently forgettable halakhic rulings. I listen to this for fifteen minutes and I'm on top of the world. Your mediocrity is my pleasure.

Shammai: What kind of a person are you?

Hillel: I think I'm pretty much like you, only successful. People follow my rulings. And I invented the illustrious Passover Hillel Sandwich. What have you invented, Shammai?

Shammai: The Passover Shammai Sandwich.

Hillel: Never heard of it, which is probably why my brilliant sandwich gets two full pages in the Haggadah,* and yours gets none. Two full pages! That's more than Moses gets! Who's the Man, Shammai? Who's the Man?

Shammai: Then maybe I should quit. It's one of the few things I do well. I come from a long line of quitters. My father was a quitter, my rabbi was a quitter. Even my mohel was a quitter. I was raised to give up.

Hillel: I'm grateful for every last Jewish minute I have. And now that I think about it, for the mohel I had.

Shammai: Grateful? You're like 100 years old. How can you be grateful when you're SO close to the end? Wait – where are you going, Hillel?

Hillel: Life's too short to waste on you, Shammai. Good luck with that sandwich, for if you are not for your sandwich who will be? Certainly not me.

The Implant

MISHNAH:

Hillel: Did you double dip that chip, Shammai?

Shammai: Yes, So what?

Hillel: That's like sticking your whole Jew-face in the dip. The House of Hillel forbids it.

Shammai: The House of Shammai allows it. And who are you calling Jew-face, chinless?

Hillel: It is forbidden.

Shammai: Moops.

Hillel: Moors.

Shammai: You're ugly and your chest can use a Mansier.

Hillel: Be that as it may, they are real, and they are spectacular.

GEMARAH:

So, fellow Sages, there are some terrific debates to be had with "The Implant," began Rav Huna, convening the meeting. I thought we would start by declaring –

By declaring, interrupted Rav Pappa, that if they are real then they ARE spectacular. Elaine is a lucky woman.

Tell me about it, said Shimon ben Pazi. The last time I tripped in the shvitz I landed on Rabbah's rotund and unusually lumpy tokhes. I cleansed myself thrice in the mikvah. Eek.

You are a pervert Pappa, said Resh Lakish. Elaine derived no pleasure from landing on Sidra's bosom. She was protecting herself from injury.

That is correct, said Abba the Surgeon. I have the opportunity to handle the bosoms of Persian fair maidens daily. It is strictly professional, and I am prohibited by oath to exact pleasure from them even when they are real and spectacular.

Isn't this how King David seduced Bathsheba, by falling on her boobies in the shvitz? asked Shimon ben Pazi. David hit the Hittite-woman on her teat, and they fell in love. I'm a sucker for fortuitous biblical romance.

Go back to your comic books, Pazi, you buffoon, said Abba the Surgeon. And it sounds like you are questioning my medical ethics. Inspecting a nipple is no different from examining a nose.

Yet, interjected Bar Kappara, Jerry stated that "You don't touch the nose! You don't aspire to reach the nose. You don't unhook anything to get to a nose, and no man has ever tried to look up a woman's nostrils."

We can thus conclude that Elaine enjoyed landing on Sidra's bosom, insisted Rav Pappa. Elaine is the one who said they are spectacular. Oh, and Abba, when can I come by your clinic to sign up for an internship?

Right after you visit Zutra the Mohel to be gelded, retorted Abba the Surgeon.

Five minutes, Doctor, that's all I need with him is five minutes and you will have a eunuch, said Zutra feverishly. And I now give warranties with all my work.

What may I ask is the warranty for, Zutra? said Abba the Surgeon. How often do your clients' foreskins grow back?

Sidra is correct, said Resh Lakish. They are both mentally ill, as are Pappa and Zutra.

I'm nothing but a lonely rabbi yearning for love, lamented Rav Pappa.

And I am here to eternally fix that yearning, said Zutra.

Master Huna, said Bar Kappara, you were rudely cut off by Pappa when you convened the meeting. Is this your conclusion as well?

Actually, replied Rav Huna, I wanted to discuss the ethics of double dipping a chip. The House of Hillel and Shammai clashed over this.

Oh Master, I am so sorry. We just assumed you wanted to discuss Sidra's spectacular bosom, said a contrite Rav Pappa.

No sweat, my disciples, said Rav Huna, because when I finally write my textbook on abnormal psychology I will be able to write off every last dinar I invested in this ferkakteh Yeshivah.

The Junior Mint

GEMARAH:

Friends, said Rav Huna, convening the meeting, this Jerry Seinfeld has turned out to be a homicidal maniac.

And one with some admittedly unique methods of execution, mused Bar Kappara.

First he killed an immigrant by mocking her pony and now he tried to knock off Triangle Boy – after they watched the doctors "slice this fat bastard up" – with a Junior Mint, said Resh Lakish.

I still don't see how you can kill someone with a Junior Mint, countered Rabbah, as George said, "People eat pounds of them."

Yes, but as Jerry replied, "they don't put them next to vital organs in their abdominal cavity," said Rav Sheshet.

Using a little mint – a Junior Mint – is a very clever MO, said Rav Pappa. I'm not surprised Elaine wanted to hire Jerry to rub out her boyfriend's cats for $28.

You are missing the elephant in the room, said Abba the Surgeon. It's not just Jerry. George is just as much of a homicidal maniac if not more so. He tried to kill the Bubble Boy and he sought to prevent Jerry from confessing to the attempted murder of Triangle Boy, accusing him of playing God.

Is it not a coincidence, asked Shimon ben Pazi, that the two victims in question are named Bubble Boy and Triangle Boy? They are both geometrical shapes.

A bubble is no more a geometrical shape than Sal Bass and Salman are both fish, retorted Resh Lakish.

But it is a shape. And it really makes you think, replied Shimon ben Pazi. Two boys named after shapes and two people named after fish, all slated for decimation on Seinfeld.

Dolores is also a kind of fish, "Dolores Tuna," noted Bar Kappara, which is why Jerry told George that Mulva's name had "something to do with a car or a fish." Moreover, Jerry met Mulva while smelling and squeezing in the produce section, which contains "a lot of melons and shapes."

Shapes and fish, shapes and fish, said the Sages in unison.

This may be the dumbest conversation we've ever had at this Yeshivah, interjected Rav Pappa, and I submit the reason is you have prevented me from talking about our anatomies. You wanted to class up the joint, and instead you get bubbles, triangles, and fish.

You're off your game Pappa. I deliberately brought up "squeezing melons" to give you an opening. And you failed, said Bar Kappara.

On the contrary, replied Pappa. I passed the test. I did not take the bait. And I refrained from broaching Gipples, Mulvahs, Celestes, and Bovarys.

Didn't Madame Bovary predict all this? that Salman or Sal Bas Rushdie would be fatwad by the Muhammedans? asked Shimon ben Pazi.

Who? asked Rav Sheshet.

Madam Bovary, the fortune teller. She saw the future from a house of worship, just like us, said Shimon ben Pazi.

You are thinking of Nostradamus, you yold, replied Bar Kappara. He saw the future.

But he did not work at a Yeshivah, said Resh Lakish. You're thinking of Quasimodo, the Hunchback of Notre Dame, said Resh Lakish. Nostradamus was the fortune teller. Notre Dame is the Yeshivah.

Then who was Madame Bovary? asked Shimon ben Pazi.

Madame Bovary was Jerry's girlfriend, whose name rhymed with a part of the female anatomy, said Rav Pappa.

OK, we are officially done here, concluded Rav Huna. We are apparently ill-equipped to talk about anything other than shmekls, shlongs, beytzim, and dingdongs.

And cleavage, said the Sages in unison.

The Smelly Car

GEMARAH:

Fellow Sages, what is the Halakhah on BO, especially when it is BBO, asked Bar Kappara convening the meeting.

Where's Rav Huna today? inquired Rav Pappa.

The Valet at Chez Shawarma stunk up his wagon, replied Bar Kappara. So he's mounting a legal case to demand restitution from the restaurant. They also stole his copy of "Rokhl, Rokhl a Sheyneh Ponim's erotic Shlepp from Minsk to Pinsk."

Here's the Halakhah, said Rav Sheshet: "What is the legal status of a foul odor that has no visible source, e.g., flatulence? He said to them: Come and see these mats in the study hall, as these students are sleeping on them and these other students are studying, and they are not concerned about foul odors. However, this only applies to Torah study because there is no alternative, but not to the recitation of Shema. And with regard to Torah study we said that it is permitted only when the odor originated with another, but not when it originated with himself." (Berakhot 25a:8)

But that passage refers to farting, not BO, replied Bar Kappara.

Yes, but at least we've established that if the odor emanates from another – the Valet – Rav Huna can continue his Torah study. Same principle with BO.

But how do we know Rav Huna did not emit the foul and unpleasant odor, asked Rav Pappa, and merely blamed the Valet to save face. The House of Hillel ruled, "whoever smelt it dealt it."

The House of Shammai thought differently, and ruled, "whoever supplied it denied it," countered Rabbah.

As usual, Shammai's aphorism sucks rocks, mused Resh Lakish.

We are at an impasse, said Shimon ben Pazi. It's like the chicken and the egg.

Is this all we got, lamented Bar Kappara?

In Avodah Zarah, offered Rav Sheshet, it is written that one who defecates malodorously should do it eastward because "the wind does not usually blow from the east, it is less likely to spread the stench." (Avodah Zarah 29a:3)

Is Chez Shawarma located in the west or the east of the city? asked Shimon ben Pazi.

People! Nobody defecated in Rav Huna's wagon, said Bar Kappara. You are supposed to be experts in Jewish law. I ask for body odor and you bring me fart and shit.

Body odor, body odor, not fart and shit, repeated the Sages in unison.

It is entirely possible Halakhah has nothing to say regarding body odor, suggested Rabbah.

Maybe, said Rav Pappa, we Jews all smell so good we have no reason to discuss it.

Or maybe, said Resh Lakish, we Jews all smell so bad we are too embarrassed to discuss it.

Well which one is it? asked Rav Sheshet.

It's like the chicken and the egg, said Shimon be Pazi.

The Handicap Spot

GEMARAH:

Friends, said Rav Huna convening the meeting, there is so much to discuss with "The Handicap Spot." This is *Seinfeld* at its most canonical, it's most talmudic. Who is responsible for what? Who should be held liable for what? Was restitution properly undertaken to Lola? To Frank? To the Drakes? How do we explain the multiple levels of irony, from Frank's arrest while receiving an award to George being sentenced to be Frank's butler?

George. George is responsible for all that transpired, from Frank's vandalized car to Lola's handicap mishap, said Resh Lakish.

I disagree, said Rav Sheshet. It was the hipster-doofus Kramer's fault. He put the idea of parking in the handicap spot in George's head. He even wanted to park in front of a fire hydrant. This from the man who burned down a '47 cabin with Cuban cigars yet.

No it was Lola's fault, said Rav Pappa. She can't drive a wheelchair. She had two accidents, and as George pointed out she should have had collision insurance. And after she got her new chair from Kramer, she had the chutzpah to call him a hipster-doofus.

No it was Jerry's fault, said Bar Kappara. He loved the Drake. George was prescient; he knew the Drake was a problem, yet nobody agreed.

The only reason Jerry liked the Drake was because of Drake's coffee cake, said Rabbah. And the coffee cake brought back fond memories of fondling Gina and the Three Stooges while Martin was in a coma.

Did Jerry actually fondle the Stooges? asked Shimon ben Pazi. That would have been a rather unusual choice for the Stooges.

Hey Huna, interjected Rav Pappa. You were supposed to show us the Stooges. You promised to show us the Stooges. And you never mentioned the fondling. You let us down.

You are missing the bigger picture, said Shimon ben Pazi. We need to discuss Jerry's doodle: the free-hand triangle he drew. That was the most important element in "The Handicap Spot."

Why? Asked Rav Sheshet.

Because Kramer was so impressed with the triangle he announced that "If I had a kid, I would name him Isosceles; Isosceles Kramer!" continued Shimon ben Pazi. And Jerry had previously tried to murder a man called Triangle Boy. Are you not following this? Triangles! It was foreshadowing an impending homicide. Forget the Handicapped, Seinfeld has it in for those who are shaped like three sided polygons. This was no coincidence.

I think Shimon is being deliberately obtuse, said Rav Pappa.

Was that supposed to be a triangle joke? asked Resh Lakish.

Uh actually it was, replied Rav Pappa. Not bad, eh?

I hate to say this Pappa, but you're much more perspicacious and even interesting when you talk about petzls, shlongs, beytzim, and dingdongs. Perverted, yes, but perspicacious at least.

And cleavage, replied Rav Pappa. The peaks and valleys make me an acute thinker. I tend to be more elliptical when our conversations enter non-carnal spheres. I apologize, we can do a 180 and circle back to our previous area of discussion. Sorry if I'm too multi-dimensional for you bunch of squares.

Hey Pappa, asked Resh Lakish, What's with all these "dad jokes"?

You know, replied Rav Pappa, I went to the library, and it turns that my name, "Pappa" means "Daddy" in French. My romantic partners have always shouted out "who's my Daddy? who's my Daddy?" during our trysts. I actually thought they meant something else. Live and learn. So I have embraced dad jokes. Funny thing is my paramours are no longer impressed with me and my trysts have diminished substantially.

I can't imagine why, mused Rav Huna. But I am still trying to fathom why you repeatedly bring your erotic escapades into our House of God.

The ladies no longer call me "God" either, lamented Pappa.

The Pilot

MISHNAH:

Jose the Galilean: Is that Akivah in the back doing laundry!?
Rabbi Tarfon: Indeed, the Prodigal Shlong has returned.

Jose the Galilean: But why is he doing laundry?

Yohanan ben Zakkai: Because the Roman court sentenced him to be my butler.

Jose the Galilean: Ah! Because he shtupped a Good Samaritan in your wagon.

Yohanan ben Zakkai: No, Roman law allows for that. Remember "Dina d'malkhuta dina"* the law of the land is the law. All such inter-ethnic matters are subject to Roman law.

Jose the Galilean: Ah! Because he was caught treating his body like an amusement park,

Yohanan ben Zakkai: Wrong again. Not only is that within the bounds of Roman law, but it is also venerated as a form of Roman sport. He even won first place in the "monotheistic and circumcised" category. They gave him a stunning award.

Jose the Galilean: Ah! because he supported Bar Kochbah's rebellion?

Yohanan ben Zakkai: Wrong again. Don't forget he left Bar Kochbah a cripple, thus inadvertently helping Rome neutralize a violent false messiah. And ironically the Romans also classify this as an ejaculatory sport and public spectacle. They gave him a stunning award.

Jose the Galilean: Then why?

Yohanan ben Zakkai: Because when granted an audience with Emperor Hadrian to receive his awards, Akivah had the chutzpah to steal Hadrian's box of raisins. Right off the table. Given that Akivah carried no dried-fruit insurance, Rome sentenced him to be our butler.

Rabban Gamliel: But why did they send him here to be OUR butler and not keep him there?

Yohanan ben Zakkai: To punish us. They know we don't want him.

Rabbi Tarfon: I'm so happy I decided to move out and get my own apartment.

GEMARAH:

Man that pilot sucked rocks, said an irritated and disappointed Rav Huna, convening the meeting. *Jerry* is certainly no *Seinfeld*.

Yes, mused Rav Pappa. Sentenced to be Jerry's butler? What kind of plot is that? It doesn't sound very Jewish. Jews don't have butlers. Occasionally a shlepper,* but no butler. I couldn't imagine a "Jeeves" or "Jarvis" walking around the Yeshivah, collecting top hats, and serving high tea and crumpets.

Indeed, said Rav Sheshet. "Butler" is only mentioned six times in the Talmud and most references are to Pharaoh's butler. So so very goyish.

Goyish, goyish, goyish, said the Sages in unison.

Yes but the judge who sentenced him did not know that Jerry was Jewish, said Rav Kahana. Perhaps this is a common practice in a goyish city like New York.

Since when is New York a goyish city? said Bar Kappara. Did Lenny Bruce not famously say "If you live in New York, you're Jewish even if you're not"? How did that bit go?

I remember it said Rabbah, it's gold I tell you, it's gold baby, to paraphrase Kenny Bania.

I can recite it from memory, boasted Rav Pappa: "If you live in New York you're Jewish, whether you are a Jew or not. Shleppers are Jewish, Butlers are goyish. Masturbation contests are Jewish, but breast implants are goyish. Junior Mints are so goyish, but Pez is Jewish even if the Pez-dispenser head is a Polish pony. Lupus is goyish, and constipation is Jewish. Exposed nipples are goyish unless rubbed for eight days with the bald head of a short stocky slow-witted Jew immersed in oil from the Jerusalem Temple. Nazis are Jewish because Nazis have been mentioned more times in *Seinfeld*'s New York than Jews have. Stinking up a car with body odor is Jewish even if it's a Limo filled with Nazis. The Bubble Boy is goyish whereas Triangle Boy is Jewish because Jews are pointy, and goys are round. Being a Good Samaritan is goyish, whereas stealing a handicap spot is Jewish, even if the car parked in the handicap spot is a Limo filled with Nazis and stunk up with the body odor of Pharaoh's Butler."

And last but not least, added Resh Lakish, *Seinfeld* is a Jewish show, but *Jerry* is Goyish television.

Well that's a wrap for season 4, folks, concluded Rav Huna. Sixty-one episodes. And lo and behold, our first episode for the new year is all about faking orgasms. You must be thrilled Pappa.

Am I!? I've been rehearsing this material in front of the mirror all month, replied Rav Pappa.

Season 5

The Rabbis Add Punctuation to the Bible but Can't Find Israel on a Map

The Mango

GEMARAH:

Friends, said Rav Huna convening the meeting, I suspect this will be the year of Pappa, since we begin our season with orgasms.

Oh yeah, exclaimed Rav Pappa, "who's your daddy, who's your daddy!"

We get the joke, Pappa, enough already, said Resh Lakish.

The question before us, said Bar Kappara, is, as Jerry put it, whether having an orgasm under false pretenses constitutes sexual perjury.

Faking orgasms is a form of idolatry, replied Rabbah. You are claiming to see the Lord's promised land when in fact you are merely bored and want to roll over and go to sleep.

I agree, said Bar Kappara. But how are we, a gaggle of bookish sweaty rabbis, supposed to know if someone is faking it?

Perhaps they've all faked it, lamented Resh Lakish. We have no women here, and nobody, with the possible exception of Pappa, has much female orgasm experience.

Oh believe me I can tell, boasted Rav Pappa. And I will contend that most of us Jewish men – excluding yours truly – lack all confidence below the equator and are incapable of finding the so-called Bat Cave.

What about Rabbi Akivah? said Resh Lakish. He delivered the most spectacular orgasms in Jewish history, first Bari Weiss, and then he left Bar Kochbah a cripple.

Maybe he had picked up some mangos from Yossel's Fruit Store, suggested Shimon ben Pazi.

Regardless, that was the last spectacular orgasm in Jewish history and Bar Kochbah's ejaculatory downfall rendered us a debilitated people in exile, said Rav Kahana. This is our exilic condition: no crippling orgasms until the messiah comes. We are the diasporic captives of those who fake it; Jewish sissies, as Daniel Boyarin put it (Boyarin, *Unheroic Conduct*).

As the Talmud states, "Va-gina d'malkhuta va-gina," quoted Rabbah. And [pointing below his equator] this is the Johnson of our affliction, bound and gagged in an impermeable casket, much like Harry Houdini, the dysfunctional Jewish magician who couldn't negate our impotence.

Jewish magicians, noted Shimon ben Pazi, they can make the Statue of Liberty disappear, but can't induce a normal orgasm.

As George put it, "if Houdini couldn't do it, what chance do I have?" lamented Bar Kappara.

Well what should we do, asked Rav Huna?

I think we should have another contest! suggested Rav Pappa. Whoever achieves the most spectacular orgasm wins. Zutra will judge, since he has the most dingdong experience and can probably spot a faker four cubits away.

And then adequately punish the faker, even from a distance of four cubits, added Zutra the Mohel, smiling.

Contest, contest, contest, said the sages in unison.

Forgive me, fellow Sages, interjected Bar Kappara. But this all sounds a bit juvenile for a community of erudite sweaty rabbis.

Not at all, said the normally reserved Rav Huna. Elaine gave Jerry another chance; Kramer admitted to faking orgasms as well-

As do I admit to having faked many orgasms, interrupted Rav Pappa.

You faked it?! Said a startled Resh Lakish. Prove it, Pappa.

OK, but this won't be a pretty site…

[CENSORED – FOR THE REST OF THE CONTENT SEE THE SHMEKL TALMUD]

The Puffy Shirt

GEMARAH:

Friends, said Rav Huna convening the meeting. "The Puffy Shirt" is an inspiring episode and I think we need to adjust our priorities.

You want to admit low talkers into the Yeshivah? asked Resh Lakish, Because our policy handbook states that only those with high, whiny, nasally voices shall be admitted to the Rabbinate.

No, not that, replied Rav Huna, though perhaps we should also take steps to stop sounding so fricking Jewish. Let's table that for now. For today, we need to start a campaign to provide clothes for the homeless, the indigent, and the imbeciles.

Do we overproduce our rabbinical getups? asked Bar Kappara. Do we have outfits to spare?

We have plenty to spare, due to mishaps on the factory floor, said Motl Komzoyl, the chief tailor of Pumbedita. Do you know how often I've made tefillin straps of the wrong length or accidentally put 614 tassels on my tzitzit? Not to mention botched shtreymels,* shirts, tallises, and everything else.

What have you been doing with these botched items? asked Rav Huna.

Nothing, except for the tefillin straps, replied Motl. There's quite the market for them. The young disorderly goys buy them in strips to shoot up. You know, to get on the Horse, White Lokshn, Yam-Yam. Shanghai Shlomo.

Can you please speak in plain Aramaic? interjected Rav Sheshet, I don't understand your marketplace jargon.

He is saying the Gentiles use our tefillin straps to inject narcotics into their veins, replied Rabbah, who grew up in a dilapidated cave on the Lower East Side of the Euphrates and knew street talk as well any Amalekite or Philistine.

That's unconscionable, screamed Rav Huna, even if you aren't selling to fellow Jews.

Uh, well I do sell the occasional botched tefillin set to some of the kinkier Israelites for BDSM, admitted Motl in shame. Isn't that right Pappa?

Pappa! said Resh Lakish in disgust.

I have an idea, said Rav Pappa, quickly changing the subject. Since nobody buys the other botched clothing items, why not give them to the homeless? The full rabbinical getup, from shtreymel on down.

Because the locals may start mistaking the homeless, the indigent, and the imbeciles for rabbis, said Rav Kahana. Imagine if they start asking and getting advice – let alone halakhic interpretations – from indigent imbeciles. The distinction between us and them may be imperceptible.

"In a place where there are no Sages, one must strive to find an imbecile," quoted Rav Pappa. From Shammai, right before he left the House of Shammai to move back in with his parents.

So then, let's do as *Seinfeld* does: we will manufacture puffy shirts and give them to goodwill, suggested Bar Kappara.

Actually, I was going to suggest that we start wearing puffy shirts ourselves, said Rav Pappa. They're cool looking and kinda kinky. And in such a getup I would no longer need tefillin straps to seduce the ladies of the Euphrates.

This could be a whole new look for us, said Rabbah. We could be "the Pirate Rabbis"!

Just like in the song! Said Shimon ben Pazi.

What song? asked the Sages in unison.

By Bubbeleh Marley, the opening line is "A pirate's just a rabbi, he sold I some magical strips…"

Never heard of this Marley, said Rav Huna. Anyone know him?

As the tune suggests, I once sold him "magical" tefillin strips to shoot up some H – Shanghai Shlomo to be exact, admitted Motl.

And he thinks we're pirates, exclaimed Shimon ben Pazi.

Wow this is turning into the coolest Yeshivah ever, said a beaming Rav Pappa.

The Glasses

MISHNAH:

Shammai: Dog Bite
Hillel: Shot
Shammai: Woof Woof
Hillel: Bang Bang
Shammai: Not Bang Bang
Hillel: Woof Woof
Shammai: Yo-Yo Ma
Hillel: Boutros Boutros-Gali

GEMARAH:

Friends, said Rav Huna, I'm letting Abba the Surgeon run the meeting today, since "The Glasses" falls into his curative domain of expertise.

Thank you, Master, said Abba the Surgeon. I am honored to have this privilege. First of all-

I'm sorry, I object! interjected Rav Pappa.

Object to what? replied Bar Kappara.

This entire episode reveals the sham that we call the medical profession, said Rav Pappa. What kind of doctor doesn't understand the difference between a dog bite and a gun shot?

Agreed, said Resh Lakish. And opticians? Just as bad. Who sells a man lady's glasses? If you can't distinguish one gender from the other, you have no business being in medicine.

Forget gender, said Rav Sheshet. This episode raises more issues regarding the equine aspects of Jerry's meshpuchah. George can't tell Cousin Jeffrey from a horse? And why, may I ask, does that police officer regularly kiss her horse?

Moreover, I suspect kissing horses runs in Jerry's family, said Rav Pappa. Remember Manya Manya who went on an erotic shlepp with her horseface brother from Minsk to Pinsk? The whole family is messed up and knee deep in horse.

Do you think when the Nazis invaded Poland, asked Rabbah, they were able to distinguish Manya's relatives from the horses? Or do you think they shot the horses as well just to be on the safe side?

Neigh Neigh, not Bang Bang, said Shimon ben Pazi.

Neigh neigh, not Bang Bang, repeated the Sages in unison.

I think it depends on whether they used medical professionals to separate man from horse. We can say with certainty, the doctors would have failed epically at this.

None of this has anything to do with me, yelled Abba the Surgeon. Some respect to doctors and veterinarians where respect is due, please.

Hey Abba: Woof Woof, not Bang Bang, said Bar Kappara.

How about some intervention, Rav Huna, this is intolerable! exclaimed Abba the Surgeon. Do you as yeshivah head have anything to say in my defense?

I have only one thing to say, replied Rav Huna: Woof Woof, not Bang Bang. Meeting adjourned.

The Sniffing Accountant

GEMARAH:

So fellow Sages, should Jake have dumped Elaine over punctuation? asked Rav Huna convening the meeting.

Absolutely, said Bar Kappara. I found it very troubling that Elaine flipped out because he did not use an exclamation point. I'm glad he walked out. And he should have taken the dinner he cooked with him. And stolen her corkscrew.

You're insane. It's an exclamation point! It's a line with a dot under it, retorted Resh Lakish. How hard is it for him to have inserted one? It would have made Elaine feel good.

I would have walked out, said Rav Pappa. I don't use my exclamation points haphazardly. My love newtons have to earn their exclamation points.

Hey Pappa, asked Resh Lakish, after one of your [cough] sessions with a [cough] love newton is brought to [cough] climax, does she always say "oooh Pappa" with an exclamation point?

If she doesn't said Rav Pappa, then I put on my tzitzit, grab my tefillin and storm out. Unless of course they're my defective set of tefillin and I'm still tied up, and I can't free myself and reach the door. (See The Seinfeld Talmud, "The Puffy Shirt: Pappa the Israelite in the House of Persian Bondage").

"Pappa Don't Reach," as Madonna sang, mused Bar Kappara.

And how, prey tell, do you know your "love newton" isn't faking her exclamation points? Asked Rav Sheshet.

I think exclamation points are superfluous, said Rabbah. God did not use a single exclamation point in the Torah. And the Torah is perfect.

I disagree, said Bar Kappara. Much of the story would be more relatable and believable if the Lord indulged in a bit of punctuation.

I agree, said Resh Lakish. "In the beginning, God created the heaven and the earth!" Exclamation point. See how much better it reads.

Let me try, said Rav Sheshet: "Oh Abraham – take this cleaver and circumcise the flesh of your foreskin! This is the covenant betwixt you, me, and Mr. Johnson!" Two exclamation points! It works!

My turn, said Rav Pappa: "Adam ate the fruit that he took from Eve that she took from the snake and then she screamed! Because she saw Adam had exposed his nuts and his snake to the beasts of the field, the fish of the sea, and the snakes that creepeth and crawleth in the Garden of nuts and fruit!" Double exclamation points. This is gold, baby, gold.

Shmendriks, intervened Rav Huna. This is blasphemy. It's sacred text, the word of God, we can't make changes to it.

I think God implied the punctuation, insisted Rav Sheshet. We're just scribbling it in. Moses didn't have time to do it on Sinai. Forty days and Forty nights is insufficient to finesse every Oxford comma or decide between a hyphen, an en dash, or an em dash, let alone exclamation points.

Agreed, said Rav Pappa. The text is simply not plausible without these exclamation points, given the number of times the Lord makes demands upon the Israelites' shlongs, dingdongs, beytzim, and foreskins. Jake Jarmel would have had none of it and would have walked out on God. And now he'd be walking around a heathen.

Agreed, said Zutra the Mohel. I provide an exclamation point with every snip. My clients find it reassuring. Otherwise, even Jake Jarmel would have none of it and would walk out on me. And now he'd be walking around with a foreskin.

This is insufferable, said Rav Huna. I'll make you a deal. We will hold a workshop to redact the Torah with punctuation if you promise to stop talking about dingdongs and circumcisions!

Agreed! said the Sages in unison. With an exclamation point.

It's go time! said Rav Pappa. With an exclamation point. And we need to finish before tomorrow's shiur.

Which episode is tomorrow? asked Resh Lakish.

I think it's "The Bris," replied Rav Sheshet.

Oy gevalt! said the Sages in unison. With an exclamation point.

The Bris

GEMARAH:

Sages, we need to discuss the depiction of our People in this rather disturbing Seinfeld episode, said Rav Huna convening the meeting.

You're right, said Rav Pappa. I realize that Rav Sheshet is a bit goofy looking, but do you think he has the countenance of a Pig Man?

We can start calling him the Pig Man of Pumbetida, said Bar Kappara, but that might be a bit cruel to our colleague.

Shmendriks, said Rav Huna, I'm not talking about the Pig Man. I'm talking about the Bris and the representation of Judaism as barbaric. They acted as if said practitioners are primitive beings, hardly better than pig men, no offense Sheshet.

I dunno, replied Rav Pappa. I think the depiction of the Mohel got our beloved Zutra dead to right. What do you say Zutra?

I'm deeply offended, said Zutra the Mohel. I've never circumcised a finger in my life. I've occasionally taken a bit too much off the edges, but I've never missed the target.

So you are admitting you're a klutz, Shaky the Mohel, retorted Rabbah.

Not at all. I used to take to much off deliberately, replied Zutra. It was an experiment. I wanted to see if it would grow back. This is why I had to stop giving out warranties.

Are you listening to this? cried out Abba the Surgeon. Zutra is a barbarian and should be expelled. I'm a trained surgeon. I can perform our community's brises. And I operate on animals too. So, Sheshet, if you ever happen to reproduce, rest assured there is a spot for your pig men offspring in my clinic.

But we have already concluded that the medical profession is a sham, said Rav Pappa. Remember Abba – "Woof Woof, not Bang Bang," you quack. And now you want to circumcise pig men. Why would Rav Sheshet trust you with his "sussoid domesticoid" offspring, let alone any of us trust you with our far more breathtaking babies.

WTF is a "sussoid domesticoid," Pappa? asked Resh Lakish.

It is the scientific term for a pig man, said Abba the Surgeon. And you have the temerity to question my medical degree. Why a layman like Pappa knows the scientific term for pig men, however, is a mystery to me.

I know, I know, interjected Shimon ben Pazi. It's as Jerry said: "No matter what the deformity you'll find some group of perverts attracted to it. 'Oooh that little tail turns me on.'" Isn't that right, Pappa? You preevert.

And yet again, lamented Rav Huna, another shiur is spoiled by talk of shlongs, circumcisions, and Pappa's carnal proclivities.

That said, interjected Bar Kappara, at least we've issued a ruling on the admission of pig men to the academy. It's halakhically sound. Sheshet can stay.

So let it be written, so let it be done, said the Sages in unison.

The Lip Reader

GEMARAH:

Fellow Sages, said Rav Huna convening the meeting, I'm setting ground rules for today. No discussing shmekls, shlongs, beytzim, and dindongs. Nothing to do with sexual intercourse, seminal emissions, or foreskins. We are going to behave like mature, adult rabbis. Whoever violates this will be thrown out on their tokhes. And no discussing tokheses either.

So what should we debate? asked Bar Kappara.

I know! Whether "six" and "sex" sound alike, said Rav Kahana.

Kahana, get out of my academy, howled Rav Huna.

Why? It's a legitimate topic from the episode, replied Rav Kahana.

OK you can stay for now, relented Rav Huna. We can discuss the intricacies behind lip reading and the halakhic challenges they pose.

Thank you, said Rav Kahana. So, I raise the question: do you think Jewish lip readers can tell the difference between the Hebrew letter "Zayin" and the word "Zayin" – as in "shlong"?

It would be difficult, said Rabbah. One would have to look at the context, at the entire sentence.

"Zalman, eifoh hazayin shelchah?," replied Rav Kahana in Hebrew. What does that mean?

That sounds like "Zalman where is your petzl?" replied Rami bar Hama.

No it could mean, "Zalman where is your letter 'Z'?" As in "I can't read your handwriting and I don't see the zayin in your signature, Zalman" replied Rav Kahana.

What about "anachnu rotsim lezayin achshav?" what does that mean? asked Rabbah in Hebrew.

"We want to shtupp now," replied Rav Kahana. That one's obvious.

Or "to shlong," interjected Rabbah.

No, replied Rav Kahana, that is a fake verb invented by Donald Trump, the Amalekite, whose command of Jewish-speak is almost as bad as his command of English.

Why can't "anachnu rotsim lezayin achshav?" mean "we want to add the letter 'Z' now?" asked Rami bar Hama.

Because "To add the letter Z" is not a Hebrew verb, replied Rav Kahana. This is all about the karnotzl shtupping the knish or perhaps shlonging the knish.

Or the knish shtupping the karnotzl, said the proud feminist Rami bar Hama. Jewish verbs of motion are multidirectional and should be gender neutral.

Rami, Kahana, and Rabbah, you're outta here, said Rav Huna. I suggest you go to the marketplace, find a lip reader and allow them to eavesdrop on your conversation about your "zayins." Send us a telegram with the verdict. Wait – where are you going Pappa?

No offense, Master, but such an excursion looks far more fun than this lesson. So I'm outta here too.

OK, now let's get back to lip reading, said Rav Huna, a proper wholesome talmudic discussion.

So the question is whether "sweep together" and "sleep together" sound alike, said Bar Kappara.

I am all but certain Gwen and Todd were talking about shtupping or shlonging after the party, said Rabbi Abbahu. Nobody says "we can sweep together" after a party. Who sticks around and sweeps? It was pure flirtation, innuendo, and euphemism. This is all about the karnotzl shtupping the knish.

Kappara and Abbahu you're outta here, said Rav Huna. Now, what's next on the ledger?

We need to discuss whether a deaf lip reader can be hired out as a novelty act to perform at weddings and bar mitzvahs, suggested Rav Zeira. Seinfeld says no, Costanza says yes.

Finally, we are getting somewhere, said Rav Huna with relief.

I for one am against it, said Zutra the Mohel. It cuts into my business, so to speak. You'd be surprised how many people want a mohel to perform at their soirees. It's right up there with human sacrifices. In fact, Motl and I have an act and a roadshow that's met with some acclaim.

Ah right, "Zutra the Impaler and Motl the Tailor: The Snip and Sew Show," noted Shimon ben Pazi. I've seen the billboards, but I assumed it was a joke. Where can I buy tix?

Ticketmaster, said Zutra the Mohel. But I will cut you a deal, so to speak.

Zeira, Zutra, Motl, and Pazi, you're outta here.

But we didn't do anything, said Zutra. Circumcision is halakhic, and, moreover, it is a skill, just like juggling. I enjoy showing it off while snipping it off.

Then go and pull a King David, find some Philistines and let loose, said Rav Huna. Like King Saul, I give you my blessing. Who's next?

It appears Rav Sheshet the Pig Man and I are the only ones left in the academy, said Resh Lakish.

Well what shall we discuss? said Rav Huna.

I want to know, asked Rav Sheshet, why you and the other sages have branded me a pig man.

So we can rent you out as a novelty act to weddings and bar mitzvahs, replied Resh Lakish.

Yes, said Rav Huna, we need to pay the bills. You think people want to fork over cash to listen to our inane discussions?

The Non-Fat Yogurt

MISHNAH:

Hillel: Hey Shammai, word in the marketplace is that you've been impersonating me.

Shammai: Well, not exactly.

Hillel: You've been going on the road and pontificating my wisdom, quoting my aphorisms, telling Jews how to live in the manner and the discourse of the House of Hillel.

Shammai: Again, not quite. I always give you credit. And, moreover, I crank it up a notch with some cussing and obscenities. I'm like the X-rated House of Hillel. I'm the Spicoli to your Mr. Hand. The Don Rickles to your Sam Levenson.

Hillel: I have been proudly PG for nearly a century, except when discussing Yoizl* Pandrek the Nazarene. And this isn't *Fast Times at Borscht Belt High*. What exactly have you done to my golden words, "Mr. Spicoli"?

Shammai: Well, for instance, I preach: "If not f*cking now, then when the f*ck?"

Hillel: That is just awful.

Shammai: How about, "If I don't f*ck for myself who will f*ck for me? If I only f*ck for myself what the f*ck am I?"

Hillel: What the f*ck are you? You're nothing but a weenie. This is unconscionable. You are tarnishing the House of Hillel. Nobody will take me seriously anymore.

Shammai: Look Hillel, judge not thy friend the shmuck until thou standest in his sh*tty place. A little rakhmones for the unemployed assh*le-philosopher, who lives with his parents, please.

Hillel: Rakhmones? Hey Shammai, thanks for ruining my career, you fat f*ck.

The Barber

GEMARAH:

Welcome back, fellow Sages, said Rav Huna, convening the meeting. I hope you all enjoyed your day off reflecting on your potty mouths.

I, for one, said Bar Kappara, felt embarrassed and humiliated in front of a large group of people, for having to walk out in shame with my tail between my legs.

Not me, said Rav Pappa, didn't bother me one bit.

Me neither, said Rabbah.

Me neither, said Rami Bar Hama.

Me neither, said Shimon ben Pazi.

OK enough of this, interrupted Rav Huna. So how exactly did you all spend your time?

I showed initiative, said Rami bar Hama. I reorganized the Oral Torah into this accordion-style folder. We can now call it the "Pensky Mishnah."

That's pretty unimpressive, said Bar Kappara shaking his head in bewilderment.

Well bear in mind I've always had the smaller office, replied Rami bar Hama.

I participated in a bachelor auction, boasted Rav Pappa.

And? asked Bar Kappara.

I fetched a lousy 5 dinars and had a "date" with the Tunisian camel jockey who purchased me.

I got a hair cut, boasted Shimon ben Pazi, and completed my high school equivalency.

You look like a 5-year-old meat head, noted Bar Kappara.

I watched Edward Scissorhands and then experimented with this intriguing appendage concept in my business, said Zutra the Mohel.

And? asked Bar Kappara.

My scissors hands scared my clients and then I ended up having a mishap with them in the toilet, said Zutra, lowering his head in shame and massaging his crotch in pain.

And, accordingly, interjected Motl the Tailor, I had more opportunities to sew things back on that shouldn't have gotten snipped off in the first place.

And you, Sheshet? asked Rav Huna. You weren't thrown out, but you walked out after we called you Rav Sheshet the Pig Man.

I went to Abba the Surgeon's clinic for a consultation, said Rav Sheshet. I told him I no longer want to bear the mark of the Pig Man. He tried to have me institutionalized and said I should accept my fate as a fat little mental patient with a pinkish hue and an upturned nose.

I think we're done for today, said Rav Huna.

That's it? Asked Bar Kappara.

Yes that's it, replied Rav Huna. I can't find a damn thing on "The Barber" episode in this new accordion-style Pensky Mishnah. We'll figure it out by tomorrow, by which time Rami bar Hama will be relocated and forced to work Newman's postal route for a pittance.

The Masseuse

GEMARAH:

Fellow sages, "The Masseuse" has made it abundantly clear that we have a problem, said Rav Huna, convening the meeting.

Not everyone has to like you Huna, said Rav Pappa.

Shmuck, that's not what I meant. The problem is that far too many of us have the same or similar names and it's very confusing.

Yes we have multiple Hillels, several sons of Gamliels, and a couple of Hunas and Ravinas; we have two Shmuels and one Samuel which makes absolutely no sense; and we have countless Judahs, listed off Bar Kappara. We even have two Abbas, only one of whom is actually a surgeon.

And to make matters worse, Abba means "Daddy" in Hebrew, and Pappa means "Daddy" in French, which greatly confuses me, said Shimon ben Pazi.

And if Abba the Surgeon says "Who's Your Abba? Who's Your Abba?" when he's with the ladies, then he's stealing my material and my reputation.

OK so we need to change Pappa's name, said Bar Kappara. I say we call him "Ned," as I've seen his irregular underwear collection. Rav Ned is a guy who buys irregular underwear.

We're going to have to call Rabbah "Alex" because of the annoying "Ahh!" sound he makes – with an exclamation point I might add – every time he takes a sip of his Maccabee Beer.

I prefer Ellis. It's the same as Alex, replied Rabbah.

Rami bar Hama will be Remy bar Hama because of that dainty beret he always wears, suggested Resh Lakish.

Zutra will henceforth be known as O.J. No explanation necessary, said Bar Kappara.

I object, said Zutra the Mohel. My clients leave my office alive. Most of the time at least.

And Rav Sheshet will have to be called "Rav Chazerman."* It's not as crude as "The Pig Man," suggested Abba the Surgeon.

I don't understand, why can't you just stop calling me a pig man, in any language, replied a distraught Rav Sheshet Chazerman.

You've given this a lot of thought Kappara, said Resh Lakish. May I ask why?

Because I need to change my name too, said Bar Kappara. Kappara makes people think of the Day of Atonement Kapparot ritual.* Little kids encircle me in the marketplace and start defiling roosters around my head. It's humiliating. I'm left disheveled and coated in that which cometh out of a rooster.

Good thing it's not a chicken or a hen, said Resh Lakish.

Maybe you should start wearing a beret for better coverage? suggested Ellis.

Then we will have to change his name to Remy, said Rav Chazerman Sheshet.

Oh no! two Remys! We're back to square one, said O.J. the Mohel.

Then the solution is for Rami the First Remy to stop wearing his hat, suggested the Second Remy. I need it more than he does. I walk the street with rooster emissions on my cranium.

Only if Pappa agrees to change his name to Ned, replied Rami the First Remy. Remy has grown on me.

No f'in way, said Rav Pappa. I'd rather ditch my irregular underwear collection. "Who's your Ned?" and "Ned Don't Reach" will not play well with my love newtons who love to come to Pappa.

May I take your underwear off your hands? Asked the First Remy.

Sure thing, said Rav Pappa, so long as you change your name to Ned.

Done and done! Replied Ned.

This was our most successful shiur this week, gloated The Second Remy. We didn't talk about shlongs, dingdongs, and beytzim.

Not quite, said Rav Pappa. You did bring up rooster emissions. And we all know the rooster is supposed to have sex with the chicken, not the cranium of the apparently perverse Second Remy.

If the rooster has sex with the chicken, asked Shimon ben Pazi the Meat Head, then who is having sex with the hen? Something's missing.

Yes Meat Head, something's missing alright, interjected Rav Huna. And that is a topic for Season 7. Wait, where is everyone going?

I'm off to the market in my new beret, said the Second Remy.

I'm off to exhibit my irregular underwear to the harlots on the Lower Euphrates, boasted Ned.

I'm off to see if my "work gloves," still fit, said O.J. the Mohel.

The Cigar Store Indian

GEMARAH:

Fellow sages, "The Cigar Store Indian" is such an important episode, said Rav Huna, convening the meeting.

I know, said Bar Kappara, who would have thought Frank Costanza collected *TV guides?* He's so prolific!

Potz,* that's not what I meant. It's important because we finally have confirmation that Jerry is a Yid. He's a Member of the Tribe.

How so? asked Shimon ben Pazi.

Because he said if "someone asks me which way's Israel, I don't fly off the handle," replied Rav Huna. Israel, get it? Zion? Our Jewish homeland.

However, interjected Resh Lakish, the Chinese mailman also said to Jerry: "Oh, hello American Joe. Which way to hamburger, hotdog stand?" thereby suggesting Jerry's nothing more than your average White American.

So which is it? asked Rav Sheshet.

Maybe he's a Native American? said Shimon ben Pazi. This would explain why he knows scalpers, has access to reservations, and felt a deep kinship with the cigar store Indian.

Hey Pazi, you Meat Head, I think you've completely missed the point of the episode, retorted Bar Kappara.

Can you imagine if we freaked out if someone asked us for directions to Israel? said Resh Lakish.

Now that I think of it, how exactly do you get to Israel from here? asked Rav Sheshet.

Beats me, said Rabbah. You think I'm in Persia in this hovel with a gaggle of sweaty rabbis by choice? I'd rather be at the Temple Mount.

Actually, someone knocks on my door and asks for directions to Israel at least once per week, boasted Rav Pappa.

And what do you say, Pappa? asked Resh Lakish.

I invite them in, and they get to see the Promised Land by mounting my Temple.

Pappa this is your last warning, admonished Rav Huna.

Would you rather I made jokes about Native Americans, much like Jerry and Kramer did, asked Rav Pappa? Because I have zero reservations about it.

Thin ice, Pappa, thin ice, said Rav Huna.

Thin ice, Pappa, thin ice, said the Sages in unison.

Then let's bury the hatchet and smoke us a peace pipe, suggested Rav Pappa.

Pappa – get out of my Academy, howled Rav Huna.

I'm not leaving without my wardrobe of irregular underwear, countered Rav Pappa.

Ned, please give Pappa back his underwear, instructed Rav Huna.

I will not, replied Ned, formerly known as Rami bar Hama and the First Remy.

Why, not? Asked Bar Kappara.

Because, replied Ned, that would make Pappa an-

A what, Ned? Do you mean an INDIAN GIVER? retorted Rav Pappa.

I'm sorry, I'm not familiar with that term, replied Ned.

QUEER TALMUD YESHIVX, 2023:

Wow what a racist episode, said an angry Rebbetzin Amirah "Cancel Student Debt" Mizrahi.

All these White people mocking an indigenous community, howled Rabba Jewliettx bat Ocasio-Cortezx.

And Asians too, said Rebbetzin Amirah. What about that East Asian actor who said "ask honolable Chinaman for rocation of lestaulant." He is complicit in performing Chinaman-face.

I think it's now called Oriental-face, said Rabba Zarah "Save Sheikh Jarrah" Al-Sabbah.

And then Jerry pledged his loyalty to Israel, kvetched Rabbx Yehudis bnei Butler. He literally erased the Palestinians.

This whole episode is anti-Palestinian, said Rabba Zarah. Did they even consult one Palestinian when writing it?

We're so done here with *Seinfeld* at the Yeshivx, concluded Rabba Jewliettx. Let's watch *The Color Purple* instead.

The Conversion

GEMARAH:

Wow what an episode, said Rav Huna, convening the meeting, we have so much to talk about.

Who knew Costanza was familiar with the basic plot: the Flood, the lepers, the Commandments, and all that? Do you think he knows more than us? Asked Shimon ben Pazi.

It's safe to assume he knows more than you Pazi, replied Bar Kappara, who was now known as Remy.

We have an issue here, said the excessively anxious Resh Lakish: George converting to Latvian Orthodoxy poses a threat to Judaism.

How so? replied a perplexed Rav Pappa.

Because Costanza is a Yid; he's one of us. His auto-erotic activities alone have exposed his yichus.

True dat, said Rav Pappa, as he leisurely leafed through the pages of his dog-eared copy of *Glamor Magazine*.

Then it would follow that Latvian Orthodoxy is our biggest rival and constitutes the ultimate danger to our peoplehood, said Rav Sheshet.

The Latvian Orthodox have so much going for them, said Bar Kappara: beautiful nuns, a theology that is at once enigmatic and vost. And the hats, let's not forget the hats.

And they are the religion that goes around mutilating squirrels, mused Zutra the Mohel. As a businessman who trades in halakhic mutilation I can see why such a ritual is more attractive than circumcision. That said, it would be an easy transition for me and my shekels to go from shmekls to squirrels.

We Rabbis are not going to mutilate any squirrels, replied Abba the Surgeon.

Hey Abba, interjected Resh Lakish, aren't you the guy who failed out of podiatry school?

Then maybe we should at least change our hats? suggested Rami Bar Hama, who never got over the forced abandonment of his beret, let alone his irregular underwear.

We need to do something, said Resh Lakish, otherwise we will be swallowed up in a sea of Latvian Orthodoxy within a few years.

Ah but we have a secret weapon, said Rav Pappa. The Kavorka. I, Pappa, have the Kavorka, the Lure of the Animal. I can draw the ladies away from the Latvians and bring them into Judaism.

Kavorka! Pappa has the Kavorka! said the Sages in unison.

Shmendriks, there's no such thing as Kavorka, said Abba the Surgeon. I'm a physician and I state for the record that Kavorka is mystical junk.

Hey Abba, interjected Resh Lakish, even Pazi got into podiatry school.

And I only received my GED last week, boasted Shimon ben Pazi with pride.

The Lure of the Animal! said the Sages in unison.

Much as Pappa disgusts me, relented Resh Lakish, I think he's the real McCoy. He has the Kavorka. He is our secret weapon.

But there are few Orthodox Latvians in Pumbedita, said Rav Pappa. Where are they? Palestine? Rome? Gaul?

They're probably in Latvia, said Resh Lakish.

Ah, Latvia! said the Sages in unison.

Where is Latvia? asked Shimon ben Pazi.

I think it's near Minsk, or perhaps Pinsk, in Poland, where Manya, Manya, Rochelle, Rochelle, and the Horseface People shot by the Nazis live, replied Rav Huna.

Neigh Neigh, not Bang Bang! said the Sages in unison.

Then we send Rav Pappa to Latvia on a fact-finding mission, said Bar Kappara.

Rav Pappa, we hereby empower you to go to Latvia and to not come back until you have seduced at least 100 Orthodox Latvian nuns, commanded Rav

Huna. Bring their habits back as proof.

And their slinkies, added Shimon ben Pazi, who had tired of his Batman comic books and Lego set.

Piece of cake, said Rav Pappa. I'll be back before Passover. And the Lure of the Animal will be known from the Baltic to the Polish Corridor. Check you later.

[Exit Pappa]

Master Huna, said Abba the Surgeon, forgive my harsh language, but we should not be encouraging this pervert.

I take inspiration from King Saul sending David to acquire 100 Philistine foreskins (1 Samuel 18:24), said Rav Huna.

Sire, if this is a foreskin hunt, then I should be accompanying him, interjected Zutra the Mohel. Latvia is fresh fertile ground for me. And I can only imagine the girth on the Horseface people.

No you yold, I'm making an analogy, said Rav Huna. It's a suicide mission. We have rid ourselves of Pappa. He'll never reach Poland let alone Latvia.

"Pappa Don't Reach," sang the Sages in unison.

The Stall

GEMARAH:

I bring news of Pappa's voyage to Latvia, said Rav Huna, convening the meeting. There was an incident.

Oh no, said Bar Kappara, did the Cossacks get him? Did he get chased into the Baltic Sea by a vost mob of enigmatic priests in those pious hats?

No, not exactly, replied Rav Huna.

Let me guess, said Resh Lakish: the Lure of the Animal wore off. He was enchanted by a Latvian temptress, and he embraced their squirrel-mutilating religion. Is he now "Brother Pappa"?

Good guess, but wrong again, said Rav Huna. The Kavorka is all to real. He will return with a collection of nun habits and – not to worry Pazi – some slinkies.

So what happened? said the Sages in unison.

Well, continued Rav Huna, while trying to seduce a Latvian nun somewhere on the road between Minsk and Pinsk he lost his way and fell off his pony, leading to severe injuries.

Oh no, said Rami bar Hama, that's terrible. What about his face? Did something happen to his face?

Why are you so concerned with his face? Asked Abba the Surgeon.

No reason, replied Rami bar Hama defensively. I've always thought Pappa has a nice face.

You have a man crush on him, don't you? said Rav Sheshet accusatorily.

That's not true, said Rami bar Hama. He's just a cool guy who happens to be a mimbo with a perfect face. You're just jealous, Sheshet, because you're a pig man who yearns for Pappa's face. So please, Sheshet, step off dude.

Step off dude, said the Sages in unison.

He has a point, Sheshet, interjected Abba the Surgeon. When you came to me seeking radical reconstructive surgery for your porcine ponim, you wanted me to transform you from Peppa Pig to Pappa the Player. That's why I told you to accept your fate as a fat little mental patient with a pinkish hue and an upturned nose. I think YOU have a man crush on Pappa.

As disturbing as this revelation about Sheshet-Peppa the Pig Man is, said Resh Lakish, I'm more convinced than ever that Rami is in love with Pappa. That explains his acquisition of Pappa's irregular underwear collection, his willingness to take the name Ned, and all those peanut butter sandwiches he made for him.

Step off, Lakish. You couldn't be more wrong. Rav Pappa hates peanut butter, retorted Rami Bar Hama.

Aha! said Rav Sheshet. You love him. You love Pappa. The Kavorka has ensnared to you.

And what will you do now if Pappa has suffered severe disfigurement, asked Resh Lakish. What will you do if he's a hideous freak, like Rav Sheshet?

Hey, howled Rav Sheshet, step off!

I was just making an analogy, chill out, Pig Man, chided Resh Lakish. Rami, will you learn to love him anyway even without the Lure of the Animal?

Lure of the Animal? I think we are avoiding the elephant in the room, interrupted Abba the Surgeon. How could a stallion like the great Rav Pappa fall off a puny Polish pony? We sent him abroad to save Judaism and he couldn't even keep his tokhes saddled on a baby horse.

He's right, this is deeply embarrassing for us, said Bar Kappara. And I dare say it is a bad sign. The future of Latvian Orthodoxy looks bright, whereas we will be a tribe extinguished in exile.

They got Costanza and they got Pappa, lamented Rami bar Hama. We're all going down in the vost enigmatic sea of Latvian Orthodoxy.

But at least you will now inherit Pappa's irregular underwear, said Rav Sheshet.

Step off, Pig Man, howled Rami bar Hama.

Friends, concluded Rav Huna, it is time to acknowledge that Rav Pappa is one of us, despite his wild sexual escapades. We will treat him with the dignity and respect he deserves when he returns, even if he, keinehora,* resembles a pig man like Sheshet.

And worst-case scenario, added Bar Kappara who always sought to put a positive spin on things, we can rent them both out as novelty acts to weddings and bar mitzvahs.

So let it be written, so let it be done, said the Sages in unison.

The Dinner Party

PREAMBLE:

The Rabbis had very little to say about "The Dinner Party" and would have passed over it entirely had it not coincided with Rav Pappa's semi-humiliating return from Latvian Orthodoxdom, tired, injured, and embarrassed for having fallen off a baby horse. So the rabbis planned a dinner party to cheer him up and to help bring the Lure of the Animal back to the Academy, for, truth be told, they had in fact missed it.

GEMARAH:

Fellow sages, thanks for helping to make our Welcome Home Pappa Party a reality on such short notice. Pappa is on his way back from his failed conquest of Latvia, and as I said in my note, word in the marketplace is that he lost a limb or two falling off a Polish pony in Pinsk. But his Kavorka lives on and there now lies an abutment in the Polish Corridor bearing his name where the heathen sex cults go to worship. "The Pappa Kavorka Abutment, The Lure of a Limbless Jewish Animal."

Limbless in Latvia, lamented the Sages in unison.

Great movie! said Shimon ben Pazi.

You're thinking of *Sleepless in Sevastopolk*, said Rav Sheshet.

No you're thinking of *Shlongless in Seattle*, you shmegegge, said Rav Huna. Please get your filmography straight.

I would think all three titles could apply to Pappa, should he ever visit Seattle.

Moving on, said Bar Kappara in the name of Rav Huna, what have you all brought for our illustrious dinner party?

I brought a hair with a cinnamon babka on it, said Rabbah,

I brought the 2-liter plastic Pepsi bottle and Ring Dings, said Rav Sheshet.

I brought the black and white cookie. We must look to the cookie for racial harmony, said Resh Lakish.

Look to the cookie! Look to the cookie! said the Sages in unison.

Pepsi and Ring Dings, but no wine and cheese? asked an astonished Bar Kappara. What kind of farkakteh dinner party is this?

Rav Huna told us to "watch *Seinfeld*, 'The Dinner Party' and plan the menu accordingly," replied Rav Sheshet. Moreover, there was a sign on the liquor store door that said, "Pagans and Pig Men not welcome," so I could not enter.

Besides, added Shimon ben Pazi, Costanza said if "I show up with Ring Dings and Pepsi, I become the biggest hit at the party."

So you're taking culinary advice from the man who ate an eclair out of a trash can? laughed Rami bar Hama.

And you brought a black and white cookie for racial harmony, Lakish? asked an incredulous Bar Kappara. This is the Orient. I have seen maybe one Black man and hardly a White man Babylon in all these years.

That's why I only brought ONE cookie, replied Resh Lakish.

Did you bring anything, Kahana? asked Bar Kappara.

Yes, I brought a copy of *Penthouse Forum*, replied Rav Kahana.

Why in the world would you bring a *Penthouse*, interjected Rav Huna? Such shmutz* has no place in our Yeshivah.

For the stories, as Kramer suggested. They are funny AF, cheerfully added Rav Kahana. We can regale in tales of lust and bondage that speak to Pappa's condition and desires.

It's as George put it, said Rabbah: "there is an unusual number of people in this country having sex with amputees."

I can vouch for that, said Abba the Surgeon. Whenever I leave town, the undisciplined nurses turn my clinic into a brothel of limited mobility. It's a sight to behold.

OK given the trauma endured by Pappa and his limbs in Latvia, relented Rav Huna, I'll make an exception this time. We can read the amputee sex stories. But please no "Pappa don't reach" jokes.

The Marine Biologist

GEMARAH:

Look who's here! announced Rav Huna, convening the meeting, as he wheeled a truncated yet beaming Rav Pappa into the Yeshivah.

How was Latvia? gingerly asked Bar Kappara.

I didn't quite make it, said Rav Pappa, at least not to Riga.

So, then, "Pappa don't Reach," laughed Resh Lakish, elbowing Rav Sheshet.

That's enough you two, admonished Rav Huna. Pappa has the floor today.

You mean he has the chair today, laughed Resh Lakish, elbowing Rav Sheshet again.

No ableist jokes in the Yeshivah! Lakish, get out of my academy, and take the Pig Man with you, howled Rav Huna.

So tell us the story Pappa, tell us what happened, said Shimon ben Pazi.

I won't lie to you boys, I was scared, said Rav Pappa. It turns out the Kavorka has limited powers in Catholic lands, which I discovered while crossing the Polish Corridor on a sojourn from Minsk to Pinsk on my Polish pony. Sure, I had conquered my way across Byzantium, seducing nuns and acquiring slinkies, but then I entered the Land of the Pontiff.

So then what happened? asked the Sages, on the edge of their seats. Continue the story.

The Holy See was angry that day my friends, like an old monk trying to return mead at a monastery.

I have no idea what that means, said a perplexed Bar Kappara.

But I pressed on, continued Rav Pappa, and triumphantly rode into Minsk on my pony, descending from Mount Kreplach into Transcarpathia, like Yoshke Pandrek on Palm Sunday. This was the land of Manya, Manya and the Horseface People. The crowds shouted "Kavorka" and surrounded me. But a strange calm came over me as I roared "I am Pappa, and I have the Lure of the Animal." I don't know if it was divine intervention or the kinship with all living things, but I tell you at that moment, I was the Kavorkian Messiah! And I was saving our Tribe.

But something must have gone wrong? Asked Rami bar Hama.

Yes, I got hit in the head by an electronic organizer and I fell off my pony, who then trampled over me, crushing my limbs. A band of traveling gypsies loaded me onto their wagon to bring me home.

So then you are not the Messiah, said Rabbah, with more than a touch of sarcasm.

I'm no longer sure he's even the Kavorka, said Bar Kappara. Who can't ride a pony?

Jews. Jews can't ride ponies. Even those Jews with Nephilim-sized beytzim like Pappa, lamented Shimon ben Pazi.

Hey, it could have been worse, said a nonetheless cheerful Rav Pappa. The beytzim broke my fall. They are now undergoing treatment with Zutra the Mohel and Motl the Tailor.

I don't believe this, howled Abba the surgeon. I'm a trained physician and you are getting your testicular torsion treated by a mohel?

Hey Abba, remember "Woof Woof, not Bang Bang"? said the Sages in unison.

You're a quack Abba, said Rav Pappa. My beytzim are now my livelihood. And besides, that's why Zutra now works with a tailor. "Snip and sew" is safer than someone who failed out of podiatry school. But rest assured I'll still frequent your amputee brothel. Yes they deliver *Penthouse* in Poland and I've been reading the Yeshivah's minutes.

Not to worry, everyone, he's in my custody now, smiled Zutra the Mohel, wheeling Pappa out of the room.

The Pie

GEMARAH:

I just came from Rabbanana Republic, said a breathless Bar Kappara entering the Yeshivah. You won't believe it; they have a mannequin in the window that looks exactly like Rav Pappa!

Are you sure it was him? asked Rav Huna. We Sages – with the exception of Sheshet and his porcine deformities – tend to look quite similar: the shtreymels, sidelocks, tzitzit, tefillin, and sweaty armpits.

Hey, I've got all of those, howled Rav Sheshet, tugging his sidelock while smelling his armpit.

No it's him, said Bar Kappara. I can tell because portions of his limbs are missing; he's the only rabbi-amputee in Pumbedita.

We need to check this out said the Sages in unison. To the marketplace!
.....

Unbelievable, said Resh Lakish. There are Pappa mannequins all over town.

And it's certainly him, said Rami bar Hama: one is riding a Polish pony; one has his ass modeling irregular underwear in the window hunched over an Assyrian lady of the evening. And they say there is a Pappa mannequin on the Lower East Side of the Euphrates in a drug den where he's using tefillin to shoot up some Shanghai Shlomo.

Hey, Abba, did you purchase one for your amputee clinic-brothel? asked Resh Lakish.

I will not even dignify that with a response, said Abba the Surgeon, while quietly placing an order via SIRI.

Poor Pappa, said Rabbah. Does he even know? Has anyone seen him since his surgery? Oy, what problems he has.

[Silence]

You know the last time I saw one of the mannequins they were changing it; Pappa was completely naked, said a blushing Rami bar Hama.

Yeah, Rami, and Pappa's the one with the problems, said Resh Lakish.

The mannequin was naked? said Zutra the Mohel in surprise. Rami did you happen to note who did the handiwork below the equator? This is cutting into my business, so to speak.

Yeah, Zutra, and Rami's the one with the problems, said Resh Lakish.

Surely, Zutra, they don't use a mohel to give a mannequin a bris? asked Rav Sheshet.

Surely they do, replied Zutra the Mohel with more than a touch of pride; it's part of our bulk snip and save volume program; we cut marble, plastic, and fiberglass. Who do you think did all the petzls on the David monuments the Nazarenes erected? Yours truly. Only my brand name for the goys is "Zutra's Clippings for Christ."

That's idolatry. Our religion does not sanction this: "Thou shalt not make unto thee any graven image and snip its shmekl," Second Commandment, said Rav Huna with some slight embellishment.

You say "idolatry," I say "successful business model," countered Zutra.

Poor Pappa, said the Sages in Unison.

What Poor Pappa? said Rami bar Hama. It is said the ladies are making pilgrimages to the mannequins in awe. The Kavorka is apparently strong in them, with or without Zutra's handiwork.

The Stand-In

GEMARAH:

Fellow Sages, said Rav Huna convening the meeting, "The Stand-In" was one of the most egregious episodes yet. There's so much to discuss.

First off, note the Seinfeld body count, said Bar Kappara, jumping in. Jerry has murdered at least two people: Manya Manya the Horse Thief and now Fulton. And he nearly killed Triangle Boy, the fat starving artist.

It seems he is most successful at offing people when he uses his comedic "talents," said Rabbah. Both Manya and Fulton died following his jokes; one who didn't laugh and one who laughed too hard. Whereas killing someone with a Junior Mint appears to be more hit and miss. Triangle Boy pulled out of his negative prognosis.

It is a little mint, after all, said Resh Lakish.

What about George? added Rav Sheshet. He almost killed the Bubble Boy. Clearly he and Jerry have a larger agenda. The body count will only increase as the envelope gets licked.

The expression is "the envelope gets pushed," you shnook, said Resh Lakish.

Forget Fulton, these homicidal tendencies are old news already, said Rav Huna. We have discussed them ad nauseam. Far worse things have transpired.

Such as? asked a rejuvenated and almost ambulatory Rav Pappa, attending his first shiur since his accident, still in a wheelchair.

Well for one, Phil Totola took it out, replied Rav Huna.

He took … it out! said the Sages in unison.

Sorry, I disagree, said Rav Pappa. As Kramer said, "maybe it needed some air, sometimes they can't breathe down there." Mine needs air all the time. For instance -

Quickly, everyone avert your eyes! howled Rav Huna.

No not now! I was just giving an example, assured Rav Pappa. My dingdong only appears with warning.

And then a phone call to the CDC, added Resh Lakish.

Look, said Rami bar Hama, I'm with Pappa here, especially for someone who has Nephilim-size Beytzim. Eh Pappa? I saw your mannequin in the shop window. It must be a sweatshop for you down there.

Rami, you are hereby requested to leave the shiur and go take a cold shower, said Rav Huna.

And what about Mickey's heightening? Said Rav Pinchas the Short, the first rabbi to attain incomparable halakhic heights from a mere four feet off the ground. As my fellow diminutive Tammy said during the "The Stand-In," "all the progress we made over the years, and you go and blow it by pulling a stupid stunt like this."

Again, I will have to disagree, interjected Rav Pappa.

You, Pappa? Why in the world? asked Bar Kappara.

Ever since my near Latvian dismemberment I've had to heighten, admitted Rav Pappa. I've been taken down several inches and I remain lopsided.

But you had surgery with Zutra the Mohel and Motl the Tailor, said Rav Huna. Were you not fixed?

Not completely, said a sullen Rav Pappa. Zutra's far better at snipping than Motl is at sewing. So I use lifts to fix my deformity.

Hey, enough with the ableist language, said Rav Pinchas the Short. We aren't lopsided or deformed. We are "unevenly divergent," much as Sheshet isn't a "pig man;" he's just a bit zaftig* with a rosy glow.

And he has a pig snout for a nose, Pinchas, retorted Rav Pappa. Hey Huna, do we have to listen to this PC narishkeit from this itsy-bitsy rabbi?

Pappa, may you be wheeled straight to hell at no more than three miles an hour! cursed Rav Pinchas the Short.

Hey Pappa, said Rav Huna, you are out of line with such ableist rhetoric, but man we all missed you in the Yeshivah! Great to have you and your beytzim back.

The Wife

MISHNAH:

Shammai: Blessed are the drainmakers for connecting pipe with pipe.

Hillel: Cursed be Shammai for he is the pee in the shower type.

Shammai: I was there! I saw a drain!

Hillel: And I am here, athwart a Sage without a brain.

Shammai: Judge not thy friend until thou standest in his place.

Hillel: No, I judge my friend for having urinated in a public space.

GEMARAH:

Fellow Sages, this is an episode that touches upon our intrinsic humanity, said Rav Huna.

Yes, public urination is the ultimate talmudic debate, said Rav Sheshet.

Which means we've covered it excessively, said Resh Lakish. Must we really waste time on this topic?

OK wise guy, said Bar Kappara, did George have the right to urinate in the shower?

Yes, replied Resh Lakish. As it says in the Mishnah: "And in general, how far must one distance himself from urine and feces in order to recite Shema? At least four cubits." (Mishnah Berakhot 3:5) We can be certain George did not recite the Shema while urinating. If only because he is now a Latvian Orthodox and they do not recite the Shema.

I disagree, said Rav Sheshet. The Mishnah speaks of the "the issue of a zav, his spit, his semen and his urine, and the blood of a menstruant, for they convey impurity both by contact and by carrying." (Mishnah Kelim 1:3) A Zav is defined as a man with abnormal seminal discharge. If anyone, that's George. And we know he conveyed his impurity through urination in a public shower. He desecrated the health club.

But as Costanza said, "it's all pipes!" insisted Rav Pappa. I stand by his right to pee in a communal shower.

Hey Pappa, have you urinated in our Yeshivah's shower? asked Bar Kappara.

I plead the Fifth, said Rav Pappa.

The fifth of what? asked Bar Kappara.

No idea, it's an expression I heard while travelling in Europe, replied Rav Pappa.

Hey Pappa, what else have you been doing with your body in our Yeshivah's shower?

I would like to call my lawyer and a plumber before I answer any questions, said Rav Pappa. And I will point out you are harassing a rabbi in a wheelchair.

Fellow Sages, said Rav Huna, despite the comprehensive attention our forefathers gave to urine we need to convene the larger Kehilla* to discuss this topic before we judge Rav Pappa, given that he is still an invalid, albeit one who still can't master his domain in any respect. We should switch topics.

QUEER TALMUD YESHIVX, 2023:

Wow what a racist episode, said an angry Rebbetzin Aluna "Black Lives Matter" Bat Filastin.

How could Kramer show up at his girlfriend's family gathering in Blackface? howled Rabba Jewliettx bat Ocasio-Cortezx.

But it was not his fault, said Rabba Zarah "Save Sheikh Jarrah" Al-Sabbah. He fell asleep in the tanning machine. What could he have done? I have reservations about these charges.

When it comes to putting on a minstrel show, intent doesn't matter, said Rabba Jewliettx, who was chairwomyn of the Yeshivx. Kramer is a very very bad man.

First they mock the indigenous, then the Asians, then the unevenly divergent little people, and now African Americans, said Rebbetzin Amirah "Cancel Student Debt" Mizrahi.

This show is so cringeworthily anti-Palestinian in every respect, said Rabbx Yehudis bnei Butler. *Seinfeld* should be canceled.

Jerry Seinfeld is a very very bad man, said the Rabbot, Rabbanx, and Rebbetzinx in unison.

The Raincoats

GEMARAH:

He was making out during *Schindler's List*! Who does that? said Bar Kappara convening the meeting in the name of Rav Huna.

I don't even think an amputee philanderer like Rav Pappa would make out during *Schindler's List*! Would you Pappa? asked Resh Lakish.

I think he would, said Rav Sheshet. My postman caught him groping a young lady of the evening during a screening of *The Ten Commandments*.

Is that true Pappa? How could you? said Resh Lakish.

Postal Employee Nudelman said Pappa moved on her like Pharoah's Chariots crashing into the Red Sea.

It was a four-hour movie! And the Golden Calf scene got us all hot and heavy, said Rav Pappa in his defense.

So while God was commanding Moses to not covet thy neighbor's ass you were literally groping thy neighbor's ass, said Resh Lakish.

In a manner of speaking, added Rav Sheshet.

Unconscionable, said Rav Kahana.

In my defense I was not making out during The Holocaust as Seinfeld did, said Rav Pappa. This was an event of liberation; I was expressing my joy at our release from bondage.

Again, in a manner of speaking, Pappa: my postman said you were bound and gagged as well. Your release from bondage came after the movie.

OK so the timing was a bit off, said Rav Pappa.

You're literally Rav Ras-Pappa-Putin, Persia's greatest love machine, said Rav Kahana.

"Ra Ra Raspappaputin, Persia's Greatest Love Machine!" sang the Sages in unison.

I'm a bit confused. If you were tied up, how did you grope her? asked Shimon ben Pazi.

Because I'm Pappa, I've got the Kavorka and I'm the Houdini of Rabbinic Judaism, boasted Rav Pappa.

Let us remember, Chevreh, said Rav Huna, this is precisely why we sent Pappa to Europe to save Judaism from Latvian Orthodoxy. His utter lack of ethics, his dissolution, and his fabled beytzim are what we needed to protect our people, much as HaShem sent the shrewd Oskar Schindler to save us, much as HaShem sent the brawny Charlton Heston to save us.

That Heston sure has some body on him, said Rami bar Hama. And that perfectly chiseled face. I should drop dead if he's not beautiful. Who wouldn't make out during the film? And what about Yul Brynner! wow, wow, wow!

Is there something you wish to share with us Rami? Asked Rav Huna.

Nothing except I agree with Pappa; making out during the Holocaust is far worse than making time during the Exodus: ten Plagues in Egypt, ten commandments at Sinai vs. millions of Jews murdered.

I disagree, said Resh Lakish. As it is written in the Haggadah: Jose the Galilean said there were 50 plagues at sea and Rabbi Akivah said the plagues were in fact fivefold; there were thus 300 plagues on land and at sea. And Moses received 613 commandments, not ten, at Sinai. 300 plagues plus 613 commandments is nearly 1000, so that makes 1000 infractions committed by Rav Pappa. 1000 infractions trump Schindler's heroism.

"Hey SIRI, how many Jews did Schindler save?" asked Shimon ben Pazi.

"According to IMDB, 'Schindler's List' was released in 1993," replied SIRI.

Approximately 1100, said Yontl the Librarian, with more than a touch of bitterness at being replaced by a flawed Apple product.

It's very close, concluded Rabbah.

Not at all, said Bar Kappara. The Holocaust constitutes history. The Ten

Commandments is Scripture. Divine revelation supersedes mass extermination in solemnity irrespective of numbers. You need to be appropriately disciplined for your transgression, Pappa.

But according to my mailman, interjected Rav Sheshet, his transgression involved being disciplined. In a manner of speaking.

Then let me discipline him, said Zutra the Mohel.

Let's put him in a basket and send him down the Euphrates, suggested Resh Lakish.

Nah, to quote *Blazing Saddles*, "too Jewish," said Rav Sheshet.

I have a solution, said Rami bar Hama. Let me take Pappa to see *The Ten Commandments* again. And I vow that our eyes shall be riveted on those chiseled bodies of Brynner and Heston the entire time. We will be entranced. I'm even willing to tie Pappa up.

Rami, are you sure there nothing you wish to share with us? asked Rav Huna.

The Fire

GEMARAH:

Friends, said Rav Huna convening the meeting, today's episode is the perfect juxtaposition of heroism and cowardice, Kramer vs. George.

I would rather discuss how prop comic Ronnie Kaye's nostrils are getting bigger, said Rav Sheshet. Is it possible for nostrils to expand?

Gee I wonder why you want to discuss expanding nostrils, Rav Pig Man? said Resh Lakish. Looking for some sussoid domesticoid companionship?

No this is a legitimate topic of discussion, countered Rav Sheshet. The Talmud relates how God sent a gnat to enter Emperor Titus's nostril, from where it "picked at his brain for seven years." (Gittin 56b:15). I'm a bit scared that a gnat will consume my brain by tunneling through my porcine nostrils.

What does one do if one's nostrils keep growing? asked Shimon ben Pazi. Is there Halakhah on this?

Only involving gnats, blemishes, and, interestingly enough, fish (see Bava Batra 73b:4), said Bar Kappara, so nothing that can be of use to our unfortunate comrade Sheshet, or to Ronnie Kaye the Prop Comic for that matter.

Yolds, enough with the nostrils, said Rav Huna. We need to talk about Kramer. Look at the pluck, the bravery, the command of the out-of-control bus. He did all that for a pinky toe. Who does that?

I know! it's just a pinky toe, hardly a valuable appendage, said Rabbah.

You could not be more wrong, said Resh Lakish. For it is the Little Piggy that went "wee, wee, wee, all the way home." Isn't that right Sheshet?

Enough with the Pig Man, you dolts, howled Rav Huna. Cracker Jack Kramer is a fearless leader, whereas George is the coward who left everyone to die.

He fled a towering inferno trampling over women, children, and old ladies with walkers, said Rabbah. He would have even knocked over Rav Pappa's wheelchair had Pappa been there.

Yes George is a coward, a selfish chicken, and a quitter, said Rav Kahana. Remember how he wouldn't even save the Pig Man, demanding that the Pig Man take the bus.

Why are pigs and buses a recurring theme in our discussions? asked Shimon ben Pazi. What do these two things share in common?

Absolutely nothing, countered Rav Huna in anger. It's because you rabbis are incapable of having an intelligent conversation about anything other than shmekls, beytzim, and foreskins.

He makes a valid point, said Resh Lakish. But we have not exhausted George's cowardice. The fire was hardly a conflagration. Eric the Clown put it out with his big shoe. Maybe if George hadn't been so consumed with Bozo, he would have exuded more valor and emerged as a hero.

What kind of name is "Eric" for a clown? said Rav Kruspedai.

What kind of name is "Kruspedai" for a rabbi? countered Rav Sheshet. Kruspedai sounds like something clinging to overly enlarged nostrils. Maybe we should change your name to Rabbi Bozo.

I think George was correct in acting as if "women and children first" is an antiquated notion, said Rav Pappa. As an amputee, I reject any special handicapped treatment. Instead of castigating him, he should be commended for treating everyone like equals.

Agreed, said Bar Kappara. Look at *Titanic*. As soon as they put women and children first what does Rose do? she takes the man who freed her from a life of bondage after shtupping him and casts his shivering body into the depths of North Atlantic.

We should find out where she works and we should go and heckle her, said Shimon ben Pazi. Costanza too.

That would be unprecedented! said Resh Lakish.

There's no precedent, baby! Said Rav Sheshet.

Actually, there is precedent: as it is written "The Lord takes revenge and furiously heckles" (Nahum 1:2), quoted Rav Huna with some slight embellishment, for he was tiring of this inane discussion. Let's disband and seek out our quarry.

The Hamptons

GEMARAH:

Friends, said Rav Huna this episode has so much implied theology we need to discuss, said Rav Huna convening the meeting.

Hang on, where's Pappa? asked Rabbah, he's not here yet, shouldn't we wait?

He won't be coming, replied Huna. I told him we were meeting in an hour from now. I didn't want him here, lest we end up discussing shrinkage and nakedness the entire time.

Good plan, said Resh Lakish. So what should we discuss?

The Sages sat in silence.

We can discuss why the tomato never took off as a hand fruit, said Shimon ben Pazi.

We can discuss which cough syrup is our favorite, said Rav Sheshet.

I'm with George: Pertussin and club soda, replied Rav Kahana.

We can discuss ugly babies, suggested Resh Lakish. I've seen plenty around the marketplace.

Yolds, there is a theologically weighty issue at stake here, said Rav Huna.

I know, said Bar Kappara: how the rebels under siege on Mount Masada in 74 CE consumed pounds of kishke to commit mass suicide and avoid the wrath of the Romans. Is suicide by kishke halakhic?

Moreso than suicide by kreplach, said Resh Lakish.

Or suicide by desiccated coarsened matzoh balls, said Rav Sheshet.

"Those aren't matzo balls," said the rabbi to the farmer's daughter, laughed Shimon ben Pazi, quoting from his favorite jokebook.

Morons, said Rav Huna, having run out of Yiddish epithets, I'm talking about the lobster. Did George commit a grave sin in feeding an oblivious Rachel lobster, thereby violating her kashrut?

The Sages sat in silence.

Nobody has any thoughts? said an incredulous Rav Huna.

It's just that Rachel outed George for his diminutive Rabbi Johnson, said Rami bar Hama. That's a major code violation.

Indeed, one could even argue that George, while perhaps going too far with the lobster, had every right to see Rachel naked, added Rav Kahana.

This is absurd, said Bar Kappara, speaking for Rav Huna. George the apikores,* the apostate, the golem, the short stocky slow witted bald man deliberately violated Rachel's covenant with HaShem. And moreover, as we discussed in "The Nose Job" this was just punishment, as Rav Ashi said: "For he who shrunk his girlfriend's shnoz will himself suffer significant shrinkage in Season 5."

I disagree, said Rami bar Hama. Rachel is a very very bad woman. She and Jerry made out during the Holocaust. She may be breathtaking, but she's already a bad Jew. And yet she's also SUCH a Jew, even a JAP.

What is a JAP? asked Shimon ben Pazi.

A Jewish Assyrian Princess, replied Rami bar Hama. It's a bit of a sexist slur, so we use it sparingly. Far worse than calling someone a pig man, no offense Sheshet.

I agree, said Rav Pappa, wheeling briskly through the doors. Looks like I'm a bit late, I guess I got the time wrong. And given my expertise on matters of the flesh, I believe my opinion, much like my beytzim, carries weight.

So what say you Pappa? relented Bar Kappara.

I, admitted Rav Pappa, have been the victim of shrinkage humiliation, rendered all the worse, because my Nephilim-sized beytzim hide much of my Rabbi Johnson. My otherwise breathtaking body has been disgraced.

Oy, this shiur is a complete a wreck, mumbled Rav Huna.

I know, whispered Bar Kappara to his mentor. We should have told Pappa we were meeting IN the Hamptons.

I'm with Pappa, boldly cried out Rami bar Hama. We have all experienced shrinkage humiliation. And it's entirely because of our traumatic visit to Zutra the Mohel's shrinkage shop.

So then blame the Covenant, blame HaShem, blame Abraham, blame Genesis 17, this has nothing to do with me, replied Zutra, keeping his cool, knowing this day of reckoning was inevitable.

He should be disciplined, said Shimon ben Pazi.

I know, replied Rami bar Hama. Zutra should be forced to strip before us and show us his nakedness. I hear he's quite breathtaking below the equator, having been lucky enough to have gotten snipped by a less shaky mohel.

No this would punish us, said Resh Lakish, and cruelly I might add. There's nothing breathtaking about Zutra.

I think we are at an impasse, relented Rav Huna, though I have gotten a bit more clarity regarding our obsession with shmekls, petzls, shlongs, beytzim, foreskins, and dingdongs.

At the very least, we owe "The Hamptons" episode for that insight, said Bar Kappara.

Yes, added Shimon ben Pazi, the entire episode was quite breathtaking.

The Opposite

MISHNAH:

Shammai: It's not working, Hillel, it's just not working.

Hillel: What's not working?

Shammai: I had so much promise. I was personable, I was bright, oh maybe not academically speaking. But every aphorism I've come up with as a Sage has sucked rocks.

Hillel: Well they certainly haven't earned the House of Shammai the fame, fortune, or dare I say fornication we at the House of Hillel have enjoyed.

Shammai: I now go up to women AND prospective students and say by way of introduction: "My name is Shammai; I'm unemployed and I live in Jesus' garage."

Hillel: At least it's not his manger. And if you live in his garage, you should no longer be called the "House of Shammai."

Shammai: Please don't strip me of my title. It's all I have left.

Hillel: You know Shammai, if every adage you avow is wrong, try speaking the opposite.

Shammai: OK, I'll give it a try:

- -"What you yourself hate, do to thy neighbor; rub his schnoz in it. This is the whole law; the rest is inane commentary."
- -"Judge thy friend and laugh at him because thou do not standest in his miserable place."
- -"He who refuses to learn from Shammai deserves extinction."

Hillel: That's not exactly what I had in mind. And this is still technically plagiarism.

Shammai:

- -"In a place where there are no strumpets, one must strive to treat one's body as an amusement park."

Hillel: OK a bit more creative. But still offensive in your idiosyncratic unsagacious way.

Shammai:

- -"If I am not for myself, I will make others be for me!"
- -"If not now, whenever, who the hell cares?"

Hillel: OK good, because whenever is now. I would like you to leave the House of Hillel now. Right now. Give my regards to Yoshke.

GEMARAH:

What an end to the Season! Said Rav Huna convening the meeting.

Agreed, said Bar Kappara. Elaine yet again showed her callousness toward Jake Jarmel. First she overreacts over punctuation and now she stops for some candy before visiting him in the emergency room.

And who buys popcorn to bring to an emergency room? It isn't the cinema or the circus! said an astonished Resh Lakish.

Those people! said Rav Sheshet. The same type of people who bring Junior Mints to watch a surgical procedure. Even Zutra doesn't distribute candy at his circumcisions.

No I'm a traditionalist in that way, said Zutra the Mohel, relieved at his partial rehabilitation. Just pastrami, pigs in the blanket, and some schnapps for me.

But Elaine finished the popcorn in the cab, said Rabbah. So the affront was not the popcorn, but the Jujyfruit, which is far more egregious than the refreshing yet elusive Junior Mint.

And dangerous, noted Rav Kahana. Whereas the Junior Mint remained undetected and may have even saved Triangle Boy, the Jujyfruit engendered the demise of Pendant Publishing. There's nothing in Lippman's future but muffin tops.

Top of the Muffin to you, Lippman! said the Sages in unison. With an exclamation point.

Yes, it was a great episode, said Rav Pappa. George finally manned up. He got a job, moved out, met a beautiful woman. He even grew a pair of beytzim, and his shrinkage shrank into a distant memory.

Goodbye to mommy, Goodbye to daddy, Goodbye my shrunken shlong! sang the Sages in unison.

OK meeting adjourned, said Rav Huna.

What's with the abrupt ending? asked a startled Bar Kappara.

I wanted to wrap it up before we went to far afield into testicle territory, admitted Rav Huna. We need to maintain our integrity and credibility over the summer hiatus.

The Rabbis adjourned, blissfully unaware of their future, replete with magic, murder, irate doormen, and even the dreaded couch urination.

Season 6

The Rabbis Debate Communism
But Can't Find Ukraine on a Map

The Chaperone

GEMARAH:

Welcome back, fellow Sages, said Rav Huna convening the meeting. We begin our new season with yet another murder on the part of Reb Seinfeld.

Jerry is a homicidal maniac, drowning those doves the way he did, said Rabbah.

Uh, technically speaking it isn't a homicide unless he killed a human, countered Resh Lakish.

You're right, said Rav Pappa. He seems to have a thing for knocking off animals. First Manya's horse and now he drowns pigeons. It's as if he's taking out all the steerage on Noah's Ark one by one. Maybe he has a beef with God's plan for Noah.

Oh boy, you better watch out Sheshet, he'll be coming for the piggies next, joked Resh Lakish, although nobody was laughing.

First off, he allegedly killed Manya, not Manya's horse, said Rav Huna. Go back and read Season 2 of The Seinfeld Talmud if you can't keep the basic talmudic plot straight.

Second, if he was trying out some bizarre reenactment of Noah's Ark gone awry, he'd be killing off the animals two by two, not one by one, said Bar Kappara.

Third, we acquitted him of Manya's murder, and his Junior Mint in fact saved Triangle Boy, said Rav Huna.

Fourth, enough with the Pig Man jokes already, said Bar Kappara. They are SO VERY Season 5. Leave Sheshet's sussoid deformities out of the discussion, except when absolutely appropriate. And trust me, you'll know when they are appropriate.

What's with you two, tag teaming like that? asked Rabbah.

We are imposing order on this Yeshivah, said Bar Kappara and his mentor Rav Huna in unison.

And not just in the Yeshivah, said Rav Huna. No more dates without a chaperone. You got that Pappa? Especially now that you are ambulatory again.

What did I do? howled Rav Pappa. You are poo-pooing on my social life.

Yes, I poo-poo, replied Rav Huna. The Pumbetida Yeshivah Rabbinate is going to the top and we're not going to step to the side while you defile women, trample the dream, and make a mockery of everything our sweaty colleagues in this Academy stand for.

Suits me fine, my chaperone will see how graceful I am with the Assyrian women of the night, said Rav Pappa. I don't mind showing off my grace.

You have no grace Pappa, said Resh Lakish. Not even a little grace. You have no ability to develop grace. We're not even convinced you recite grace.

If he recites grace, I can assure you it's not after eating, said Rav Sheshet.

Why are all you sages poo-pooing on my lifestyle? howled Rav Pappa.

Yes, we poo-poo-Pappa, said the Sages in unison.

Given the course of this discussion, it seems that Rav Pappa is far more the sinner than Reb Seinfeld, said Resh Lakish.

I agree, said Rav Kahana. Rhode Island is such a small shrunken state. Kramer's right, "they're never in contention." With anything. It's not even an island. Who cares if he killed some of their pigeons.

I disagree, said Rabbah. Jerry the bird killer also did George in. He knew changing the Yankee uniforms to cotton was a bad idea, yet he didn't say anything. He suspected Costanza would turn the Yankees into a shrunken mess.

That's perfect irony, said Rav Pappa. He who endured humiliating shrinkage ends up triggering humiliating shrinkage. And thus Costanza's penile predicaments became enshrined into the collective memory of America's favorite pastime.

Do you really think America's favorite pastime is masturbation? Asked Rami bar Hama.

No you shmendrik, countered Rav Huna, I'm pretty sure Rav Pappa's unexpectedly profound statement refers to baseball.

But Jerry insisted that baseball and sex are intimately connected, recalled Rami bar Hama.

What's your game Pappa? asked Rav Huna. It sounds like you are trying to play us.

To "Jerk us" around, to be more exact, added Rami bar Hama with a devious smile.

Rami, watch your mouth or get out of my Yeshivah.

So much for taking control, Master, said a gloating Rav Pappa. I poo-poo on YOUR Academy, he added, walking out the door, accompanied by Rami bar Hama and an animated Zutra the Mohel. We are not even getting to first base in this debate. We three amigos are off to play the field elsewhere.

...

It was a nice effort at decorum, Master, said Bar Kappara. Though admittedly you could have handled these apostates with a little more grace.

You can't have a little grace, countered Rav Huna. You either have grace or you don't have grace. I have no grace.

You know, you're right, said Bar Kappara. TBH, I'm not really sure how you even managed to get this job.

The Big Salad

GEMARAH:

Fellow Sages, said Rav Huna, it appears we have an episode filled with duplicity, murder, and pencil mating rituals. So much Halakhah to discuss

Poor Little Pinkus, said the Sages in Unison.

It's true, "Pinkus" could have been one of our own, said Bar Kappara.

He is one of our own, said Resh Lakish. Where is Pinchas the Short, our four-foot rabbi?

Do you think Pappa took him out, asked Rav Sheshet? Last time Pinchas was here they had a shouting match and Pinchas cursed him, wishing that Pappa be "wheeled straight to hell at no more than three miles an hour." ("The Stand-In," s5e6).

Poor Little Pinchas, said the Sages in Unison.

This is just a coincidence, friends, reassuringly said Bar Kappara. The names aren't even the same: Pinkus vs Pinchas.

But they both sound like "Pink Ass," noted Shimon ben Pazi. It's not a good name for a rabbi.

Or a drycleaner, said Rabbah. No wonder he was murdered. And Kramer was deeply complicit.

Kramer was no more responsible for Pinkus's death than Elaine was for the Big Salad, said Rav Sheshet.

I disagree, said Resh Lakish. The Seinfeld body count increases yet again: Manya, Fulton, Pinkus, and the near death of the Bubble Boy and the Triangle Boy. They are very very bad people.

Elaine hasn't killed anyone, noted Rabbah. Yet she is in many respects the meanest of the bunch. She might as well have killed Jake Jarmel. And there is no doubt she will stomp on the heart of that poor pencil salesman.

Much as Jerry stomped on Margaret's heart, just because she had dated Newman, said Bar Kappara.

Would you kiss someone who swapped spit with that postman, asked Resh Lakish?

Newman is an enigma, replied Rav Sheshet.

You mean he is a twinkie, not even wrapped in a riddle, said Rabbah.

He is a ring ding with what is by all appearances a big fat pink ass, said Rav Kahana.

No body shaming at my Yeshivah, said Rav Huna, especially in light of the disappearance of our own itsy-bitsy Pinchas.

Poor little Pinchas, said the Sages in unison.

What kind of name is "Pinkass" anyway? said Shimon ben Pazi.

It's a sacred name, countered Rav Huna: Pinchas was Aaron's grandson, and Priest of the Israelites during the Exodus.

Yes, Pinchas saved the Jews at Shitim right after God gave Balaam's ass the power of speech, said Bar Kappara.

So Balaam's ass spoke and Pinkass found salvation in Shitim, and you expect me not to laugh? said Shimon ben Pazi.

What are you, five year's old, Pazi? said bar Kappara.

See, this is what happens when Pappa, Rami, and Zutra aren't here to talk about petzls, beytzim, and foreskins, noted Resh Lakish. We end up making potty jokes.

I'm telling you if it's the last thing I do, I'm going to class up this Yeshivah, avowed a dejected Rav Huna.

Master, said Bar Kappara, our only hope is to have a fundraising pledge drive.

The Pledge Drive

"Welcome to NPR – The National Pumbedita Rabbinate's – first annual pledge drive," said Rav Huna, launching what was the Sages first public performance in the market square, tzedakah box held prominently athwart by Shimon ben Pazi.

"Hi, I am Resh Lakish, and I tell jokes at the Yeshivah all the time; but there's no joking about the financial crisis here at NPR, the National Pumbedita Rabbinate. Show you care about Jews and donate now."

"And if you donate now you get this lovely tote bag and a piece of shmurah matzoh," added a beaming Bar Kappara.

"Hi, I'm Rav Pappa and I need to get help for my deep psychosexual problems. I have a hankering for being bound and gagged with our tefillin, while the Assyrian dominatrices have their way with me. Your donation will get me the psychiatric help from Vienna that I need."

"Or at the very least some leather straps that aren't intended for Judaic ritual," added Rami bar Hama, always looking out for his admittedly perverted friend.

"Hi, I'm Rav Sheshet, often mocked for my porcine-like deformities. Please give your dinars and shekels to NPR today so I can get the reconstructive surgery I desperately need."

"Hi, I'm Zutra the Mohel and my circumcision kit is all rusty. Giving your dinars and shekels to our Yeshivah will prevent a tetanus outbreak in Pumbedita."

[Murmuring from the townsfolk]

"Hey, are you the guys who catered my son's bar mitzvah last year?" came a shout from the crowd.

"Yes that was us, but rest assured that day was a fluke. Our kreplach is usually the best," said Bar Kappara defensively.

"Hey, so are you the guys who performed and staged my son's disastrous bris?" came a shout from the crowd.

"Yes, but rest assured I was having an off day. Our snip and sew is usually seamless. But we can offer you a corrective procedure at Abba the Surgeon's clinic," said Zutra the Mohel, preparing to make a quick exit.

"With a $50 pledge I will give you a coupon for any free operation you like, from head to pinky toe, shmekl included," jumped in Abba the Surgeon, who suspected a lynch mob was not far off from forming.

"Wait, YOU ARE the Rabbis who provided the Pig Man cabaret show at our wedding," screamed a couple of voices from the distance. Let's get these Jewish charlatans!

Master, dare I say that this pledge drive was not the greatest idea, said Bar Kappara. What ever shall we do now?

We move on. There is a "Chinese Woman" – Donna Chang she is called – in town and she offers the wisdom of Confucius to help the downtrodden. We shall consult her.

The Chinese Woman

GEMARAH:

Fellow Sages, today we have a fascinating episode about the immense wisdom and talents of the Chinese people, said Rav Huna convening the meeting.

I disagree, said Rav Pappa. The Chinese are, as Jerry put it, "hanging in there with the chopsticks. Because if you think about it, you know, they've seen the fork by now." Why use chopsticks when you have a fork and spoon available?

You're wrong, Pappa, said Bar Kappara. Jerry meant it as a compliment. It demonstrates the tenacity of a 3000-year-old civilization. And they're using the chopsticks for food, unlike George's girlfriend Patrice who wore them in her papier-mâché hat.

I agree, said Shimon ben Pazi. That Donna Chang was a miracle worker: saving the Costanza marriage the way she did, using the brilliant wisdom of her illustrious ancestor Confucius.

Ancestor? said an incredulous Resh Lakish. Donna Chang isn't really Chinese.

But she took acupuncture classes, and ate Chinese food with Jerry. They probably even used chopsticks, said Rav Sheshet.

I say this is cultural appropriation, no different from Patrice putting Chinese eating utensils in her hair, said Resh Lakish.

And I disagree with you, Lakish, said Bar Kappara. I think it demonstrates the fluidity of ethno-cultural boundaries in our postmodern age. Much as Schindler's List speaks to the universality of human suffering, Donna Chang demonstrates that anyone can become Chinese.

Except for Patrice. No Chinese woman would put chopsticks in her hair.

This discussion is ridiculous, or rather, I should say "ridicurous," countered a skeptical Resh Lakish. One doesn't become Chinese by mispronouncing words.

Agreed, said Rav Sheshet. She's nothing but a woman from Long Island. And nobody should take advice from people from Long Island.

I think we are missing the elephant in the room, said Abba the Surgeon. Her family name was originally Changstein. Changstein. Get it? She's one of us, she's of the Tribe, an Israelite.

She is a Jew who converted to "Orientalism" at Ellis Island, noted Shimon ben Pazi.

Uh they're called Asian Americans now, replied Abba the Surgeon with reproach. The Changsteins became Asian Americans at Ellis Island.

And what about us? asked Shimon ben Pazi. We order Chinese food every Christmas. Does that make us Asian Americans as well, or are we just cultural appropriators?

The Chinese want us to appropriate their culture, said Rav Pappa. Look at the fortune cookie. After a hearty meal complete with an indefatigable struggle to master the chopsticks the Chinese try to brainwash us with their zippy aphorisms and inspiring wisdom. Name one other culture that does that.

We do, said Rabbah. We stick a Bible in the drawer of every hotel room.

That's not us, that's the Nazarenes, countered Bar Kappara

Who appropriated our words of wisdom and wrote a cheap sequel, retorted Resh Lakish.

Well at least we don't put rolled up bits of our wisdom into our knishes, as Jerry put it, said Rav Sheshet.

Imagine getting a knish or a latke that said "thou shalt snip the flesh off thy foreskin," said Rav Pappa

What a great idea! said Zutra the Mohel, who was now preparing to partner with a Rav Hunan Chen Yehudim-Sum, a local Chinese Jewish apostate in Pumbedita.

Let's change the topic because all this food talk is making hungry, said Rav Huna. We can discuss Kramer's adventures in reproductively suitable underwear. I find it fascinating that Kramer treating his body like an amusement park in the middle of the day constitutes a disruption of his otherwise "busy" schedule.

Just like it does for you, eh Pappa? said Resh Lakish.

Hey, I am master of my Manchurian Candidate.

QUEER TALMUD YESHIVX, 2023:

Wow, this was the most racist *Seinfeld* episode yet, said Rabba Jewliettx bat Ocasio-Cortezx.

Pure Oriental-face, and at the hands of a Jew no less, added Rebbetzin Amirah "Cancel Student Debt" Mizrahi.

I can't believe how anti-Palestinian it was. Did they even consult one Palestinian when writing the script? Howled Rabbx Yehudis bnei Butler.

Agreed, said Rabba Jewliettx. Let's cancel *Seinfeld* and go watch *Tora! Tora! Tora!* instead.

The Couch

GEMARAH:

Friends, there is a weighty talmudic debate to be had concerning "The Couch," said Rav Huna convening the meeting. Who wants to start?

I will start, said Shimon ben Pazi. I will start by avowing without fear of recrimination or ostracism: it is not a pizza until it comes out of the oven!

The Sages remained silent.

And? said Bar Kappara.

Meaning Kramer is right, one can put cucumbers on the pizza pie, clarified Shimon ben Pazi.

I disagree, I am siding with Poppie on this one, said Rav Kahana. Unregulated pizza building engenders chaos. Tohu vavohu.* And we can't have tohu vavohu in Poppie's kitchen.

Yes God forbid we have disorder in the kitchen of the man who goes potty without washing his hands, said Resh Lakish with more than a hint of sarcasm.

Which brings me to the ACTUAL subject of today's debate, said Rav Huna, finally losing his patience, but having been reluctant to interrupt: Poppie's urinary proclivities.

So the question is, did Poppie have the right to pee on Jerry's couch? Said Bar Kappara jumping in and taking control of yet another unwieldy bathroom discussion.

Poppie had no business desecrating Jerry's furniture, said Rav Pappa. As it is written, "His spittle, his seat, his couch and his urine are unclean; his bread, his oil and his wine are clean." (Tractate Gerim 3:2).

But it was defensible urination, countered Rav Kahana. Jerry destroyed Poppie's business with alacrity, as he later told George: "And I have to say...it was pretty much all my fault." Then he and Elaine tried to kill Poppie with a bottle of wine and five-alarm chili, resulting in his hospitalization. Jerry's body count almost went up. Manya, Fulton, and now Poppie? Poppie had every right to get a little sloppy.

Poppie got a little sloppy, repeated the Sages in unison.

Too bad Manya's pony didn't urinate on Jerry's couch, said Rabbah.

That would have been perfect irony, said Rav Kahana.

Polish poetic justice, said the Sages in unison.

What did Poppie do wrong? All Poppie did was oppose abortion, and abortion is murder, insisted Rav Sheshet.

Not always, replied Rami bar Hama.

When is it not? countered Resh Lakish.

For instance, as Elaine suggested, what if a woman became impregnated by her troglodytic half-brother? replied Rami bar Hama.

Or for that matter, what if she was impregnated by a pig man, added Shimon ben Pazi, trying hard but failing to not look at Rav Sheshet.

Then she would give birth to little pig men, and we would lovingly embrace them, said Bar Kappara, discreetly winking at Rav Sheshet.

Agreed. I've seen Rav Sheshet's children, said Resh Lakish. They should be welcomed into our Yeshivah despite their inherited Sussoid deformities. Don't worry Sheshet, I have your back.

Rav Sheshet, do you have an opinion on this subject since it directly pertains to you? asked Rav Huna.

Yes, I do, replied a disconcerted yet irate Rav Sheshet. Once we adjourn, I intend to visit Shimon ben Pazi's place, pee on his couch, and then go wee wee wee all the way home.

The Gymnast

GEMARAH:

Fellow Sages, said Rav Huna convening the meeting, I have no doubt that many of you are disconcerted by what transpired in "The Gymnast." The geopolitical ramifications are astounding.

Thank you, said Abba the Surgeon. These Romanians do not come off as particularly likeable people.

Please elaborate, Abba, said Bar Kappara.

What kind of sick person screams curses at elephants, blaming them for the ills of Communism? said Abba the Surgeon in anger.

I disagree, said Rabbah. It's as Jerry said: they do take up a lot of space, thereby precluding an equitable distribution of resources in the Workers Revolutionary Paradise.

Agreed, the elephants should have been divided up among the poor suffering Romanians, said Rav Kahana, to each according to his need.

Who needs an elephant? Asked a bemused Shimon ben Pazi. Are Romanian elephants the equivalent of Polish ponies? And why would anyone come from a country packed with elephants to a non-elephant country?

Because the elephants were not equitably distributed among the proletariat by the ruling class, said Yontl the Librarian, consulting his copy of *The Great Soviet Encyclopedia*.

Agreed, this is precisely why Katya was so perfunctory in bed, said Rav Pappa. Imagine spending your entire life listening to Ceausescu demand muffins from you. Had Communism worked, she would have treated Jerry like the balance beam or the parallel bars, as he deserved. The proletariat deserves first-rate sex and first-rate muffins. Accordingly, I support the Revolution, proclaimed Rami bar Hama!

Jerry is no proletarian working class stiff, said Resh Lakish in astonishment. And by Katya's account he was also lousy in bed. No virility, no potency. He does not even warrant the title of comedian, as she put it.

"You may tell jokes, Mr. Jerry Seinfeld, but you are no comedian," said the Sages in unison.

You are wrong Lakish, replied Rav Pappa. I traveled through Romania on my way to Latvia. Not one gymnast treated my body like a balance beam. They didn't even laugh at my jokes. Nobody called me a comedian. Yet my virility is legendary throughout the Levante and the Orthodox Romanians know the Kavorka.

While I acknowledge that Pappa is as usual thinking with his petzl, said Rav Sheshet, the episode was very much a critique of capitalism from a gastronomic Marxist perspective.

What, pray tell is gastronomic Marxism? interjected Rav Huna.

The bourgeois capitalist pigs, continued Rav Sheshet, don't think twice about ostentatiously wasting eclairs, the food of emperors, dandies, and aristocrats.

Sheshet, interrupted Rav Huna, while I would normally not condone calling human beings "pigs" in my Yeshivah, I will grant you some leeway, given your... um... condition.

Yes! Jumped in Rav Pappa. George WAS launching the Revolution. He moved on that squandered éclair like the storm troopers moved into Poland.

Is that why Mr. Pitt vowed to annex Poland by the Spring at any cost? asked Shimon ben Pazi. I assumed it was to exact vengeance against Manya for having abandoned her pony.

Mr. Pitt, or rather Herr Justin Adolf Pittler was in fact on his way to ride his own horse, Jenny, added Resh Lakish.

Did Hitler have a soft spot for the animal kingdom? asked Shimon ben Pazi. Is that why Poland was dismembered?

Not a chance, said Abba the Surgeon. If that were so he would have occupied Romania as well, given that cursing elephants is their national pastime.

And we know that Hitler spared neither Manya's horse-faced relatives nor the pig men during the Holocaust, added Rav Pappa. Remember I traveled the Polish Corridor and I prayed at the Tomb of the Unknown Pig Men.

I think this was one of our most productive debates yet, said a beaming Rav Huna. We covered Nazism, gastronomical Marxism, the dismemberment of eastern Europe, and their dialectical relationship to the utopian redistribution of elephants, éclairs, and pig men.

I feel as if we could have devoted more attention to Ceausescu and his muffins, said Shimon ben Pazi. Do you think Ceausescu would have eaten one out of the trash as George did with the éclair?

Now you're just getting silly, Pazi, replied Rav Huna. We don't deal with such foolishly illogical hypotheticals in this Yeshivah. Our debates are firmly grounded in the realm of historical plausibility. So let's call it a day.

The Soup

GEMARAH:

Fellow Sages, we have a choice today. We can debate whether or not soup constitutes a meal, or we can debate whether finding something positive in "manure" should be grounds for terminating a date.

This is a Talmudist's dream come true! said Rav Pappa.

What?! replied Resh Lakish.

Where I come from, Lakish, we say "Paahrdon." Saying "What" is considered rude, retorted Rav Pappa.

Pappa, you live next door to me, and I've known you since we unfortunately attended "The Itsy-Bitsy Rabbi Preschool" together! said an exasperated Resh Lakish.

Nevertheless, I see Pappa's point, said Rav Sheshet. Once we cease discussing shlongs, beytzim, and foreskins, all our debates revolve around food and going potty. This entire week was about eating fortune cookies and couch urination.

And disturbingly, it still got Pappa horny, noted Resh Lakish.

May I point out that "manure" is mentioned 101 times in the Talmud and 41 times in the Mishnah, whereas "soup" is only mentioned 22 and 5 times, respectively, said Rami bar Hama. Manure is the hot topic, not soup.

What if we combined the two subjects? suggested a bemused Shimon ben Pazi. Does manure constitute a meal or not?

I'd rather eat a pile of horse manure than a acquire an Armani suit, if it came with a Kenny Bania appended to it, said Rav Pappa.

Paahrdon?! said Resh Lakish.

Yes I am siding with George on this one, said Rav Pappa. There's nothing wrong with putting a positive spin on feces during a first date. George is a true Gaon, maybe even a Lomed Vovnik. He knows how to take the quotidian and make it enticing, attractive, and irresistible for his lady friend, much as our ancestors Yohanan ben Zakkai and Rabbi Judah the Prince took the cataclysmic decimation wrought by the Romans and built the mighty edifice we now call "Rabbinic Judaism."

Pappa, may I point out that you are comparing the Oral Torah to horse manure? said an incredulous Resh Lakish.

Shame on you Lakish, replied Pappa. You don't know your Talmud. And I quote: "To say to you, just like an almond, even though it is dirty with mud and manure, what is inside it is not spoiled, so too a scholar, even though he has rotted, his Torah is not spoiled." (Chagigah 15b:10). Clearly, I am not the first to view food, manure, and Torah as one through the Rabbinic gaze.

Master, I'm afraid Pappa is correct, chimed in Yontl the Librarian, who was furiously searching keywords on Joogle, the Oral Torah search engine. "Manure" quite literally intersects with all of our frequent topics of discussion.

Indeed, replied Rav Pappa, if I may quote the great Rav Judah: "If one is uncertain whether excrement is present, it is forbidden to read the Shema. If one is uncertain whether urine is present, it is permitted." (Berakhot 25a:13) "And it is also written "A pig's snout is to be regarded as passing manure for the purpose of reading the Shema. That is obvious!" (Berakhot 25a:12)

Oh no here come the Pig Man jokes, lamented Bar Kappara.

[Rav Sheshet promptly gets up and makes for the door].

Sheshet, may we ask upon whose couch you will be urinating today? said Rav Huna.

First off, that's for me to know and you to find out, replied Rav Sheshet looking directly at Rav Pappa. Second, who said anything about urine?

Oh don't look so distraught, Pappa, said Resh Lakish in his least consoling voice. It's just "nure" which is good with a "ma" in front of it. When you consider the other choices, "manure" is actually pretty refreshing.

The Mom & Pop Store

GEMARAH:

Chevreh, today's episode is all about imposture, said Rav Huna, convening the meeting. Sadly, it is a topic we have encountered before.

I for one was aghast to learn that John Voight is not really Jon Voight, said Bar Kappara.

Yes, but that pales in comparison to the travesty of Mom-and-Pop not being a mom and pop, said Rabbah.

It was a scam of epic proportions, said Bar Kappara, one hell of an operation. Pretending to have children, just to make off with a comedian's sneakers? said Rav Kahana. Feigned parenthood is a cardinal sin.

Say, Abba: what right do you have to go by the name "Abba the Surgeon"? asked Rav Sheshet, his porcine countenance exuding the suspicion of a little piggy getting hoodwinked in the marketplace. You don't have any children.

My fellow Sages, replied Abba the Surgeon, I am the father of all the animals in my care at my clinic, much as our forefather Noah was the father of two of every animal on his ark.

You? Abba "Woof Woof, Not Bang Bang" the Surgeon? laughed Resh Lakish. You are a fraudulent parent and a medical quack. Can you even pilot a ship?

Uh, no, replied Abba defensively. I'm like George in the Coast Guard. The land guy who unhooks the boat so it can leave the place.

Abba, You need to return everyone's sneakers forthwith, said Bar Kappara.

But I don't have anyone's sneakers! screamed Abba "Woof Woof, Not Bang Bang" the Surgeon.

That's just an expression, said Bar Kappara, Now moving on-

Wait a sec, interrupted Resh Lakish. What about Rav Pappa? He has no children either. Why does he have the right to go and reap the benefits of fatherhood?

Hey, replied Rav Pappa, much like Abba, I have nobody's sneakers in my possession!

But neither do you have animals in your care, noted Rabbah.

Not quite, noted Resh Lakish. Has anyone eavesdropped on his wild nocturnal revelries? You'd be shocked at the sounds that emanate through his walls. It's like a pack of feral hyenas.

But is that not why his name is Pappa? countered Rami bar Hama, sticking up for his perverse hero: because he shouts "Who's your Pappa, Who's your Pappa?" during his foreplay?

During foreplay, in-play, and post-play, said the aroused Sages in unison.

Maybe he should change his name, suggested Rav Kahana.

Not again, exclaimed Bar Kappara. Are we going back to this whole "Ned wears irregular underwear" business? I thought we had settled this in Season 5.

We have matured since Season 5. Hence, we should rename him "John Voight," with an "H," suggested Shimon ben Pazi, who as usual struggled to keep up, but as always remained faithful to the *Seinfeld* script.

I have no doubt Pappa's teeth marks are ubiquitous where they shouldn't be, all along the Tenderloin District of the Euphrates, laughed Resh Lakish elbowing Rav Sheshet.

Unless the teeth marks are on pencils, he is no John Voight, with or without the "H," ruled Bar Kappara in the name of Rav Huna.

Everyone needs to get off my back, cried Rav Pappa.

That's what she said, laughed Resh Lakish, elbowing Rav Sheshet.

Look, continued Rav Pappa, I do not deny the serendipity of my moniker for fornicatory purposes-

Boy that is quite the mouthful, Pappa, interrupted Rabbah.

That's what she said, laughed Resh Lakish, elbowing Rav Sheshet.

Oy gevalt, groaned an increasingly pallid Rav Huna from the corner.

As I was saying, I am lucky to have this name during my nocturnal escapades, said Rav Pappa. But I submit that if I am forced to change my moniker, then and only then would I be committing an act of imposture, for every time I would cry out "who's your Pappa?" I would no longer be "Pappa."

He has a point, said Rav Kahana.

The bottom line is that I've done more with this name than Abba "Woof Woof, Not Bang Bang" the Surgeon ever has and ever will with his.

The Yeshivah hereby rules, interjected Rav Huna, that Rav Pappa can keep his name, so long as he agrees to repair our sneakers.

So let it be written, so let it be done, said the Sages in unison, while removing their sneakers.

The Secretary

GEMARAH:

Friends, said Bar Kappara, convening the meeting, Rav Huna is taking a short mental leave of absence. We have sent him on a long shlong, dingdong, foreskin-free vacation.

How does one take a shlong-free vacation? asked Rav Pappa.

You WOULD ask that, retorted Resh Lakish.

I could easily arrange such a vacation, replied Zutra the Mohel.

You WOULD offer that, retorted Resh Lakish.

And if this keeps up, warned Bar Kappara, I'm afraid I will be next.

OK Captain K., so how are you steering this ship today, said Shimon ben Pazi.

Thank you for asking, replied Bar Kappara. We're going to try something different today. We will use this *Seinfeld* episode, "The Secretary," as our guide for classing up the joint. Thank you for everyone who brought what I asked to the academy.

Here are our new suits, said Rami bar Hama. They're vintage. I bought them from the ancient Parthian* population at the marketplace. They needed the dinars desperately. I took the suits right off their backs and left them naked.

I don't understand, what did they wear home? asked Bar Kappara.

Apparently, they didn't think that far ahead, concluded Rami Bar Hama.

And that explains why we rabbis are now living in the Sassanid and not the Parthian Empire, noted Yontl the Librarian. I'll update the recorded chronicles to include "unexpected nudity" among the Parthians' epic failures.

Please add a note to the record that "unexpected nudity" is not, in and of itself, an epic failure, added Rav Pappa.

I brought the super hydrating total protection moisturizer with UVA to rejuvenate our aging countenances, said Rabbah. Our faces are inexorably turning to leather. Our deterioration proceeds apace.

Please add a note to the record that wearing leather on one's face is not, in and of itself, a sign of deterioration, added Rav Pappa.

I brought skinny mirrors to promote a positive body image, said Rav Kahana.

This is all inappropriate, interjected Rav Pappa. We rabbis are not supposed to be vain.

You're one to talk Mr. Kavorka, retorted Resh Lakish. I'm sure you spent most of the episode imaging how you could score with Uma Thurman and Demi Moore.

Actually, I have a confession, said Rav Pappa.

Here we go, grumbled Bar Kappara.

I became very attracted to Elaine in that dress from Barney's, admitted Rav Pappa.

Which dress? Asked Motl the Tailor. You mean the one that made her arms look like something hanging in a kosher deli?

Yes, said Rav Pappa without shame. I find kosher salami the most erotic of all the salted cured meats.

OK Caligula, you need serious help, said Rav Sheshet.

Actually, I need the afternoon off, replied an aroused Rav Pappa. I'm outta here. I'm not digging this new format. Hey Captain K. let me know when Rav Huna is back. Check you later.

The Race

GEMARAH:

Friends, I am back, said Rav Huna, My vacation was restful, splendid, magnificent. In fact, next time I'm planning on going to Corfu.

Where is Bar Kappara? asked Rabbah.

Uh … he needed to take an admittedly predictable mental leave of absence. I tried to talk him out of it. But then I got to the "unexpected nudity" portion of yesterday's minutes, and I granted him his leave.

We are thrilled to have you back Master, said Shimon ben Pazi, for this much anticipated discussion about Superman and Lois Lane.

We are not discussing Superman, you yold! said Rav Huna. We are beyond such puerile conversations in my Yeshivah.

I disagree, said Rav Kahana. Remember when Jerry killed Fulton? He was in the middle of doing his Superman routine. And now in "The Race" he was impersonating Superman, even dating his girlfriend.

The entire Fulton fiasco was likely a setup, said Rav Pappa, so Jerry could shtupp Superman's main squeeze.

Speaking of squeeze, said Rav Huna, doing his best to maintain his composure and dignity, we need to continue discussing how the capitalist fat cats are squeezing the proletariat into destitution. We began this conversation during "The Gymnast." Where did we leave off?

We were talking about the dialectics of gastronomical Marxism and debating the equitable redistribution of elephants in a worker's paradise, said Yontl the Librarian, reading from the minutes.

Intellectually weighty questions, precisely what Sages such as ourselves SHOULD be discussing, said a beaming Rav Huna, passing around a copy of *The Daily Worker*.

Master, does the stereotype of Judeo-Bolshevism – Jew as Communist – not bother you? asked Rabbah. "The Race" gives us a bad name.

What are you saying? replied Rav Huna. They didn't mention Jews once.

Not so, interjected Rav Pappa, yet again demonstrating there was more to his rabbinic mind than his unremitting quest for orgies. Ned Isakoff is obviously Jewish. He has a Jewish name, Elaine likened him to Trotsky, and he dresses like Trotsky.

He dresses like us, noted Rabbah, in this drab, olive colored clothing. Which means we dress like Trotsky.

And he eats Chinese food, just like we do, said an alarmed Shimon ben Pazi.

Look on the bright side, said Rav Pappa, holding up the circulating copy of *The Daily Worker*. Their publications have great personal ads: "uninhibited woman seeks forward and inclusive thinking comrade. Appearance and disabilities not important." I think I'm going to give her a call to discuss modes of production.

You mean modes of reproduction, said Resh Lakish derisively.

Wait let me see that, said Rav Sheshet, grabbing the paper from Rav Pappa. She doesn't care about appearances. I'm going to call her. The Pig Man will be getting a date.

I saw her first, shouted Rav Pappa. And I'm disabled. My disability trumps your goofy appearance.

My sussoid countenance is a disability, replied Rav Sheshet. So I'm both disabled and, as you put it, goofy looking. That's two handicaps to one. The girl is mine. The doggone girl is mine.

Settle down, please! howled Rav Huna.

[Rav Pappa lunged at Rav Sheshet and grabbed him by his enlarged porcine nostrils.]

Master Huna, can you please issue a ruling, implored Rabbah. We can't have such fighting in the Yeshivah. And the last thing we need is to have Jewish communism associated with violence.

It looks like Rav Huna has passed out in the corner, said an alarmed Resh Lakish. What shall we do?

I know, I know, we will do like King Solomon proposed with the baby. Let's cut the woman in half, suggested Shimon ben Pazi, bewildered as usual, yet faithful to his Bible.

Five minutes, Chevreh, that's all I need with her is five minutes, said Zutra the Mohel feverishly.

Yes go ahead and divide the woman in two, said Rav Sheshet.

No, give the woman to Rav Sheshet, said Rav Pappa. I'd rather see the Pig Man get laid than see this poor woman suffer.

Wow, what a predictable ending said, Rami bar Hama. It's almost as if we are sitting around reenacting inane events from the Bible like a bunch of monotheistic clowns.

As Marx himself said, "history repeats itself, first as tragedy, second as farce," noted Yontl the Librarian.

How exactly would you have handled this, Rami? asked an incredulous Resh Lakish.

I would have suggested that an equitable distribution of the woman would be in keeping with the principles of Communism, replied Rami bar Hama.

Hard to believe the Soviet Union was a failure, said Resh Lakish sarcastically.

Well we've still got China, said Rami "the Red" bar Hama. But I know, I know it's not the same.

The Switch

GEMARAH:

Friends, said Rav Huna convening the meeting, we might as well get this over with and hand the mic to Rav Pappa. I suspect we'll be talking about orgies for the duration of what will be a painfully childish shiur.

Thank you, thank you very much, said Rav Pappa taking the floor. So "ménage à trois" – what is it and what can it do for you? Personally, I think-

Not on my watch, said Bar Kappara, cutting him off. I anticipated this inappropriately carnal turn of events, so I took the liberty of instructing the Sages to bring note cards with relevant topics of discussion. Shlongs, beytzim, foreskins, and the ménage à trois will not dominate our discourse. Who, among our mature flock would like to start?

I will, said Shimon ben Pazi.

Go ahead, you have the floor, Rabbi Shimon.

Can anyone tell me, began Shimon ben Pazi, what is the plural form for ménage à trois? Is it ménages des troises?

Stop! who's next? asked Bar Kappara, struggling to retain his composure.

I'll take a stab at this, said Rami bar Hama: If we use the plural form for ménage à trois because there are six people present, should the proper term not be "ménages des six"?

We said no shtupp talk in the shiur, howled Bar Kappara.

That's not shtupp talk, interjected Rav Kahana. We are having a halakhic discussion about grammar, mathematics, and history.

First of all, nobody mentioned anything pertaining to Halakhah, retorted Bar Kappara. Second, What history? There's nothing "historical" about your question. To be sure, historical topics are always on the table in our Academy. That's why Yontl the librarian is here. Please rephrase.

OK then, how about this? asked Rav Kahana: did they have ménages des six in the Middle Ages?

I don't think this question is appropriate, said Shimon ben Pazi.

Thank you Shimon, said Bar Kappara.

Because we don't know what the Middle Ages are, admitted Shimon ben Pazi.

You mean when are the Middle Ages? that's the question, said Rav Kahana.

The Sages sat in silence.

The Middle Ages must have come between the beginning and the end, suggested Yontl the Librarian, flipping through the pages of his Hebrew Bible.

The Sages sat in silence.

But there is no end, said Rabbah. The Hebrew Bible just kind of stops, no conclusion. No happily ever after. No End of Days.

It's true, said Yontl. The Nazarene-Jesus people have an ending in that so called sequel they wrote. It's called "Revelations." Fire, brimstone, apocalypse, and the promise of Yoshke Pandrek's return.

How can that be "The End" if Yoshke will return after it is over? asked Shimon ben Pazi.

An excellent philosophical question, but one for a Christian seminary, said Bar Kappara. We are Jews in this academy. So please, let's stick to the original Bible, before it was cheapened with a sequel and placed in a drawer in every hotel nightstand.

So the Middle Ages must be whatever took place in the middle of our Book, said Shimon ben Pazi.

The Middle Ages are the middle pages, said the Sages in unison.

So this is the question for debate, interjected Rami bar Hama: did they have ménages des six in the middle pages of our book?

Please, everyone let's stick to the actual *Seinfeld* episode, said an increasingly unnerved Bar Kappara.

Then let me rephrase the question, said Rami bar Hama: did they have roommates in the middle pages?

Good question, let's roll with it, said Bar Kappara, breathing a sigh of relief.

I believe the Philistines had roommates, said Rav Sheshet.

OK, I'll bite, said Bar Kappara. Why must the Philistines have had roommates?

Because, began Rav Sheshet, King Saul instructed David to massacre 100 Philistines and bring home their foreskins. Yet he came home with 200 foreskins. So David must have killed each of the 100 Philistines and then massacred each one's roommate as well. 200 Philistines, and hence 200 foreskins. The foreskins doubled because they were living in pairs.

I agree, said Zutra the Mohel. This is my favorite chapter in the Bible. I cite it in my brochure, under the heading "Volume Business for Heathens"

But just because the Philistines had roommates, does it necessarily mean they had ménages des six? asked Rami bar Hama. I see no evidence these roommates were sleeping with each other.

Is there any evidence the middle-paged Philistines performed the roommate switch as per George's brilliant plan? asked Rabbah.

People, we are not interested in the sex life of the middle-paged Philistines. That's not within the purview of the Talmud. We are having these discussions in order to live our lives as better Jews.

Not so, chimed in Rav Sheshet, and I quote: "Rabbi Yitzhak of the school of Rabbi Ami says: Samson desired something unclean, as he was driven by lust to Philistine women." (Sotah 9b:20)

Samson was a prime candidate for a ménages des six, said Rami bar Hama. I'm certain he was an orgy guy, stocked up with robes and weirdo lotions.

Meeting adjourned, screamed Bar Kappara.

The sages got up to leave. An unusually silent Rav Pappa complacently made his way to the door and winked at his mentors.

Well that worked out splendidly, said Bar Kappara to Rav Huna with more than a touch of sarcasm.

I told you Kappara, we should have just handed the mic to Pappa when the meeting started. We would have had the same discussion, minus the frayed nerves, and we may have actually learned *something* valuable about the ménage à trois.

Thank you, said Rav Pappa, emerging from the shadows. Now would you please get down on your knees and thank God that you know me and have access to my dementia?

The Label Maker

GEMARAH:

Friends, said Rav Pappa who was granted permission to convene the meeting because Rav Huna and Bar Kappara were at the end of their wits, I find this entire episode, "The Label Maker," implausible.

Why? asked Rav Huna, content to have taken a back seat.

For starters, continued Rav Pappa, Bonnie's roommate Scott didn't look a thing like George.

He looked exactly like George, countered Resh Lakish. Short, stocky, slow-witted, and wearing glasses.

No he did not, said Rav Pappa. Because unlike George, Scott had hair.

That is true, conceded Rav Sheshet. How could someone who looks "exactly" like George have hair? That should have been the focal point of the episode's plot.

Maybe he ordered hair from China – "grow hair like Stalin" – suggested Rabbah, but unlike George, he committed to the cream of the Orient. George can't commit to anything, except quitting.

One single "cream of the Orient" joke and you're out on your tokhes Pappa, interjected Rav Huna.

So the question is, mused Rav Sheshet, why would Bonnie give up a "George with hair" and all that furniture for a "George without hair," who had nothing but a portable TV?

And what about the ménage à trois? asked Rav Pappa.

And ... here we go, mumbled Bar Kappara.

Why would anyone want to sleep with two Georges at once? asked Rav Sheshet.

Given George's unpredictable orgasms, suggested Rami bar Hama, a second George is a logical safety precaution, an insurance policy without paying a higher premium, if you will.

OK, then I raise a different question, said Rav Pappa without missing a beat, thus demonstrating his talmudic acumen: Why would a "George with hair" want to participate in a ménage à trois with a "George without hair"?

For the same reason that a successful handsome dentist would take postal employee Newman to the Super Bowl: these people are all sick. Sickos, all of them, said Resh Lakish.

Do you have a thing for dentists, Lakish? asked Abba the Surgeon. Those people are butchers who flunked out of medical school. We don't call them "mouth mohels" for nothing.

Watch yourself Abba, rumor has it you got your medical degree in Ukraine after flunking the admissions test to podiatry school, countered Zutra the Mohel, always at the ready to defend his professional integrity.

Ukraine, laughed the Sages in unison.

Ukraine has some of the finest medical schools on the continent, replied Abba the Surgeon.

On which continent? asked Rav Sheshet. I can't even find Ukraine on the map.

That's just an expression, said Abba the Surgeon.

Ukraine is a weak, feeble, sitting duck, which was occupied by Newman and threatened by Kramer during "The Label Maker," noted Rabbah.

So, Abba, this is really all about Newman, isn't it? said Resh Lakish. Do you have a little thing for the guy?

Well he is merry, noted Rav Pappa.

He is merry, we'll let him have that, said Rabbah. And we'll be diplomatic and let Kramer have part of Ukraine.

Uh, I'm not sure the Rabbinic Academy of Pumbedita has the power to dismember a foreign state, noted Yontl. But I will be happy to look into it.

Friends, said Rav Pappa, let's call it a day. I have proved once and for all I can run our shiurs without it degenerating into shtupping and Zutra's dismemberment program.

Not so, said Resh Lakish. We did discuss George's orgasms.

And we had to visualize Bonnie's Double George Fantasy, said Rav Sheshet.

So that would be two Georges, two Orgasms, and one ménage à trois, counted Shimon ben Pazi on his fingers.

You also presided over the slurring of various branches of medicine and our colleagues who practice them, not to mention the violent dismemberment of Ukraine in a game of world domination played by two guys who can barely run their own lives.

Oh who cares, meeting adjourned! exclaimed Rav Pappa.

Do you feel better, Kappara? asked Rav Huna after the other Sages exited.

Much better, thank you, replied Bar Kappara.

As I told you, said Rav Huna, we're far better off letting these shmendriks debate their way into inanity while we take notes and craft our literary masterpiece.

Agreed, said Bar Kappara. They will be reading *A Confederacy of Dummkopfs* for generations to come. It will become part of the Canon.

The Scofflaw

MISHNAH:

Shammai: If not mine, whose?
Hillel: If not now, when?
Shammai: Scofflaw
Hillel: White Whale
Shammai: Gary Fogel
Hillel: Jake Jarmel
Shammai: Malaysian glasses
Hillel: Eyepatch
Shammai: Your Smugness is not a good quality
Hillel: Send Jesus my regards
Shammai: No, I'll tell him you say hi!
Hillel: Then I'll go to the Mount of Beatitudes and tell him you lie
Shammai: Moops
Hillel: Moors
Shammai: Moops
Hillel: You're ugly in that toupee
Shammai: That's what you say
Hillel: That's what I know

GEMARAH:

Friends, sometimes our Yichus is just so utterly embarrassing, said Rav Huna convening the meeting.

The House of Hillel was excessively cruel to the House Shammai, said Rav Pappa.

Are you kidding? Shammai's main claim to fame is his inane backward menorah (Shabbat 21b), said Resh Lakish. Lighting eight candles on the first night and one candle on the last is just so anticlimactic.

But what about the Passover Shammai Sandwich? asked Rav Pappa.

Never heard of it and it ain't in the Mishnah, said Yontl the Librarian.

Well maybe if they hadn't wasted two full pages in the Haggadah on the Hillel Sandwich, there would have been room for the Shammai Sandwich, countered Rav Pappa.

Let me guess. The Shammai sandwich starts with 8 layers of matzoh, and we eat one on each day of Passover, said Resh Lakish. Pathetic.

But what about his brilliant adage, "If not mine, whose?" said Rav Pappa. I feel that phrase is a necessary corrective to Hillel's overused "If not now, when?."

Agreed, said Rami bar Hama. It was touching to see the House of Costanza quote the House of Shammai in "The Scofflaw."

It is a rather selfish expression, very fitting for Costanza, said Rav Sheshet.

Why is Shammai even a "House" if his penury forced him to live in Jesus the Nazarene's garage? asked Resh Lakish.

Now that, for once, is a good question, said Bar Kappara.

Perhaps we should downgrade him from being a "House," suggested Shimon ben Pazi.

We can call him "The Garage of Shammai," suggested Shimon ben Pazi.

Except he was shacked up in Jesus' garage, said Resh Lakish.

OK, how about hovel, shanty, hut, shed, shack, hole? offered Yontl the Librarian, flipping through the dictionary.

The House of Hillel vs the Shack of Shammai. I like it! said Bar Kappara.

It reads much better with the alliteration, said Yontl the Librarian.

Actually, "The Shammai Shack" sounds more like an eatery that serves eight-layer matzoh sandwiches than a House of Wisdom, noted Rabbah.

So then it's apt, said Bar Kappara.

Yontl, I authorize you to rewrite the Mishnah, accordingly, said Rav Huna. Let's disband the meeting on this high note. We accomplished more today than we have since Season 3.

The Highlights of a Hundred

PREAMBLE:

Yohanan ben Zakkai: It's time we start writing our conversations down. It will serve as the basis for a sacred text, or at the very least a sitcom.

The topic at hand is "why our lessons are like a *Seinfeld* episode" said Rav Sheshet.

We not only know about each others deep dark secrets, but we sit here debating them, said Rav Huna. I can tell you more about the hemorrhoids and boils that plague the beytzim and buttocks of Hanan bar Rava than I can tell you about my own wife's cycles.

Our bowels are the affliction of our exile, the burden of Babylon, and the proof of the matter is that toilets and bathrooms are discussed 120 times in the Talmud, said Bar Kappara in the name of Rav Huna.

THE TEXT:

What is a Mobydick? asked the probing Shimon ben Pazi. I've heard of Pesachdick and Shabbosdick, but not Mobydick.

Torah was given to Moses at Sinai, Moby-Dick was given to Melville in New York. There were as many Israelites in the Big Apple as there were at Sinai, perhaps the texts are related? proposed Rav Sheshet.

What is a Poland? asked Shimon ben Pazi.

It is a place, said Rabbah, filled with plenty of living space, ponies, and inhabitants who do not know how to change a light bulb.

What is a Guggenheim? asked Shimon ben Pazi?

It is a Temple in the Big Apple named for an "immigrant" who went down on the Titanic after it was rammed by Noah's Ark, killing all the ponies on board, said Rav Sheshet. He probably knew Manya. Maybe even killed her pony, a makher like Guggenheim surely hated anyone who owned a pony.

What is a Dingo? asked Shimon Ben Pazi.

Dingo is one of the few non-Yiddish words for penis, said Rav Pappa.

What are AstroTurfs? asked Shimon ben Pazi.

They are transphobes who believe hermaphrodites, tumtums, and eunuchs come from outer space, specifically celestial objects between Mars and Jupiter, said Bar Kappara.

Why hasn't George ever had a normal, medium orgasm? asked Rav Pappa the Player, who always put his virility first.

I can literally set my clock to Rav Pappa's emissions, said Resh Lakish.

Treating one's body like an amusement park is only mentioned nine times in the Talmud, said Rav Pappa.

Do you really think America's favorite pastime is masturbation? Asked Rami bar Hama.

You think this is all a big joke, don't you? said Mar Buchman the Library Cop. Are you a comedian?

I've performed at a bris or two, retorted Rav Pappa.

We need to discuss public urination, this is the major halakhic issue raised in the episode, said Bar Kappara.

Agreed, said Rav Pappa. "Urine" is mentioned 76 times in the Mishnah and 189 times in the Talmud.

Maybe we should make Rav Pappa take the IQ test? suggested Resh Lakish. At least we know he will get the questions about testicles correct.

My female love newtons leave me dirty messages all the time. And for this I am a better Jew, a tzaddik if you will, perhaps even a Lomed Vovnik, said Rav Pappa.

How exactly is that so? interjected Resh Lakish, you are the horniest Israelite in Babylonian Exile. The Alexander Portnoy of the Levant.

I don't even think a philanderer like Rav Pappa would shtupp a Nazi, said Resh Lakish. Would you Pappa?

Of course not, how can you even ask me that? replied Rav Pappa. OK maybe I would. Rav Huna, what is the Halakhah on sexual intercourse with an antisemite?

We've ruled it is halakhically permissible to shtupp a Nazi in order to avert a pogrom against the Jews, said Rav Pappa. Does it not follow that it is permissible to play the girlfriend of a Nazi who has the power to avert a pogrom against the Jews?

Why, asked Resh Lakish, must our discussions always revolve around shmekls, petzls, shlongs, beytzim, foreskins, dingos, and dingdongs?

Dingo Starr has a rather Jewish nose, pointed out Rav Pappa. Now it makes sense why his name sounds like penis.

Maybe we should measure each other's noses, proposed Rav Huna.

Isn't that getting a bit too personal? said Rav Sheshet.

Why? Asked Rav Hama. We know the location of all of Resh Lakish's boils. And we can literally set our clocks to Rav Pappa's nocturnal emissions.

Season 4 has just begun, Pappa, concluded Rav Huna. You will never survive "The Contest." You'll be out before your Rabbi Johnson manages to get through the interlocking metal teeth.

THE SAGES:

What do you do if the Dingo eats your baby? repeated the Sages in unison.
And cleavage, said the Sages in unison.
Kavorka! Pappa has the Kavorka! said the Sages in unison.
He took … it out! said the Sages in unison.
Poor Little Pinkus, said the Sages in Unison.
Woof Woof, not Bang Bang! said the Sages in unison.
Giddy up, said the Sages in unison.
Moops, Moops, Moops, said the Sages in unison.
Booby Boy, Booby Boy, Booby Boy, said the Sages in unison.
Body odor, body odor, not fart and shit, repeated the Sages in unison.
Yes, we poo-poo-Pappa, said the Sages in unison.
Cheap, cheap, cheap, cheap, said the Sages in unison.
Goyish, goyish, goyish, said the Sages in unison.
Jews, Jews, Jews, Jews, repeated the Sages in unison.
Step off dude, said the Sages in unison.

CONCLUDING REMARKS:

I think we have concluded, said Rav Huna, that the New York subway system is an abomination, worse than a leper colony, where the rats converge and the sewage of our exile flows. The Seinfeld Four endured a great tribulation of biblical proportions, one that puts Noah's Ark and the Titanic to shame.

Antisemitism is the longest hatred, lamented Rav Sheshet. Oh wretchedness of our exile! Nevertheless, In spite of everything, I still believe that Long Islanders are really good at heart.

And this is why, added Rav Sheshet, Ted Danson makes so much more money than us. I'm sorry, I can't live knowing Ted Danson makes that much more than me. Who is he?

I declare that we, Israelites, will embrace the "Jewish Nose." I predict our noses will be the envy of the nations, declared Rav Huna. What could go wrong?

The Beard

MISHNAH:

Hillel: Melrose Place
Shammai: 90210
Hillel: Dallas
Shammai: Dynasty
Hillel: Luke & Laura
Shammai: Patch & Kayla
Hillel: Who shot JR
Shammai: Jesus Christ Superstar

GEMARAH:

Friends, said Rav Huna convening the meeting, I'd like to begin by asking what you thought of the toupee.

I think it looked great on that homeless man, said Shimon ben Pazi.

Shimon you yold, obviously Rav Huna is referring to Costanza, said Bar Kappara. Who cares about the homeless man?

You are wrong said Rav Sheshet, we share a great deal with the homeless man, toupee or no toupee.

Please elaborate, said Rav Huna.

He eats Chinese food; we eat Chinese food. We marvel at the Chinese people's culinary abilities; he marveled at the Chinese people's culinary abilities.

So then maybe the homeless man is Jewish, suggested Rabbah.

There is no way that homeless Tupperware gonef* is Jewish, said Bar Kappara.

Then maybe we're homeless, suggested Shimon ben Pazi.

I've been in your home, Pazi, said Resh Lakish derisively. I've peed in your toilet. We may have even discussed me peeing in your toilet at one of our previous ever so enlightened shiurs.

Urination was discussed once during Season 2, twice during Season 3, once each in during Seasons 4 and 5, and multiple times during Season 6, said Yontl the Librarian, reading from the archived minutes.

Lakish, I think Shimon means "homeless" in the metaphorical sense, said Rav Pappa, yet again demonstrating there was more to his talmudic mind than the logistics of emissions, ménage à trois, and Resh Lakish's urinary habits. We live in diasporic captivity dependent on the good will of the goyim around us.

We are a nation in exile, added Rav Sheshet. "By the rivers of Babylon, we eat Chinese from Tupperware, and weep for Zion." (Psalm 173, Kung Pao Edition)

But we have no Tupperware! exclaimed Resh Lakish.

Lakish, I think Sheshet means "Tupperware" in the metaphorical sense, added Rav Pappa.

This is quite possibly the silliest discussion we've had since the day we debated whether or not Moby Dick swallowed George in New York Harbor, said Resh Lakish.

And I still say George sojourned in the belly of the great fish! exclaimed Shimon ben Pazi.

Mammal, interjected Rabbah.

Whatever, replied Shimon ben Pazi.

The homeless man, with or without the hair piece, is not Jewish and we Jews are not homeless. Moreover, we have no Tupperware, insisted Resh Lakish.

So then maybe the homeless man is Chinese, suggested Shimon ben Pazi.

Paahrdon? said Resh Lakish marshalling his finest English accent.

Donna Chang's meshpuchah converted from Jewishness to Chinese – Changstein to Chang – at Ellis Island, insisted Shimon ben Pazi. So maybe the Jewish homeless man pulled an Ellis island as well.

So why is it that the Moby Dick swallowed Costanza but not the Changs in New York Harbor? asked Rav Sheshet.

Maybe whales do not eat Chinese, offered Shimon ben Pazi.

Objection! yelled Resh Lakish. No Orientalism in the academy. And we've already established that Moby Dick ate George because God was testing him. God did not put the Changsteins to the test.

Unlike the homeless man, who failed God's test miserably, noted Rav Sheshet. Thou shallt not steal Tupperware.

And, moreover, noted Abba the Surgeon, showing off his continental Ukrainian credentials, whales cannot digest Tupperware.

I think we've ... uh ... covered a lot of ground today, said a discombobulated Bar Kappara in the name of a once again catatonic Rav Huna. There are a number of motions coming in from the flock, which we need to take up at tomorrow's meeting, so let's disband.

The Rabbis disbanded, intrigued about tomorrow's shiur, yet alarmed over their increasingly erratic Master.

The Kiss Hello

GEMARAH:

Welcome to the shiur, friends, said Rav Huna convening the meeting. We have a proposal on the table from the normally silent Rav Yehudah.

Who is Rav Yehudah? asked Rabbah.

He's that haughty fella who sits behind Sheshet, said Resh Lakish. The one with that bad hairdo, he looks like something out of a Yemenite Yeshivah Yearbook

The floor is yours Rav Yehudah, said Rav Huna. Don't listen to those shmendriks in the peanut gallery.

Thank you, began Rav Yehudah. I would like to propose that we all hang etchings of ourselves in the lobby. This way we will know who everyone is.

We already know who everyone is, said Resh Lakish.

Nobody knew who I was, countered Rav Yehudah.

That's because you hide out silently in the back, replied Resh Lakish, acting as if you are too good for us. Like you are some sort of delicate genius. The delicate genius has profound thoughts on his mind and can't be disturbed.

First off, I apologize for my lack of contribution to yesterday's discussion, which near as I can tell, amounted to little more than Lakish confessing to having peed in Shimon's toilet. Second, I'm not hiding and I'm no more delicate than anyone else who has undergone the knife at Zutra the Mohel's Chopshop, replied Rav Yehudah. I remain invisible because my face is blocked by Rav Sheshet's enormous porcine head.

Well we know who you are now, said Resh Lakish, so I say motion denied because it is superfluous. I don't want my pic hanging in the lobby.

Are you scared someone may deface it with pee-pees and wee-wees, Lakish? asked an irritated Rav Sheshet.

OK, then let me put my own motion on the table, countered Resh Lakish. We should relocate Sheshet to an area from which he will no longer obstruct the view of the delicate genius nor our view of the genius's outmoded hairdo.

I was not done yet, interrupted Rav Yehudah. I also want to institute a "kiss hello" policy, much as said kissing transpired on *Seinfeld*.

I have zero interest in kissing anyone from the midst of this gaggle of sweaty rabbis, retorted Resh Lakish. I'm down to one kiss hello in my life: my chiropodist.

I see both Yehudah and Lakish's points, said Rav Pappa. So I propose the following amendment to Yehudah's motion: I motion "to touch a breast" as part of the "kiss hello."

We have a "bosom touching" motion on the table, said Rami bar Hama. Shall we vote?

Objection! said Resh Lakish.

On what grounds? asked Rami bar Hama.

Nobody in this yeshivah of men has breasts, insisted Resh Lakish.

Are you that sure Lakish? countered Rav Pappa. It seems someone forgot to peruse next week's *TV Guide*.

TO BE CONTINUED

The Doorman

GEMARAH:

Today we get to talk about boobies, said Rav Pappa, jumping up in excitement, preemptively starting the meeting.

Alas, it is true, conceded Rav Huna. "The male bosom" and how to best manage it is the topic at hand. We don't have a doorman at the Yeshivah, so discussing doormen seems rather pointless.

Why don't we have a doorman? asked Shimon ben Pazi. It would give us a level of class the other yeshivahs lack. The goys would all say, "Rav Huna must have the greatest yeshivah, he's even got a doorman."

No, it would be very uncomfortable for us have one, said Rav Sheshet.

Why? asked Rabbah.

Because we'd have to make idle chatter with someone who by all accounts is a pain in the ass and a simpleton, replied Rav Sheshet. Everyday we'd have to come in and say, "How about those Nicks?" as if we mean it.

What are the Nicks? asked Shimon ben Pazi.

The Sages sat in Silence.

And, accordingly, the doorman is a dead end, said Rav Pappa. Now getting back to boobies.

But this is absurd, said Resh Lakish. None of us has boobies. So why should we have a conversation that is clearly intended to give Rav Pappa material for his nocturnal emissions.

Objection! shouted Bar Kappara. Keep it clean Lakish. This is the *Seinfeld* episode, this is the script, this is our Talmud.

Thank you, said Rav Pappa. Allow me to elaborate. The Jew Costanza, descendent of Alexander Portnoy in everything but name, clearly carries the bosom gene. We learned this when Frank disrobed and much to George's horror exposed his cleavage. I am all but certain that some of us rabbis here carry the bosom gene as well.

I object to this line of discussion, said a disconcerted Resh Lakish.

Lakish, may I ask if your grandmother was bosomy? inquired Rav Pappa.

You want to know if my grandmother was bosomy!? retorted an incredulous Resh Lakish. I once again object.

I've seen your father, Lakish Senior, with his shirt off, while brushing his hair by the moonlight at his bedroom window, which lies directly astride from mine, said Rav Pappa. And dare I say he should be wearing an undergarment for support.

You want my father to wear a bra? said Resh Lakish, beginning to lose his patience.

No of course not, said Rav Pappa. A bra is for ladies. He needs either a bro or the less ethnic mansier.

No offense Lakish, but I agree, said Bar Kappara. I used to see your father at the shvitz. He's got some serious boobage. Gimel-cups at least.

Don't look so embarrassed Lakish, consoled Rav Pappa. If those are real, and I assume they are, then they are spectacular. The bosom gene may be a Jewish gene, and perhaps George Costanza is your distant progeny.

So now that we've established that Lakish has inherited the bosom gene, began Rav Sheshet, relishing the opportunity for vengeance against he who has branded him the Pig Man, we need to return to yesterday's motion.

With all due respect, Sheshet, I have no interest in either kissing or feeling off Resh Lakish every time he enters the Yeshivah, said Rabbah. But I am all for purchasing him and his father a mansier.

I can take care of this, interjected Yontl the Tailor.

I object, said Resh Lakish. I am not wearing female undergarments. My body my choice. My family chooses to live in discomfort.

Have you considered having a surgical reduction? suggested Rav Sheshet, who was not giving up that easily. I still have a "snip and save" coupon for Zutra the Mohel, that's good until Pesach.

Come in around Pesach, Lakish, said Zutra the Mohel. Your chest shall emerge unleavened much like the bread of our affliction. An end to your breasts of affliction. It will be another Pesach miracle.

I think we've covered enough ground for today, said Rav Huna. A very productive shiur fellas.

Bar Kappara: I don't get your game, Master. These last few shiurs have been totally, pardon my French, bananas.

Rav Huna: Relax, Kappara, I'm letting these shmegegge hot heads take each other down one by one.

Bar Kappara: Remember that your previous scheme to make Pappa disappear in Latvia failed.

Rav Huna: Yes, which is why the better solution is far simpler – have them mock each other with extreme prejudice until we have the most well behaved Yeshivah in Babylon. Sheshet is down, Lakish is down, and Pazi is going down next.

Bar Kappara: What a diabolical plan, Master. What could possibly go wrong?

The Jimmy

MISHNAH:

Hillel: Hey Shammai, I heard you finally got your own place.

Shammai: Yes, I'm on my own.

Hillel: Well I think that's the tops. You're really independent.

Shammai: You're not doing so bad yourself.

Hillel: And you know Shammai, when you're smiling, the whole world smiles with you!

GEMARAH:

Fellow sages, said Rav Huna convening the meeting, we have an interesting Mishnah for today's *Seinfeld*.

Yes it appears the House of Hillel was mocking an oblivious House of Shammai for being mentally challenged, like Kramer.

Well..., joked Rav Pappa.

It would explain a lot, said Rav Kahana. Shammai and Kramer share a great deal in common. Classic luftmenshes* whose greatest achievements were an uncanny ability to mooch off their neighbors.

Kramerica Industries would have made a good home for the aphorisms produced by the House of Shammai, added Rav Pappa. Kramer's revolving tie contraption could have dispensed Shammai's pearls of wisdom.

The Shammai-Tie. I like it! Said Rami bar Hama.

Can we please dispense with such hypotheticals and discuss "The Velvet Fog" instead? said Rabbah.

What is a Velvet Fog? asked Shimon ben Pazi.

It is the nickname of that classic crooner Mel Tormé, said Rav Pappa.

But George previously claimed he would drape himself in velvet if it were socially acceptable, said Shimon ben Pazi. Does that not imply George seeks to drape himself in Mel Tormé? How does one drape oneself in a classic crooner?

Me thinks Shimon's goyishe kop is hopelessly enveloped in a velvet fog, said Rav Sheshet.

No mocking of our fellow rabbis, said Bar Kappara, surprised by Huna's silence.

And no mocking of Mel, said Rav Pappa. Many a night do I play his discography in the candlelit company of my lady friends. Pappa loves the Velvet Fog.

You just said, "Pappa loves the Velvet Fog," said Rav Sheshet. You're pulling a Jimmy. And Jimmy is a boor and a weirdo.

Pappa thinks that Sheshet is jealous of Pappa, sardonically replied Rav Pappa.

Pappa just did it again, retorted Rav Sheshet. And I'm Jealous of what, Pappa? Mel Tormé is as clueless as Pazi. He actually thought Kramer was mentally challenged.

Is Kramer not mentally challenged? asked Rabbah.

The Sages sat in silence.

Well we issued an earlier ruling that Kramer is in fact Jerry's pet, said Bar Kappara. It stands to reason that he is intellectually disabled since we've already branded him a domestic companion.

I disagree, said Rav Kahana. First off, we also branded Rav Sheshet a sussoid domesticoid pig man, yet he still comes to our shiurs with most of the trappings of a sentient being. And second, we also ruled that Kramer "is a parasite, a sexually depraved Hellenizer, who is seeking only to gratify his basest and most immediate urges."

You are insulting his great vulnerability, said Bar Kappara, his cry out for love. He is merely an innocent primate in the post-modern world.

Are you referring to Kramer or Sheshet? asked Rav Kahana.

Uh, both I guess, said Bar Kappara.

Much like Pazi, joked Rav Sheshet.

I was impressed too, said Shimon ben Pazi. Kramer has a beautiful voice. And I think it's the tops that he is able to live on his own.

Much like Pazi, joked Rav Sheshet.

Hey Sheshet, who died and appointed you the Yeshivah's Don Rickles? said Rav Pappa.

Lakish is not here today, so someone needed to fill his giant clown shoes, replied Rav Sheshet.

Say, where is Resh Lakish? asked Rabbah.

He is still undergoing post-op recovery at Abba the Surgeon's for his breast reduction, said Bar Kappara. We're not sure when he'll be returning. He was rather offended, having come home only to find the tree in his front yard covered in brasiers. Witnesses claim to have seen a gaggle of sweaty rabbis retreating in laughter, singing "I Am Woman, Hear Me Roar."

Pappa is completely innocent, said Rav Pappa. Pappa is not threatened by Lakish's sexuality.

Pappa is a liar, said Rav Sheshet. Pappa was directing this gaggle of sweaty rabbis from his window which faces Lakish's house. Sheshet knows because Sheshet, I am willing to admit, was there too.

Pappa is a troublemaker much like Woody Woodpecker, said Rabbah.

Let Pappa just say, started Rav Pappa, that in Pappa's defense-

Pappa don't speak, said Bar Kappara, cutting him off. Pappa don't speak, you're in trouble deep. You misused a gaggle of sweaty crooning rabbis. You are a big baby.

This meeting is adjourned, said Rav Huna. We will rule later on whether there is something mentally wrong with Pazi – sorry I mean Kramer – when Resh Lakish returns, and we can formally apologize to him for defacing his foliage and defaming his boobage.

QUEER TALMUD YESHIVX, 2023

I can't believe how offensive this episode was, howled Rabba Jewliettx bat Ocasio-Cortezx.

I know, lamented Rebbetzin Amirah "Anti-Maskers Are Fascists" Mizrahi, mocking Kramer's neurodivergence the way they did, and with Mel Tormé's complicity yet. It was pure what's that word-face.

I don't think there is a term for cosplaying the handicapped, said Rabbx Yehudis bnei Butler

Well we should coin one, suggested Rebbetzin Amirah. Because that's what this episode was – "something something disabled-face."

I also can't believe how anti-Palestinian "The Jimmy" was.

I know, concluded Rabba Jewliettx. Did they even consult one Palestinian when writing the script?

The Doodle

PREAMBLE:

It was said that on the morning of the day of "The Doodle" Rav Pappa arrived at the Yeshivah hours before the other Sages, recited the Shema and then oiled up with his weirdo lotions in his orgy robe.

Bar Kappara [upon entering the academy]: You're here early Pappa, what's going on?

Rav Pappa: I was told they were sending in an Asian woman.

GEMARAH:

Friends said Rav Huna convening the meeting, we are gathering and then disbanding very quickly. The building needs to be evacuated. Apparently we have fleas.

Fleas? said Shimon ben Pazi. Is this because Kramer is a pet?

Is it my imagination or is Pazi mentally depreciating? asked Rav Sheshet.

Sheshet, watch your ableist discourse, cautioned Bar Kappara.

Sorry, replied Rav Sheshet. Is it my imagination or is Pazi … achieving special excellence in his neurodivergence?

I would comment, said Shimon ben Pazi, if I understood a word of what you just said.

We think you're just the tops, Pazi, said Rav Sheshet, and the whole world smiles with you.

OK we're all here, we need to leave the building, said Rav Huna.

Where shall we go? asked Rabbah.

I booked us a swanky room at the Pumbedita Plaza Hotel, said Bar Kappara.

The Plaza Hotel! exclaimed Rav Pappa. They have pay-per-view, peanuts, champagne, massages, and Asian women.

We are going to study Talmud, said Bar Kappara, right after you change out of your orgy robe, Pappa.

And if you all behave, added Rav Huna, we can conclude by having an affectionate doodling contest.

Hey Kappara, whispered Rav Pappa, on the way out the door. Is it just me or is Rav Huna beginning to lose it? Has he been reading one too many Billy Mumphrey stories?

In a manner of speaking, replied Bar Kappara. Huna is a simple country boy; you might say a cockeyed optimist. He was unprepared for the love, deception, greed, lust, and the unbridled enthusiasm of the Pumbetida Yeshivah's gaggle of sweaty Rabbis. And much like Billy Mumphrey, this will ultimately lead to his downfall. This flea infestation may be the last straw.

The Fusilli Jerry

GEMARAH:

Today, exclaimed Rav Pappa, jumping up in excitement and preemptively starting the meeting, we get to deliberate everyone's favorite anatomical topic: Butts! The storied yarns of the multitudes of assmen out there among Israelites and goys alike. With, to be sure, some musings on the incomparable Jewish tokhes, which is famous throughout the land.

Uh, where is Rav Huna, asked Rav Sheshet, looking around the room in disgust.

He is sitting at home on his, to be sure, incomparable Jewish tokhes, having frightfully anticipated the inexorable direction of this already catastrophic meeting, replied Bar Kappara.

I object! said Resh Lakish, raising his arm in anger while howling "Ouch!" in pain for having stretched out his wounded truncated bosom, far beyond what Abba the Surgeon had recommended ("stay off the boobies for a fortnight, Lakish," said the Ukrainian-credentialed "Doctor").

You're objecting to what? asked Bar Kappara.

To everything, to anything, to this tokhes-laden discussion, grumbled Resh Lakish.

Me thinks Lakish is worried we will be discussing boobies again, said Rav Pappa, given that Kramer stopped short with Estelle, which, incidentally, is my patented move. Kramer stole the bosom-move from me, not from Frank.

That's your move, Pappa? asked Rabbah. But your camel vanity plate reads "ASSMAN." Is it the butt or the bazongas you crave?

I'm but a simple Jew who loves both butts and bazongas, said Rav Pappa, but as far as the state of Persia is concerned, I am "the Assman."

The Assman is but a simple Jew who loves both butts and bazongas, said the Sages in unison.

And we're all very impressed, interjected Resh Lakish.

I think it would be far more fruitful to discuss the statistical improbability of Fusilli Jerry getting corkscrewed into Frank Costanza's rectum, said Rabbah.

It's as Frank said, added Rav Sheshet: "a million to one shot, Doc. Million to one."

Unless of course Frank wanted Fusilli Jerry comfortably ensconced where no light tends to go, suggested Rami bar Hama. Some people enjoy these things.

Did Frank look like he was sustaining pleasure? asked an incredulous Resh Lakish. You and Pappa need to keep your sexual perversions to yourself.

OK Boobie Boy, said Rami bar Hama, smiling at Resh Lakish. You are the last person who should be lecturing us on cis heteronormativity.

A dejected Resh Lakish glanced down at his still swollen nipples and left the shiur with a tear in his eye.

I think we are ignoring the elephant in the room, said Abba the Surgeon. "Buttocks" and "Rectum" are mentioned a mere 19 times in the Talmud. Moreover, as it is written "a male, whose genitals are not covered when he sits, may not recite the blessing over the separation of challah. The Mishnah teaches that exposed buttocks do not constitute nakedness." (Berakhot 24a:10)

But Frank was not separating challah, countered Rav Pappa.

On the contrary, his butt cheeks were being separated by corkscrew pasta, noted Rami bar Hama.

What's the Halakhah on the parting of butt cheeks with graven images laden with carbs? asked Rav Pappa.

That's precisely my point, said Abba the Surgeon. There is no Halakhah. In Jewish law, the tokhes is not considered genitalia: it's just another orifice, so the entire debate surrounding Frank's anus is moot. We might as well discuss shoving pasta into one's nostrils.

Who possesses nostrils large enough to accommodate corkscrew pasta? asked Rav Pappa.

Some have nostrils with a diameter wider than the widest of anuses, noted Abba the Surgeon, especially those with the documented porcine deformity. I've seen it in my clinic.

Before everyone's gaze fell upon Rav Sheshet, Bar Kappara jumped in and said, let's end on this graphic note; we've appeared to have exhausted the Halakhah on the rectum. Uh…good…job Rav Pappa.

For me, concluded Rav Pappa, it was just another day at the orifice!

The Diplomat's Club

GEMARAH:

I'm deeply troubled, said Rav Pappa, beginning the meeting before Rav Huna had a chance to speak.

What's wrong? Did DIRECTV remove the adult channel, joked Rav Sheshet, elbowing Resh Lakish.

Ouch! howled Resh Lakish, who had yet to heal from his Ukrainian breast reduction.

No, said Rav Pappa, taking the insult (which he in fact took as a compliment) in stride. I was at the marketplace and Arram, the Makher who runs the Mackinaw

Peach stand, told me I looked like Moses. I accused him of thinking all Jews look the same, and I called him a rabid antisemite. He banned me from the marketplace.

He probably meant it as a compliment, said Rabbah.

Indeed, to have the countenance of that chiseled Charlton Heston, said Rami bar Hama. Wow, wow, wow! I should be so lucky.

And don't forget that all of Jethro's seven daughters, in addition to Nefertiti, threw themselves at Moses, said Rav Kahana. He was a real stud, and not just among the Israelites.

Yes, you should take it as compliment, insisted Rav Sheshet, especially from such a big mouth lout like Arram. The last time I was there he told me I looked like Wilbur from Charlotte's Web. So I called him a rabid anti-Piglite. He banned me from the marketplace.

I don't think "anti-Piglitism" is a thing, said Yontl the Librarian, flipping through the dictionary.

Surely, there must be a term for discrimination against pig men, said Rabbah.

We can add "anti-Piglitism" to the dictionary, said Rav Kahana. We're the Sages of Pumbetida, our words carry as much weight as those bequeathed by Moses, even if he looked like Pappa.

Done and done! said Yontl the Librarian. Perhaps one day anti-Piglitism will be known as the world's longest hatred.

It would certainly be a lucky break for us Jews, said Rabbah, no offense Sheshet.

Should we call it a day? Coining a term has taxed my intellect, said Rav Pappa.

No, replied Bar Kappara. I am very concerned that the goyim think we all look alike, much as George thinks all Black people look the same.

Indeed, it is troubling, said Abba the Surgeon. My Ukrainian medical training included a course in phrenology, and it seems that the stereotypes about our shared appearance go far beyond the Jewish nose.

Please elaborate, Abba, said Bar Kappara.

Let's just say that in Slavic lands, we are all Manya's horse faced relatives, replied Abba the Surgeon cryptically.

So what can we do about it? asked Bar Kappara.

We need to parade a group of Jews around the marketplace who are so vastly different in appearance, nobody will harbor any doubt henceforth, replied Abba the Surgeon.

Well we've got the Pig Man, said Rami bar Hama. Sticking him side-by-side with our chiseled Moses is like juxtaposing a fox and a chicken. But I fear that isn't sufficient. If only we had a horseface, like Cousin Jeffrey.

Abba, you should have never operated on Lakish, said Rabbah. His spectacular bosom would have been a real asset in this situation.

Do breasts grow back? asked Shimon ben Pazi.

No but I could put them back, said Yontl the Tailor brimming with confidence.

What say you, Lakish? Willing to undergo the knife – or rather the needle and thread – again? asked Rami bar Hama.

I can't help but feel as if everyone is making fun of me, lamented Resh Lakish.

We are, said Rav Sheshet, elbowing Resh Lakish in his greatly reduced sore bosom.

People, I think we need to embrace our commonalities, said Rav Huna, speaking up for the first time in days. There's no shame in being part of a community of sweaty large nosed Rabbis.

With unkempt beards and elongated sidelocks that could choke a small horse, added Rav Pappa.

But still, Arram was out of line, much as Costanza was out of line, said Bar Kappara. What can we do?

I think we should send Pazi to pee on his couch, suggested Resh Lakish.

You know that Arram insulted me as well, said Shimon ben Pazi. He called me neurodivergent. What does that mean?

It means, said a relieved Rav Huna, they will think it isn't your fault when you do pee on his couch.

Then I'd be honored to be the designated urinator, replied Shimon ben Pazi. This is just the confidence booster I need!

That's the tops Pazi, that's the tops! said the Sages in unison.

The Face Painter

GEMARAH:

Fellow Sages, said Rav Huna convening the meeting, let's discuss the Halakhah behind face painting, especially where the devils – what in the New Jersey Devils is THAT doing in here, Abba?

This is a Chimpanzee, we call him Baruch, replied Abba the Surgeon. He is depressed, so I brought him to the shiur.

I believe we have a "no animals in the Yeshivah" policy, said Resh Lakish.

We let Sheshet the Pig Man in, countered Rabbah.

Technically speaking, a pig man is a humanoid, said Yontl the Librarian.

Technically speaking a chimpanzee is a hominid, countered Abba the Surgeon. So if Sheshet the humanoid can stay, so can my hominid.

OK, the monkey can stay, ruled Rav Huna. Pray tell, Abba, why is your monkey depressed?

Because Resh Lakish threw a banana peel at him while he was recovering from his breast reduction. He has not been the same ever since, said Abba the Surgeon.

The monkey or Lakish? said Rav Sheshet, elbowing Resh Lakish.

He threw it at me first, said Resh Lakish and that was after he made fun of me for undergoing ... uh ... my reconstructive operation. The monkey is guilty of ableism.

And one could argue transphobia as well, mused Rav Pappa.

How exactly can a monkey make jokes about the disabled and the gender queer? Can he even speak? asked Bar Kappara.

Objection! howled Resh Lakish.

Baruch here is a very intelligent primate, said Abba the Surgeon. He knows sign language better than Kramer, and, I would argue, would make a much better pet than Kramer.

But can he sing like Kramer? asked Shimon ben Pazi.

Keep up the good work Pazi, said Rav Sheshet, we think you're the tops, the tops, and the whole world smiles with you – even if I've peed on your couch.

So how can you tell he's depressed? asked Rabbah.

He barely sleeps, replied Abba the Surgeon. And the nurses tell me that he has curtailed his auto-erotic activities; even with their help, he's not interested.

Maybe Pappa should help the monkey get reacquainted with his little monkey, suggested Resh Lakish.

I'd be happy to, said Rav Pappa, so long as Abba provides us with the nurses in question as well.

You're a misogynist Pappa, said Abba the Surgeon.

And you all are coming mighty close to asking me to engage in bestiality, retorted Rav Pappa.

As it is written: "The following are stoned: He who has sexual relations with his mother, with his father's wife, with his daughter-in-law, with a male; with a beast; a woman who commits bestiality with a beast; a blasphemer; an idolater." (Mishnah Sanhedrin 7:4). I have no intention of spilling my seed with Baruch the monkey spilling his by my side.

Yes, your request is a bit problematic, and perhaps even blasphemous, interjected Bar Kappara.

Is it blasphemous because Jesus threw the monkey-spankers out of the Temple? asked Shimon ben Pazi.

Wait, so then the nurses in Abba's clinic should be tried for bestiality, said Rabbah.

First rule of Abba's Clinic is we do not judge what transpires inside Abba's clinic, said Zutra the Mohel, who, in recent times, decided it best to form a tacit alliance with Abba, having realized their common surgical practices were coming under greater scrutiny.

Nevertheless, Lakish is responsible! said Abba the Surgeon. I demand that Lakish take Baruch home and not return until he has a full psychiatric recovery.

Agreed, said Rav Huna. Lakish, he is in your custody now. Or maybe you're in Baruch's custody now. Both of you go get the help you desperately need. Today's lesson is over.

Bar Kappara: Master, do you think we will ever see that monkey again?

Rav Huna: If all goes as planned, we will never see either of them again. Lakish is a troublemaker, and expelling a rabbi who treats his monkey like an amusement park will be simple enough.

Bar Kappara: How devilishly clever Master. What could possibly go wrong?

The Understudy

GEMARAH:

Friends, said Rav Huna convening the meeting, today we have to – who in the name of the New Jersey Devils are you there, sitting in the front?

Hi, I'm Hesh Lakish, I'm new here. I'm your venerable sage Resh Lakish's understudy. I'm assuming his role while he is in "recovery."

Our Yeshivah has a "no understudy" policy, said Rav Pappa. Those understudies are a shifty bunch, they are the substitute teachers of the rabbinic world. They're always looking to subvert those above them.

And lo and behold, Pappa is right, added Rabbah, we now have a Hesh and no Resh.

Respectfully, interjected Hesh Lakish, you also had a "no monkey" policy, yet you sent my master home with a chimpanzee yesterday, and instructed the two of them – in the most ableist and transphobic language imaginable – to explore each other's bodies like amusement parks. So I have every right to be here.

Boy the little rascal is rather verbose, noted Rav Sheshet.

For the record, I also speak Korean, much like Frank Costanza, boasted Hesh Lakish.

And you apparently have Frank's foot odor problem as well, said Rav Kahana.

Yes, I have seen him around town with his understudy buddies, said Rabbah. I can confirm that he wears his shoes in the mikvah.

That's a halakhic violation! said Bar Kappara in judgment.

I take my shoes off for nobody, insisted Hesh Lakish.

Does he also have man boobs? asked Rav Pappa.

Maybe we should throw him out, suggested Rabbah.

Or at least give him a mansier, said Rav Pappa.

Or operate on him, said a hopeful Abba the Surgeon.

Throw me out, replied Hesh Lakish, and I promise that MY understudy Lesh Lakish will show up to take my place. And I can assure you his foot odor is far worse than mine.

Does he have a tail? joked Rav Sheshet, elbowing Hesh Lakish.

You mean there exists a Resh Lakish, a Hesh Lakish, and a Lesh Lakish all under one roof? said Bar Kappara. It's Larry, Darryl, and Darryl all over again.

What a country! said the Sages in unison.

Yes, replied Hesh Lakish. And now there's also a monkey under our roof, who rumor has it, will be replacing me as Resh Lakish's new understudy once I've moved up in the Yeshivah world.

Maybe Baruch the Monkey should just replace all three of them, suggested Rav Pappa. That seems to be the most equitable approach.

OK I think we're done here, concluded Rav Huna. Hesh, it's been a pleasure. Please tell Baruch Lakish to come back tomorrow, wearing his full rabbinic garb, with that very soft, huge shtreymel, those drawstring tzitzit, and an aerodynamic tallis perfect for jumping into a gondola.

What about Resh Lakish? said Hesh Lakish.

Tell Resh he's on indefinite hiatus for treating his monkey – and quite possibly his understudy – like an amusement park.

We expect the monkey at 8am PST tomorrow, said Bar Kappara.

Pumbedita Standard Time? asked Hesh Lakish.

No, Primate Standard Time, replied Rav Huna. According to HR, it's far more inclusive.

Season 7

The Rabbis Debate Jewish Law
on Buying Soup From a Nazi

The Engagement

MISHNAH:

Shammai: What is this? What are we doing? What in God's name are we doing!?

Hillel: What? -

Shammai: What kind of lives are these? We sit around coining aphorisms. Who does that? We're not men.

Hillel: You're right. We're not men. We have no jobs, nor do we have the proverbial 2.4 children, dog, or white picket fence.

Shammai: We spend our days arguing menorahs, Pesach sandwiches, and the Moops. Will we be doing this like two idiots when we're eighty?

Hillel: Moors

Shammai: Moops

Hillel: Moors

Shammai: Moops. But you see my point. We should be having dinner, preferably Chinese, with our children.

Hillel: Moors. You're correct for once, Shammai. No more arguing, no more dissecting the minutiae of every excruciating bit of Halakhah. No more zippy aphorisms. No more trite expressions.

Shammai: We're pathetic. Time for a change. Time for us to be normal.

Hillel: If not now, when?

Shammai: There you go, you're doing it again!

Hillel: That's just an expression.

Shammai: But it's your trite expression.

Hillel: I know, I know. It's as if we're trapped.

Shammai: It's like that Twilight Zone episode where the Rabbi wakes up and he's the same but everyone else is different.

Hillel: Which episode was that?

Shammai: Oh they're all like that.

GEMARAH:

Friends, said Rav Huna convening the meeting, we have finally arrived at the weighty topic of that shmendrik Costanza's engagement. So much to discuss.

Motion to postpone this discussion to address a more pressing topic, said Abba the Surgeon.

Which would be what exactly? asked Rav Huna.

We need to discuss Elaine, Kramer, and Newman's plot to rub out that helpless dog, said Abba the Surgeon.

Agreed, said Rabbah, and we should note that Elaine had previously tried to hire Jerry to exterminate a couple of cats.

Jerry is himself far from innocent, said Abba the Surgeon. He murdered Miss Rhode Island's pigeons and quite possibly killed Manya's pony.

Oh who cares, said Rav Pappa. These are just a bunch of animals. As God said to Adam and Eve: "have dominion over the fish of the sea, and over the fowl of the air, and over every living thing that moveth upon the earth." (Genesis 1:28)

You are a callous pig, Pappa, said Abba the Surgeon. God gave man dominion over beast to sustain himself and to be fruitful and multiply, not to engage in wanton zoocide. And let's be honest: you are ignoring the monkey in the room.

Zoocide? said Shimon ben Pazi. And I think you mean "the elephant in the room." That's the expression.

No, I mean that we are ignoring – quite literally – the monkey sitting in this room, countered Abba the Surgeon. Baruch bar Chimp Lakish is here in his finest rabbinic garb as we commanded, and you have the temerity to act as if canicide, avicide, and felicide are no big deal.

The Sages sat in silence while Yontl the librarian frantically searched the tattered 1960s *Audubon Nature Encyclopedia* the Yeshivah inherited from a Jewish Baby Boomer hoarder.

He has a point, said Rav Huna. We did invite Baruch Lakish to replace Resh Lakish, assuming he fully recovered from his depression and auto-erotic dysfunction. Let's extend Baruch a laurel and hearty welcome to the Academy.

Are you back to spanking the monkey, eh Baruch? joked Rav Sheshet, elbowing his new companion.

In my defense, I never spoke of cercopithecide, retorted Rav Pappa. God forbid we accidentally offend the precious monkey. And what about you calling me a pig, Abba? Don't you think that's offensive to Rav Sheshet?

He has a point, said Rav Huna. Abba, please be more respectful of Sheshet's …um…special condition. And I have no idea what "cercopithecide" means.

I believe it is the technical term for "murdering a monkey," said Rav Pappa. And no offense Baruch. You're as handsome and well dressed and therefore as welcome as virtually anyone else in this room. Just try to fit in.

There's something very familiar about this scene, said Rav Bilko.

It's déjà vu in a hominoid key, said Rabbah.

We thus have a new policy in place at the Yeshivah, said Bar Kappara, once again taking the lead: we are to respect beast, swine, and all that creepeth and crawleth, in deference to our fellow Rabbis who cannot help their hominoid and humanoid conditions. We shall judge the zoocidal Seinfelders accordingly.

Then it is clear, said Rabbah. These four New Yorkers, enabled by the diabolical Newman, behave unconscionably towards man and beast alike.

I'm afraid we're out of time, concluded Rav Huna. We will have to save the discussion of George and Susan for tomorrow. Meeting adjourned.

The Rabbis disbanded, unaware that tomorrow's shiur would be upended yet again because one of their own – a man of the rabbinic cloth – had moved into Elaine's building, causing a tzimmes* that would not be good for the Jews.

The Postponement

GEMARAH:

Friends, said Rav Huna convening the meeting, I think we all know that a matter of great importance in need of discussion has come up in "The Postponement."

Agreed, said Rav Pappa, and I'll begin: for the record, I concur with George that visiting a prostitute while one is engaged to be married does not constitute cheating.

The Sages stared at Pappa in unison.

You're a shmendrik of the highest order, Pappa, said Bar Kappara. Rav Huna is obviously referring to the depiction of the Rabbi on *Seinfeld*.

Yes, said Rabbah. I do not think this Rabbi, Glickman is it? – Glickman! what kind of a name is Glickman for a Rabbi!? – is good for the Jews.

Agreed, said Rav Kahana. He made our people look like a bunch of yentas, and worse, like a gaggle of lemechkes* who surely lack the wit and aptitude to survive the dark night of exile.

I don't know, I kinda liked the way he reached out to Elaine, the shiksa, countered Rami bar Hama. It was a mitzvah.* We are supposed to be a Light unto the Nations. He even offered to find her a companion from the Jewish faith.

Agreed, said Rav Pappa. And I'll admit that it gave me the idea of starting an inter-faith matchmaking venture as a side business: "Shiksa dot com."

You're out of order Pappa, halakhically and, I might add, in terms of your employment contract. You signed a conflict-of-interest form. Expect a visit from HR.

Are we sure the Rabbi is supposed to be symbolic of the Israelite nation? asked Rav Sheshet. As Jerry said, "Elaine, if I could say a word here about Jewish people. That man in no way represents our ability to take in a nice piece of juicy gossip and keep it to ourselves."

You know Sheshet is right for once, mused Rabbah. Perhaps they were just making rabbis look like a bunch of shmegegges, not the Jewish people as a whole. It was the same with Shaky the Mohel who circumcised Jerry's finger in Season 5. The writers really nailed our beloved Zutra.

So how is this any better? asked Bar Kappara. *Seinfeld* is mocking the Rabbinate writ large. It's almost as if we are the Wise Men of Chelm.*

Who are these Wise Men of Chelm? asked Shimon ben Pazi.

Really, Shimon, of all people, we assumed YOU would know the Chelmites, joked Rav Sheshet, elbowing his new chum Baruch bar Chimp, who replied by giving his human companion a hearty "ooh ooh aah aah" in approval.

I think the lesson is clear, said Bar Kappara. We need to pass down a favorable image of the Rabbinate to our progeny. This is why Yohanan ben Zakkai, Z"L,* had the seychel* to begin writing down our insight. This is why, under my stewardship, we are compiling The Seinfeld Talmud.

Through our musings, added Rav Huna, future generations will view our sagacity as a contribution not only to Halakhah but dare I say the jurisprudence of western civilization. Now let's disband for the day. And before I forget, Baruch, can you please stick around to sign your conflict-of-interest forms?

The Maestro

GEMARAH:

Friends, said Rav Huna, convening the meeting, I am not sure we have much to discuss today with "The Maestro."

Indeed, it is a rather straightforward episode. And although Bobb Cobb, AKA Maestro is a bit of a yold, there were no great debates and nothing that implicates our Yeshivah in any way, said Bar Kappara.

We can debate changing our honorific titles and salutations from rabbi to maestro, suggested Shimon ben Pazi.

The Sages groaned and Baruch the Chimp facepalmed in unison.

We can debate whether or not our security guard should have a chair, suggested Rav Yehudah.

We don't have a security guard, replied Bar Kappara.

Then maybe we should debate whether or not we need a security guard, said Rabbah.

This will inevitably force us into a debate about getting the security guard a chair, said Rav Pappa. You see the problem?

Yes I see the problem, said Rami bar Hama. And then we would have to debate what kind of chair we would have to purchase.

There are so many different types of chairs out there, said Shimon ben Pazi, passing around the Ikea catalog he swiped from Resh Lakish's coffee table before peeing on his couch.

The chair should definitely swivel, said Rabbah. He must have radial omniscience, like HaShem.

But he can't have a nicer chair than the throne upon which HaShem sits in the Kingdom of Heaven, said Rav Kahana.

It would also be wrong for the security guard to have a nicer chair than the ones we have, said Rav Sheshet.

It all depends on whether or not the security guard is Jewish, said Rav Pappa. If he's one of us, we don't want to make him feel inferior with a lesser chair.

According to HR, we are not allowed to ask employees whether they are Jewish or not, said Rav Huna. So the chair we buy can't be contingent upon the security guard's race, ethnicity, faith, ability, or sexual orientation.

Are you suggesting we can't take our security guard's disabilities into account when choosing his chair? said Abba the Surgeon. This flies in the face of everything I learned in Ukrainian medical school.

And moreover, added Rabbah, we gave the damn monkey the same chair we use and I'm fairly certain Baruch the Chimp is not Jewish.

Ah, but he is a talmudic scholar, said Rav Sheshet. Baruch knows his Torah. He's my new evening chevrutah* partner. We meet at 7 Primate Standard Time right after he's done with his auto-erotic activities. Then we recite the Shema and watch Jeopardy together.

And Baruch is content with his chair, right Baruch? asked Rabbah.

Ooh Ooh Ahh Ahh, replied Baruch bar Chimp Lakish, while signing his evening schedule for those in the academy who knew sign language.

So maybe the chair we buy should be contingent upon the extent to which the security guard knows Talmud, suggested Rav Kahana. Surely that's not against HR's hiring policies.

Don't you think we should ask the security guard whether he wants a chair or not in the first place, before we pick one out for him? asked Rav Sheshet.

But how can we ask him if we don't actually have a security guard? said Bar Kappara.

And therein lies the problem, said Rav Kahana.

This is like the chicken or the egg, said Shimon ben Pazi.

Maybe we should drop this discussion, said Rav Huna. I've never heard of a Jewish institution needing armed security. The very idea seems preposterous.

The Wink

GEMARAH:

"The Wink," was an intriguing episode, said Rav Huna, convening the meeting.

It hit too close to home, said Rav Pappa. A sloppy Resh Lakish once squirted matzoh ball soup into my eyes and I subsequently winked myself into a submissive BDSM session with a-

Do we really need to hear this? asked an exasperated Abba the Surgeon.

Objection! said Rav Pappa. I have every right to discuss the bitter irony of flying matzoh balls leading to my own matzoh balls' bondage.

Objection! said Bar Kappara. This isn't a second-rate club in the Catskills, and I am tired of indulging Pappa's hackneyed Henny Youngman jokes.

But this isn't a joke, insisted Rav Pappa. These are my beytzim of affliction.

Save it for the marketplace, Pappa, concluded Rav Huna. No we need to discuss the dogs, those hounds from hell who pervade the streets of New York, going after Elaine like the SS raiding a shtetl in Poland.

Objection! said Abba the Surgeon. Elaine brought this on herself. She was walking around with semi-masticated mutton in her pockets. That's every doggie's dream.

What exactly is mutton? asked Rabbah.

I have no idea but I'm sure it had parents, retorted Rav Pappa.

Then I object on the grounds that Elaine had this coming, said Abba the Surgeon. This is poetic justice for having previously kidnapped an innocent dog.

Abba has a point, said Bar Kappara. We've already implicated her in attempted canicide and felicide. Conversely, it seems Jerry, by going meatless, is making amends for having taken out pigeons and a pony, not to mention Fulton.

Moreover, added Abba the Surgeon, out of deference to our colleague Baruch, we should refrain from discussing wanton cruelty to the animal kingdom. It's in the HR policy manual: "species-inclusive language is required at all shiurs once your Yeshivah has admitted hominid-divergent rabbis."

So we can never talk about animals, again? said an incredulous Rav Pappa. This is absurd. Admitting Baruch the Chimp, sorry Rav Baruch the Hominid-Divergent, was supposed to enrich our discussions, not inhibit them.

[Baruch the Chimp lowered head in embarrassment to the point that his Yarmulkeh fell off and landed in his matzoh ball soup splashing some into Rav Pappa's eye.]

Ouch! screamed Rav Pappa. Look what the Hominid-Divergent Rabbi did to me!

I'm taking Baruch out of the lesson to cheer him up, said Rav Sheshet. We'll hit the marketplace before we begin his evening routine. You all need to reflect upon what you did here today and do better.

So what else can we discuss, friends? asked Rav Huna.

Perhaps we can discuss the relative merits of a blind date vs. a deaf date, suggested Rabbah.

I agree with Jerry, said Rav Pappa. 90-95% of the population is goofy looking and accordingly undatable.

And yet, you still continue to date them, noted Yontl the Librarian, browsing the archival minutes.

I have been to the DMV lately, said Rav Kahana. And it is indeed a leper colony down there.

How can a leper conduct a moving vehicle, asked Shimon ben Pazi. What if one of their limbs becomes dismembered while driving? There must be Halakhah on this.

Lepers are mentioned 625 times in the Talmud, said Yontl the Librarian, though most instances deal with ritual purification, not dismemberment in traffic.

Objection, said Abba the Surgeon. The HR policy manual states that we cannot use the term "leper" anymore.

But it is a genuine medical condition, Abba, said Zutra the Mohel. We are not talking about someone who had a body part inadvertently severed at one of our clinics. And we have no lepers in our academy.

Jerry meant "leper" in the metaphorical sense, i.e. to use Pappa's favorite phrase, "goofy looking," countered Abba the Surgeon. In deference to Rav Sheshet's porcine deformity, we can no longer say "leper."

But mocking Sheshet is the highlight of our lessons! countered Rav Pappa. This is egregious. We can't talk about beytzim, cruelty to animals, or pig men. What have we got left? This is the script. This is our Torah.

I got nothing, said Rabbah.

Neither do I, admitted Bar Kappara.

So let's call it a day, concluded Rav Huna.

Master, said Bar Kappara, it appears you judged incorrectly. Expelling Lakish, while keeping Sheshet and adding that simian has only worsened our problems, stifling our discussions.

It's my fault, said Rav Huna. I admit that I hadn't read the new HR guidelines, except for the section on antisemitism. I assumed we were in the clear.

So what's the solution? asked Bar Kappara.

It's simple. We need to get rid of Abba the Surgeon. He's the only one who listens to HR anyway. I have a plan.

TO BE CONTINUED.

The Hot Tub

GEMARAH:

So are we sons of bitches ready to begin? said Rabbah, in the spirit of "The Hot Tub."

I don't know about this bastard, said Bar Kappara, pointing at Rav Sheshet, but this son of a bitch, said Bar Kappara pointing at himself, is ready to proceed.

Well this mamzer* is as ready as the next mamzer, said Rav Kahana, adding some biblical inflection to the discourse.

This is fun, we are all a bunch of sons of bitches, even Baruch, added the normally reticent Shila of Kefar Tamarta.

Ooh ooh aah aah, said Baruch bar Chimp Lakish, jumping up and down while signing "sons of bitches"

Friends, said Rav Huna, I hate to be the son of a bitch who breaks up the party, but I'm afraid I have some bad news.

What happened, asked Rabbah?

It seems as if Abba has gotten himself into a bit of a pickle. When he didn't show up for Shacharit prayers, I called 911 in panic. They sent the fuzz to his clinic, busted down the door, and walked in upon the rumored house of ill repute the nurses allegedly operate in the building. They busted the nurses, then found Abba and arrested him too. They also put his animals in quarantine.

Where was Abba? asked Rabbah.

He was at home in bed. Turns out he overslept. His alarm didn't go off. He likely got the AM/PM on his alarm clock mixed up.

And where's Pappa? asked Rav Kahana.

He was also busted at the scene, said Rav Huna. Ironically he was already handcuffed to a nurse when the cops arrived.

Perfect irony, said the Sages in unison.

But he was released on his own recognizance, added Rav Huna. He'll be back soon.

Also perfect irony, said the Sages in unison.

So it may be some time before we see Abba again, lamented Rav Huna. The authorities are also investigating his so-called Ukrainian medical license.

OK, Sages, I think you all need to go down to the slammer and visit Abba, instructed Bar Kappara. And please act with the decorum one would expect from a rabbi. Tempting as it may be, no mocking him, no throwing banana peels at him. Yes I'm looking at you Sheshet. Yes I'm looking at you Baruch.

Meeting adjourned, said Rav Huna. Kappara, please stick around.

Rav Huna: We need to fill out these HR forms regarding our ignorance of Abba's, if you will, extra-clinical affairs.

Bar Kappara: Sure, master.

Rav Huna: Something on your mind, K.?

Bar Kappara: So he got the AM/PM mixed up, and now we have no Abba. Master, did you-

Rav Huna: Don't ask me about my business, K., not even this one time.

The Soup Nazi

GEMARAH:

Nazis, I hate these guys! said Rav Huna convening the meeting.

What is the Halakhah on buying soup from a Nazi? Is it permissible? asked Bar Kappara.

I would think not, said Yontl the Librarian, flipping through the Mishnah, but admittedly coming up with little.

Purchasing soup from someone complicit in the extermination of six million Israelites is abhorrent, said Rabbah. I don't even think a gourmand like Rav Sheshet would buy soup from a Nazi. Would you Sheshet?

Of course not, said Rav Sheshet, how can you even ask me that? And my porcine countenance does not mean I eat "like a pig," if that's what you were implying, Rabbah.

Actually I think he was calling you fat, speculated Rav Pappa.

Baruch the Chimp nodded in agreement.

Does it matter what kind of soup it is? Asked Rabbah. It's a mitzvah to consume matzoh ball soup, whereas lobster bisque is treyf.*

A Nazi with matzoh balls is still a Nazi, replied Bar Kappara.

But what if you are starving in the ghetto, and the only soup available is being dished out by the Nazi, should it not be permissible then? asked Shimon ben Pazi.

There is no evidence in "The Soup Nazi" of a famine in progress, countered Bar Kappara. George was seen munching – albeit with little joy – on cereal in Jerry's apartment.

You cannot blame the Seinfeld Four for succumbing to the Nazi soup, said Rav Pappa. Much like Fascism, the soup was an alluring temptation. It was an opportunity to be part of something bigger than yourself, so long as you obeyed the rules. The Soup Nazi demanded perfection from his soup; how could he tolerate anything less from his customers?

I'm surprised at you, Pappa, said Rav Sheshet. I assumed you would have been deeply offended by Jerry's betrayal of Sheila to the Fascist thugs for a bowl of soup.

I didn't care for that Sheila, said Rav Pappa. I don't care for this whole "Shmoopy" business.

Maybe we should call Pappa "Shmoopy" from now on, suggested Rav Kahana.

You're Shmoopy, said Rav Pappa.

No you're Shmoopy, said Rav Sheshet

No you're Shmoopy, said Rav Pappa.

No you're Shmoopy, signed Baruch the Chimp.

Everyone, settle down, howled Bar Kappara. This is exactly what the Fascists want.

For us to start calling each other "Shmoopy"? asked a bemused Shimon ben Pazi.

No you yold, replied Bar Kappara, for us to start turning on each other. It is the first step in the process of social atomization. And look at the ingenuity of doing it with shmoop.

You mean soup, said Rabbah.

No I mean shmoop and soup, replied Bar Kappara. Brilliantly diabolical.

This is precisely why we need to applaud those who resisted the soup artisan's Nazi regime, said Rabbah.

Right, agreed Rav Kahana. Resistance is built upon the practices of everyday life. George asking for bread: it may seem like a small act, but in fact it constitutes a powerful weapon of the weak, as argued by James C. Scott.

Or in this case, the weapon of the short, stocky, slow-witted, bald man, added Rav Sheshet, elbowing Baruch the Chimp.

Agreed, said Abba the Surgeon, marching through the door, though HR now insists we call George: "an altitudinally-compact, full figured, neurodivergent, follicly-challenged person who identifies as male."

Abba, you're back! said the Sages in unison.

How did he get out so soon? asked Bar Kappara.

I pleaded no contest and promised to implement state guidelines in this institution of higher learning. They empowered me.

Can you believe this guy? said Rav Pappa.

Oh you better believe it. And my pronouns are they, them, and their.

I don't want to live under his – sorry their – Nazi regime. Next thing we know they'll be unleashing the Gazpacho Police on us, said Shimon ben Pazi.

Hey Pazi, said Rav Huna, are you making a clever pun, or did you happen to vote Republican in the last election?

The Secret Code

GEMARAH:

Friends, said Rav Huna convening the meeting, there are some interesting things to discuss with "The Secret Code."

Where's Abba? asked Rav Pappa.

I made sure to schedule the shiur at the time of his – sorry I mean their – court hearing, replied Rav Huna. In light of this episode's plotline, I expect the fat and crippled jokes to be flying from my ever so mature flock. Abba is the last thing we need.

Hey, give me some credit, Huna, retorted Rav Pappa. Ever since my accident in eastern Europe, I have been very sensitive to the feelings of the disabled. All my lame jokes will be accompanied with trigger warnings. Get it? I made a pun.

And we are all very impressed, said Bar Kappara.

But seriously, said Rav Pappa. Why would a disabled man call his store "Leapin' Larry's," employ a co-worker who laughs at his handicap, and then get mad at Jerry for imitating him? Shouldn't Larry have more of a sense of humor?

One can only make jokes about the disabled if one is disabled, replied Rabbah. Jerry is not disabled. Hence that joke, even if it was inadvertent, was punching down. Jerry, like us, is a Jew. So Jerry, like us, can make Jewish jokes without being branded an antisemite.

So given that I am handicapped, I can make fun of Leapin' Larry? asked Rav Pappa.

In theory, yes, replied Rav Huna.

Then I say he's a lame-o and Jerry did the right thing by burning down his store, declared Rav Pappa. Larry may have a wooden leg, but he also has a stick up his ass.

The astonished Sages stared at Rav Pappa in unison.

You are a cruel man Pappa, said Rav Sheshet. What did Leapin' Larry ever do to you?

Nothing, replied Rav Pappa. I'm just exercising my entitlement as a disabled person. But I will say this: Abba the Surgeon is responsible for exacerbating more people's disabilities than healing them. For starters, he left me all lopsided – sorry I mean "unevenly divergent." He's more of a butcher than Zutra the Mohel.

Thank you, replied Zutra the Mohel, who knew when it was best to keep his objections to himself.

Why are you people speaking of Abba's ineptitude and Larry's disability rather than the key takeaway from "The Secret Code"? said Bar Kappara. The Seinfeld body count has risen again, this time at the hands of Costanza. George killed Peterman's mother and would have let the guy at the bank machine burn to death had he gotten his way.

First off, Jerry and to a certain extent Kramer, not George, are responsible for the fire, replied Rav Sheshet. And second, I see no evidence that George killed Mrs. Peterman.

"Bosco" triggered her death, said Rabbah. It was the last thing she heard, and it was the final word to emanate from her mouth in horror as she entered the great beyond. "Bosco."

That's absurd, said Rav Pappa. Words can't kill someone.

Did you not read your HR manual, Pappa? asked Rabbah. The office of Diversity, Equity, and Inclusion has made it clear that linguistic violence is as deadly as physical violence. Thus if one of us made fun of your "lame jokes," we'd be guilty of perpetuating linguistic violence against you, a disabled rabbi.

How exactly is "Bosco" a form of linguistic violence? asked Shimon ben Pazi.

The Sages sat in silence.

Because Bosco, to quote Kramer is "the dark master," replied Rav Sheshet. It evokes images of brutality and enslavement.

Believe it or not, it also evokes images of chocolate, added Rav Pappa. So if you are suggesting that George's mentioning of chocolate syrup is an instance of him committing homicide, then I will quote Resh Lakish from an earlier shiur: "This is quite possibly the silliest discussion we've had since the day we debated whether or not Moby Dick swallowed George in New York Harbor."

And I still say George sojourned in the belly of the great fish! exclaimed Shimon ben Pazi.

Mammal, interjected Rabbah.

Whatever, replied Shimon ben Pazi.

On that note, let's end this incredibly successful shiur, said Rav Huna. That makes two in a row.

Successful? Have you lost your marbles, Master? asked a dubious Bar Kappara.

Yontl, can you please read through the minutes from the past two meetings, asked Rav Huna, and tell us how many times we discussed shmekls, petzls dingdongs, shlongs, and beytzim? Or for that matter urine and feces?

Aside from one rather oblique reference to matzoh balls yesterday, not once! said Yontl the Librarian.

I think we can now claim to be a fine institution of higher learning, packed with mature and intelligent rabbis, said Rav Huna. Even Baruch has contributed in his own way.

Ooh ooh aah aah said the Sages in unison, as they headed for the door.

The Pool Guy

GEMARAH:

And the Seinfeld body count continues to rise, said a gleeful Abba the Surgeon, convening the meeting.

Objection! Why is Abba running the shiur? asked an already irritated Rav Pappa.

Because the office of Diversity, Equity, and Inclusion empowered him to clean up our discourse, lamented Bar Kappara.

It's "them," not "him," replied Abba the Surgeon. Mind your pronouns.

See what I mean, replied Bar Kappara.

Objection! said Rav Kahana. Torah was divinely revealed at Sinai and *Seinfeld* was divinely revealed at Monk's; both are perfect. Abba is not above either of them, even with a mandate from HR.

The script is our Scripture and *Seinfeld* is our Sinai. If our Talmud evokes petzls and beytzim, such is the content of our discussions, insisted Rav Pappa. End of discussion.

Please say "sexual organs usually identified as male," interjected Abba the Surgeon.

PENIS, DINGDONG, SHLONG, retorted Rav Pappa.

You see what's happening, said Rabbah: worlds are colliding. HR and *Seinfeld* are having a conflict of interest.

A Yeshivah divided against itself cannot stand, said Rav Kahana.

And we Sages are caught in the deep end of the pool clutching our Rabbi Johnsons. Our beytzim will bear the brunt of this, added Rav Pappa clearly trying to get a rise out of Abba.

That was your last warning Pappa. I am reporting you to HR forthwith for referring to your anatomical member with a sagely honorific. You're in deep trouble now, you and your "Little Rabbi" will be disciplined, said Abba the Surgeon, leaving the room in a huff.

Well what should we do? asked Shimon ben Pazi.

Maybe we should get our fat porcine friend Rav Sheshet to pull a Newman and jump on Abba the next time he's in the mikvah, suggested Rav Pappa. He will never be able to withstand the weight of a portly pig man.

I would be happy to, said Rav Sheshet, who saw this as an opportunity to demonstrate that even pig men are a useful contribution to diversity, for he too had read the HR brochure. And I will take Baruch with me as well. And if necessary, neither of us will give him mouth to mouth.

Perfect, said Rav Pappa.

But then Sheshet and Baruch will be in trouble with HR, said an alarmed Bar Kappara.

No they won't, interjected Rav Huna. The office of DEI would never prosecute either the humanoid or hominid divergent. And yes, I am taking this straight from their policy manual. Sheshet and Baruch are ideal for the task.

Terrific, said Rav Pappa. Then may I suggest once they're at it, they should also pee on Abba's couch for good measure. They will have urination immunity as well, which ironically Seinfeld and Costanza have been trying to acquire since Season 3.

Ooh Ooh Aah Aah, assented Baruch the Chimp who also gave the international sign for "accidental couch urination."

With any luck, concluded Rav Huna, by this time tomorrow, Abba will be in a coma, and we will show him all the respect that a good coma deserves. But this is my Yeshivah, damnit, and all future rulings on petzls and pronouns will come from me alone.

The Sponge

GEMARAH:

Friends, said Rav Huna, convening the meeting. Today we need to discuss … um … birth control.

Yo-Yo Ma! exclaimed Rav Pappa.

Ooh Ooh Aah Aah! exclaimed Baruch the Chimp.

To be discussed with all the dignity one expects from Jews. And monkeys. Added Bar Kappara.

Master, is it not a problem for us to discuss this topic? asked Rabbah.

How so? replied Rav Huna.

Because during our discussion of "The Shoes" we concluded that we possess little ability to know what women think, let alone how to write them into the script, said Rabbah.

Indeed, said Rav Sheshet. If I may quote our absent colleague Resh Lakish, from Season 4: "I don't even know what women think. That's why I'm never with any, but instead sit in this Yeshivah day after day poring over the excruciating minutiae of every single event with a gaggle of sweaty rabbis. No offense."

Good ole Lakish. Maybe we should invite him back, said Rav Kahana. That's the second time we've quoted him in recent days.

Sheshet has a point, said Bar Kappara. How in good conscience can we, a bunch of hirsute men, discuss Elaine combing the underbelly of New York in order to hoard sponges so she can turn her apartment into Bourbon Street?

She bought an entire crate, said Rav Kahana. Does that not make her a fallen woman driven by insatiable carnality?

Beats me. As a responsible monogamous rabbi, I have no way of knowing if a crate of sponges is excessive or not, said Bar Kappara. Is it debaucherous or just responsible planning? What say you Pappa?

Are you asking if I'm sponge worthy? replied Rav Pappa. I have yet to fail an interview.

No we are asking your opinion of Elaine's hoarding, replied Bar Kappara.

I for one admire Elaine's tenacity, said Rav Pappa. And she is sexually judicious. Did you note the interrogation she gave her prospective mate before consenting to treat his body like an amusement park? She even forced him to agree to trim his sideburns.

Agreed, said Rami bar Hama. How many of us would trim our peyos for a woman?

I cut my sidelocks for no one, said Rav Yehudah.

And perhaps that's why you haven't gotten laid in two years, Yehudah, retorted Rav Pappa.

Objection! said Rav Yehudah.

No I'll allow it. You need to get out more Yehudah, and perhaps trim those sideburns, said Rav Huna, relishing every moment of Abba the Surgeon's absence.

No I agree with Rabbah, said Bar Kappara. Look at Jerry. He couldn't figure Lena out. She was such a kind, giving person, a tzaddik by any yardstick who even took the trouble to check what kind of soup they had at the soup kitchen. Yet she was running a sponge empire out of her closet without shame. Like Jerry, I just can't figure women out.

Yes, Pappa? asked Bar Kappara, you look like you want to add something.

No, it's just that "soup" and "sponges," there's a matzoh ball joke in there somewhere, but I'm drawing a blank, replied Rav Pappa. Just try to ignore me.

We usually do, signed Baruch the Chimp.

Friends, I'm afraid we need to raise the topic of admitting women into the Yeshivah again, said Rav Huna. It's our only hope of understanding the opposite sex.

Torah study is for men, a woman's place is in the home, said Rav Sheshet.

May I point out, said Rav Yehudah, that we have admitted a monkey to our study hall, and as of last week we have a rabbi – granted a rabbi in a coma, but a rabbi nevertheless – who has come out as non-binary. Surely admitting a woman is hardly contravening any of our current practices?

By the way, interjected Rav Huna with a devious smile, Abba is out of their coma, and they will be back at the Yeshivah once Zutra finishes operating on them.

A third-rate mohel who got his smicha from a Cracker Jack box is operating on a man in a coma? said Rabbah in shock.

As luck would have it, Zutra was on the scene of Abba's "accident." And Abba's a "they" now, not quite a man. Zutra of course took this into account in performing the surgery. Please, let's get back to the topic at hand. I agree with Yehudah. We need to admit women. Now if only we knew some women.

And here comes Pappa to the rescue! said Rav Pappa. Pappa will bring women to us. Pappa will roam the streets. Pappa will preach, beseech, and unleash his best "come to Pappa" charm until you have women begging to study *Seinfeld* in our Academy.

But any woman admitted has to be an intellectual, said Rav Huna.

Pappa says no problem, boasted Rav Pappa.

And she has to know both Torah and *Seinfeld*, said Bar Kappara.

Pappa says piece of cake, boasted Rav Pappa again.

And most importantly Pappa cannot have had slept with her, said Rav Huna. You got that Pappa?

Pappa will inevitably have to plead the Fifth, lamented Rav Pappa.

I still don't know what that means, said Bar Kappara.

Oy gevalt, we are screwed, said Rav Huna. Pappa, take Baruch with you, he'll keep you an honest man. We're adjourned until our academy has a female student enrolled who is Pappa-free.

Or she'll need a little shot of penicillin, added Rav Sheshet.

The Gum

GEMARAH:

Fellow Sages, said Rav Huna convening the shiur, welcome back. Look around and you will see the room is a bit more crowded today. We have some new members and some...unexpected... returnees.

First let's welcome back Abba the Surgeon, said Bar Kappara. Their surgery was only a partial success, which explains the silence we anticipate from them today. And let's also welcome back Resh Lakish, whose recovery from surgery also took an unanticipated turn for the worse.

What happened? asked Rabbah, feigning concern.

Let's just say HR's DEI policy guidelines for neurodivergence are now particularly relevant.

I don't follow, said a bemused Shimon ben Pazi.

Let's just say they are living on their own, the whole world is smiling with them, and we think it's the tops, added Rav Huna.

He means they spent time in the loony bin, said Rav Pappa. Complete mental breakdown because they were mishandled by questionably credentialed surgeons.

But we are convinced they are still industrious fellows who can accomplish anything they set their minds to, added Bar Kappara beaming with confidence. And that's the tops.

And now let me welcome the Pumbedita Yeshiva's first two female rabbis, said a glowing Rav Pappa. Over here we have Deena Lazarovich whose father tuned up my "ASSMAN" Camel in his body shop, and next to her we have Ruthie Cohen, who knows all about horses.

I have a question, said a sluggish Abba. Am I crazy or are those, women in the Aca-aca-academy?

No you're not crazy, Abba, replied Bar Kappara. We had a policy change.

But that's no reason to get excited, you're still the tops, said Rav Sheshet slowly. Here let me help you with your comic book.

Why is he speaking to that Rabbi like that? asked Rabba Deena.

Because Abba was in the nuthouse and Sheshet thinks it necessary to coddle the crazies because of his own unfortunate pig man condition. A bit ironic, no? Welcome to our gaggle of sweaty humanoid and hominid adjacent special needs rabbis! quipped Rav Pappa.

There you go again, Pappa. Just like last night. Taking pleasure in the misfortune of others! replied an angry Deena.

It's not just me, all the rabbis do that, insisted Rav Pappa.

Last night? said Bar Kappara. Rabba Deena, may I ask– how shall I put this – did you deem Rav Pappa sponge worthy?

Don't lie Pappa, said Resh Lakish, finally speaking up. I heard animal noises emanating from your house and they weren't from Baruch who had already left for Sheshet's to watch Jeopardy.

Rav Pappa and Rabba Deena lowered their heads in shame.

Rabba Deena, we will have to ask you to leave, said Rav Huna. Your membership presents a conflict of interest.

But feel free to take this vial of penicillin on your way out, added Zutra the Mohel, who was now the acting chief physician and pharmacist for the community.

Well what now? lamented Bar Kappara.

Hey, we still have Ruthie Cohen, said Rav Pappa. And I guarantee you we have not shtupped.

But beyond horses, what are her qualifications? asked Rabbah.

Isn't it obvious? said Shimon ben Pazi. She's a Cohen, a descendant of the priesthood.

OK she can stay, said Rav Huna. Let's celebrate. Anyone for gum?

The Sages sat around chewing lo-mein gum from Chinatown.

Now this is what the rabbinate is all about, said Shimon ben Pazi. The most brilliant minds in Judaism sitting around enjoying a chew.

The Sages continued to chew their lo-mein-y gum from Chinatown.

And we think this is just the tops, said Abba the Surgeon and Resh Lakish in unison, while Baruch the Chimp signed for them.

The Rye

GEMARAH:

Friends, said Rav Huna, convening the meeting, we need to discuss the many layers of this historic Ross and Costanza clan gathering.

It was the ultimate clash of Jew vs. Gentile, said Bar Kappara.

The Merlot represented the blood of the Christ, whereas the marble rye was Costanza's bread of affliction – our Jewish affliction – preached Rabbah with great erudition.

Yet they almost found common ground over the chicken, the hen, and the rooster, noted Rav Kahana. A perverse and fowl ménage à trois. Pun intended.

There is nothing foul about the fowl fornication in question, said Rav Pappa. As the resident orgy guy, I believe that diversity, equity, and inclusion entails extending these carnal privileges to the animal kingdom.

Is it true that they're all having sex with the chicken? asked Shimon ben Pazi? I'm not sure why the chicken would want to get it on with both the rooster and the hen.

Is this like Bonnie wanting to have sex with "two Georges" in "The Label Maker"? As an insurance policy against unpredictable orgasms?

Close, but not exactly, replied Rav Pappa. It's because the rooster does not always want to do everything, much like John Germane. The chicken is all hot and heavy, but the rooster's repertoire is devoid of a few numbers. The hen picks up some of the slack. Yet the goys hunt the poor hen for game. That's the great perversion here.

That is so perverse, said Shimon ben Pazi. And hot and heavy.

And the chicken will remain unsatiated by the surviving rooster after the poor game hen gets massacred by goys with guns.

Maybe we should get some female input, said Rami bar Hama, given the nature of the topic.

All eyes turned to Ruthie Cohen.

I would rather talk about horse manure, said Ruthie Cohen.

Rabba Cohen, I'm afraid we already discussed manure during Season 6, when George almost stepped in it, said Bar Kappara. And we likely discussed it on other occasions as well. We are a "manure positive" Yeshivah, as HR would put it. After all it's just a "nure" with a "ma" in front of it. It's pretty refreshing.

So we invite you to peruse our archive for what you have missed, suggested Rav Huna. It's searchable by keyword, but be sure to enter "dung," "fart," and "poopoo" along with "manure" into the Oral Torah search engine.

But there is a talmudic conundrum here, replied Ruthie Cohen. Kramer proved grossly negligent and demonstrated cruelty to his horse by feeding it Beefarino. He then allowed it to defecate in the street, ruining the Rosses' anniversary while soiling the city. It was his burden to remove the manure from the streets of New York, yet he did no such thing. There's nothing refreshing here. Kramer has no business conducting carriage rides. He has no business being around horses. And I know my horses.

Perhaps this is why Manya got chased out of Poland, suggested Rav Sheshet. She never cleaned up her pony's manure.

Incorrect, countered Rav Pappa, because we have already established that Manya's pony was in fact a horse-faced relative from the Horse-Faced House of Seinfeld. It is an equinoid family, much as yours, Sheshet, can be classified as a sussoid domesticoid one.

Baruch nodded in agreement, while frantically signing the various scientific terms denoting his fellow animals and the animal adjacent.

Then Manya had an obligation to clean her horse-faced relatives' manure from the streets of Poland, maintained Rav Sheshet.

You people seem to have a bizarre obsession with the animal kingdom, mused Ruthie Cohen. Pappa, you never told me this was the nature of your shiurs.

What do you mean? replied Rav Pappa.

Well in the past 10 minutes we've discussed chickens, hens, roosters, horse-faced Jews, and pig men, with the insinuation that some may be shtupping others. Then you all turned to an ape for validation.

Do you not concur with Baruch's zoological conclusions? said Bar Kappara. I must point out that Baruch has seniority over you, Rabba Ruthie.

Baruch bowed his head in recognition.

I'm leaving, said an exasperated Ruthie Cohen, as she stormed out the door.

Well, we gave the woman thing a shot, said Rav Pappa. Perhaps they are not ready for the rabbinate.

Or at least the few in town you haven't slept with are not equipped for the rabbinate, noted Rav Sheshet.

Still, we need to commend Baruch on his erudition and patience, said Rav Sheshet. I think he deserves a promotion. We should bestow him with a new title. Let's call him Maestro because of how well he has conducted himself.

You guys are the best colleagues an ape could ever ask for, signed Maestro Baruch the Chimp, as he headed out the door for his auto-erotic evening activities.

The Caddy

GEMARAH:

Friends, said Rav Huna, convening the meeting. This episode leaves me perplexed. I fail to see how Sue Ellen Mischke, the bra-less wonder, could wreak such havoc across the New York landscape.

Indeed, said Rav Pappa. It makes no sense. I know parts of Pumbedita where women wear nothing on their upper bodies.

Where exactly is this? asked a curious Rami bar Hama.

Uh … nowhere you know, replied Rav Pappa sheepishly. But my point is that wearing a top without a bra is no big deal. After all, Resh Lakish walked around without a bro or a mansier for years before we finally said anything about his man boobs.

Yeah and look at what happened to the poor zhlob, said Rabbah. We talked him into getting superfluous surgery at the hands of Abba the Ukrainian butcher, who was then forced into surgery himself by our resident mohel Zutra, also a butcher and even less talented than Abba.

Indeed, Lakish's gimel-cup bazongas created a chain of events that led to the psychiatric crippling of two of our finest minds, said Bar Kappara.

Finest minds!? exclaimed a doubtful Rav Kahana. I would say the change in them is barely perceptible, except they are far less voluble.

Fair enough, said Bar Kappara.

OK, I can now understand, how this *Seinfeld* episode makes sense, said Rav Pappa. Sue Ellen's convention-flouting bosom-flaunting engendered a car crash and George's alleged death. Lakish's bosomy yichus likewise engendered the near death of two rabbis. Both in our academy and on *Seinfeld* unfettered boobies precipitated calamity.

And I can't help but wonder what would have been, had Lakish taken our advice and worn a mansier, said Rav Huna. This entire catastrophe could have been averted.

But what if Lakish had walked the streets of Pumbedita wearing a bro with no top? asked Rabbah.

Then the residents of Pumbedita would have fled in horror, joked Rav Sheshet, elbowing Baruch the Chimp.

You are wrong, squawked Resh Lakish with great effort from the special needs corner of the study hall. They were real and they were spectacular.

And sadly the only person who can vouch for this, lamented Bar Kappara, is our erstwhile surgeon who now sits in the corner drooling.

I think we should disband on that note, said Rav Huna. Besides it's five o'clock Primate Standard Time. As per the DEI policy manual, it is time for Lakish and Abba to be taken for their walks. And it's your turn to walk them, Baruch.

The Seven

GEMARAH:

Friends, said Rav Huna convening the meeting. There are a handful of issues that came up in "The Seven" that we need to debate. Who wants to start?

OK, said Rabbah, here's the first issue on the table: Why in the world would Costanza make such a tzimmes over a silly name like "Seven."

Actually, "Seven" – "Shevah" – is a pretty common Jewish name throughout eastern Europe, said Rav Pappa. I made it with quite a few of them in the Polish Corridor.

This would be so much more Seinfeldesque if you made it with someone named "Six," noted Rav Sheshet: "I had sex with Six" brings to mind "The Lip Reader."

A good point, Sheshet, said Rav Pappa giving his porcine colleague a rare compliment. I'll be on the lookout for "Sixes" on my next sojourn.

So I guess in choosing the name "Seven" Costanza is merely a Jew being true to his heritage, said Rav Kahana. We've already established his Israelite yichus.

You know you're right, said Bar Kappara. This really isn't much of an issue.

OK, second issue on the table: Why does Jerry's girlfriend Christie wear the same outfit on every date? asked Bar Kappara.

I don't see what the big deal is, said Rabbah. We wear the same outfits every day, and they are far less dazzling than that superhero dress.

Then perhaps she's a Jew and a rabbi to boot, said Shimon ben Pazi.

That's ridiculous. A Jew named Christie?! said Bar Kappara. There has never been a Jew, let alone a rabbi, with THAT Goyish name.

Sure there has, said Rav Pappa. That superhero superstar Jesus the Christ was a Jew and his flock called him "Rabbi."

You know you're right, said Bar Kappara. This really isn't much of an issue.

OK, third issue on the table, said Rav Pappa: Newman ruling that the bicycle should be cut in half.

I know. It's a complete appropriation of our culture, said Rabbah. All he did was plagiarize from our Scripture.

Well perhaps Newman is a Jew, suggested Shimon ben Pazi.

That's ridiculous, said Bar Kappara. He's someone, as Jerry put it, "whose heart is so dark, it cannot be swayed by pity, compassion, or human emotion of any kind." He's also a sadistic mailman. There has never been such a vicious diabolical Yid in the uniform of that goyish postal profession.

Sure there has, said Rav Pappa. The Son of Sam, David Berkowitz, was a Jew, though admittedly nobody on his postal route called him "Rabbi."

You know you're right, said Bar Kappara. This really isn't much of an issue.

So it would seem everyone in this *Seinfeld* episode is unexpectedly Jewish, said Rav Huna.

Not quite, interjected Rav Pappa. No way Kramer's friend Jay Riemenschneider is Jewish. Kramer said Riemenschneider "eats horse all the time." Jews don't eat horse; it is treyf of the highest order; the food of peasants.

I disagree, said Rabbah. I would say it is more than likely that Manya ate her horse and was thus required to flee Poland. And Manya was certainly Jewish. Why else would she leave a country packed with ponies to come to a non-pony country unless she had eaten her pony?

I disagree, said Rav Pappa. We've already established that Manya's horse was in fact her horse-faced relative from the House of Seinfeld, a Polish cousin Jeffrey, if you will.

Eating a horse-faced sibling is not kosher, noted Yontl, perhaps not quite as goyish as eating an actual horse, but treyf nonetheless.

So we can conclude that this entire episode was oozing with Jewishness, save for Jay Riemenschneider, the eater of horse meat, said Rav Huna.

Unless Jay Riemenschneider ate horse-faced Cousin Jeffrey.

The Sages meditated on this point, chewing their leftover Chinese gum.

Ah but did Jay Riemenschneider wear the same outfit everyday? added Shimon ben Pazi.

Or did he ever rule that a horse should be split in two to satisfy two rival claimants? added Rav Pappa.

Neither of which would make him Jewish, said an exasperated Bar Kappara.

You know Einstein wore the exact same outfit everyday and for all we know he ate horse, said Shimon ben Pazi, and Einstein was Jewish.

Well, if Jay Riemenschneider ever splits the atom, we can admit him into the Tribe.

The Cadillac

GEMARAH:

Friends, said Rav Huna convening the meeting, today we shall discuss whether or not having coffee constitutes cheating.

Obviously it does, replied Bar Kappara, how is this even a question?

I disagree, said Rav Pappa.

And...here we go, said the Sages in unison.

We need to take several factors into account, continued Rav Pappa. First, Susan is a horrible person, universally hated among critics of the show. Second, we are talking about Marisa Tomei, not some random shiksa from the marketplace. Third, George does not understand the implications of "coffee." We already established that in "The Phone Message" during Season 2.

Agreed, said Rami bar Hama, who as usual felt it necessary to stick up for his perverted friend. George thinks an invitation to coffee is a request to be on 24-hour missile watch. Forgive Costanza, fellow Rabbis, for the short stocky slow-witted bald man, knows not what he does.

You mean the short quirky, funny, bald man, retorted Rav Sheshet shaking his head. Costanza knew full well what this was all about, much as he did when he indirectly asked the Rabbi in Elaine's building if visiting a prostitute while engaged constitutes cheating.

But it's Marisa Tomei, countered Rav Pappa. She even took pleasure in Costanza's musings on manure.

Again, with the manure, grumbled Bar Kappara.

If we are going to debate manure again, perhaps we need to invite Ruthie Cohen back, suggested Rabbah.

No she's not welcome, said Bar Kappara. Why? Because I believe she has NOW been violated by our insatiable Rav Pappa. Isn't that right Pappa?

It's true, concurred Rav Kahana. I saw her riding around town with Pappa, and they were neither on a horse, nor Pappa's "ASSMAN" camel, but on a luxury two-humped camel.

Care to explain yourself, Pappa? asked Rav Huna.

About the sex or about the camel? replied Rav Pappa.

No, the camel, you shmendrik, replied Rav Huna. We've come to know your carnal proclivities, but your camel proclivities remain a mystery. We want to know how someone on your paltry rabbinic salary could afford a two-humped Bactrian camel – The Cadillac of camels – when the rest of us are riding around on one-humped Dromedaries.

Uh, well, I decided to expand my importing business into the realm of exporting, replied Rav Pappa.

What exactly do you trade in, Pappa? asked Bar Kappara.

I run a dating service, as I mentioned a few weeks ago. I fix up eligible Gentile maidens with sweaty large-nosed Jewish men, said Rav Pappa.

You went ahead with "Shiksa dot com"? said an angry Rav Huna. We put the kibosh on that!

I cleared it with HR, replied Rav Pappa. And, moreover, that's why I have the two-humped camel, for business. Makes transportation easier. That's also why Ruthie Cohen was riding with me. I was fixing her up.

But Ruthie Cohen is Jewish, so how could she be eligible to participate in "Shiksa dot com"? said Rabbah.

She's not Jewish, replied Rav Pappa.

Her name is Cohen! exclaimed Bar Kappara.

She spells is Cone, replied Rav Pappa. And she hates being mistaken for a Jew. She's a bit of an antisemite if you ask me.

If she hates being mistaken for a Jew, then why does she want to be fixed up with one, asked Rabbah. And for that matter why would she enter our Yeshivah as our first female Rabbi?

I'm beginning to suspect that Ruthie Cone is really Jewish, much as Donna Chang is really Jewish, said Rav Huna.

Do we also suspect that Ruthie Cone is from Long Island? asked Shimon ben Pazi.

Pazi, that's absolutely ridicurous, joked Rav Sheshet, elbowing Maestro

Baruch who had finally caught up on Season 6.

Well if HR gave Pappa the go ahead, there's little we can do, said Rav Huna. But I suggest we open an investigation, lest he is embezzling Yeshivah funds to afford a Bactrian camel.

I say no investigation, declared Rav Sheshet, with Baruch nodding vigorously in agreement.

The Sages stared at Rav Sheshet in disbelief.

I know what's going on here, said Resh Lakish, who was slowly regaining some of his faculties. Sheshet and perhaps his Simian companion are making use of Pappa's services.

It's true, conceded Rav Sheshet. Pappa has an inclusive humanoid and hominid adjacent policy, so long as you're Jewish. And Baruch is of the Tribe now. He took the plunge in the mikvah last week.

Who the hell converted an ape to Judaism? asked Bar Kappara.

The Reconstructionists, replied Rav Sheshet. And HR says we have to accept their Halakhah on matters of conversion. Again, it's all about inclusivity, and, as a recovering pig man once in denial, I'm inclined to agree with their policy, lest I suffer humiliating exclusion and excommunication myself.

Has he been circumcised yet? asked Rav Huna with growing disbelief.

Tomorrow, replied Zutra the Mohel. It will be the 8th day since his rebirth, as the Reconstructionists call it. My knives are being sharpened as we speak. And you're all invited!

I object! said Abba the Surgeon, who was also regaining some of his faculties. You can't circumcise an animal.

Not so, replied Zutra. As the Lord said to Abraham: "For the generations to come every male among you who is eight days old must be circumcised, including those born in your household or bought with money from a foreigner – those who are not your offspring." (Genesis 17:12). According to the office of Diversity, Equity, and Inclusion, "foreigner" includes the human adjacent. So no, perhaps you can't circumcise an elephant, but a monkey is very much on the table. And, accordingly, Baruch will be on MY table – tomorrow at 5 Primate Standard Time.

And you're OK with this Baruch? asked Bar Kappara.

Baruch nodded in agreement.

Actually, he was on the fence, said Rav Sheshet. But it was the opportunity to qualify as a candidate for Pappa's ritual mating and dating service that won him over.

Meanwhile, I have business to attend to, said Rav Pappa getting up to leave. If anyone is interested in being mated, please swing by. And yes, Ruthie Cone is still available.

The Shower Head

GEMARAH:

Friends, said Rav Huna convening the meeting, this episode raises some existential issues about the very essence of our being.

Agreed, said Rav Bar Kappara. Who would have thought Uncle Leo could experience antisemitism in such a Jewish milieu.

There's no evidence that Monk's is a Jewish milieu, said Rabbah. Moreover, as Rav Pappa suggested recently, the cashier Ruthie Cone seems to possess a touch of anti-Jewish bigotry herself.

Is this the first instance in history of an antisemite trying to smite a Jew by overcooking their hamburger? asked Rav Sheshet.

Surely, someone must have overcooked a Jew's meat in Nazi Germany, suggested Rav Pappa. Yontl, is there anything in the history books?

Art Spiegelman's *Maus* depicts a bunch of cats distributing undercooked meat to a bunch of mice deemed unfit for labor, read Yontl the Librarian. With extreme cruelty, they also withheld the requisite ketchup and side of fries.

The Sages grumbled in unison.

Perhaps this is why Manya ate her horse? The Nazis forced her to consume her pony after invading Poland, suggested Rav Sheshet.

I wouldn't be surprised if they did so, and I'm sure they withheld the ketchup and fries as well, said Rav Kahana.

Does *Maus* depict any mice eating horse? asked Rav Pappa.

Again, we've already established that her horse was in fact a horse-faced relative from the House of Seinfeld, said Rav Pappa.

Is it possible Manya ate her horse-faced relative under the gun of the antisemites? asked Shimon ben Pazi.

Imagine being forced to eat Cousin Jeffrey, said Resh Lakish. With or without a side of fries.

But this makes no sense, said Bar Kappara. If Uncle Leo's burger was overcooked because of antisemitism, then why was Jerry oblivious to it?

Isn't it obvious? replied Rav Pappa. Because he was making out during *Schindler's List*, probably during the notorious cheeseburger scene. He was not equipped to pick up on the warning signs of anti-Jewish burger bigotry.

This is the great tragedy of the American Jewish diaspora, said Bar Kappara. They erroneously believe they are safely ensconced in security and empowerment, until Goebbels overcooks their meat and it is too late to act.

Instead they do the talk show circuit, making jokes about Jewish paranoia, said Rabbah. They mock their own relatives and nation for having a persecution mentality. Ruthie Cone is even worse; she denies her Jewish identity, she shortchanged George, then she rode off like a Cossack into Central park on horseback.

But nobody forced her to eat her horse, said Shimon ben Pazi. If she ate it, then it was, much like Jay Riemenschneider, by choice, in which case she's not Jewish.

The Sages stared at Shimon ben Pazi in silence.

No comment about Ruthie Cone, but I disagree as far as Jerry and George go, said Rav Sheshet. This is why they were both trying to ship their parents off to Florida. They wanted to save them from the Meat-Nazis by sending them to an Early Bird Jewish state. A land of Israelites where Jews preside over condo associations in nothing but swimming trunks, and where you can get a tenderloin, salad, and baked potato for $4.95.

Theodor Herzl's dream, said Rav Pappa. As Abba Eban put it, "There is no difference whatever between antisemitism and the denial of Jewish meathood."

With all due respect, said Resh Lakish, sharing ethno-national space with Jack Klompus would be a nightmare, I don't care if everyone's Jewish and I don't care how good the meat is.

Surely, Lakish, you don't enjoy living among every Jew in this room? replied Rav Sheshet. Surely you must find some of us large-nosed sweaty rabbis grating?

To quote Rav Pappa, I'm pleading the Fifth.

The Doll

GEMARAH:

Friends, said Rav Huna convening the meeting, Resh Lakish, who has almost fully recovered, has asked if he could run the shiur today. He says he has a special topic for discussion.

Thank you, Rav Huna. But I'm afraid there is a problem. I bought this disturbingly hysterical piggy bank at the market that looked exactly like Rav Sheshet. It would have been conducive for a fruitful debate. But I tripped on my way over, dropped it, shattering it beyond recognition. So I've got nothing.

The Sages sat in silence looking at Rav Huna.

Well this is unexpected, said Bar Kappara. What will we debate, Huna?

I've got nothing, replied Rav Huna. I'm out of material.

The Sages sat in silence.

I can tell some Henny Youngman jokes, suggested Rav Pappa.

The Sages sat in silence.

We can discuss Styrofoam, suggested Rabbah, citing Reb Kramer.

Please, go ahead, said Rav Huna.

What is this stuff? Why do we need this stuff? And why do they make it so small? said Rabbah in his best Krameresque voice.

Probably because "they" need to seamlessly ensconce it in the packages "they" fill for safety purposes, replied Bar Kappara.

If only I had Styrofoam protecting my Sheshet piggy bank, lamented Resh Lakish.

The Sages sat in silence.

We can discuss our peyos and our beards, suggested Shimon ben Pazi.

Please, go ahead, said Rav Huna.

Why are our beards so long and our sidelocks oh so long and curly. Why do we need this stuff on our faces? said Shimon ben Pazi in his admittedly inferior Krameresque voice.

Because it is written: "Ye shall not round the corners of your heads, neither shalt thou mar the corners of thy beard." (Leviticus 19:27).

The Sages sat in silence.

But why do they have to be so long, persisted Shimon ben Pazi.

My fellow neurodivergent colleague Pazi has a point, said Resh Lakish. There's no reason they have to be this long. The Torah says nothing about length. It's a safety hazard. I tripped over my left sideburn this morning. That's how I fell and broke my little piggy bank at the market.

I also tripped over my sidelock recently, said Rav Pappa, and I dropped my roast beef and cried wee wee wee all the way home.

I think this is antisemitism, said Shimon ben Pazi.

How is this antisemitism? asked Bar Kappara.

Pazi's little hamster has gone to sleep at the wheel again, said Rav Pappa. You're the Tops, Pazi. Keep up the good work.

No I get it, said Rabbah, Pazi is correct. Because Pappa lost his roast beef! Yesterday we established that the breakdown of the Jewish-meat encounter in the diaspora is an instance of Jew-hatred. Pappa's soiled and spoiled roast beef is akin to Uncle Leo's overcooked hamburger.

But Pappa tripped and ruined his meat because he's a klutz, said an exasperated Bar Kappara. Goebbels neither tripped Pappa, nor overcooked his sandwich.

No there is very much a connection here, said Rav Sheshet. Much as there is a connection between Uncle Leo's hamburger and his equine adjacent relatives.

Are you suggesting that Cousin Jeffrey looks like a horse because of antisemitism? said Resh Lakish.

Yes, and the roots lie deep in Eastern Europe, going back to Manya and her horse-faced relatives in the Polish House of Seinfeld, said Rav Sheshet. In fact this may explain so much about the Holocaust.

Perhaps this is why Spiegelman drew his characters as animals, said Rav Pappa.

Then shouldn't he have drawn the Jews as horses rather than mice? said a vexed Bar Kappara.

Oh stop being such a literalist Kappara, said Rav Huna. The graphic novel is a metaphorical genre.

So drawing the horse-faced Jews as mice and Nazis as the cats is a metaphor, mused Bar Kappara.

And the Poles as pigs, no offense Sheshet, added Resh Lakish.

Poor Cousin Jeffrey, said Rav Kahana. What will he do when the Nazis come for him?

They're already coming for him, said Rabbah in alarm. That's why they overcooked Uncle Leo's hamburger.

Hey, has anyone noticed that Cousin Jeffrey's favorite animal is the Leopard? asked Rav Pappa.

Yes, and according to our records it is because he likes the spots, said Yontl the Librarian reading from the archived *Seinfeld* scripts.

Don't you see? said Rav Pappa. Cousin Jeffrey is attracted to the cat. much like the Jews of Germany couldn't resist the alluring culture of their Teutonic overlords, the horse-faced mouse is drawn to the cat. This is what Spiegelman had in mind.

The Second Holocaust has already begun, said Bar Kappara. First they came for Leo's hamburger and Jerry didn't speak up.

Then they came for my roast beef, and you all didn't speak up, added Rav Pappa.

Yontl, update the archive to include this warning to future generations, instructed Rav Huna. Chevreh, look what we achieved here today. We had nothing but a broken piggy bank, Styrofoam, and some soiled roast beef, yet we put our yiddishe kops together and may have averted genocide using nothing but our wits and a touch of literary theory.

The Friars Club

GEMARAH:

Fellow Sages, said Rav Huna convening the meeting, it appears Cosmo received some cosmic justice.

Yes, if anyone deserves to be drowned in a sack, it's one of the Seinfeld Four, said Rabbah.

Their wanton cruelty to animals and humans alike has finally caught up to them, added Abba the Surgeon with a sneer.

I too learned a great deal from this episode, said Shimon ben Pazi.

Why, Pazi? Because you are now prepared to follow Hillel the Elder's golden rule, "That which is hateful to you, do not do to your fellow man"? The Seinfeld Four clearly don't follow it.

No, replied Shimon ben Pazi. I learned that "Leonardo da Vinci" means "from Vinci." That must have been some book Kramer was reading. Did you know this, Yontl?

To be honest, I never really gave it much thought, said Yontl the Librarian, increasingly livid that his hard-earned doctorate was going to waste in the company of this gaggle of sweaty large nosed rabbis.

I've also taken up Kramer's sleep regimen, said Shimon ben Pazi with pride.

So have you woken up in the Euphrates in a sack yet? asked Rav Sheshet.

That would entail Pazi actually getting a date, retorted Rav Pappa.

Hey, you promised to set me up, Pappa, complained Shimon ben Pazi. We were going to be like the Gatsbys.

I tried, Pazi, but Ruthie Cone didn't think you were sponge worthy, said Rav Pappa. She only wants to date horseback riders and entertainers, like the kind who frequent the Friars Club.

Can we please get back to discussing the attempted "murder" of Cosmo Kramer? interjected Abba the Surgeon. How are you all not concerned that Kramer's girlfriend Connie is being unjustly charged for the crime?

But she had her thugs dump Kramer in a sack in the East River! exclaimed Rav Pappa. I don't care how many animals Kramer and his friends have killed over the years; no man deserves a watery grave. I have been scared to bring a woman home ever since watching this episode.

And we've all heard the cries of joy and relief from the fair maidens of Pumbedita, noted Resh Lakish. We are now a Pappa-petzl-free community. And the Persian government in gratitude has named us a model city and bestowed upon us a tax-exempt status.

Far be it from me to be ungrateful, given that my dating service has benefited from tax-exemption, replied Rav Pappa. Nevertheless, I take this as a personal insult. The government is acting as if Pumbedita is now a safer place because I remain celibate.

Safer and cleaner, added Rav Sheshet.

And far more hygienic, added Resh Lakish.

And far more dignified, added Rabbah.

And far less pregnant, noted Bar Kappara.

Objection! said Rav Pappa. I have always been deemed sponge worthy.

Really, Pappa? said Bar Kappara. You've never slipped one past the goalie in all these years?

I am hereby ending this shiur using my now patented aphorism, "I plead the Fifth." Meeting adjourned.

The Wig Master

GEMARAH:

Imagine someone coming to stay with you for two weeks, said Rav Huna, convening the meeting. Feh!

Poor George, said Rabbah. And his only refuge was a distant parking lot where the attendant worked as a pimp, with prostitutes turning tricks out of parked cars.

I dunno, I sort of admire the business initiative, said Rav Pappa. In fact, I'm surprised it wasn't an idea concocted by Kramerica industries.

You think Kramer can come up with something that sophisticated? said Resh Lakish. His last idea for Kramerica was a restaurant that only served peanut butter and jelly sandwiches.

Moreover, Kramer is a law-abiding primate, signed Baruch the Chimp.

Yet he got busted for being a pimp in "The Wig Master," noted Rami bar Hama. Perfect irony.

Perfect irony, said the Sages in unison.

It was his own fault for gallivanting around town with that hat, coat, and Squire's Walking Stick, said Rav Sheshet.

I object! said Rav Pappa. Everyone's unfairly picking on Kramer again, simply because he lives a rather erratic yet colorful lifestyle.

It's not his fault, said Rami bar Hama. How do you think you'd behave if Bob Sacamano moved into your place for a year and a half.

According to the Mishnah, a destitute and intellectually discarded Shammai lived in Jesus' garage for a year and a half, said Yontl the Librarian.

However, as Hillel told Shammai, he should count his blessings that it wasn't Jesus' manger, noted Bar Kappara.

Sacamano's worse than Shammai, and probably worse than Yoshke, said Rabbah.

How do you know? replied Bar Kappara. We've never actually seen Bob Sacamano.

We do know that, unlike Jesus, Sacamano's been in the loony bin for electric shock treatment, said Rav Pappa.

Shhh, you mean he visited an "exceptional home for the neurodivergent," Pappa. Mind your language, said Bar Kappara tilting his head toward Resh Lakish and Abba the Surgeon.

Nobody here is crazy, said Rav Huna, reassuringly. We're all on our own and doing just fine.

Didn't Sacamano also have rabies, much like Elaine almost had, thanks to Doctor "Woof Woof, not Bang Bang."?

No wonder Kramer took him in, said Rav Pappa. Kramer is a good friend. There's nothing wrong with him.

But didn't Kramer move in with Bob Sacamano after Bob had a botched hernia operation? asked Rabbah.

No you're thinking of Len Nicodemo, when he had the gout, corrected Yontl the Librarian.

What is a Nicodemo? asked Shimon ben Pazi.

St. Nicodemo was a prominent Pharisee mentioned in the goys' so called "New Testament." He allegedly helped embalm Yoshke Pandrek's body after the crucifixion, said Yontl the Librarian.

Did Nicodemo get the gout from touching the body of Christ? asked Shimon ben Pazi. This is why I will never touch a corpse.

I thought the body of Christ is supposed to heal? asked Rav Sheshet. Isn't that the basis of Communion? How could Christ pass on the gout?

It's as Kramer said, citing Scripture, "He who cureth, can maketh ill," said Rav Kahana.

Then why didn't Shammai get the gout from living with Jesus? Or why didn't Kramer catch it from St. Nicodemo? asked Rav Sheshet.

Or for that matter, why didn't Kramer get rabies from Bob Sacamano? asked Shimon ben Pazi.

Maybe he did. Maybe that's why Sacamano moved in with him for a year and a half, suggested Bar Kappara. To take care of Kramer.

I think we should conclude that George has no business kvetching over the wig master shacking up with him and Susan for two weeks. It would be far worse – and possibly more contagious – to have Jesus, Bob Sacamano, St. Nicodemo, or even Kramer as a house guest.

The Calzone

GEMARAH:

Fellow Sages, said Rav Huna convening the meeting, we need to discuss several pressing matters regarding "The Calzone." Let's lay them all out on the table.

I would like to know if "Todd Gack" is really Dutch. It is such a nice name, evocative of scenes with windmills and tulips, said Rav Sheshet.

And with Anne Frank and attics during a Nazi invasion, added Shimon ben Pazi.

I would like to know why Dustin Hoffman was not in Star Wars, said Rav Yehudah, and why is it that we assume a Darth Vader or another supervillain couldn't be taken down by a short Jewish guy.

Like Elie Wiesel in eastern Europe during a Nazi invasion, added Shimon ben Pazi.

I would like to know if we could start warming up our shirts during the shiur in our communal ovens, said Rav Yehudah.

No Holocaust comments, Pazi! said Bar Kappara, in dread.

Great idea! said Rav Pappa, who was already disrobing. And, he added, would it be halakhically sound to hire a Shabbos goy to heat up our shirts on Saturdays and yontef?*

I would like to know whether or not Rav Pappa has already tried out the dating loophole Todd Gack discovered, said Resh Lakish. I'm willing to bet he did and FAILED to score a date with the same Star Wars bet Gack used.

I would like to know why postal employee Newman doesn't go to work in the rain, and whether or not precipitation is what causes his colleagues like the Son of Sam to, if you will, "go postal," said Rabbah.

I would like to know if a tip counts as a tip if the tippee doesn't see the tipper placing the tip in the tip jar, whether or not Costanza be exonerated of any wrongdoing? said Rav Kahana.

I would like to know what's so special about Nikki, said Abba the Surgeon. She would never be able to pull that mesmerism shtick with me.

I would like to know at what point Elaine's encounters with Gack do in fact constitute a date, said Bar Kappara. And with all due respect to my fellow rabbis, my question is the only legitimately talmudic question that's on the table.

You don't think debating whether or not Gack is a Dutch name constitutes a genuine talmudic debate? said Rav Sheshet.

No, it's a simple etymological question, replied Bar Kappara. There's no Halakhah involved. And whether he's Dutch or not has zero impact on any other question raised by this Seinfeld episode.

I disagree, said Rav Pappa. The name "Todd Gack" rolls off the tongue mellifluously in such a way that explains why he was able to keep scoring dates with Elaine, bamboozle Jerry into purchasing junk cigars from Peru, and then steal Nikki from Jerry. The name's Gack, Todd Gack. I just can't help but say it.

The name's Gack, Todd Gack, said the Sages in unison while Barry signed it in Dutch.

He got together with Elaine because of the dating loophole, and that's it, said Bar Kappara. It has nothing to do with the name Gack, Todd Gack, however much it reminds us of windmills and tulips.

And the Holocaust, added Shimon ben Pazi.

But no idiot would think a short Jewish guy like Dustin Hoffman or Elie Wiesel was actually in Star Wars. She would have seen through it in a second, said Rav Pappa. Me thinks Elaine had a knack to hit the sack with some Gack.

Did you even watch the episode, shmendrik? retorted Resh Lakish. Elaine did NOT hit the sack with Gack. Gack was the one hit by the sack when he was attacked and smacked by Kramer and his pack of pennies.

Kramer whacked Gack, said the Sages in unison.

You see how versatile his name is, said Rav Pappa. Maybe I should change my name to Gack.

Or to Pennypacker, as Kramer did, suggested Rav Sheshet.

Again, I know what this is all about, said Resh Lakish. Pappa tried out Gack's dating loophole and it didn't work. Am I right, Pappa?

I'm going to end this shiur, as usual, by stating that "I plead the Fifth," said Rav Pappa.

We still don't know what that means, and I'm willing to bet you don't either, said Bar Kappara.

OK what are the stakes? replied Rav Pappa.

I'm so confident you're being dishonest, you can name whatever stakes you want, said Bar Kappara. I swear.

OK, here they are: If I am right, your lovely daughter Sara Kappara has to treat me to dinner, if I am wrong then I have to take her out for dinner, said a beaming Rav Pappa.

Well played Pappa, well played, said the Sages in unison.

The Bottle Deposit

GEMARAH:

Friends, said Rav Huna convening the meeting, I find it rather troubling how attached Jerry's mechanic became to that car.

Especially since Newman clearly treated his precious mail truck with such reckless abandon, said Rabbah. For shame.

Not his fault, Newman was ejected by Kramer from the mail truck! countered Rav Pappa. Plus it worked out in his favor, he had the chance to make time with the farmer's daughter. Go Norman, go! Norman is da man!

I love you Norman! said the Sages in Unison.

Have you ever made time with a farmer's daughter? asked Resh Lakish.

He certainly made time with Bar Kappara's daughter after losing his bet over Todd Gack, said Abba the Surgeon with derision.

Where is Kappara? Asked Rav Huna.

He felt as if his family was so violated he needed to check into Zutra the Mohel's clinic for special neurodivergent people, said Rabbah.

And how is his daughter, asked Rav Huna?

She's doing just fine, said Rav Pappa, and in fact, she's still at my place.

And she's not being held against her will? asked an incredulous Resh Lakish.

Well, she may be tied up at the moment, but that's got nothing to do with it. I've got the Kavorka, replied a beaming Rav Pappa.

Those poor Kapparas, said Rav Huna.

And Bar Kappara has insufficient funds to pay his medical bills. If he doesn't come up with money forthwith, Zutra will have to use his "bottom shelf" medical equipment on him, said Rabbah.

God, even Rome banned the "bottom shelf" equipment because it constituted cruel and unusual punishment. And why is he being treated by Zutra – a third-rate mohel? asked Rav Kahana.

Because Abba the surgeon lost his Ukrainian medical license since the Persian board of physicians couldn't find Ukraine on any map, said Rabbah. And believe it or not there are no other Jewish doctors in Pumbedita.

No doctors!? said Shimon ben Pazi in shock. And we have the chutzpah to call ourselves Jews.

No lawyers, either, noted Rabbah. Just rabbis and Zutra, the used camel salesman of the mohel world.

Well we need to help the Kapparas out, said Rav Huna. I say we have an auction, like they did on Seinfeld.

Screw the auction, I say we just whack Rav Pappa with a set of golf clubs for causing this situation, said Resh Lakish.

But we don't golf, noted Rav Sheshet. And as pleasurable as that may be, it won't help Bar Kappara.

OK so what have we got to auction off? asked Yontl the Librarian, taking notes.

I can offer the bro I once sewed for Resh Lakish, said Motl the Tailor.

I can offer the rope I used to tie up Bar Kappara's daughter, I mean once we're done with it, said Rav Pappa.

These items are either irrelevant or cruel, said Rav Huna.

We can auction Baruch the Chimp, suggested Abba the Surgeon.

No way, he's a valuable member of the Academy, replied Rav Huna.

We can auction off Rav Sheshet as a natural curiosity, suggested Resh Lakish.

Great! I hear the Romanian circus is in town, said Rav Huna. All they have are a handful of clowns and animals. They'll want him. I say we do it.

Uh, doesn't this go against HR's policy of diversity, equity, and inclusion? said an alarmed Rav Sheshet. And why can't you auction Baruch instead of me?

Because we looked at their policy manual, said Rav Huna. We are only required to have one human adjacent member. Baruch the Chimp has filled that role admirably. Plus the Romanians already have monkeys.

The Wait Out

GEMARAH:

I would like you to meet my lady friend, Sara bat Kappara, said Rav Pappa, walking into the Academy.

Seriously? said Rabbah. Boy she could have done a lot better than you, Pappa.

What are you talking about? I'm a great catch. I have the body of a taut preteen Armenian minstrel.

You aren't Armenian, you can't sing, and you're too fat to fit into a pair of jeans, replied Resh Lakish.

And guess what, said an unfazed Rav Pappa. We're engaged to be married.

Seriously? said a flabbergasted Rav Huna. Sara do you actually love him?

I do, very much, replied Sara bat Kappara.

May we ask why? said Shimon ben Pazi.

He's very persistent, said Sara.

And after several hours of convincing, added Rav Pappa, she finally said those magic words: "OK I'll marry you, now please untie me."

Well given this ... um ... appalling turn of events, said Rabbah, I propose that Sara bat Kappara join our Yeshivah as our new female rabbi, especially in light of her father's continued absence.

I'd be honored, said Sara bat Kappara.

What? said Rav Pappa. As the Talmud says, "Three things enlarge a man's mind: a beautiful home, a beautiful woman and beautiful utensils." (Berakhot 57b:12). "Utensils" are an allusion to the kitchen. My wife should be in my beautiful home tending to my kitchen and our future baby Papas.

You're a misogynist Pappa, said Abba the Surgeon. I've seen Sara in action. She's got a sharp talmudic mind.

But I should have been consulted, said Rav Pappa. My worlds are colliding!

YOUR world's are colliding?! said Rav Huna. Think about poor Bar

Kappara, who now has to welcome you into his family. You'll be in his home, ushering in the Sabbath, eating his food, drinking his schnapps, watching the Superbowl, and essentially ruining his tranquility of mind.

Has anyone broken the news to Bar Kappara yet? asked Rav Sheshet.

No, he's still under the care of Zutra, said Rabbah. This may be the straw that breaks the camel, and we do not want him to end up under suicide watch.

I suppose we now have a wedding to plan, relented Rav Huna. But I still say you could have done a lot better than him. And I'm not being folksy. You could throw a dart out the window and hit someone better than him. Let's disband and figure out how to break the news to Bar Kappara.

The Invitations

GEMARAH:

Friends, said Rav Huna convening the meeting, once again we have homicide at the hands of the Seinfeld Four on the table for discussion.

Poor Lily, said the Sages in unison.

What's to discuss? said Resh Lakish. George is clearly guilty. He was looking for any and every possible way out of the wedding. He even hoped Susan would be in a plane crash. He was ready to move to China and blend into the masses.

How could George blend into a sea of a billion Asians? Said Rav Sheshet. He looks nothing like them.

He didn't look that different from Donna Chang, said Shimon ben Pazi. He could have easily fit into a nation of a billion Donna Changs.

She's from Long Island you yold, said Rabbah. That's why Jerry told him it would be easier to blend in on Staten Island.

I never knew there was such a large Chinese community on Staten Island.

But do you all agree? asked Rav Sheshet, George is responsible for Susan's death?

How is he responsible? Fault lies with the company that manufactured the invitations, said Rav Kahana.

No, the company took them off the market, perhaps for that very reason, said Rav Yehudah. It's the store's fault for continuing to sell them.

Maybe it's the doctor's fault, suggested Rami bar Hama. He couldn't have been particularly competent if she died so easily.

I agree, said Rav Huna. That's why George asked the doctor "are you sure?" when he broke the news to him. George recognized his incompetence.

Why? asked Abba the Surgeon. People ask me "are you sure?" all the time when I convey their diagnoses.

Well unlike you, retorted Rabbah, the doctor on *Seinfeld* didn't get his medical degree in Ukraine.

People say "are you sure" to me all the time as well, said Zutra the Mohel. "Excuse me sir, I may have taken a bit too much off your son along the edges," I convey. "Are you sure?" they respond suspiciously. And I didn't get my mohel license in Ukraine.

Wait a second, said Resh Lakish. Isn't this doctor the very same proctologist who is known as "The Assman"? Didn't he previously extract Fusilli Jerry from Frank Costanza's tokhes? Why is a proctologist-assman pretending to be a toxicologist?

Maybe the toxins had traveled from Susan's mouth to her ass, infecting her entire system, suggested Abba the Surgeon. You'd want a doctor familiar with the point of exit.

Toxins always emerge from the anus, added Rabbah. That was why Frank's life was in danger. Fusilli Jerry had corked up his exit passage. "It was a million to one shot."

But Susan didn't have her butt corked up with pasta. Why couldn't the toxins have exited? asked Shimon ben Pazi.

That is a question only the Assman can answer, concluded Rav Sheshet.

Speaking of Assmen, where's Pappa? asked Rav Huna.

As Seinfeld described in his opening monologue, replied Sara bat Kappara, my shmoopy is driving around sticking our wedding invitations on people's windshields. It inspired him.

Windshields? asked a confused Rabbah. I don't understand. Camels don't have windshields.

I'm being metaphorical, replied Sara bat Kappara. He's gluing them to our friends' camel humps. He's trying to save money; he didn't want to send them out in the mail.

What a cheapskate, said the Sages in unison.

He's also paranoid that toxic glue on the envelopes may kill me, so he said he'd rather risk his own life than mine, added Sara bat Kappara.

What a romantic, said the Sages in unison.

Actually I think he fears being put on trial for murder more than anything, admitted Sara bat Kappara.

What a coward, said the Sages in unison.

Either way, he thinks one of us would end up on either Abba or Zutra's operating table and we'd end up dying because of their medical ineptitude, added Sara bat Kappara.

What a wise decision, said the Sages in unison.

Season 8

The Rabbis Debate Jewish Law on Buying PLO Blended Coffee and Eating Japanese Tourists

The Foundation

GEMARAH:

Friends, said Rav Huna convening the meeting, today's topic for discussion is the relationship between eating a block of cheese the size of a car battery and living the dream of freedom.

I can see it, said Rami bar Hama. Who doesn't yearn to be free to eat a big block of cheese at will?

Cheese at last, cheese at last, thank God all mighty, we have cheese at last, said the Sages in unison.

But we need to discuss what has transpired with some of our flock, said Rabbah. The engagement is apparently off; there shall be no Pappa-Kappara wedding.

Oh no, said Rav Sheshet, don't tell me, did toxic glue on the wedding invitation envelopes put the kibosh on one of them in?

Nope, said Rav Huna.

Did Zutra, emulating a proctologist accidentally shove something into Rav Pappa's anus, corking it up? asked Shimon ben Pazi.

Hey, my petzl-work has transitioned perfectly fine to the anus and other orifices, said an angry Zutra the Mohel. And I cut things, I don't cork things. There is no Fusilli Jerry corking up Pappa's tokhes.

Nope, replied Rav Huna. One of them caught the other up to no good down by the banks of the Euphrates. I shall not mention any names.

And they determined this constituted cheating? said Rami bar Hama. But we ruled at an earlier shiur that being with a prostitute while engaged does not constitute cheating.

We never issued any such ruling, retorted Rabbah. Only one person in the academy came to that conclusion. Only one. And he is one of the parties involved in this obscene incident. Got it?

So with the engagement off, where is Bar Kappara? asked Resh Lakish.

He survived his commitment and frontal lobe surgery at Zutra's clinic. But he's now busy at his ka-ra-TE lesson, regaining his strength, confidence, and composure. It is therapeutic for him, said Rabbah.

Ka-ra-TE? asked the Sages in unison.

Yes, some of us practice Kabbalah, some of us practice ka-ra-TE, replied Rabbah. The lifetime pursuit of balance and harmony, but with punching and kicking.

Yes he needs his confidence restored, said Rav Huna. So we stuck him in the kids group, the "Mazal Tots." Kappara is dominating the dojo. He took down little Stuart Rifkin, the one who likes to go shopping with his mommy.

And please, when he returns, no "wax on, wax off" jokes, added Rabbah.

I still can't believe Pappa was with a prostitute, said Rav Sheshet. I thought he was willing to abandon his decadent lifestyle for the dignified Sara bat Kappara.

Oh it wasn't Pappa, replied Rav Huna. Pappa wasn't with a prostitute.

Sara bat Kappara was with a prostitute??? said Rav Sheshet in astonishment. I'm flummoxed. We don't even have any orgy guys – let alone male prostitutes – in Pumbedita, except of course for her fiancé Rav Pappa.

No, this has nothing to do with prostitution, orgies, ka-ra-TE, or corked anuses, replied Rabbah.

So what happened? asked Rav Sheshet.

Pappa found Sara at the riverbank down to her panties eating a block of cheese the side of a car battery, replied Rav Huna. I told you this was the subject of discussion today. Why isn't anyone listening to me?

The Soul Mate

GEMARAH:

Friends, said Rav Huna convening the meeting. We have some Sages to welcome back today. Say hello to Bar Kappara and to Rav Pappa, who have agreed to put this entire engagement travesty behind them.

I'm not done with you yet, Pappa, said Bar Kappara. You stole my little girl. Rest assured I will strike first, strike hard, and show no mercy.

Wax on, wax off, Rabbi, retorted Rav Pappa. My tzitzit are quaking. I concluded I was no longer gaga over your little girl. She wasn't my soulmate. I wouldn't even trade a two-hump camel for her.

What happened, Pappa? You were so gaga! said Shimon ben Pazi. Was it because she pranced around with that giant block of cheese in her undergarments down by the Euphrates?

Not at all, said Rav Pappa. Who do you think bought her the block of cheese? We were planning on integrating it into our love making. But then she decided to start eating it without me.

Watch yourself Pappa, you are upsetting the balance of my katra, admonished Bar Kappara.

Kindly watch yourself, Mr. Motto, replied Rav Pappa. No she wanted to move to Armenia and have a baby. "We've got to have a BAY-Bee," she kept repeating. She said the city is a toilet. So I said no and went to Zutra's and had a vasectomy, and then she broke it off.

Is that why you're walking funny? asked Shimon ben Pazi. I thought it was because Bar Kappara kicked you.

Nope, just recovering from my surgery, said Rav Pappa. Zutra said the excessive pain is only temporary, but I think he lied.

The Sages laughed and Baruch the Chimp facepalmed in unison.

Why in God's name did you have a vasectomy? said Rav Huna

I was just following the *Seinfeld* script for the Shiur, said Rav Pappa. Oh I'm just like that Kevin. So, so very impulsive. I never think things through!

Well, these procedures are reversible, said Rabbah reassuringly.

Not the way we do it Chez Zutra, replied Zutra the Mohel. Suffice it to say, Bonnie Raitt will not be singing "Pappa come quick" anytime soon.

Damn, lamented Bar Kappara, and I was looking forward to being the one who put Pappa out of commission.

The Bizarro Jerry

GEMARAH:

Friends, said Rav Huna convening the meeting, today we need to talk about James Polk.

What is a James Polk? asked Shimon ben Pazi

I think it's a creature out of Greek mythology, part woman and part man-hands, replied Rami bar Hama.

So Jerry was dating a James Polk? replied Shimon ben Pazi.

No I think a Polk is a person who comes from Poland, like Manya, said Rav Sheshet.

And the Polkas are known for having giant man-hands? asked Rami bar Hama.

Could be, said Rav Sheshet.

Then perhaps that explains what happened to Manya's pony, suggested Rabbah. Manya strangled the pony to death with her giant man-hands.

And then she ate it, like Jay Riemenschneider, added Rabbah.

But we've already established that Manya's pony was actually a horse-faced relative from the House of Seinfeld, like Cousin Jeffrey, countered Resh Lakish. You are now accusing Manya of strangling a sibling or a cousin to death.

So that's the connection to Greek mythology, posited Bar Kappara: The Polkas are a people with gigantic man-hands and horse faces.

Perhaps this is why Jerry wanted to chain Gillian to the refrigerator and sell tickets, suggested Shimon ben Pazi. That is just so cruel. We never even considered doing anything of the sort to Rav Sheshet, despite his pig man deformity.

And I am am…uh…deeply appreciative of this, fellow rabbis, said Rav Sheshet sheepishly.

Maybe we should have chained Sheshet and sold tickets, interjected Rav Pappa, then we wouldn't have had to have that stupid failure of a fundraiser. That was so embarrassing. We looked like shnooks.

I can't believe the cruelty of this conversation, said an incredulous Abba the Surgeon. I am all but certain Bizarro Jerry and his friends would never discuss this, let alone do any of these abhorrent things.

What do the Bizarro Seinfeld three do all day? asked Rabbah. They seem to lead a rather dull existence.

I think they sit around reading books, and they buy each other groceries, said Bar Kappara.

That's pathetic, said Rav Pappa. Imagine if they were the TV show – *Bizarro Seinfeld* – we'd never have anything to discuss at our shiurs.

You're right, said Rami bar Hama. There's no way Feldman has friends who eat ponies. There's no way Kevin ever conspired to steal a marble rye. And I'm sure Gene has perfectly normal orgasms.

Do you think the three of them had a "contest"? asked Rav Pappa. How would that even have worked?

They would probably have done it together in Kevin's apartment, suggested Rabbah. It would have been a three-way tie, then they would have hugged each other, compared "notes," and used the communal pot to buy each other groceries.

Real sickos, said Resh Lakish. Even Pappa wouldn't participate in anything like that. Would you Pappa?

Of course not, retorted Rav Pappa. How could you even suggest such a thing? OK maybe I would, depending on how much money was at stake.

Do they have contests like this in Poland? asked Shimon ben Pazi. I imagine giant man-hands would be an asset for treating one's body like an amusement park. Tell us Pappa, you were there.

Pappa's never going to tell us, replied Resh Lakish. If he tells us then he'll have to admit to having participated. No, Pappa won't speak.

I admit to nothing, said Rav Pappa. What happened in Poland stays in Poland, but suffice it to say, my delicate digits were considered a liability. It hurt my claim to have the Kavorka.

But tell us, was crossing into Poland like entering the forbidden city, Pappa, with models as far as the eye could see? Was the road from Minsk to Pinsk awash with Rochelle Rochelles?

No it was more like entering a meat packing plant, said Rav Pappa. With manure as far as the eye can see, and butchers with giant man-hands and horse faces.

I don't remember reading any of this in Greek mythology, said Rav Kahana. And I don't recall Manya having man-hands, so I'm questioning the veracity of this entire discussion.

Maybe Manya had reconstructive surgery when she got off the boat, like the old lady from *Titanic*, suggested Rabbah.

But Rose didn't have man-hands, replied Resh Lakish.

She must have – look at how easily she unhooked Jack's far more delicate frozen hands and cast him into the depths of the ocean. Only someone with meaty paws like Gillian could have had the strength to do that, contended Rav Pappa.

Alternatively, Rose could have gotten her great strength from eating horse meat on the Titanic, much like Jay Riemenschneider, suggested Rav Sheshet.

This discussion is absurd, interjected Abba the Surgeon.

Not at all, replied Rav Pappa. This is why they called the boat "Titanic": it was an homage to the Titans of Greek mythology, the meaty-pawed and horse-faced gods who resided on Mount Olympus.

And then the ship collided with an iceberg because Captain James Polk couldn't steer it with those gigantic meaty paws, suggested Shimon ben Pazi

That's perfect irony, said the Sages in unison.

Chevreh, I think we learned how important it is to study other cultures today, especially the Greeks who were known for their humanistic practices. I think we have grown as rabbis. But before we disband, let's chain Sheshet to the refrigerator and sell tickets. I'm kicking myself for not having thought of this sooner.

The Little Kicks

GEMARAH:

What a dark and disturbing episode, said Rav Huna, convening the meeting.

I know, said Bar Kappara, and it opened with one of the great talmudic debates between Jerry and Kramer: would you rather get sideswiped by a taxi or hit on the head by an 80-pound air conditioner? Which is more dangerous?

The Sages sat in silence.

Maybe we need to put it to the test, suggested Shimon ben Pazi.

Oh don't be such a shmegegge, Pazi, said Resh Lakish. We don't have any air conditioners in Pumbedita. Moreover, Pappa was trampled by a pony in the Polish Corridor, and he is unfortunately still with us.

We are not going to solve this debate, said Rav Huna, so let's move on: is it good or is it bad to be "the bad seed"?

I say "yeah baby!" replied Rav Pappa.

OK, please elaborate, said Rav Huna.

Objection! said Resh Lakish.

On what grounds? asked Rav Huna.

Because all that will emanate from Pappa's foul mouth in the coming minutes is bound to be utterly offensive to women, minorities, the LGBT community, and HaShem knows who else. HR will be breaking down our door within the hour, replied Resh Lakish.

Please proceed Pappa, but keep it clean, said Rav Huna.

Until my accident in the land of Polish man-hands, began Rav Pappa, Pappa was "the Bad Seed of Pumbedita." Pappa got all the chicks, man. And you people were envious. Pappa was the dark horse until he got taken down by a Polish horse. And now that Pappa is crippled, he dances like Elaine. Pappa is all little kicks and thumbs. The women aren't into it. Sure, Pappa still gets laid by playing the handicapped card, but it's just not the same.

With the exception of Resh Lakish, the Sages stared at Rav Pappa in deep admiration while Baruch the Chimp gave Pappa a thumbs up.

See what I mean? interjected Resh Lakish. Such drek, such filth, coming out of one egotistical rabbinic mouth who is still pulling a "Jimmy" and referring to himself in the third person.

I disagree, said Rami bar Hama. While he was admittedly a tad sexist and ableist, Pappa has offered us some insight through his tale of tribulation and horror. To wit, it is good to be the bad seed. Rami would love to be the bad seed.

I disagree with you Hama, said Bar Kappara. The concept of "the bad seed" is replete with Nazi overtones and yet again the Seinfeld Four have inappropriately deployed Holocaust terminology in this episode.

How so? asked Rav Sheshet. I do not understand.

As Elaine herself said, Bar Kappara began, "The bad seed" is like a "virus" infecting the system. "He attaches himself to a healthy host company, and the next thing you know the entire staff's infected." Do you know what that sounds like?

Actually, it sounds like Elaine has described Rav Pappa to a tee, said Resh Lakish. Hey Kappara, isn't that how Pappa seduced your daughter, by being the bad seed?

Shmuck, retorted Bar Kappara, you don't get it. This is exactly how the Nazis described the Jews before the Final Solution. They were likened to a parasitical virus that infected the German host.

So Kappara, do you not feel this way about Rav Pappa? Is he not the bad seed who infected your family by attaching himself to your daughter? asked Rav Huna, relishing this weighty talmudic battle that would go down as Judaism's greatest confrontational moment ever since Hillel and Shammai fought over their respective Passover sandwiches.

Uh yes, that does sound like Pappa, but that's not the point, said Bar Kappara shifting uncomfortably in his chair.

No I think the point is you just used Nazi rhetoric to describe Rav Pappa – your fellow Jew – said Rav Sheshet. For shame Bar Kappara, for shame.

Wait – maybe Kappara is suggesting that the Nazis adopted this rhetoric after encountering a gaggle of Jews who resembled Rav Pappa, mused Resh Lakish. Are you insinuating, Kappara, that Nazism had a basis in reality?

The Sages let loose a chorus of oohs and aahs, led by Baruch the Chimp.

Please explain yourself Kappara, said Rav Huna.

Sorry meine Süßen, I, Bar Kappara, am hereby pleading the Fifth.

Before I challenge your use of that idiom we have yet to define, Kappara, let me ask you one question, said Rav Pappa, seizing the moment: are there any more daughters in your household?

The Package

GEMARAH:

I can't believe Jerry and Kramer committed mail fraud, said Rav Huna, convening the meeting.

Yes it seems the Seinfeld Four all sank to a new low in this episode, said Bar Kappara. Look at Elaine, tampering with medical records.

Which is worse? asked Shimon ben Pazi, mail fraud or stealing your chart?

Certainly mail fraud, replied Rav Sheshet. It's a federal offense. The post office wields an incredible amount of authority. That's why they are run by a general.

The Polkmaster General, added Shimon ben Pazi.

Shmendrik, that's Postmaster General, not Polkmaster General, interjected Bar Kappara.

I thought the position was named after James Polk, replied Shimon ben Pazi. Isn't that why Polk was Gillian Man-Hands' favorite President?

Regardless, it's a serious offense, said Rabbah. Once again we see Jerry for what he is, a very very bad man. And he knows it. That's why he thought the package he received might have been a bomb.

Agreed, George was dead wrong, not taking Jerry's bombability seriously, added Resh Lakish.

Agreed, said Abba the Surgeon. It's not just the airlines that want to take him out "for all the stupid little peanut jokes." Virtually every woman he dated has a reason to knock him off.

Sorry, but if we are bringing women into the picture, then George is far more bombable than Jerry, countered Rav Pappa: Karen of Risotto fame, papier-mâché Patrice who spent time in the nut house, Noel the pianist, humiliated by an apathetic Pez dispenser, and of course the entire Ross family. George claiming that "there are a couple of people that wouldn't mind having me out of the way," is, to put it mildly, an understatement.

Yet Jerry treated his Uncle Leo like a bomb defusing robot, said Abba the Surgeon. What kind of sicko does that?

What would you do if you had to listen to the astonishing tales of Cousin Jeffrey every week? said Rav Sheshet. Besides, if it were a bomb and Leo survived, he would have blamed it on antisemites. It was a rather clever ploy on Jerry's part.

And ironically George is the only one who did nothing wrong in this episode, said Bar Kappara. His courting of Sheila at the photo store was endearing.

I disagree said, Resh Lakish. He cruelly led on Ron, the large gay Black man, with those racy photos. Then George rejected him with extreme prejudice. The homophobia is appalling.

George never led him on, countered Rav Sheshet. It's hardly George's fault that Ron happened to develop that particular roll of film.

Still, at that point George should have done the honorable thing and proposed a ménage à trois with Sheila and Ron, insisted Rav Pappa. It was incumbent upon him to become an orgy guy for Ron's sake.

And now George can add Sheila and Ron to the list of people who want to knock him off, concluded Rabbah. George is the most bombable member of the Seinfeld clan.

If bombability is tied to promiscuity, then Rav Pappa is certainly the most bombable member of our Yeshivah, said Rav Sheshet. There are more women who want to see him disappeared than the population of Poland.

Including the entire female population of Poland, added Resh Lakish. Yes the

Slavs speak of a Kavorka who entered their forbidden city like the Nazis moved on Warsaw.

It was those meaty paws, conceded Rav Pappa. I couldn't resist the Polish people's man-hands. I admit it.

And what about their horse faces? said Bar Kappara. Does that turn you on as well? Sicko! And you want to make time with my daughters? Maybe you should be putting the moves on the relatives of the humanoid and hominid adjacent members of the Yeshivah?

Leave Sheshet and the monkey out of this Kappara, said Rav Huna. You are accusing Pappa of having an animal fetish, all because he violated your daughter. Your comment is also anti-Polish. The Polkas may have horse faces, but they are still human. There's no evidence Pappa practices bestiality.

Excuse me, said Rav Sheshet. I feel it necessary to add that sleeping with my sister does not constitute bestiality, whether she looks like a pig man or not. Moreover, nobody here has ever seen my sister.

Well that should be rectified, added Rav Pappa. I'll head over to her place forthwith to "evaluate" the scene. Pappa's back, baby!

[Rav Pappa left the shiur]

Let's call it a day, Chevreh, said Rav Huna, concluding the meeting. And, please, if anyone needs to deliver something to Rav Pappa, send it to his home, not his Yeshivah mailbox.

The Fatigues

GEMARAH:

Friends, said Rav Huna convening the meeting, "The Fatigues" raises some troubling questions about the fate of our community in exile.

Something seems very off with this New York Jewish community, said Bar Kappara. It's almost as if we've degenerated into a bad joke.

It's undoubtedly because of centuries of poor mentorship, added Rabbah. With no prophets to guide us, it appears that our rabbinical heirs have completely failed.

Yes, I can't even tell who is a Jew anymore, said Rav Kahana. Eddie Sherman is Jewish? He works in a mailroom, walks around in military fatigues, fantasizes about his knife, "the only friend who won't be dead by sunup," and has no sense of humor. He's a Jew? He's straight out of one of those 1980s Vietnam movies.

Or maybe he's a Zionist, suggested Rabbah. He's the negation of the big nosed sweaty Borscht Belt diasporic Jew.

Then why is he writing for the Peterman catalogue and not chasing terrorists in the middle east? questioned Rav Pappa. And how do you know he isn't sweaty? Those fatigues look like they could use a good wash.

He appears to have lost his way, like Lomez, replied Rabbah. Yet another unexpected Jew. I've never heard of a Jew with a name like Lomez.

What about Jose the Galilean? Or Juan Epstein? suggested Rav Sheshet. He may be a Puerto Rican Jew. I believe Kramer. Lomez is old school Orthodox, and he's doing a mitzvah by running Jewish singles night.

Agreed, said Rav Pappa, and that is very much my domain. My service, "Shiksa dot com," hosts singles nights all the time.

Perhaps we need to establish a mentor-protégé program at the Yeshivah, suggested Rav Huna, in the interest of Jewish continuity. Much as Pirkei Avot* documents the passing down of Torah from Sinai to Hillel and Shammai, we can pass down our Seinfeld Talmud to the righteous of future generations.

So who shall mentor whom? asked Shimon ben Pazi.

I volunteer to be a mentor, said Rav Pappa. With me guiding you, you shall inherit the Kavorka, you will be the dark horse of Pumbedita, you will possess power over the sheyneh meydl and the shiksa alike.

I volunteer to be a mentor, said Zutra the Mohel. With me guiding you, you shall inherit my knife, which, much like Eddie Sherman's, will be your only friend. You will wield power over every sheyneh shmekl in the land.

With me as your mentor, I promise you will get laid, interjected Rav Pappa.

With me as your mentor, I promise your daughter will never get laid by Rav Pappa's protégés.

As God promised Abraham, with me, you will be exceedingly fruitful, thy seed will multiply as the stars of heaven, said Rav Pappa. This is my covenant.

And as God promised Abraham, with me, you will be exceedingly prolific in ensuring every man-child from the House of Pappa shall have his Rabbi Johnson put out of commission for good, countered Zutra the Mohel. This is MY covenant.

This is outrageous, said Bar Kappara. Mentorship is about bequeathing wisdom to future generations; it's not about transforming our religion into a "catch my dingdong if you can" contest.

I disagree, said Rav Pappa. It is in our Torah at the very onset of humanity: "be fruitful and multiply"

And I disagree as well, said Zutra the Mohel. It is in our Torah at the very onset of Jewish peoplehood: "snip your dingdong and then good luck with your fruitful multiplication."

But who will mentor us on "risk management?," asked Shimon ben Pazi, yet again struggling to stick to the *Seinfeld* script.

Certainly, not Pappa or Zutra, replied Rav Sheshet. Maybe Bar Kappara should take on that role, as he is the most circumspect of our flock.

I want no part in this program. It's fraught with danger, bad publicity, and the collapse of our religion, insisted Bar Kappara. Moreover what we're offering is so infused with hyper-masculinity HR will be breathing down our necks.

See Kappara is perfect for the job, concluded Rav Huna. And he makes a valid point too: let's add Sheshet and Baruch to the list of mentors, just to satisfy HR's DEI requirements. And Lakish as well, should anyone need man-boob mentoring. Yontl, please highlight the minutes from today's shiur; it will be the foundational document of our new great chain of tradition. This is our gift to the future Eddie Shermans of our exile.

The Checks

GEMARAH:

Friends, said Rav Huna convening the meeting, as you can see I've purchased several sets of oversized Karl Farbman drawers for us to sleep in. They will be useful for our late-night shiurs should anyone decide to spend the night. Think of them as a communal space where you can get some much-needed sack time.

But how are we to decide who rooms with whom? said an alarmed Bar Kappara. I have no interest in bunking with half the people in this gaggle of sweaty rabbis, especially the monkey, whose evening routine is known to all.

Baruch the Chimp hid his face in shame.

And how do we decide who gets the top drawer? added Rabbah. I wouldn't want to get stuck in the middle.

Imagine getting stuck between Sheshet and Baruch, said an irate Abba the Surgeon. It would be like living in a barn.

I like the idea, said Rav Pappa. And I am willing to throw some dinars into the communal pot if I can have two adjacent drawers all to myself.

Why do you need two drawers? In case you bring a girl back for the evening? asked Resh Lakish.

No comment, said Rav Pappa.

And how would that even be of any use, if you and your "friend" are in separate drawers? added Abba the Surgeon.

Again, no comment, said Rav Pappa, who was already powering up the drill he borrowed from Zutra the Mohel when the discussion began.

I want to know if it's true that the Asians really sleep in cubicles like these drawers, as Kramer maintained, asked Rav Kahana.

Does Donna Chang sleep in a chest of drawers? asked Shimon ben Pazi. Or is it only the Japanese and not the Chinese?

Despite their mutual animosity, the Japanese and Chinese borrow a great deal from each other's culture, said Yontl the Librarian. So it stands to reason both peoples live in oversized chests of drawers.

But their cuisine requires such intricate utensils, said Rabbah. I just can't see anyone scooping up dumplings with chopsticks in such a confined space.

Too bad Jerry didn't ask Donna Chang when he had the chance, said Shimon ben Pazi.

For the last time, Donna Chang is not Chinese, said Bar Kappara.

Right, she is just some Jew from Long Island who decided to "become Chinese" at Ellis Island, said Rav Sheshet.

Then it stands to reason she started sleeping in an oversized Farbman chest of drawers once she converted, said Shimon ben Pazi.

You're a meathead Pazi, a genuine meathead, said Bar Kappara.

No Pazi is correct, said Rami bar Hama. Why? Because in acquiring these drawers we have now made it into a Jewish tradition. Who knows maybe the kibbutzniks in Israel will one day adopt our new form of Farbman communal living.

Agreed, said Rav Huna. Let's end for today, but first, everyone please choose two bunkmates.

Except for me, I only need one, and preferably one with poor hearing, said Rav Pappa as he began drilling his "home renovations."

The Chicken Roster

GEMARAH:

"Co-STAN-za!" [to the tune of "By Mennen"] it's got a nice ring to it, said Rav Huna convening the meeting.

Yes, he is like a jingle, first a little irritating, then you hum it in the shower, and then it's "Buy MEN-nen!" added Rabbah. I now understand how he's secured dates with all these beautiful women.

Agreed, said Rav Pappa. I admit to having used this technique. If you travel across the Fertile Crescent you can still hear "Rav-PA-ppa" emanating from the lips of Sassanid damsels near and far.

Rav-PA-ppa sang the Sages in unison [to the tune of "By Mennen"].

Jeez, do you also show up at their doors inside a wooden horse? asked Resh Lakish sardonically.

Yes, but unfortunately that doesn't work as well, admitted Rav Pappa.

Well now that we've gotten our daily dose of Pappa's Playhouse what else should we discuss from "The Chicken Roaster"?

I think we should get a gigantic neon sign like Kenny Rogers Chicken Roaster; it would be good for business, suggested Zutra the Mohel.

But we aren't in business, countered Bar Kappara. We are a respectable academy of learning.

For my circumcision business, replied Zutra the Mohel.

But you're the only mohel in town, countered Bar Kappara. People have no choice but to use your services. That's the only reason you have any business. And, moreover, almost everyone in this room wants to put you out of business.

Then maybe we should do like Kramer and hang a banner outside our window that says "BAD MOHEL," suggested Resh Lakish.

Now that's an idea, exclaimed Rav Pappa. I say we get to work on it immediately.

May I point out, interjected Zutra the Mohel, that the Yeshivah relies on the income generated from my business. Every snipped shlong is a shekel in your pocket.

It's true, chimed in the normally reticent Ahasuerus the Bookkeeper. Should we keep Zutra in business we can purchase those new sable hats we've been considering. Should we cut him loose, so to speak, we won't even be able to afford Bob Sacamano's rat hats.

Well it looks like the petzls of Pumbedita are in a pickle, said Rabbah. We need those hats, so I say we nix the "BAD MOHEL" sign.

Listen, replied an irritated Zutra the Mohel. My services are like a commercial jingle. During the first few snips, people find me a bit irritating. Then they watch a few more brises and they start imagining it in the shower. By the tenth snip, it's "My DING-dong!" [to the tune of "By Mennen"]

With no self-control, the Sages sang "My DING-dong" in unison.

And then the dismayed Sages got up and left the shiur, having been outwitted yet again by one of the more perverse members of the flock.

The Abstinence

GEMARAH:

Friends, said Rav Huna convening the meeting, "The Abstinence" is a terrific gateway into numerous weighty halakhic matters.

Indeed, said Rami bar Hama. As George and Jerry debated, whom would we eat first should our plane crash in the Andes and we faced the prospect of starvation?

How is this a halakhic question? asked Bar Kappara shaking his head in disgust.

It is a halakhic issue, replied Rav Pappa, as it pertains to the violation of kashrut.

Then it is a no-brainer, said Bar Kappara: eating humans is treyf.

So it is a simple question, mused Rav Huna: at what point of starvation are we allowed to eat non-kosher food.

It is not so straightforward. Perhaps there are degrees of treyf when it comes to eating humans, said Rav Pappa.

Please elaborate, said Rav Huna, to the irritation of Bar Kappara.

Well, said Rav Pappa, perhaps ordained Rabbis and members of the priesthood are more kosher than regular Jews. In that case our rank in the Yeshivah is important. It would be less of a sin to eat Rav Huna, than to eat Yontl the Librarian, who merely holds a doctorate.

What about Rav Sheshet? asked Shimon ben Pazi. It can be argued that his humanoid porcine condition makes him the most sinful to consume. Pig is the ultimate treyf, the great temptation of bacon that has taunted us Jews since biblical times.

So eating Huna is almost a mitzvah compared to eating Sheshet the Pig Man, mused Shlomo the Mashgiach* who was also the resident chef at the Academy.

Shouldn't we eat Baruch first? asked Rav Kahana. Apes are not kosher, but at the very least he's not human.

Yet he is a rabbi, and as of last week a Jew as well, noted Rav Sheshet.

But we have not discussed whether we should eat a goy before we eat a Member of the Tribe, added Rami bar Hama.

Everyone here is a Jew, said Zutra the Mohel, so it's a non-issue.

Wrong, it's possible we might have a Gentile among the flight crew, countered Resh Lakish.

Is it better to eat a pig man or a horse-faced Seinfeld? asked Shimon ben Pazi.

Definitely a horse-face, replied Rav Pappa. Eating pig men is a far greater infraction.

Then perhaps this is why George was so eager to eat Jerry, whereas Jerry was not eager to eat George, suggested Shimon ben Pazi. Perhaps George, like Jay Riemenschneider, enjoys horse meat.

Then I would say, concluded Rav Huna, it is better to eat a Jew than a Gentile, a rabbi than a layman, a monkey than a human whether the monkey is a rabbi and a Jew or not, but consuming a pig man should be a last resort. Horse-faced Jews can be eaten before pig men, especially in Poland, where it is safe to assume Manya consumed her horse-faced cousin, the pride of Krakow, after the Nazi invasion.

So let it be written, so let it be done, said the Sages in unison.

Hey Huna, said Resh Lakish, you mentioned there were multiple questions raised in "The Abstinence."

Yes, replied Rav Huna. There are two others, to be precise. First off, what would happen if Rav Pappa abstained from sex? Would he develop into a brilliant mind, like George, or would he become a bumbling yold, like Elaine? Second, we need to discuss whether we can call Abba the Surgeon "Doctor" or not, since he received his "medical degree" in Ukraine after failing out of podiatry school.

I think we should force Abba the Surgeon to abstain from sex to see if he develops into a brilliant doctor, or if he becomes more of a bumbling yold, assuming that is mathematically possible, said Rav Sheshet, elbowing Baruch the Chimp.

A simple joke from a simple man, retorted Abba the Surgeon as he got up and stormed out of the shiur.

We are out of time, anyway, noted Rav Huna. But the important thing is we have issued a halakhic ruling on human and human adjacent consumption in the event of a plane crash. The rabbinate will be guided by this for centuries to come.

So let it be written, so let it be done, said the Sages in unison.

The Andrea Doria

GEMARAH:

So friends, said Rav Huna convening the meeting, who should have gotten that apartment, George or Mr. Eldridge?

Of course it should have been George, said Rav Sheshet. He suffered far more all those years right up to and including that very minute!

The astonishing tales of Costanza were gut wrenching, said Rav Pappa. Had I been caught with my shrunken marble rye dangling from my fishing pole, it would have been straight to the loony bin – I mean the special neurodivergence bin – for me.

I disagree, said Rabbah. In virtually every instance, George was responsible for his own misery. He skipped out on the job interview and ended up handcuffed to the bed; he decided to shamelessly flirt with a card-carrying Nazi; he concluded that smuggling the marble rye back into the Rosses' house was a good idea; and he was happy the envelopes that killed Susan were toxic. Mr. Eldridge is the true victim. The Andrea Doria was a nautical catastrophe. It was a real ordeal.

Are you kidding? interjected Resh Lakish. Only 51 people died. The craft eased into the ocean like an old rabbi into a nice warm mikvah. The Titanic was far worse and yet we sit here mocking Rose with extreme prejudice.

That's because Rose killed Jack with her meaty man-hands after consuming horse meat on board, much like Jay Riemenschneider, countered Rav Sheshet.

Much as George killed Susan with the toxic envelopes, added Rav Kahana.

Both shipwrecks, said Rav Pappa, paled in comparison to the greatest calamity ever to take place at sea – Noah's Ark. Virtually every man, woman, and child, every beast in the field, and every creature that creepeth and crawleth perished. Noah's Ark was a much more harrowing ordeal than the Titanic. The apartment should have rightfully gone to Noah.

And unlike Rose, added Rami bar Hama, Noah didn't drown his companion when all hope seemed to be lost.

But Noah tried to kill a bunch of birds, countered Abba the Surgeon. He sent them out into the great flood to see if the waters had receded. This was attempted avicide, much as Jerry put the kibosh on Miss Rhode Island's pigeons.

Well, concluded Bar Kappara, I guess we've established that Noah didn't deserve that apartment.

Maybe that's why he was so restless after reaching land, suggested Shimon ben Pazi, and decided to get drunk while loafing around buck naked. And then the poor shlepp was mocked by his son Ham, father of Canaan.

I disagree, said Rav Pappa. I'm drunk and naked every night and I have neither been in a shipwreck nor have I ever been homeless. I even have the most deluxe set of oversized drawers of all the Sages in the academy. And I am the envy of every Jew in Pumbedita and beyond.

Hey Pappa, interjected Resh Lakish, has anyone ever stabbed you, thrown scalding coffee in your face, or jammed a fork into your forehead?

No, replied Rav Pappa. And why do you ask, big head?

No reason, replied Resh Lakish.

The Little Jerry

GEMARAH:

What an episode! said Rav Pappa, starting the meeting. Fugitive sex and cock fights!

Where is everyone? asked Bar Kappara looking around the half-empty room.

Where do you think? Replied Resh Lakish. Obviously they anticipated the direction of this discussion, and preemptively terminated their presence in disgust.

But that's not fair! said Rav Pappa. These are among my favorite topics, and they need to be discussed.

I think, said Rav Huna, most of the Sages were concerned they were also among your favorite pastimes, and you would feel they needed demonstration.

Have you ever had fugitive sex or been to a cock fight, Rav Pappa? asked

Shimon ben Pazi.

Well actually, replied Rav Pappa, I've had a cock fight with a sexual fugitive.

What does that mean? asked Shimon ben Pazi.

Here, replied Rav Pappa. Allow me to demon-

Objection! shouted Resh Lakish as Baruch the Chimp covered his eyes in horror. Pappa is a pervert and Pazi is too stupid to participate in this discussion.

Overruled, retorted Rav Pappa. This is the *Seinfeld* script. And you are not allowed to mock the sexually or neurologically divergent. We've established this already.

Sustained, intervened Rav Huna. Sorry Pappa: Fugitive sex? Cock fights? We need to keep it clean, and there's plenty to discuss with "The Little Jerry." But mind your manners Lakish, or I will green light some good-natured ribbing about your breast reduction.

So what shall we discuss, Huna? asked Rabbah.

How about: is George responsible for Celia's continued incarceration? asked Rav Huna.

Of course he is, replied Bar Kappara. He was trying his best to live out his sexual prison fantasies while simultaneously ensuring his girlfriend remained behind bars. And when his scheme went south, he sabotaged her parole hearing.

I disagree, said Rav Pappa. Celia was an embezzler who landed herself in the clink. George was just looking for some companionship. He even gave her some smokes which is like gold in the joint. If he truly wanted to live out his fantasy he would have had the warden throw her in the box. But Celia chose to go on the lam instead of doing what was either a bullet or a nickel. He then salvaged what he could with some TLFS.

TLFS? Asked Bar Kappara.

"Tender Loving Fugitive Sex," replied Rav Pappa.

Wow, you really know your prison lingo, Pappa, noted Shimon ben Pazi.

Have you by chance done time, Pappa? asked Bar Kappara. If you lied on your HR forms then you get the boot, said Resh Lakish. There can be no compromising on this.

Screw the boot, let's throw him in the box! said Resh Lakish.

Throw Pappa in the box, chanted the remaining Sages in unison.

We have no box, said Rav Huna. This is a minimum security yeshivah.

Then let's lock him in one of the Karl Farbman oversized chest of drawers.

Lock Pappa in the drawers, chanted the remaining Sages in unison.

Rav Pappa made a hasty exit through the fire escape with a gaggle of sweaty rabbis close on his heels.

I told you we should have cancelled today's shiur, said Bar Kappara. What transpired was all too predictable.

And I told you Kappara, as I have said in the past, replied Rav Huna: We leave no stone unturned, no exposed nipple unexamined, no rooster unexplored. This is the script. This is our Torah.

The Money

GEMARAH:

Friends, said Rav Huna convening the meeting, "The Money" is all about the clash of cultures: The Gentile high-society Petermans of the world versus the economical Jews who eschew extravagance in favor of utility.

That's why the Seinfelds did not feel comfortable in a Cadillac, said Bar Kappara.

And that's why Estelle refused to buy a Mercedes, said Rabbah.

Whereas Peterman is a man of adventure and intrigue who sells luxury garments by peddling tales of extravagance and mortal danger, Morty is a peddler of shmatahs, who moves chintzy merchandise through dim lighting, mused Resh Lakish.

Whereas Peterman acquires fine fabric from the Dark Continent and the Burmese Jungles, Morty gets his rags from "a couple of Chinamen on 43rd Street," added Rav Sheshet.

Whereas George, began Shimon ben Pazi trying his best to keep up, only purchases the boldest Arabian Mocha Java...

Please continue, Shimon, said Rav Huna.

That's it. I have nowhere to go with this, said an embarrassed Shimon ben Pazi.

Why is George the Jew drinking Arabian Mocha Java PLO-blended coffee? asked Resh Lakish. Is it not antisemitic to support terrorist coffee?

I know, it's a bit of a conundrum, since it is the same episode where Estelle declared her refusal to ride in anything German, mused Rabbah.

Damn Nazis, I hate those guys, added Bar Kappara.

So the Costanzas are supporting one batch of antisemites while boycotting another. It makes no sense, concluded Rav Huna.

Maybe George is doing it for the sake of peace, much as Jerry told Joel Horneck in Season 1, "Male Unbonding," that he would be performing at Hezbollah's "annual terrorist Luncheon," suggested Rav Kahana.

Maybe the Seinfeld gang IS anti-Israel, speculated Rabbah. It's possible.

Yes they are clearly lefty assimilationists, said Resh Lakish. That's precisely why Jerry sought to date a Chinese woman and reacted with dismay when he discovered she was merely a Jew who had converted to Orientalism.

Is this why Morty buys his fabric from "Chinamen" and not from fellow Jews? asked Shimon ben Pazi.

Impossible, said Motl the Tailor. The Chinese have bargain priced fabric and, moreover, they tend to be staunch supporters of Israel.

As is Jerry, interjected Rav Pappa. Remember, in the "Cigar Store Indian," Jerry stated that if "someone asks me which way's Israel, I don't fly off the handle." An anti-Zionist WOULD fly off the handle.

Then perhaps the PLO just happens to make good coffee and there's nothing more to it, suggested Bar Kappara.

I think you are correct, concluded Rav Huna. After all, the Seinfeld Four sold their souls to the Soup Nazi. Jerry even abandoned his beloved Shmoopy for a bisque.

Which is worse, to buy soup from a Nazi or coffee from Palestinian terrorists? asked Rami bar Hama.

Definitely the soup, said Rav Sheshet. It's much easier to fight back after a cup of coffee than a bowl of soup.

Perhaps this is why European Jews went to their deaths in the Holocaust whereas the Israelis are kicking ass all over the middle east, said Bar Kappara.

But what if "coffee" doesn't mean "coffee," but means "sex" as it did in "The Phone Message"? asked Rav Kahana.

Then the question is whether it is worse to buy soup from a Nazi or to shtupp a terrorist, replied Rav Pappa. And I think the answer is a no-brainer.

You are wrong Pappa, said Rav Huna. We have extensive Halakhah on the impermissibility of shtupping an antisemite unless our people face mortal danger. Clearly, in this case, the PLO is using coffee as a means to seduce and disempower the Jews.

And the Nazis are using soup to render the Jews powerless before they send in the Gazpacho police to round them up and "evacuate" them eastward.

I think we are at an impasse, said Rav Huna, but we have made tremendous progress in codifying the halakhic intersection between food, sex, and antisemitism. Next time someone overcooks Uncle Leo's hamburger, we shall have all the answers.

The Comeback

MISHNAH:

Shammai: Milosh

Hillel: Manya
Shammai: Man-hands
Hillel: Horse face
Shammai: Tennis pro
Hillel: Architect
Shammai: Poland
Hillel: Ukraine
Shammai: James Polk
Hillel: Martin Van Buren

GEMARAH:

So what's the Halakhah on pulling the plug on a rabbi in a coma? asked Rav Huna, convening the meeting.

I think it would depend on the identity of the puller and the pullee, replied Bar Kappara.

Please elaborate, said Rav Huna.

Well it goes without saying that a cantankerous old fart like Resh Lakish would pull the plug on any one of us given the opportunity, said Bar Kappara.

That's true, replied Resh Lakish. I've got a lot of problems with all you people.

And I have no doubt that any one of us would relish the opportunity to pull the plug on Rav Pappa, continued Bar Kappara.

On the other hand, interjected Rabbah, Abba and Zutra would check if the comatose victim has any usable body parts before rendering their decision.

So would Abba and Zutra remove what they need and then still keep the person on life support? asked Rav Sheshet. You two are as bad as those infamous Chinese organ thieves.

If anyone makes a Donna Chang joke, interjected Rami bar Hama, I'm going to walk out of this ridicurous discussion. Pun intended.

That isn't a pun, Hama, that is a racist joke, admonished Bar Kappara. You're out of order and we should have no reservations in pulling out the hatchet and disciplining you.

Objection! said Zutra the Mohel. You're all sitting around, besmirching my good name while mocking ethnic minorities. Let the record show that I, Zutra, exclusively operate on the living, and the sole body part I consider usable is the foreskin…ok, and perhaps some of the surrounding region, depending on the patient. Whether he's in a coma or not is immaterial. Moreover, I'm the only one here licensed to use a hatchet.

Let the record show that Zutra will henceforth be known as Dr. Hannibal Lecter, said Rav Pappa.

So noted, replied Yontl the Librarian, but as the only one present with a doctorate, I object to calling him "Doctor."

Shmucks, what you are debating has nothing to do with Halakhah, said Rav Huna. You are rendering judgment based on the personalities of individual rabbis. Jewish law is clear on this matter: Pikuach Nefesh – life must be preserved at all costs superseding all other Halakhah (Yoma 85b).

What if the life in question is something we could eat after pulling the plug? asked Rav Pappa. I'm only asking because we have humanoid and hominid-adjacent members in the academy.

Who are considered treyf. Neither Sheshet nor Baruch are kosher for consumption, said Rav Huna.

Baruch the Chimp lowered his head in embarrassment, while Rav Sheshet slunk out of the room in humiliation.

But we determined that if we were in a plane crash and faced starvation then eating one another would be kosher even if it's treyf, noted Bar Kappara. Should it not follow then, that our "who will eat whom" foundational halakhic ruling will be applied to determine life support procedures?

You have a point, conceded Rav Huna. Yontl: add to the records that should one of us end up in a coma during a famine we need to apply the Halakhah on "who will eat whom" before we pull the plug.

I think it goes without saying that Jerry would have pulled the plug on Milosh, that jackass, said Bar Kappara. He prostituted his wife and he's a lousy tennis player to boot.

What's wrong with those people? asked Resh Lakish in disgust.

Based on his name and accent, I think they are east European, possibly Polish, said Yontl the Librarian.

But neither had a pony, noted Rabbah.

But they probably had meaty man-hands, conjectured Rami bar Hama. That would explain why Milosh was such a lousy tennis player. How humiliating.

Now that makes sense, added Rabbah. It's perfectly understandable why someone would leave a country with ponies but no tennis to come to a non-pony country with tennis.

There's no way Manya played tennis, insisted Rav Pappa. Look at what terrible shape she was in.

So? Look at that portly Newman, countered Bar Kappara. He's a zhlob who's too lazy to deliver mail in the rain, yet he's a fantastic tennis player. There's no reason to think Manya wasn't a tennis pro as well.

Or at least she would have been a tennis pro, if she didn't have those giant Polish man-hands straight out of Greek Mythology, added Rav Pappa.

I have no doubt Abba would pull the plug on a comatose Manya to use her meaty paws in some deranged surgical procedure, said Resh Lakish.

Just like on the Island of Dr. Moreau, noted Yontl the Librarian.

Wasn't that the Forbidden City of Dr. James Monroe, where Gillian Man-Hands had the surgery resulting in her meaty paws? asked Shimon ben Pazi.

Shmuck, you are conflating her affection for President James Polk with another President, retorted Rav Huna.

So President Polk performed genetic experiments on animals and humans? asked Shimon ben Pazi.

Stay focused Pazi, we are talking about Abba the Surgeon and his barbaric medical practices, said Rav Huna struggling to retain his composure.

Maybe this is why Abba chose to get his medical degree in Ukraine, which was once part of Poland: an endless supply of meaty pawed patients, added Rabbah.

But who would we eat first: Milosh or Manya? asked Rami bar Hama.

According to the records, the House of Hillel and the House of Shammai split on the question.

The Rabbis disbanded without reaching a conclusion, but confident that a hearty Slavic meal was only a heartbeat away.

The Van Buren Boys

GEMARAH:

I find "The Van Buren Boys" a perplexing episode, said Rav Huna, convening the meeting.

So do I, said Bar Kappara. Why did Kramer not bring anything to wear on his way home from the store when he was returning Bob Sacamano's pants?

Hey Kappara, interjected Rabbah, were you even listening? Kramer never made it to the store because he lost track of time and slipped in mud, ruining the very pants he was returning.

That's perfect irony, said the Sages in unison.

It is a ripping good yarn, said Shimon ben Pazi. I'm not surprised Peterman bought all of Kramer's stories.

But those are not really stories, said Resh Lakish. They are inane discussions about quotidian events, collections of conversations without beginning or end, rhyme or reason, often little more than inventories of Kramer's meager possessions.

Hey what do you suppose Kramer has in his apartment? asked Rav Sheshet.
You mean aside from Jerry's toaster oven? asked Rabbah.
Yes, why don't we make a list? said Rav Huna. Everyone: call out anything you can think of, and Yontl be sure to document this conversation.

-A hot tub!
-Fusilli Jerry and Macaroni Midler!
-A Karl Farbman oversized chest of drawers that may or may not contain three diminutive Japanese men!
-A rooster named Little Jerry!
-But no refrigerator!
-Mr. Marbles!

I don't understand what he feeds Little Jerry or his Japanese tenants if he has no refrigerator, mused Bar Kappara.

Kramer previously said that he only eats fresh produce, and we know he keeps his chicken feed in Jerry's apartment, replied Rav Sheshet.

Is it possible Kramer ate his rooster? asked Rabbah. We haven't seen it in a number of episodes. Maybe eating Little Jerry briefly quenched his appetite.

But if Kramer ate the rooster, then who would be left to have sex with the hen and the chicken? asked Shimon ben Pazi, drawing from his knowledge of previous episodes. Something is missing.

Stay focused Pazi, said Rav Huna. Kramer only owned a rooster; he never had a chicken; he never had a hen. There were no fowl ménage à trois happening in that apartment.

But what about Kramer's Japanese tenants? asked Rami bar Hama.

There's also no evidence they were having a ménage à trois, or, assuming Kramer participated, a ménage à quatre, interjected Bar Kappara.

No, continued Rami bar Hama, what I mean is that Little Jerry would not have offered enough servings or calories to satiate the hunger of all four of them.

Is it possible Kramer ate the three Japanese men? asked Shimon ben Pazi.

Out of the three of them, which one would Kramer have eaten first? asked Rav Sheshet.

It's hard to say, replied Rami bar Hama. Our halakhic guidelines for human consumption only deal with Jews vs non-Jews, Rabbis vs non-Rabbis, humanoids vs hominid adjacent. We didn't discuss eating Japanese tourists.

I say they would have eaten Mr. Oh first, replied Rav Pappa. He's the one who occupied the middle drawer and insisted on sleeping longer. Kramer, Tanaka, and Yamaguchi probably conspired and took him out while he was snoozing.

I don't think Karl Farbman would have ever given Kramer that drawer set had he known Kramer would turn it into Bates Motel, mused Bar Kappara.

I dunno, it's pretty innovative, especially for a failed corporation like Kramerica Industries, said Rav Pappa.

Kramer has become the most homicidal of the bunch, said Resh Lakish. I don't think the Van Buren Boys were such sociopaths.

Agreed, said Rami bar Hama. Given the Van Buren Boys' commitment to city planning, you can be sure nobody would have been sleeping in oversized drawers in the neighborhood they ruled.

They probably run a joint like the Plaza Hotel, complete with pay-per-view, peanuts, champagne, massages, and Asian women, said Rav Pappa.

And they probably don't eat their guests, Japanese men or otherwise, said Shimon ben Pazi.

Is it just me or is there something eerily familiar about our discussion of this episode, said Rav Huna.

I know, said Bar Kappara. It's just like that *Twilight Zone* episode where the guy wakes up and he's the same, but everyone else is different, yet they keep having the same inane conversation over and over again.

Which episode was that? asked Rav Pappa.

Oh they were all like that, said Rav Huna. Meeting adjourned.

The Susie

GEMARAH:

Friends, said Rav Huna convening the meeting, I don't think there's much to discuss with "The Susie."

Agreed, said Bar Kappara, it's an elusive episode, much like the coward Costanza going on the lam to avoid his girlfriend. And who thinks a pair of sunglasses and an answering machine is sufficient gear to disappear.

Agreed, he should have followed through with his earlier plan, to go to China and vanish in a sea of Chinamen, said Rav Pappa.

Pappa, said Abba the Surgeon, how many times do we have to tell you they are not called "Chinamen" anymore. As Elaine corrected Morty in "The Money," the correct term is "Asian Americans."

How can they be "Asian Americans," if they are located in China? asked Rav Sheshet.

The Sages sat in silence, pondering this problem.

Anyways this is immaterial, said Bar Kappara. We have nothing to discuss.

Sure we do, said Shimon ben Pazi. Jerry murdered Susie after breaking Mike Moffitt's thumbs. He's a thug and a murderer, and he now has a gambling problem.

Pazi, were you not following the plot? said Rav Kahana. Susie took her own life, probably because Peterman jilted her after their one-night stand.

Kahana, interjected Resh Lakish, were you not following the plot? Susie didn't really exist. Elaine invented her. There was no one-night stand, no suicide, and no murder.

So why would Peterman invent this tale of the two of them surrendering to temptation? Asked Rabbah.

Same reason he told Elaine to throw herself into the memoirs she was ghostwriting. He's a sicko. A white-poet warlord who got yellow fever and what not in the Burmese Jungle, concluded Abba the Surgeon.

OK, so why would Jerry take credit for murdering someone who didn't exist? asked Rabbah.

Because he's a homicidal maniac, replied Resh Lakish: Manya, Fulton, Triangle Boy, and the pigeons. A very very bad man.

Maybe he's the one who ate Kramer's rooster, suggested Rav Sheshet.

And the three little Japanese men, added Shimon ben Pazi.

Pazi, interjected Abba the Surgeon, how many times do we have to tell you: they are not called little Japanese men anymore; the correct term is "Asian American."

But how can they be "Asian American," if they are Japanese tourists who were here on a brief visit? asked Rav Pappa.

Remember they ran out of money and ended up staying in Manhattan, said Rav Sheshet. So they became American when they moved into Kramer's oversized Farbman drawers.

That's perfect irony, said the Sages in unison.

And if Kramer ate them, added Rav Pappa, then they are permanently stuck on the continent.

At least until Kramer becomes incontinent, joked Rav Sheshet as he elbowed Baruch the Chimp.

I guess that depends on where the pipes empty out, said Rav Pappa. Unfortunately the HR DEI policy manual offers zero guidance on this matter. We will need to consult a plumber.

I say we adjourn the meeting, said Rav Huna. We will let the question stand on what is the proper term for consumed Japanese tourists until we speak to professionals. We have reached the limits of rabbinical knowledge.

The Pothole

GEMARAH:

"Holy Cow!" what an episode, said Rav Huna, convening the meeting. There is so much Halakhah we need to discuss.

Agreed, said Rabbah. What does the Torah say about delivering Chinese food – sorry Asian American food – to your side of the street if the restaurant's delivery boundary ends on the other side of the street?

Potz, that's not what I meant, interjected Rav Huna. While that question may of interest to those obsessed with trivialities and the minutiae of everyday life, we rabbis have bigger flounder to fry.

I know! said Bar Kappara. What is the Halakhah on using a toothbrush that has fallen into the toilet?

Exactly, said Rav Huna. Has it been rendered impure? And if so, can it be purified?

I think no matter what, an object that falls into the toilet has been rendered impure. And anyone who touches it has been rendered impure as well and needs to go through a purification ritual, said Resh Lakish. Until such time, the person who removed the toothbrush cannot study Torah.

Does it not depend on whether or not there was anything in the toilet at the time the toothbrush fell in? asked Bar Kappara.

Yes, if someone had gone to the bathroom and the toilet remained unflushed then it is far more complicated, said Rav Huna.

I think it depends on what was in the toilet, suggested Rav Kahana. Whether it was a number 1 or a number 2.

If it's urine then the purification process would be the same as if there was nothing in the toilet, said Rabbah. If it is feces, then purification becomes impossible, and the toothbrush must be discarded. And whoever removes it must head straight to the mikvah before reciting his prayers or studying Torah.

But why? asked Shimon ben Pazi. After all, feces is just another word for manure. And we've determined that manure is just a "nure" with a "ma" in front of it. As George concluded, it's actually pretty refreshing when you think about it.

Shmuck, he was talking about horse manure, not human feces, said Resh Lakish.

So then it depends on what kind of feces is in the toilet, countered Rabbah. If it's human feces then the object has been rendered impure, if it's horse manure then it's as if the toilet is empty.

But if the manure is "refreshing," then wouldn't the toothbrush landing on the manure constitute an act of purification, negating the desecration that transpired when the toothbrush fell in? asked Rav Pappa.

Hey Pappa, would you have kissed Jenna had she brushed her teeth with a toothbrush that had come into contact with horse manure? asked Resh Lakish.

Pappa would have kissed Jenna even if she herself had fallen into horse manure, retorted Abba the Surgeon in disgust.

That's true, said Rav Pappa, but I'm also a rabbi. I would not have recited the Shema or studied Torah after kissing her until I took a plunge in the Mikvah. I respect the Lord.

Leaving Pappa aside until he undergoes psychiatric evaluation, began Bar Kappara, can we conclude that Jerry took proper ritual purification steps before kissing Jenna?

Absolutely, said Rav Sheshet. But I think he went too far when he fled after the toilet exploded on her toward the end of the episode. They could have gone through ritual purification together.

I disagree, said Resh Lakish. Given that plenty of number 2 would have come out of the detonated toilet, Jerry had no choice but to discard her. Feces is a deal breaker.

Unless of course there was horse manure, then the very act of detonation would have purified her and he should have run up to her and consolingly kissed her, countered Shimon ben Pazi.

Why would horse manure have come out of her toilet? asked Resh Lakish.

Because, speculated Rabbah, it's as George had previously stated: they are all pipes, and those pipes are all connected. All it would take is one horse to have used one networked toilet and, boom, she'd be covered in horse manure.

May I point out that horses do not use toilets, said Rav Huna.

Well what about a horse-faced relative of Jerry's, like Cousin Jeffrey, said Shimon ben Pazi. Would that count as horse manure?

I guess that depends on where Cousin Jeffrey's pipes empty out, said Rav Pappa. Unfortunately the HR DEI policy manual offers zero guidance on this matter. We will need to consult a plumber.

Isn't this how we ended yesterday's shiur? said a puzzled Rav Huna.

I know it's just like that *Twilight Zone* episode where the guy wakes covered in manure, but everyone else is clean, said Rav Pappa.

Which episode was that? asked Rav Sheshet.

Oh they were all like that, replied Rav Pappa.

The English Patient

MISHNAH:

Hillel: The English Patient
Shammai: Sack Lunch
Hillel: Neil Armstrong

Shammai: Neil Diamond
Hillel: Cubans
Shammai: Dominicans
Hillel: World's Greatest Sage
Shammai: Number One Sage
Hillel: Mandelbaum
Shammai: Mr. Peanut

GEMARAH:

Friends, said Rav Huna, is it just me or does this episode contain a touch of antisemitism?

Why do you say that? replied Rav Sheshet. Do you think Mr. Peanut is supposed to be Jewish?

Shmuck, I'm talking about the Mandelbaums, retorted Rav Huna. I got the sense that they were making fun of diasporic Jewish weakness.

Oh come on, said Shimon ben Pazi. Izzy Mandelbaum is a champion weightlifter. He took on Charles Atlas in the 1840s.

Hey Pazi, do you have any idea who Charles Atlas is? asked Resh Lakish.

Actually, I don't even know what the 1840s are, admitted Shimon ben Pazi.

I think Jerry was making an ageist joke about Mandelbaum, suggested Rabbah. You know like, the 1840s were a long time ago, around the time of the Civil War.

What civil war? asked Shimon ben Pazi. Do you mean the Maccabee Revolt? The civil war that pitted the Hellenizers against the anti-Hellenizers? That sure was a long time ago.

So that's why he mentioned Atlas, inferred Rav Kahana. Charles Atlas was the Greek God that held up the heavens.

Right, so the feats of strength pitted the Jew Mandelbaum against the Hellenizer Atlas and caused the war that led to Hanukkah, added Bar Kappara.

So then why don't we commemorate the "Mandelbaum Revolt" on Hanukkah? asked a perplexed Shimon ben Pazi.

And how do we even know Mandelbaum is supposed to be Jewish? asked Rabbah.

What do you mean? said Rav Pappa. Just look at him!

Potz, interjected Abba the Surgeon, keep your racist phrenology out of the Yeshivah.

The name Mandelbaum is a Jewish term for "Almond Tree" said Yontl the Librarian consulting the Academy's prized copy of Leo Rosten's *The Joys of Yiddish*.

But why would a Jew be named after an almond tree, asked Rabbah. And shouldn't the Mandelbaums be named after crepes, since they are makhers in the crepe business and have all that crepe money?

You think he should have been named Izzy Crepelbaum? asked Shimon ben Pazi. That sounds a little off.

I agree, interjected Rav Kahana. And if nuts are going to be involved, given the plot of the episode, he should have been named after Mr. Peanut.

The Yiddish name for Mr. Izzy Peanut would be "Pan Izzy Nussbaum," said Yontl the Librarian, consulting Leo Rosten once again.

So then I was right, said Rav Sheshet, Mr. Peanut is supposed to be Jewish.

In that case this episode was replete with antisemitism. Mr. Peanut was the victim of a combustible crepe, manufactured by Dominican terrorists who then went on to hijack an airplane.

It's true. They failed to get a living wage from their Jewish employers in that crepe emporium, said Bar Kappara.

And yet another layer of gastrointestinal anti-Jewish bigotry surfaces, concluded Rabbah: first we have the Soup Nazi and the Gazpacho police, then Uncle Leo's hamburger is overcooked by an antisemitic chef, and now Mr. Peanut is nearly roasted to death in the House of Mandelbaum.

You mean the House of Nussbaum, insisted Rav Kahana.

Yet George admired Mr. Peanut's skills, even after his calamity, noted Rav Pappa, all because he yearned for Danielle's companionship. Hey Huna, what is the Halakhah on emulating a victim of antisemitism in order to get laid?

Pappa, how can you even ask such a question, said Rav Huna in disgust. A Jew almost perished and this is your thought process? Wait where are you going?

I'm off to get a top hat, a monocle, and a cane, replied Rav Pappa. I will be Mr. Peanut, and you will all admire my skills.

Bar Kappara: Master, why do we continue to indulge Pappa?

Rav Huna: Because his escapades actually bring a great deal of money into the Yeshivah.

Bar Kappara: How is that possible?

Rav Huna: I could tell you, but then I would have to kill you. And you know better than to ask me about my business, K.

The Nap

GEMARAH:

Friends, said Rav Huna convening the meeting. What shall we discuss from

"The Nap"? What pressing halakhic issues did this episode raise?

Whether or not it is permissible to take naps under our desks, suggested Shimon ben Pazi.

That isn't a halakhic question, retorted Bar Kappara.

OK, countered Rav Pappa: can we take a nap under our desk if it has been exposed to feces within the past 12 hours?

Good question! said Rav Sheshet. I think it depends on how far the feces was located from the napper. "We learned in the Mishnah: And how far must one distance himself from urine and from feces in order to recite Shema? Four cubits." (Berakhot 26a:2)

That would imply one can take a nap under one's desk even if the feces is still present, so long as the feces is more than four cubits from the napper, said Resh Lakish.

The question is moot, countered Rabbah. Have you ever seen a desk that had more than four cubits of space underneath? I have seen no such desk. George certainly had no such desk even after Conrad built that extension for him.

That said, It was a brilliantly expanded desk, added Shimon ben Pazi.

Yes, because we know how good George is at pretending to be an architect. Only an imaginary architect could have designed such an intricate desk, said Rav Kahana.

I disagree, said Shimon ben Pazi. If he was so brilliant, he would have left more than four cubits of space to accommodate the presence of feces.

Why would there be feces under his desk, Pazi? asked Resh Lakish.

In case he had to go to the bathroom, replied Shimon ben Pazi.

Pazi has a point, said Rami bar Hama. George is also a toilet buff. He should have had Conrad install some sort of waste management system.

So then it's settled, said Bar Kappara: one cannot take a nap under a desk should feces have also been present within the preceding twelve hours.

I disagree, said Rav Pappa. Because I think it would depend on the kind of feces. If it were horse manure, which George finds so refreshing, then the desk would not be rendered impure.

How in the name of the Lord would horse manure have ended up under George's desk, asked Bar Kappara? And don't tell me a horse could have come by and relieved himself under a desk. The horse would have been far too big to fit.

What if it wasn't a horse but a pony from Poland, suggested Rabbah. Manya's pony could have easily fit under the desk.

But we've already established that Manya strangled her pony in Krakow, possibly even eating it, retorted Resh Lakish. And, moreover, it may not have even been a pony, but a horse-faced relative.

Then it stands to reason that if a horse-faced member of the House of Seinfeld, like Cousin Jeffrey, should defecate under George's desk, the desk is not rendered impure, for it is essentially horse manure, insisted Rav Pappa.

Agreed, said Rami bar Hama. And I would further argue that napping under a manure-laden desk is far more halakhically sound than swimming in the East River, as Kramer did. Did you notice how much Elaine's mattress stank?

Thus we can assume, said Rav Pappa, that if someone is rendered impure by swimming in the East River they can subsequently purify themselves by napping under George's horse-face manure laden desk. And when they awaken, they can recite the Shema, so long as the manure came from Cousin Jeffrey.

This is a sound conclusion, said Rav Huna, but hardly practical in our daily lives. We don't even have desks in our Yeshivah.

We can apply the same principle to our oversized Farbman drawers, said Rav Pappa. We nap in them all the time.

But we neither have horses nor horse-faced rabbis at the Academy, countered Bar Kappara.

Would George's "manure is refreshing" principle apply to that which emanates from a pig man? asked Resh Lakish.

Absolutely not, said Rav Huna. When George nearly stepped in manure it was clearly horse manure, not pig man manure.

But how can you know the Pig Man didn't defecate in Central Park after he escaped from the hospital? asked Rami bar Hama.

He escaped by stealing George's car, noted Rabbah. Perhaps he defecated in George's car as he fled.

Yes! said Rav Pappa. And this is how George arrived at the conclusion that manure is refreshing. Pig Man manure falls under the same halakhic category as horse manure.

So let it be written, concluded Rav Huna. Should Rav Sheshet ever defecate in our oversized Farbman drawers we can nap in them to purify ourselves.

Colleagues, interjected Rav Sheshet, would there be any point in me objecting to this entire line of reasoning or is that a silly question?

The Sages laughed at Sheshet in unison and then disbanded to take a nap in their oversized drawers.

The Yada Yada

GEMARAH:

Friends, said Rav Huna convening the meeting, today's shiur is all about who has the right to make Jewish jokes.

I think Jerry is correct in concluding that Tim Whatley converted to Judaism solely for the jokes, said Bar Kappara.

Agreed, said Rav Sheshet. He is a scoundrel that dentist, trying to achieve total joke immunity.

I didn't understand what Jerry meant when he said that if Whatley "ever gets Polish citizenship there'll be no stopping him," said Shimon ben Pazi. What does that mean?

It means that people love to make Polish jokes, said Abba the Surgeon. But according to the logic of political correctness as outlined in HR's DEI policy manual, only Polish people can make Polish jokes.

But we make Polish jokes all the time, countered Shimon ben Pazi. Ukrainian jokes too. And we're neither Polish nor Ukrainian.

And I've been complaining about this unseemly behavior all along, said Abba the Surgeon. You people have no shame.

Abba is, technically speaking, correct, interjected Rav Huna. You can only make fun of a particular group if you happen to belong that particular group. So we are only permitted to make Jewish jokes. And rabbi jokes.

Like the one Pappa told us about the rabbi and the farmer's daughter, noted Shimon ben Pazi.

Uh that wasn't a joke, said a beaming Rav Pappa. That really happened to me.

The problem is you people constantly make mohel jokes, countered Zutra the Mohel, and I'm the only one here authorized to be a mohel. So I should be the only one who is allowed to make mohel jokes.

No Zutra, the joke is that someone allowed YOU to become a mohel, retorted Resh Lakish. We are actually making fun of YOU, not the profession.

So given that I am disabled, mused Rav Pappa, I am allowed to make disabled jokes, right? And I'm also allowed to make Polish jokes because I received honorary Polish citizenship during my sojourn to Latvia. Finally, I will also postulate the following: given that Resh Lakish had upper body surgery, he's allowed to make LGBT jokes, am I correct about that?

Objection! shouted Resh Lakish.

No, Pappa is correct, said Rav Huna. It's clearly laid out in the HR policy manual.

Wonderful! Tell us a gay joke, Lakish!

Objection! shouted Resh Lakish.

Pappa, said Bar Kappara, may I point out that you can't force a minority to make a joke about themselves. They have to do so voluntarily. If Lakish wants to make fun of his gender queer condition, it's entirely up to him.

Objection! shouted Resh Lakish.

OK fine, said Rav Pappa. Then I would like the proverbial microphone so I can make some disability jokes. For instance: "Why did Helen Keller's dog run away?"

The Sages sat in silence waiting for the punchline.

Objection! Shouted Abba the Surgeon who had cared for numerous dogs that had run away from their disabled masters.

OK, how about this one: "Why did the Polack put ice in his condom?"

Objection! shouted Abba the Surgeon. I don't care if Pappa has Polish citizenship. We have the right to opt out of listening to such drek.

Actually, countered Zutra the Mohel, that last joke sounds like it could be a mohel joke as well, since it involves the numbing of a Polish shlong. That means I have the right to decide whether we hear the punchline or not.

Shmendriks, shouted Rav Huna, we convened this session to discuss who has the right to tell a Jewish joke, not to make fun of Helen Keller or east Europeans. I'm declaring this meeting adjourned.

Pathetic, said Rav Pappa. And not one person here told a single Jewish joke.

Not even the one about the rabbi and the farmer's daughter, lamented Rami bar Hama.

The Millennium

GEMARAH:

Well the Seinfeld body count is up again, said Rav Huna, convening the meeting.

There was an attempted homicide at the hands of Kramer and by extension Elaine, added Bar Kappara.

And this is the second time the Seinfeld Four resorted to poisoning as an MO.

I disagree, said Rav Pappa. Kramer did not deliberately poison Mrs. Hamilton, he should not be held accountable for his ineptitude.

Yet the poisoning of the salsa transpired while he was committing a deliberate act of sabotage at Putumayo, countered Rav Kahana. At the very least it was criminally negligent homicide.

I think Kramer was framed, said Rami bar Hama. This was an allusion by the writers to a common antisemitic stereotype: that the Jews have tried to kill the Mexican Catholics by deliberately poisoning their salsa bowls.

I think the Pope declared that those charges were fabricated, said Yontl the Librarian, flipping through "How to Fight Mexican Antisemitism" by Bari Weiss.

The point is that Jerry exhibited a callous indifference to Mrs. Hamilton, said Resh Lakish. Instead of calling 911, he took pleasure in the fact that he was elevated from "Number 1" to "Poison Control" on Mrs. Hamilton's speed dial.

May I ask whom you would put as "Number 1" on your speed dial, Lakish? Inquired Rav Pappa.

To be sure, I would put HaShem in the "Number 1" slot, replied Resh Lakish. I have a close personal relationship with my God.

The Sages stared at Resh Lakish in disbelief.

You're better off putting Baruch the Chimp on your speed dial, said Abba the Surgeon. At least then someone would actually answer the phone.

Ooh ooh ahh ahh, said Baruch the Chimp in annoyance.

When I speak God listens, said Resh Lakish. Who would you put first on your speed dial, Pappa?

If Pappa were smart he would put "Poison Control" in the "Number 1" slot, said Bar Kappara, who was still livid about Pappa's affair with his daughter.

Maybe I will, Kappara, retorted Rav Pappa. The spot is free, now that I have demoted your daughter from "Number 1" to "Number 9."

Oooh! said the Sages in unison.

Actually, my "Number 1" slot is now filled by the farmer's daughter, boasted Rav Pappa.

From the joke? asked Shimon ben Pazi.

No joke! replied Rav Pappa.

Morons, said an exasperated Rav Huna. This is literally the dumbest discussion we have ever had in this Yeshivah.

Well this is all "The Millennium" has to offer, replied Rabbah in annoyance. This is the Script. This is our Torah.

Then there's nothing left to discuss, concluded Rav Huna. Meeting adjourned. Let's order some Chinese food. The House of Wong is "Number 1" on the Yeshivah's speed dial.

The Muffin Tops

GEMARAH:

Friends, said Rav Huna convening the meeting, we need to discuss Jerry's latest infraction.

His shaving of his chest? Asked Rabbah. Yes, what is the Halakhah behind that?

It is strictly prohibited, said Bar Kappara. Jews are barred from shaving their face, so it stands to reason they cannot shave their chest hair either.

I disagree, said Rav Pappa. If it makes one's female companion happy then it is permitted. Look at how Gaga Alex went over the Mexican hairless dog. "Ooh hairless, this is where it's at," she said.

Jerry is not a dog, countered Resh Lakish.

Moreover, added Abba the Surgeon, Alex was not pro-shaving. She favored the naturally hairless, as was the case with the Mexican dog.

How do you know the dog was naturally hairless? Maybe the dog had a Mexican wax, said Rav Pappa. Hence Mexican hairless.

What the hell is a Mexican wax? asked Bar Kappara.

When one gets all their body hair waxed, replied Rav Pappa. It's an extension of the more famous Brazilian wax. I think it would be kosher for Jerry to get a Mexican wax, much as I routinely get a Brazilian wax.

First of all, replied Rav Huna, TMI. Second, I think Brazilian waxes are for women. And third, where exactly are you getting a Brazilian wax?

What do you mean where? Around my privates, of course, replied Rav Pappa in confusion.

Shmuck, I mean where in Pumbedita, countered Rav Huna.

Actually, Zutra performs them, said Rav Pappa.

Indeed I do, said Zutra the Mohel. I've been trying to supplement my income.

And how many clients have you gotten? asked Rav Sheshet.

Just one, replied Zutra the Mohel: Rav Pappa.

So how exactly does one lousy client supplement your income? asked Resh Lakish.

It doesn't, said Zutra the Mohel. Hence my other business: stump disposal.

How do you dispose of the stumps? asked Rabbah. Do you have a bus?

No, replied Zutra the Mohel, I dump the stumps behind Abba the Surgeon's homeless shelter.

That's you? I object! replied Abba the Surgeon in anger. The indigent I shelter have no interest in your stumps. It's cruel, it is a sign that you think of them as less than human. Nobody wants a bunch of stumps.

And it's politically incorrect, said Rav Pappa. You should never refer to people as stumps just because they are amputees. As a disabled man I take offense to this.

Uh, I think they are talking about muffin stumps, not people, interjected Bar Kappara.

Then why did Kramer refer to the stumps as war veterans? asked Rav Pappa.

Because Kramer is a mentally disabled idiot, said Resh Lakish.

Objection! said Abba the Surgeon. We concluded that it was cruel and exclusionary to refer to Kramer as an idiot. He is neurodivergent.

And a pet, interjected Shimon ben Pazi.

I disagree, said Resh Lakish. Any man who rents a bus and drives around Manhattan trying to convince passengers that his mediocre life is really someone else's life is clearly an idiot.

And I disagree with you, Lakish, retorted Rav Pappa. Any man who can get people to fork over $37.50 for a bite sized Three Musketeers is clearly a genius. I sense major things on the horizon for Kramerica Industries. No, the true idiot in this episode is George.

Agreed. He pretended to be a tourist and it ended up costing him his job with the Yankees. He's the idiot, said Rami bar Hama.

I think you are all ignoring the monkey in the room, said Abba the surgeon.

Again, the expression is "elephant in the room," unless of course you have Baruch in mind, but I don't see what "The Muffin Tops" has to do with our sagacious chimp, said Rabbah.

It has everything to do with Baruch, countered Abba the Surgeon. George's girlfriend visited his apartment and said, "It smells like the last tenant had monkeys or something." Does Baruch smell bad to you?

Everyone, said Rav Huna, please smell Baruch.

The Sages smelled Baruch in unison.

I don't understand, said Shimon ben Pazi. He smells just like we do.

So then maybe we smell like monkeys, suggested Rav Kahana while sniffing his armpit.

Objection! howled Abba the Surgeon. You are implying that a monkey is the yardstick to measure someone or something that smells bad.

Well what other idiom do you propose? asked Bar Kappara We can't say "it smells like manure" since we concluded that horse manure is refreshing.

Perhaps everyone smells bad because of our excessive body hair, discreetly suggested Zutra the Mohel.

Maybe we should all visit Zutra's for a Mexican wax, suggested Rav Pappa.

I will offer a volume rabbi discount, added Zutra.

Baruch thinks he should not have to pay for his, said Rav Sheshet.

Why should he get a freebie? asked Abba the Surgeon.

Because his feelings were deeply hurt by the expression, "to smell like a monkey." And HR's DEI manual states that the humanoid and hominid adjacent members of the academy are entitled to special equitable treatment, since they can't help the bodies God gave them.

Then as a stump, I should be entitled to a discount as well, insisted Rav Pappa.

Objection! said Abba the surgeon. Will you stop referring to disabled people as stumps! We went through this already.

But as a disabled man I am entitled to make jokes and use objectionable terms to describe myself. We already established this as well, earlier this week. Huna, can you please intervene.

Sorry, this one has me stumped. On the one hand it's deeply offensive, on the other hand it is in line with HR's guidelines, replied a perplexed Rav Huna.

Let's all head over to my place and think it through while we have a salubrious Mexican wax, suggested Zutra the Mohel. Complimentary muffin stumps for all.

The Sages disbanded and headed to Zutra's intent on improving their scent.

The Summer of George

GEMARAH:

Friends, said Rav Huna convening the meeting, it appears as if most of the Seinfeld Four finally got what was coming to them.

Two of them taken down by Raquel Welch, said Rav Sheshet. Who would have thought!

And George hospitalized by party invitations, said Bar Kappara. Poetic justice.

Perfect irony, said the Sages in unison.

Sorry to be a stick in the mud, interjected Abba the Surgeon, but I think you are all missing the bigger picture. This episode was deeply offensive.

Yes, they belittled the sexism women are subjected to in the workplace, said Resh Lakish. Elaine experienced harassment, and everyone responded with mockery. This is why Rabba Ruthie Cone left our academy.

Oh stop being so catty, Lakish, said Rav Sheshet.

Reer, said the Sages in unison.

If that is a comment about my upper body surgery, Sheshet, then I have every intention of reporting you to HR, you pig. Or maybe I'll just stick a fork in your forehead.

Woof, said the Sages in unison.

Your use of the word "pig" is an insult to Rav Sheshet, Lakish, said Rav Pappa. You are nothing but a hypocritical callous baboon.

And that brings me to my point, retorted Abba the Surgeon, you are once again missing the monkey in the room.

And...here we go, grumbled Rav Huna.

What is it today, Abba? How was this episode offensive to apes? Or was it offensive to cats perhaps, because they were likened to women. Do you have a thing for felines, now?

You are all focused on the episode's misogyny, but far worse was its affront to our simian friends. Peterman's employees said that Sam "walks like an orangutan" and Kramer later told Raquel Welch that she dances like a gorilla. Have you no shame? Our poor companion Baruch is humiliated, yet again.

Baruch the Chimp lowered his head in embarrassment.

I object to using a monkey as our yardstick to measure someone's comical gait, continued Abba the Surgeon.

Didn't we just do this yesterday, Abba? interjected Bar Kappara. You've already vetoed the expression "to smell like a monkey" and now you want to put the kibosh on saying someone "walks like an ape"?

Yes I do, insisted Abba the Surgeon.

But using monkeys as a yardstick to measure our human achievements is a cornerstone of civilization. We simply can't erase this into oblivion, insisted Rav Sheshet, more thrilled than ever to have monkeys, not pigs, at the center of attention.

Why not? asked Abba the Surgeon. We rabbis can do anything we want! We are the interpreters of God's will here on earth. If we can rule that horse manure is refreshing, why can't we give our simian friends the respect they deserve?

Because there are too many valuable expressions involving monkeys, insisted Rav Pappa: to monkey around; to make a monkey out of someone; monkey business; monkey see, monkey do; a monkey's uncle; that's bananas.

Yontl, is there any Halakhah to support Abba's proposition? asked Rav Huna.

Believe it or not, replied Yontl the Librarian, the Talmud for once supports Rav Pappa's position: "all people compared to Sarah are like a monkey compared to a human, as Sarah was exceedingly beautiful; Sarah compared to Eve is like a monkey compared to a human; Eve compared to Adam is like a monkey compared to a human; and Adam compared to the Divine Presence is like a monkey compared to a human." (Bava Batra 58a:6)

And elsewhere, it is written, interjected Rabbah: "Since the priest arranged the shewbread at a time that was not in accordance with the procedure dictated by its mitzvah, it is considered as though a monkey had arranged the shewbread, and it is not consecrated by the Table." (Menachot 100b:2).

I have no idea what that passage means, said Rav Sheshet.

Neither do I, replied Rabbah, but it does suggest our rabbinic colleagues routinely use "monkey" as an analogy for "idiocy."

Ahh, the Sages said in unison.

Well there you have it Abba, concluded Rav Huna. Halakhah clearly supports the use of monkeys as a yardstick to measure our beauty and idiocy. No offense to Baruch of course who is better looking and smarter than half the rabbis in this academy, especially with his Mexican wax.

Permission to reintroduce the phrase "to smell like a monkey," into our talmudic lexicon, asked Yontl the Librarian.

Actually, replied Rami bar Hama, we never banned the expression "to smell like a monkey." No, we took measures so that we would no longer smell like monkeys, and I for one am enjoying my Mexican wax.

I am also loving the scent of my fellow hairless primates, signed Baruch the Chimp, while sniffing his armpit.

Yes we do smell nice, said Rav Huna, also sniffing his armpit.

You haven't heard the last from me on this subject, said Abba the Surgeon in anger.

Perhaps not, but Season 8 is over. Your kvetching will have to wait until the end of the Summer of George.

Season 9

The Rabbis Convene After Their Mohel Buys a Deli Slicer to Streamline Business

The Butter Shave

GEMARAH:

Friends, said Rav Huna convening the meeting, I gather some of you have some rather strong feelings about this episode.

Yes, this episode trafficked in far too much humor regarding society's most vulnerable, said Abba the Surgeon, who had not forgotten the commitment to fight for simian rights he had made in Season 8.

And once again, Abba is going apeshit, said Rav Sheshet, elbowing Baruch the Chimp, who laughed even though the joke was at his expense.

There were no damn monkeys in this episode, Abba, said Rabbah, so what's your grievance?

No he's right, interjected Resh Lakish. The episode was extremely cruel to Magnus.

Who the hell is Magnus? asked Shimon ben Pazi.

That poor shlepp who sat next to Elaine on the airplane: Vegetable Lasagna.

Aahh, said the Sages in unison.

He was a bit of a lemechke that one, said Rabbah. Where is the cruelty?

Because calling him Vegetable Lasagna is an affront to vegetarians everywhere, insisted Resh Lakish. It implies that vegetarians are weak, pathetic, effeminate, and, well, lemechkes. This is precisely how the story of Cain and Abel transpired.

What in the name of HaShem do you mean? said Bar Kappara.

Cain killed Abel because his vegetarianism was mocked by God, said Resh Lakish. He sought to prove one didn't need to be a carnivore to be tough. So he knocked off his brother.

I'm not certain that is supposed to be the main takeaway from this early event in human history, said Rav Huna. But OK, let's appease Resh Lakish. All in favor of banning the ridicule of vegetarians – whom I will add are NOT a protected group according to Title VI or HR's DEI policy – say "aye."

Aye, said the Sages in unison.

Oh come on, said Rav Pappa, this is absurd. You're all ignoring the elephant in the room.

Please tell me this isn't about a monkey, said Rav Huna.

No it's about the true affront perpetrated in this episode, continued Rav Pappa: George pretending to be handicapped in order to secure employment.

But that was not his fault, said Rav Sheshet. Mr. Thomassoulo assumed he was handicapped, even as George tried to set the record straight.

Ah, but George subsequently embraced this identity, and he expressed an entitlement to special treatment and company resources because of his "disability." As a disabled person, as a genuine "stump," if you will, I take offense.

What exactly did George mean when he said "Jerry, let's face it, I've always been handicapped. I'm just now getting the recognition for it."

The Sages sat in silence contemplating this conundrum.

Perhaps his imposture is sincere; he's genuinely taken on this false identity, much as Rachel Dolezal claimed to be African American or Resh Lakish now claims to be gender queer because he had a breast reduction to avoid having to wear a mansier.

Objection! shouted Resh Lakish. I've never claimed to be "gender queer." This is an identity you foisted upon me in order to amuse yourselves.

And amuse ourselves we have, said Rav Sheshet, elbowing Baruch the Chimp.

So perhaps George genuinely thinks he's disabled, suggested Shimon ben Pazi.

I think it's metaphorical, suggested Yontl the Librarian. Perhaps George means "disabled" in the sense that he is the embodiment of the Jew in exile, the neurotic and effeminate coward; he is the antithesis of the martial warrior oozing with brawn and masculinity, anchored to Zion. He is emblematic of our sickly diasporic condition. And in claiming his recognition by Play Now is well-deserved, George is expressing Israel's chosenness, which had been unjustly revoked by an angry God who abandoned us to our miserable fate.

The Sages sat in silence for an extended period of time.

I don't think we understand what that means, said Bar Kappara on behalf of the gaggle of rabbis who were no longer sweaty because of their Mexican wax.

Yes why are we are not grasping what you have said, Yontl? repeated Rav Huna.

Perhaps because I'm the only one in the f*cking Academy who has an actual degree in Jewish studies, grumbled Yontl the Librarian under his breath.

The Voice

GEMARAH:

HellOOO said Rav Huna, convening the meeting, La La La.

HellOOO, Hola, ShalOHHHM, La La La, replied Bar Kappara.

I gotta tell you something, said Rav Pappa. That voice is played. So so very played. Calling each other "bastards" and "sons of bitches" was far more interesting. Can we move on?

OK, said an undermined Rav Huna. Let's discuss whether or not George had the right to stay at Play Now after he was caught fake handicapping.

Do you mean legally or halakhically? asked Rav Sheshet.

Excellent question, said Bar Kappara, and I think George was doing a mitzvah by staying because this episode, yet again, had antisemitic overtones.

How so? asked Shimon ben Pazi.

George said he was "like a weed," replied Bar Kappara. Much as the Nazis likened the Jews to a virus attaching itself to a healthy host, they also viewed the Jews as weeds that needed to be eliminated from their well-kept imperial Aryan garden. George is the tenaciously stubborn Jew; the weed who refuses to obey marching orders.

I disagree, said Rav Pappa. George also likened himself to Hitler in his last days in his bunker. How can he simultaneously be Adolf Hitler and a weedy Jew?

Because, replied Bar Kappara, George subsequently said he's like a "weed in Hitler's bunker." He's a Jew who's infected Hitler's fortress of solitude. George finally exhibited beytzim on behalf of his tribe.

I'm skeptical, replied Rabbah. You'd think the bunker would be the first place Hitler would check for weeds. And I don't see why a Jew would even want to be in Hitler's bunker. Feh. It must have stunk in there by 1945.

George wouldn't have noticed the stench, given that we have established he smells like a monkey, said Rav Pappa.

Objection! said Abba the Surgeon.

What now Abba? grumbled Rav Huna. We've already ruled that "smells like a monkey" is a halakhically sound expression. It's straight from the script. It's straight from our Torah.

Ah, retorted Abba the Surgeon. But the Nazis likened the Jews to apes, so in this particular context, the expression "to smell like a monkey" has antisemitic overtones.

Then it follows that Hitler would have definitely removed any weeds from his bunker since they were Jews who smelled like monkeys, countered Rabbah.

This isn't adding up, said Rav Sheshet, especially since George had previously expressed his sexual attraction to a Nazi in "The Limo." And worse, Eva the Nazi was deeply attracted to George. She was ready to die for him. Why would she be attracted to a weed who smelled like a monkey?

So he's a self-hating Jew, said Rav Pappa. And one who fakes being handicapped as well. And he IS a faker. No handicapped person could survive the asbestos they sandblasted into his office.

What is asbestos? asked Shimon ben Pazi.

I think it's a chemical the Nazis used to exterminate disabled people, replied Bar Kappara.

So as a disabled Jew who stank like a monkey, hiding out in Hitler's bunker, George should have been doomed, noted Rav Sheshet.

Yet he survived, even after the collapse of the Play Now Empire, said Rav Huna.

So George is a Survivor, said Shimon ben Pazi. Like Elie Wiesel and Primo Levi.

Yontl, did George compose any memoirs to document the tribulation he endured? asked Rav Sheshet.

Just *The Astonishing Tales of Costanza*, replied Yontl. And that play *La Cocina*. But we have a copy of neither.

I think we've determined here today that George not only deserved that handicapped restroom, but he also deserved that plush apartment, said Bar Kappara. He certainly suffered more than the Andrea Doria Survivor. George is the Survivor, an unrecognized hero.

Agreed, said the Sages in unison.

So now what? asked Rav Huna.

I know! replied Shimon ben Pazi. How about ketchup and mustard in the same bottle?

The Serenity Now

GEMARAH:

Friends, said Rav Huna convening the meeting, this episode has revealed that a major catastrophe has befallen our tribe, abetted by a renegade member of our flock. You know who you are, come forth!

But I didn't do anything wrong, I swear to God, said Zutra the Mohel. I really thought that was part of the patient's foreskin when I began my surgery. And Motl the Tailor sewed it back up.

The Sages stared at Zutra the Mohel mouths agape.

Zutra, said Rav Huna, we will bookmark this admittedly bizarre revelation and come back to it later. No I am speaking of Rav Pappa and his unethical business that is destroying our people.

I object! shouted Rav Pappa. If you are referring to "Shiksa dot com," I can assure you that my clients never renounce their Judaism.

Ah, but your clients are only interested in shiksas BECAUSE they are Jewish men, Pappa, countered Bar Kappara. You are playing on their imagined revulsion toward Jewish women.

Not so, Kappara, insisted Rav Pappa. Let's not forget my engagement to your daughter. Pappa was pretty sweet on Sara and Sara was no Shiksa.

That's it Pappa, it's go time, shouted Bar Kappara. You and I are going to take this outside right now.

A rabbinic brawl, exclaimed Rav Sheshet! And people make fun of us for being a cowardly effeminate nation.

To be honest, I don't think our Mexican waxes have helped disprove that reputation, noted Resh Lakish. Maybe an old-fashioned cat fight between rabbis is just what we need.

C-c-c-at fight, said the Sages in unison.

Nobody is going to rumble in my Yeshivah, shouted Rav Huna. Calm down Kappara.

Serenity Now! howled Bar Kappara.

Serenity Now, what the hell is that? Asked Shimon ben Pazi.

I'm trying Frank Costanza's relaxation technique, said Bar Kappara. Serenity now!

People, we have a halakhic question with far deeper implications on the table, said Rav Huna. Is "Shiksa dot com" against Jewish law and worse, is it destroying our peoplehood?

Scripture is clear, insisted Resh Lakish: "For they have taken of their daughters for themselves and for their sons; so that the holy seed have mingled themselves with the peoples of the lands" and it is an abomination (Ezra 9:1-2).

Ah, but that's only if they marry and reproduce, countered Rav Pappa. I have a rigorous interview process to determine if my clients are sponge worthy, and then proceed to facilitate hook-ups for one night stands only. That's the policy of "Shiksa dot com." My business is solely about getting laid. And kinky shtupping at that. Nobody is marrying, reproducing, and starting wholesome families on my watch. Our Jewish seed remains pure. So I resent this character assassination.

Gee, forgive us Pappa, we thought you were promoting some sort of immoral activity, replied Resh Lakish sarcastically.

Absolutely not, said Rav Pappa. In fact, the data we've collected suggests 9 out of 10 clients go on to marry Jewish women. I'm merely offering these Jewish men the chance to wet their toes on the other side of the pond, so to speak.

As a client of Pappa's I agree, said Rami bar Hama. It's as Rabbi Glickman suggested: "shiksappeal" is a myth, like the sasquatch, or his Israelite cousin, the golem.

I don't think there's any relationship between the sasquatch and the golem, interjected Rav Sheshet.

I think you're right, said Rabbah. The sasquatch is a humanoid monkey-like creature who inhabits the woods, whereas the golem is a soulless creature of clay brought into existence through kabbalist mysticism. As Lenny Bruce put it, sasquatches are goyish, golems are Jewish.

If that's so why do we have a monkey in the Yeshivah but no golem? asked Shimon ben Pazi.

Aha, said Rav Pappa, It is you people, not me, who are diluting our peoplehood with goyish simians. You should have brought a golem, not a sasquatch, into the rabbinate.

First off, Baruch isn't a sasquatch, he's a chimpanzee. And second, Baruch converted to Judaism, countered Bar Kappara, so you are wrong yet again, Pappa.

And we know Baruch converted to make use of your services Pappa, said Rav Sheshet. He needed to be a Jew before he could hook up with a shiksa.

All the more reason for my business to continue, countered Rav Pappa.

I am issuing an official ruling, concluded Rav Huna. Pappa has one week to transform "Shiksa dot com" into a Jewish-only dating site. We are going to eliminate the myth of "shiksappeal" once and for all. You need to fill the ranks of your clientele with Jewish women.

Now if only we knew some women, lamented Bar Kappara.

The Blood

GEMARAH:

Fellow Sages, said Rav Huna convening the meeting. We need to discuss one of the Seinfeld Four's monstrous descent into the domain of Caligula.

Agreed, said Rav Pappa. Hoarding blood in one's freezer suggests Kramer has become a vampire. Jerry was right to fear being across the hall. And sure enough Kramer's blood ended up coursing through Jerry's veins.

Excuse me, but doesn't a vampire suck the blood of other people, not insert their blood into an injured friend to save their lives? countered Resh Lakish.

No, it's as Jerry said, replied Rav Pappa: he could feel Kramer's blood borrowing things from his blood. This was an all-out vascular invasion. And then he used his blood to take over Jerry's car. Schnorring in a bloody key.

Shmucks, Rav Huna was talking about "George the Fornicating Gourmet" and his depraved amalgamation of food and sex. Hence the Caligula reference, interjected Bar Kappara

I don't see why that's a problem, countered Rav Pappa.

Me neither, said Shimon ben Pazi, and I for one was thrilled to finally understand one of *Seinfeld*'s political references.

Sure, Caligula the monstrous Roman Emperor, said Rabbah. He was a very very bad man. He sought to erect a statue of himself in the Jerusalem Temple, a blasphemous scheme that was fortunately thwarted.

Desecrating the Temple is a far greater sin than incorporating a pastrami sandwich into a mid-afternoon tryst, said Rav Pappa. So unless George erected a statue of himself on the premises of a Jewish holy site, he did nothing wrong.

You're a pervert Pappa, said Resh Lakish. Do you engage in such wanton depraved behavior?

I've been known to munch on some Salami while in the sack, replied Rav Pappa. The ladies rather like it.

I agree, said Rami bar Hama. The visual record suggests that the fusion of food and sex has dotted the landscape of Jewish history.

For example? asked Bar Kappara.

For example, replied Rami bar Hama: Don't you remember the Matzoh Ball scene in *Yentl*? Or the Schnitzel scene in *Schindler's List*?

Yontl, can you please check if there is any Halakhah on augmenting intercourse with food? requested Rav Huna.

This is what I have found, said Yontl the Librarian: "Rav Judah said in the name of Shmuel in the name of R. Hanina: I saw a non-Jew buy a goose in the market, have sex with it, and then strangle it, roast, and eat it. R. Jeremiah of Difti said: I saw an Arab who bought a side [of meat], pierced it in order to have sex with it, and then roast it and eat it." (Avodah Zarah 22b:12)

That sounds just like Pappa to me! said Resh Lakish in satisfaction.

Objection! said Rav Pappa. That passage describes bestiality. Neither I nor George have actually had sex with the beast from which the pastrami came, nor from the chicken or the hen from which the soft-boiled egg was extracted. This talmudic passage is not applicable here.

Well that's it, there's no other Halakhah, conceded Yontl the Librarian.

Then I guess it is permissible to eat during sexual intercourse, relented Rav Huna.

But what is the Halakhah if we were all in a plane crash in the Andes and, facing starvation, we started to eat each other during sexual intercourse? asked Shimon ben Pazi.

Then I suppose the procedures we earlier compiled governing the order of who would eat whom first would kick in, mused Rav Huna. Yontl please amend the text in light of our new ruling on food fused with sexual intercourse and read it:

> "Should sexual intercourse transpire during a famine, it is better to eat a Jew than a Gentile, a rabbi than a layman, a monkey than a human whether the monkey is a rabbi and a Jew or not, but consuming a pig man while fornicating should be a last resort. Horse-faced Jews can be eaten before pig men, especially when starving during sex in Poland, where it is safe to assume Manya consumed her horse-faced cousin during sexual intercourse, because only those on Schindler's List received schnitzel to survive the Nazi invasion," read Yontl the Librarian from the archival minutes.

But who would we eat last during sexual intercourse? asked Rav Sheshet. Does it depend on who is the least kosher or who would provide the most pleasure during sex? For instance, George would rather eat pastrami than strawberries and chocolate sauce because "they just aren't a meal." Pastrami satiates him in a way fruit doesn't. How do we apply this to our Halakhah?

That's an easy one, said Rav Pappa. We'd eat Chef Shlomo last during sex.

Why? asked Bar Kappara.

Because, replied Rav Pappa, he is the only one who could tell us how best to cook and prepare the other rabbis.

The Junk Mail

MISHNAH:

Shammai: Hillel, this is my landlord, Jesus the Christ.

Hillel: Look who it is, it's the "Christian me."

Jesus: And look who it is, it's the "Jewish me."

Shammai: So where does that leave me?

Hillel and Jesus together: Like Whitey Fisk, forgotten to history.

GEMARAH:

Friends, said Rav Huna, convening the meeting, it seems there are no halakhic issues to discuss in "the Junk Mail."

Indeed, said Bar Kappara. The plotlines from Season 9 are just too wacky.

And our discussions are not wacky? retorted Resh Lakish. Yesterday we debated whether Kramer is a vampire or not, and then argued over whom among us we would eat last during sexual intercourse should a famine transpire in the Andes.

Precisely, said Bar Kappara – we had those outlandish discussions because we were following the *Seinfeld* script, which I will remind you included Kramer putting his blood in Jerry's car, not to mention George's culinary sexual escapades, which induced him to have an orgasm while eating his lunch at Monk's.

Kappara is right, said Rav Huna. We never even discussed how in "The Butter Shave" Kramer morphed into a chicken and Newman tried to eat him. Perhaps if we were better rabbis we would have found pertinent Halakhah with that one. This is the script, the is our Torah. If they eat each other, we are bound to follow suit.

OK, so let's discuss mail, suggested Shimon ben Pazi: What's the deal with all these catalogs and envelopes, said Shimon ben Pazi in his best comedic Seinfeldesque voice, and why do men in blue keep stuffing all those envelopes in mailboxes? What's up with that?

Because they are mailmen and their job is to deliver the mail, retorted Bar Kappara. Next!

What's the deal with Seinfeld's van and why does is beep when you go in reverse? offered Rav Sheshet in his best comedic voice.

I think that's a safety feature, surmised Bar Kappara. You both suck. Next!

Why should you not come a knockin' if this van's a rockin'!? asked Rav Pappa.

Because nobody wants to see Frank and Estelle Costanza having sexual intercourse, replied Rav Huna. Next!

What's the deal with the Wiz, and why does nobody beat him? asked Rabbah in a rather mediocre comedic voice.

This is an absurd discussion, said Resh Lakish. I'm wasting my day. I could have stayed at home and watched my face break out.

So instead you came here and allowed us to watch, retorted Rav Sheshet.

Maspik! Genug shoyn! I've had enough of this. We are officially disbanded until tomorrow, when we will try out a new format. Adjourned!

TO BE CONTINUED

The Merv Griffin Show

GEMARAH:

Hi everybody, said Rav Huna, beckoning his flock into a now sparkling academy that may have smelled a bit like a garbage dumpster. Welcome to "The Jew Filerman Show"!

What in the name of HaShem is going on here? asked Rabbah. And why are you reading from cue cards, Huna?

This is our new format, replied Rav Huna. I told you we were shutting down and retooling. So our shiurs are now called "The Jew Filerman Show."

What is a Jew Filerman? asked Shimon ben Pazi.

He's the host, interjected Bar Kappara. Rav Yehudah "Jew" Filerman, one the brightest rabbis in our academy.

Then why have we never seen him before? asked Rav Sheshet.

Because he's a real sidler, he just sidles up to you, noted Bar Kappara.

And for those of us who don't know what sidling is, please explain, Kappara, interjected Rav Huna.

Again with the note cards, Huna? Seriously, are you OK? asked Resh Lakish.

And what did you do to our academy, asked Rabbah. Where are our oversized chests of drawers? Where are we supposed to sleep?

They're backstage. And this is the new format, said Rav Huna. I'm turning the floor over to Jew Filerman.

[Cue music and lighting]

Jew Filerman: Hi everybody, I'm Jew Filerman, but I'm not really new here. Everyone come and take a seat for The Jew Filerman Show.

Jew Filerman: So, Rav Pappa, could you be even more dashing than the last time I saw you? What a dreamboat rabbi!

Rav Pappa: Thanks for noticing, Jew! I got my chest waxed at Zutra the Mohel's Bodyshop.

Jew Filerman: Ah Zutra the Mohel's Bodyshop! I spent a month there one night.

Baruch the Chimp: Ooh ooh aah aah.

Resh Lakish: Why does Baruch get to sit next to the host?

Jew Filerman: He's my sidekick. He takes some of the pressure off. So Pappa, please tell us, are there any romantic scandals in your life we should hear about?

Rav Pappa: Funny you should ask, Jew. I recently had a fling with Bar Kappara's daughter Sara. And believe it or not, his three other daughters – Lara, Tara, and Dara Kappara – all answered my very first personal ad in my retooled dating site, now called "My Sheyneh Meydl* dot com: Wholesome Jews Looking To Be a Little Bad." I'm seeing all three of them after Shabbos. We may be talking ménage des quatres here!

Bar Kappara: That's it Pappa, it's go time. Let's take this backstage right now. I'm going to sew your ass to your face and stuff you in a manure-laden oversized drawer.

Jew Filerman: No fighting on my set. We run a clean show here.

Bar Kappara: Pappa is bragging about shtupping three of my daughters at once and you're telling me to keep it clean!

Jew Filerman: He's tonight's star guest for this episode's theme, "Scandals and Animals."

Rav Huna (from the audience): He's right Kappara, this is the format, this is *Seinfeld*, this is the script, this is our Torah.

Resh Lakish: So who do you have lined up for the animal portion of the show, or is Baruch going to introduce this?

Jew Filerman: Ladies and Gentlemen, tonight we have the pleasure to host the first documented Jewish pig man in history. Rav Sheshet, come on down [theme music plays].

[Rav Sheshet took a seat on stage]

Jew Filerman: Great to have you back Sheshet! Is it possible you look even more like a pig man than the last time I saw you?

Rav Sheshet: I don't recall agreeing to this.

Jew Filerman: So Sheshet [reading from his cue cards], for those of us who don't know, can you explain the difference between humanoid and hominid adjacent, and which box you checked off on HR's form when you applied for this job?

Resh Lakish: That's it, I'm out of here. This new format stinks, Huna, and this Filerman is a lousy host. He's a hack.

Rabbah: Me too. I'm sidling my way out of here.

Rav Sheshet: Me too.

Abba the Surgeon: Me too.

Rav Pappa: Hey come on, I have so many more romantic yarns to share with the audience.

Bar Kappara: Let's go Pappa [Kappara grabbed Pappa and dragged him off stage]

Rav Pappa: These are my fans. I have the right to be here. You're hurting my elbow.

[Most of the Sages left and the lights went out]

Well at least you tried, Master, said Bar Kappara, but the new "talk show" format didn't work.

I know, admitted Rav Huna. I suppose that the Jews are just not cut out for the entertainment business.

The Slicer

GEMARAH:

Hey Huna, said Rabbah, preemptively starting the meeting, why is Zutra handcuffed to the chair in the corner?

Given that the most memorable line from this *Seinfeld* episode was "No, you're not taking a deli slicer to my boss," I would think the reason was obvious, said Rav Huna.

I am trying to run a legitimate snip and save business, howled Zutra the Mohel, and you assume that I am going to start treating my patients like meat in a kosher butcher shop?

Nice try, Zutra, said Bar Kappara. But we know you purchased a slicer this morning at the marketplace. Yes, we had you followed. Why? Because the frickin' episode is called "The Slicer" and we have a whack job for a mohel in our employment.

Why is he still in our employment? asked Shimon ben Pazi.

According to HR, he has tenure. And botched circumcisions with crude utensils, however much he may repeatedly miss the target, is not sufficient grounds for dismissal, said Rav Huna bitterly.

Sure, him they give tenure! grumbled Yontl the librarian, the only one among the gaggle of formerly sweaty rabbis to hold a doctorate or for that matter any degree from a nationally recognized institution.

What's that Yontl? asked Bar Kappara.

Nothing your Holy Rabbiness, replied Yontl the Librarian. And that's Dr. Yontl, he continued, grumbling.

Your concerned about Zutra, interjected Abba the Surgeon, yet this episode made a mockery of my profession: "Dr. Van Nostrand" treating Mr. Kruger's skin cancer, Kramer suggesting that medical healers are also poisoners, it's unconscionable. It's downright antisemitic.

How is it antisemitic? asked Rav Pappa. There's no evidence Dr. Sitarides is Jewish. The name sounds Greek, actually. I think they were just making fun of doctors, which is well in keeping with our practices.

Indeed, Abba, we see you as little more than an Aloe pusher who is one step above the woman behind the Clinique counter, joked Rav Sheshet paraphrasing George.

I do not have to stand for this, howled Abba the Surgeon.

Woof Woof, not Bang Bang, "Doctor Abba Van Nostrand," said the Sages in Unison.

Do you even have a degree from the Julliard, like the real Dr. Van Nostrand? asked Rabbah.

Obviously not, countered Abba the Surgeon.

And how do we know you won't someday take a deli slicer to your superior? asked Shimon ben Pazi. Maybe that's how they perform surgery in Ukraine?

Maybe we should shackle him to Zutra, suggested Rav Pappa.

Settle down, Rabbis, said Rav Huna. We'll give Abba the benefit of the doubt, for the moment at least. We had him followed as well and he did not purchase a slicer, so as they say, innocent until proven guilty.

For how long should we leave Zutra shackled to the chair? asked Bar Kappara.

At least until the series finale, replied Rav Huna. We may not be allowed to fire him, but there's nothing in the policy manual preventing us from imprisoning him. Now let's go ransack his apartment and find that slicer. I'm suddenly in the mood for a mile high.

The Betrayal

GEMARAH:

Rav Pappa: Ouch, that hurt!

Bar Kappara: You are a dead man Pappa. Kavorka my tokhes, you home wrecker.

Rav Pappa: But how was I supposed to know she was related to you.

Bar Kappara: Serenity Now!

Rav Pappa: I'm apologizing. I'm very sorry. I'll enter sex addicts anonymous.

Bar Kappara: You can stuff you sorries in a sack, mister! Serenity Now!

[Crash]

[FIVE MINUTES EARLIER]

Rav Huna: Kappara why are you bringing that matzoh ball packed with ice inside the Yeshivah?

Bar Kappara: I'm going to nail that perverted little weasel Pappa with it. There he is, I see him outside.

[ONE WEEK EARLIER]

Oh my God what's that smell in here! There's nothing refreshing about this, screamed the naked Sages in unison.

[TWO MINUTES EARLIER]

In the heat of passion, the Sages all started to rip off each others' clothing down to their dangling tzitzit and glistening Mexican waxes. The gaggle of naked rabbis made a mad dash for the oversized drawers.

[FIVE MINUTES EARLIER]

Regardless, Ranawat is from none of those places. He isn't Dutch, he didn't live in an attic, and even if he did live in an attic his attic wouldn't have been underwater. And he committed a very grave sin. As they say in India, he is a very very bad man.

I disagree. First off, they say that in Pakistan. Second, we should be discussing how Jerry, not Pinter, is the very very bad man.

I Agree, said Rami bar Hama. Jerry should be ashamed of himself for having slept with Nina, and he should have come clean and told George about it. Who does that to their best friend?

Yes, who indeed? said Bar Kappara. Almost as bad as shtupping the daughters of one's colleague.

It wasn't his fault, countered Rabbah. There was an extended awkward pause in the extended conversation. And awkward pauses lead to passionate sex.

The Sages sat awkwardly in silence for an extended period of time.

[TWO MINUTES EARLIER]

Maybe Holland sank like Atlantis, suggested Shimon ben Pazi.
Then wouldn't Anne Frank's attic have been underwater? asked Rav Sheshet.

[TWO MINUTES EARLIER]

Who exactly are the Dutch? asked Rav Sheshet.
What do you mean who are the Dutch? They are a people. They live in Holland, said Resh Lakish.
No that's the Netherlands, not Holland, said Rabbah.
So if they're from the Netherlands, what happened to Holland? I don't see it on the map, said Rav Sheshet.

[TWO MINUTES EARLIER]

Objection! said Rami bar Hama. People are not obligated to reveal their entire dating history when they get married. Ranawat is innocent.

Agreed, said Rav Pappa. When I meet a new love newton, I tell them nothing and they tell me nothing. That's my policy. Last week I went out with a Lara, a Dara, and a Tara, and for all I know they could have been sisters, but we didn't discuss it.

It's a nice name Ranawat, mused Shimon ben Pazi. Is that Dutch?

It's Indian, you shmendrik, said Bar Kappara. That's why the episode took place in India. He's not Dutch.

[TWO MINUTES EARLIER]

I have "mechanical sex" all the time, it's a Pappa specialty, boasted Rav Pappa, but I suspect Elaine meant something different.

As her bridesmaid, continued Abba the Surgeon, Elaine had an obligation to tell Sue Ellen about their encounter. Ranawat should have also come clean.

[THREE MINUTES EARLIER]

The horror, the horror, said the Sages in unison.

I still can't believe she slept with the groom, said Abba the Surgeon.

She did nothing wrong, insisted Rav Sheshet. It was years before Pinter got engaged to Sue Ellen. Where is the sin?

Moreover, they only went out a few times, and, as Elaine put it, the sex was rather mechanical, said Rami bar Hama.

What exactly is mechanical sex? asked Shimon ben Pazi.

[TWO MINUTES EARLIER]

Elaine would do something like that, replied Bar Kappara. Remember how she tried to put Putumayo out of business: out of spite.

She also went all the way to the Burmese Jungle to show Peterman "the Urban Sombrero," said Rav Kahana.

[TWO MINUTES EARLIER]

I don't see how or why, replied Rav Pappa. We have the plague in Pumbedita, and I urinate in public all the time.

Agreed, said Abba the Surgeon. I resented the way they portrayed India as a land of barbarism. George just needed a 4-cubit buffer, and he could have peed anywhere. It's in the Mishnah.

I don't understand who goes all the way to India out of spite, said Rav Sheshet.

[TWO MINUTES EARLIER]

What a bizarre trip to India, said Rav Huna.

Is it possible that George didn't go to the bathroom during the entire trip? asked Rabbah.

[TWO WEEKS EARLIER]

Guest: I'm here about the ad for a night's rest in the oversized drawers.

Rav Huna: OK you look sufficiently like a horse. You can grab a blanket from the other room.

[TWO DAYS EARLIER]

Ahasuerus the Bookkeeper: Master, our Yeshivah is in dire need of funding.

Putting "Shiksa dot com" out of business has broken us financially.

Rav Huna: What if we turn our oversized chests of drawers into a Japanese-style hotel? Would that generate income?

Ahasuerus the Bookkeeper: Yes, and if we follow through with our previous discussion about freshening them up with horse manure we can market them as ritual purification chambers as well.

[300 YEARS EARLIER]

Shammai: Hi, I'm Shammai. I'm unemployed and my nemesis is Hillel. May I stay in your garage?

Jesus: Of course my sagacious brother. Help yourself to anything in here. What's mine is yours.

Shammai: But you don't have anything.

The Apology

GEMARAH:

Friends, said Rav Pappa preemptively convening the meeting, I perused our corpus of Halakhah, and it seems we have no guidance on good naked versus bad naked. Let's discuss.

Pappa, we wear our clothes on at the Academy, we keep our clothes on in public, and what we do in the privacy of our own homes is nobody's business, replied Rav Huna. What's to discuss?

Let me point out that we have all seen each other naked, said Rami bar Hama. I can relate in great detail the extent to which our Mexican waxes had an impact on each and every rabbi's body. I know whose bodies are riddled with boils and warts, and I know whose bodies are as smooth as a baby's tokhes.

He is right, Huna, interjected Rav Sheshet. We see each other naked in the shvitz all the time. Is what we put on display good naked or bad naked?

I think it depends on the rabbi, said Rami bar Hama. Some of us, like Rav Pappa, look terrific naked. He's got the most sublime buttocks I have ever seen on anyone who has been ordained.

Why thank you for noticing Rami, replied Rav Pappa. You should see me squatting on all fours with my belt sander.

What time should I pop over, asked an eager Rami bar Hama.

I'm sorry, I disagree, said Resh Lakish. Elaine is correct. The male body, is especially hideous. All hair and lumps. As she put it, it's "simian." No offense, Baruch.

Baruch the chimp tightened his kaftan and pulled his shtreymel over his eyes.

Then why did God create Adam naked and in his image, asked Rav Pappa. Are you suggesting the Lord also has a lumpy, ape-like body?

We can never know, because nobody has seen the Lord's naked body, said Bar Kappara.

Not so, Moses saw him on Mount Sinai, when God divinely revealed himself, countered Rav Pappa.

Yet the Torah contains no description, other than the bush that did not burn, said Shimon ben Pazi. Is the bush not a reference to God's body hair?

Objection! said Resh Lakish. This is blasphemous. We are not permitted to discuss whether God is hairy or not. Why do you think the Second Commandment proscribes the carving of graven images of the Lord.

Perhaps the Second Commandment was issued because the Lord is goofy looking, said Rav Pappa. And when Adam and Eve – who were created in God's image – ate from the Tree of Knowledge they came to know their own goofiness and accordingly covered themselves up.

Objection! said Resh Lakish. I call for convening a tribunal and prosecuting Rav Pappa for blasphemy. We are not permitted to discuss what God looks like naked.

You're actually wrong, Lakish, said Yontl the Librarian. Halakhah strictly prohibits physical depictions of God. There's no prohibition against discussing what such depictions would look like should they be allowed.

Yontl is correct, said Rav Huna. This conversation is well within bounds.

Of course I am right, you potz, I have a f*cking PhD in Jewish theology, grumbled Yontl the Librarian under his breath.

Well if God is ashamed of his appearance, much like Adam, then I feel bad for him, said Rabbah.

Perhaps this is why he is angry all the time, said Rav Pappa. Perhaps he needs a lady friend.

Objection! howled Resh Lakish. You are not permitted to discuss the Lord using perverse sexualized imagery.

You're actually wrong, Lakish, said Yontl the Librarian. Kabbalah is filled with divine sensuality bordering on the carnal.

Yontl is correct, said Rav Huna. This conversation is well within bounds.

Of course I'm right, you potz, I have a f*cking PhD in Jewish theology, grumbled Yontl the Librarian under his breath.

So then why is it that God isn't depicted as goofy looking in the iconography of the goys? asked Rav Sheshet. They worship the same god as us. They even depict Yoshke as a divinely dashing being, and he, by all our Jewish accounts, was nothing more than a goofy looking Israelite.

Perhaps it is because Father and Son – as the Nazarenes call them – went for a Mexican wax, suggested Rav Kahana.

So that's the fundamental difference between the Jewish God and the Christian God, mused Bar Kappara. Body hair. The goys put them through a de-simianization program.

You mean de-Semitization, interjected Yontl the Librarian. That's the literary critic Irving Howe's concept. To make a Jew look like a goy: de-Semitization.

No I mean, de-simianization, corrected Bar Kappara. To make the Jew look less like a monkey.

What, they didn't teach you that in grad school, Dr. Yontl? said Rav Sheshet with a touch of rebuke. We coin terms too, Doctor-Librarian, and we don't have your fancy-shmancy degree.

I think we've established some important Halakhah today regarding the naked Jewish body, said Rav Huna. And all I have to add is that it's a damn shame we couldn't have invited God to come for a Mexican wax with us, concluded Rav Pappa. We could have taken his bad naked and transformed it into good naked. Imagine if God had gotten a wax much earlier on in Jewish history.

Then he would have had no bush that didn't burn, noted Shimon ben Pazi. What body part would have been besieged by flame if not a bush on Mt. Sinai?

Alas, that is a discussion for another day, concluded Rav Huna.

The Strike

GEMARAH:

Happy Festivus everyone! said Resh Lakish, in a rare jovial mood. I've had so many problems with you people this past year and now I'm going to beat the crap out of all of you!

It's April 8 today, replied Bar Kappara. We already celebrated Festivus on December 23. It always falls around Hanukkah and the birthday of Yoshke Pandrek the Nazarene. Remember?

Right, when we removed the aluminum pole from the crawlspace we found it next to Zutra's jar of foreskins, said Rav Sheshet.

A Festivus miracle! shouted Shimon ben Pazi.

And then I rubbed it and it turned into a jug of foreskins, said Rav Pappa.

Another Festivus miracle! shouted Shimon ben Pazi.

You're jokes are so old, Pappa. You're hung up on petzl humor from the 1960s, said Rav Huna. And, be forewarned, if you also rubbed the aluminum pole, we don't want to hear what it turned into.

The 1960s were my formative decade, in a metaphysical sense, replied Rav Pappa cryptically.

In any case, said Rav Huna, finally intervening, on December 23 we celebrated Festivus. Today we discuss "Festivus" as a ritual practice, because "The Strike" is the current episode in our *Seinfeld* lineup.

What's there to discuss? asked Rabbah. Frank Costanza is a meshugeneh whack job who goes around inventing painful holidays. Who does that?

We do, said Rav Pappa. We Jews do it all the time.

For example? said Bar Kappara.

Yom Kippur, said Rav Pappa. We need to apologize to everyone we have wronged and then repent before God while depriving ourselves of food and pleasure. Otherwise God will put us in the "Book of Death." That's downright sadistic. It has always scared the crap out of me.

Gee, I wonder why, retorted Resh Lakish.

Pappa, Yom Kippur was ordained by God; it's in the Torah: "On the tenth day of the seventh month you must deny yourselves ... because on this day atonement will be made for you, to cleanse you. Then, before the Lord, you will be clean from all your sins." (Leviticus 16:29-30).

OK, so what about the Kapparot ritual? countered Rav Pappa. Where in the Torah does it instruct us to defile a rooster by spinning it around our head?

The Sages stared off into space in silence.

It appears there is no mention of Kapparot anywhere in the Torah, Written or Oral, noted Yontl the Librarian.

I'm with Pappa on this one, said Bar Kappara. Do you know the ridicule I experience because of my name's etymology? And come the Ten Days of Awe each year, the hooligans in the marketplace torment me; I walk around with my cranium covered in chicken sh*t.

For the official record, Kappara, asked Yontl the Librarian, would that be chicken sh*t, rooster sh*t, or hen sh*t?

All three of them said Rav Sheshet. They're all defecating on Bar Kappara.

That's perverse, said Shimon ben Pazi.

And unlike horse manure, there is nothing refreshing about chicken sh*t, added Bar Kappara.

Then maybe we should start spinning ponies around our heads; we can cast all our sins upon the equine instead of the avian, suggested Rabbah.

Would a horse-faced relative of Seinfeld, like Cousin Jeffrey, also work? asked Shimon ben Pazi.

Sure, then our Jewish rituals will appear to be normal, said Rav Pappa, rolling his eyes.

Perhaps not, but at least we will enter Yom Kippur exuding a far more refreshing scent, said Rabbah.

Yom Kippur and horse manure, it even rhymes, noted Shimon ben Pazi.

So what's your point Pappa? asked Rav Huna. Our rituals are divinely ordained by HaShem. We don't question them, and if it be His will that Bar Kappara walk around covered in avian feces for ten days of the year, it is not our place to judge.

All I'm saying is that there is nothing meshugeneh about Festivus when compared to some of the bizarre rituals we Jews practice, said Rav Pappa. Spinning a chicken around your head is far more whacky than the Feats of Strength.

OK, all in favor of replacing Kapparot with the Feats of Strength, say "aye," said Rav Sheshet.

Aye, said the Sages in unison.

But we're so out of shape, said Shimon ben Pazi. The Feats of Strength is a ritual for Philistines, Roman Gladiators, and Crusaders, not for effeminate Jews.

Then we need to practice our martial abilities, suggested Rabbah.

Alright, let's rumble! said Rav Pappa.

Wait, wait, we need to start off slowly, said Rav Pappa. we need an easy target.

I know! exclaimed Rabbah. Let's attack Zutra, he's already shackled to the chair in the other room.

Everyone on Zutra! said Rav Pappa.

The is the best Festivus ever! said the Sages in unison.

The Dealership

GEMARAH:

Fellow Sages, said Rav Huna convening the meeting, given that we have neither cars nor candy bars in Pumbedita, I don't think there's much to discuss with "The Dealership."

Really? Has nobody here ever ridden their camel until it has run out of gas? asked Shimon ben Pazi.

Keep up the good work Pazi, said Resh Lakish. You're an asset to the Rabbinate.

I think he is asking if anyone has ridden their camel without quenching its thirst, suggested Rabbah.

Why would I do that to my precious "ASSMAN" camel? asked Rav Pappa. I've got the hottest two humped camel in all of Babylon. Shmerl, as I call him, gets nothing but respect from me.

There was an animal disrespected in "The Dealership," interjected Abba the Surgeon, but it was no camel. Yes, I will say it again, you are ignoring the monkey in the room.

Oy, I can't take any more of this, cried Rav Huna. Kappara get the spare set of shackles, Abba's gonna get up close and personal with Zutra.

No, Abba has a point, countered Baruch the Chimp, using the finest sign language one had ever witnessed from an ordained rabbi. The entire discourse around "grease monkey" was deeply offensive to simians everywhere.

Baruch is correct, said Resh Lakish. Both Jerry and Puddy were insulting the human adjacent. For Jerry "grease monkey" denotes someone engaged in an occupation devoid of skill, someone who is little more than an imbecile.

And Puddy took it as the insult it was intended to be. "I don't know too many monkeys who could take apart a fuel injector."

Before we cast aspersions, interjected Rav Pappa, I have to ask: can Baruch take apart a fuel injector? I suspect not.

Baruch lowered his head in shame.

That may be true, noted Rabbah, but this shortcoming has far more to do with him being a Jew than a monkey. Jews don't work well with machinery.

We must also point out that Jerry redeemed himself by extolling Koko the Chimp's command of sign language, said Rav Sheshet.

So what? said Abba the Surgeon. The implication is that the only ape worthy of respect is an ape who knows sign language. What if Baruch didn't know sign language? Would we call him a grease monkey? This is ableist rhetoric of the worst kind. And it's downright anti-simian. We have a room full of anti-simianites and it's going in my report to HR.

The shackles, Kappara, get the damn shackles, repeated Rav Huna. And some sort of gag.

Sure Huna, go ahead, continued Abba the Surgeon just as Kappara slipped on the handcuffs and prepared a bucket to cover Abba's head. You can prick the chimp, but I assure you he will bleed. Just remember, we may use a monkey as a yardstick to measure our refinement, but monkeys everywhere use humans as a yardstick to measure barbarity. And perhaps maybe one day they will rule our planet. They certainly deserve it. I am hereby taking a stand on behalf of monkeys everywhere.

Shouldn't you be out on a ledge somewhere? retorted Rabbah.

You want I should shackle him to the ledge? asked Bar Kappara. Piece of cake.

That would be perfect irony, said the Sages in unison.

Well, let's call it a day, friends. We can disband in confidence that tomorrow's discussion will be monkey-free, and to prove our lack of anti-simianism, I am even willing to let Baruch lead the shiur. Adjourned.

The Reverse Peephole

GEMARAH:

Fellow hominoids, what would you like to discuss from the Reverse Peephole?" signed Baruch the Chimp, who was leading the shiur just as Rav Huna had promised.

I would like to discuss why "Dr. Zaius" is leading the shiur, said Rav Pappa. He can't even speak Aramaic.

We made a promise, and a Jew always keeps their word. said Rav Huna. Plus his sign language is impeccable and he can mouth a few dozen words of biblical Hebrew.

What's a Dr. Zaius? asked Shimon ben Pazi.

It's Pappa trying to be funny, replied Rav Sheshet. Elaine called Puddy "Dr. Zaius" because he was walking around in that grotesque fur coat, which made him look like an ape, a talking ape to be exact, like Dr. Zaius, a character from the classic film, *Planet of the Apes*.

Isn't that the movie with Charlton Heston, said Rami bar Hama? We can't rebuke a film that features our beloved dashing chiseled hunk of a liberator, our Moses of Blessed Memory.

Be that as it may, Puddy looked like an idiot in that fur coat, said Rav Pappa. He did look ape-like, which is apt for someone widely known as a grease monkey.

Wait a second, said Rav Sheshet: what's wrong with a human being taking on simian attributes, unless you are some sort of Nazi blood purity fanatic, Pappa?

Agreed, said Rav Huna. If we can permit Baruch to convert to Judaism and be ordained a rabbi, I fail to see why Puddy can't convert to monkeydom. The fur coat finalizes his transformation into a hairy burly grease monkey, who not coincidentally has a smaller vocabulary than Baruch.

And Puddy doesn't even know sign language, let alone biblical Hebrew, added Rabbah.

As HR stipulated: identity boundaries are fluid, and should anyone come out as simian, it is incumbent upon us to accept them, said Rav Huna with authority.

So then Elaine was wrong to throw his coat out the window, speculated Rav Sheshet.

Yes, and Joe Mayo was right in forcing Elaine to replace it, replied Resh Lakish.

But it was for the wrong reason, countered Rav Pappa. Joe Mayo wanted her to replace it because she was in charge of the coats. Joe Mayo had no idea she threw the coat out the window.

Elaine was in charge of the coats, said Rabbah. So it follows she is responsible for any coat that disappears.

I disagree, said Rami bar Hama. Have you never been to a restaurant and seen the sign at the coat check that states, "we are not responsible for lost items"? That policy should have been in force by default at Joe Mayo's.

And who the hell has a party like that anyway? said Rav Pappa. Putting burdens of responsibility upon your guests? Joe Mayo throws the worst parties. I'm glad Silvio ambushed him with a sock full of pennies.

But Joe Mayo was innocent, countered Rav Kahana; he wasn't shtupping Silvio's wife.

Much as Elaine was innocent as the coat check girl at Joe Mayo's apartment, said Rav Pappa.

So what's your point, Pappa? asked Rav Huna.

My point is simple, continued Rav Pappa, I learned a valuable lesson from this episode.

That simians are just like us? asked Rav Sheshet.

No that I did the right thing in reversing my peephole. I came home last night and Bar Kappara was inside waiting – for quite some time it seems – to ambush me with a sock full of shekels. I caught him in the act. And let me state for the record, he should not be comfortable with his body.

The Cartoon

GEMARAH:

Friends, said Rav Huna convening the meeting, there is some troubling matters to discuss with "The Cartoon."

Agreed, said Rav Pappa. First and foremost I am wondering, if Janet looks like Jerry does that also mean Janet looks like a horse and, if so, is George attracted to horses? Does he have a horse fetish?

It would help explain why he finds manure so refreshing, suggested Rabbah, and it raises some disturbing questions about his bathroom habits.

This conversation is gross and has nothing to do with Halakhah, said Bar Kappara, who was tending to a black eye with a frozen piece of horse manure.

I disagree, interjected Rav Huna. This conversation is in line with the script. And the script is Torah.

So then the issue raised is not whether George is secretly attracted to Jerry, not that there's anything wrong with it. That much is clear, mused Rav Sheshet. The question is whether George is openly attracted to horse manure, and whether horse-faced Janet is his gateway to it.

Had George gone straight to manure he'd be branded a fetishist, said Rav Kahana. Had he struck up a relationship with Cousin Jeffrey he'd have to come out as gay.

Or as someone attracted to the equine adjacent, suggested Rabbah.

But Freud insisted that "a certain degree of fetishism is habitually present in normal love," quoted Yontl the Librarian. So why must George have kept this a secret?

For halakhic reasons, noted Rav Pappa, citing one of his favorite rulings: "And in general, how far must one distance himself from urine and feces in order to recite Shema? At least four cubits." (Mishnah Berakhot 3:5).

Nope, that doesn't apply, said Rav Huna. We earlier ruled that there is a distinction between feces and horse manure, because the latter is refreshing, as per George Costanza's own halakhic ruling. So it follows that George has no reason to hide his attraction to manure, which I will add he never has in the past.

Agreed, said Bar Kappara. He even managed to charm Marisa Tomei with his musings on manure, and she doesn't even look like a horse.

So then maybe George is embarrassed that he's attracted to horses, said Rabbah, and this has nothing to do with manure. You know not everything has to do with manure.

And maybe this has nothing to do with horses, said Rav Kahana. Maybe he's just attracted to people who look like horses.

And, accordingly, this explains why George is secretly attracted to Jerry, ruled Rav Huna, which was the main takeaway from the episode: George is attracted to horse-faced people. I think we're done here.

So we're not going to debate whether Jay Riemenschneider is secretly attracted to horse manure? asked Shimon ben Pazi.

Pazi, said Bar Kappara, why do you have so much trouble following our discussions?

The Strongbox

GEMARAH:

Let's cut to the chase: they murdered a bird and then dug up his corpse, said Rav Huna, jump starting the meeting.

Jerry and Kramer are not to blame, said Rav Pappa. Nobody told Fredo to eat the damn key. It was his fault.

"I know it was you Fredo!" said Shimon ben Pazi doing his best Al Pacino impression, which admittedly fell short and was thus ignored.

But it was an accident, said Rav Pappa.

Yeah, right, it was an "accident," said Resh Lakish. Why is it that the Seinfeld gang keeps killing birds "by accident"?

Yontl, please read back the minutes on the Seinfeld Four's ongoing alleged avicide, said Rav Huna.

Dead birds on *Seinfeld*, began Yontl the Librarian: Jerry took out Miss Rhode Island's doves because they were causing a ruckus; George accidentally ran over some pigeons while trying to impress his lady friend with his car wash; Kramer fed Fredo the key to his strongbox.

And every one of those cases was an accident, countered Rav Pappa. As George said, "we had a deal with the pigeons," and they violated the deal.

That's true, but then George deliberately stomped on some pigeons in the park, as a mother and son looked on in horror, said Bar Kappara.

That's because he was testing the stability of the deal, countered Rav Pappa again. He later swerved his car to avoid hitting a pigeon, in an effort to make peace with our feathered friends.

He wanted to make peace solely to appease his girlfriend, since he wasn't, as you would put it Pappa, "getting any," said Bar Kappara. And in the process he ran over a squirrel and then petitioned the doctor to put the squirrel to sleep.

But he ultimately agreed to save the squirrel, said Rav Pappa, and he had those tiny little instruments flown in. Then George, being such a Good Samaritan, agreed to take the squirrel into his home as his pet, even though the squirrel was "a wild invalid" who knew Costanza had tried to kill him.

Again, countered Bar Kappara, he did all that to get laid. He would have gladly pulled the plug on the squirrel, much as he took out the pigeons. And this, I will argue, fits the pattern of the Seinfeld Four's ongoing zoocide, with Fredo being the most recent victim. We haven't even mentioned the kidnapped dog, the prospective extermination of a couple of cats, and that infamous pony in Poland.

I have to agree with Kappara, said Resh Lakish. Even if we allow that Kramer's imbecility exonerates him from Fredo's death, he and Jerry nevertheless became grave robbers.

It was a barbaric act and, dare say I say, the writers depicted it with antisemitic overtones, insisted Bar Kappara.

Antisemitic overtones? said Rav Huna. Please elaborate, Kappara.

The Jews are often falsely accused of digging up animal corpses and mutilating their bodies for malevolent ritual purposes including the reenactment of the crucifixion, said Bar Kappara. They call it "the Bird Libel."

The Sages laughed in unison.

Potz, said Rav Huna, that's "the Blood Libel" and the alleged victims are young Christian boys, not parakeets. There is no such thing as Bird Libel.

Forgive my intervention, said Yontl the Librarian, but were we not recently discussing the etymology of Bar Kappara's name, insofar as it possibly originates from the Jewish habit of spinning a chicken around one's head.

Yontl has a point, said Rav Pappa. That's why Kappara often gets attacked with chicken sh*t, rooster sh*t, and hen sh*t in the marketplace. Kappara is regularly subject to Bird Libel.

But those are Jewish hooligans who are making fun of him, countered Rav Huna, not enraged Christians accusing us of Christ-killing. This has nothing to do with antisemitism, let alone with the exhumation of Fredo's corpse.

Nevertheless, said Bar Kappara, we see the pernicious harm that the Kapparot ritual has done to our reputation. Bird Libel is a reality and I'm its principal victim.

But if the Seinfeld Four attacked our feathered friends with such vicarious cruelty, does it not imply that Bird Libel has a basis in reality, asked Rabbah.

A valid point, Rabbah, said Rav Huna. Even if we stopped spinning chickens around our head we would still be a persecuted people because of Seinfeld and company's ruthlessness toward animals.

So maybe Abba was correct all along, mused Resh Lakish. We are so anthropocentric. We treat animals like garbage, like our playthings, with the worst sadism imaginable. Yet we'd never do that to our fellow man.

"In a place where there are no humans, one must strive to be human," as Hillel the Elder put it, mused Rav Sheshet.

Where is Abba anyway? asked Shimon ben Pazi.

I'm pretty sure, noted Rav Pappa, that we left him shackled by his beytzim to the ledge of the fifth story window and then had Baruch swallow the key to the handcuffs.

The Wizard

GEMARAH:

Well my rabbinical colleagues, said Rav Huna convening the meeting, it looks like we need to discuss race relations today.

Why? asked Rav Pappa.

Because the principal plot of the episode has Elaine dating an alleged Black man, replied Rav Huna. What else is there to discuss?

We can discuss what kind of name is Snoopy for a horse, suggested Rav Pappa.

Absolutely! Snoopy is a dog, said Shimon ben Pazi. Why would George name his horse after a dog?

The Sages chose to ignore Shimon ben Pazi, since even their jokes mocking his imbecility were over his head.

Are we even allowed to discuss race relations? asked Bar Kappara. HR's policy manual stipulates that we can't discuss a minoritized community behind their backs.

And what's to discuss? Elaine wasn't even dating a Black man in the end, said Rav Sheshet. They both turned out to be White.

Aha, said Rav Huna. Precisely. It suggests racial identification is more complex than many would have us believe.

Are we Jews white? asked Shimon ben Pazi.

The Sages sat in silence.

Pazi, that's either the most inane question ever to emanate out of your mouth or a conundrum that defies easy answer, said Rav Huna. Let's debate it.

On the one hand, we are a sweaty group of Semites from the Middle East who ride camels.

Not White! said the Sages in unison.

On the other hand, we have delicate alabaster skin waxed in the Mexican style which glistens under the scorching sun of the desert.

White! said the Sages in unison.

We also worship an angry deity who divinely revealed himself to us in the scorching sun of the desert.

Not White! said the Sages in unison.

But we only worship one God whose law is enshrined in writing, yet we live amid a sea of idol and tree worshipers.

White! said the Sages in unison.

We gave the Nazarenes their Chosen one.

White! said the Sages in unison.

And then we allegedly killed him and have been severely persecuted for it.

Not White! said the Sages in unison.

We were once slaves in Egypt.

Not White! said the Sages in unison.

And now we have slaves of our own.

White! said the Sages in unison.

We will one day be accused of occupying Palestine and colonizing the land's indigenous people.

Extra White! said the Sages in unison.

But we are the indigenous people of Palestine, and were chased out by White Europeans.

Extra not White! said the Sages in unison.

We can't ride horses without severely injuring ourselves.

Not White!

But we have a horse manure fetish.

The Sages sat in silence.

Where does horse manure fall on the racial binary? asked Bar Kappara.

I don't think it does, replied Yontl the Librarian.

So then what are we? asked Rav Sheshet.

We're Jews, replied Yontl the Librarian. And, based on the 100,000 words of debate I have compiled since Season 1, we are Jews with some serious psychological problems.

See, said Rav Pappa, this discussion was pointless.

Yontl, let's bury this transcript, said Rav Huna. I rather doubt that anyone will raise this ridiculous question about the whiteness of Jews ever again.

The Burning

THE GREAT ENCYPLODIA OF JEWISH AILMENTS:

All, said Rav Huna, convening the meeting, given that our two "medical practitioners" are "in disposed of" for the foreseeable future, we need to augment our own abilities to diagnose Jewish illnesses.

Yes, said Bar Kappara, "The Burning" has made this abundantly clear.

So we should do as Kramer and Mickey did, said Rav Pappa. Let's each perform a disease and see if anyone can guess it.

OK, I'll begin, said Rabbah. "I feel tired, weak, and thirsty all the time."

It's diabetes, he's got diabetes, diabetes! said the Sages in unison.

Correct! exclaimed Rabbah. That's it for me, goodnight everybody.

"I've got an uncontrollable itch all over my face and my body," said Rav Kahana.

Have you been wearing a fake beard? asked Shimon ben Pazi.

Wrong, said Rav Kahana.

He's got hives! Said the Sages in unison.

Wrong again, said Rav Kahana.

Fleas! He's got fleas! said the Sages in unison.

Correct! exclaimed Rav Kahana. That's it for me, goodnight everybody.

"I, I don't know what's wrong with me," cried Rav Sheshet. "I went for a biopsy. Nobody can tell me what's wrong. God will never let me be successful."

Is it lupus, Oh my God it's lupus, he's got lupus! shouted the Sages in unison.

Alright! exclaimed Rav Sheshet. That's it for me, goodnight everybody.

"I have an aching pain in my kidneys," said Resh Lakish. "Ow! I got it while being denied the lavatory in a Red Chinese Prison."

He's got uromycitisis! said the Sages in unison.

Alright! exclaimed Resh Lakish. That's it for me, goodnight everybody.

"My body has not been behaving," said Bar Kappara, "and consequently you need to keep four cubits from me before reciting your morning prayers."

What is irritable bowel syndrome? said the Sages in unison.

Alright! exclaimed Bar Kappara. That's it for me, goodnight everybody.

"My body has also not been behaving," said Rav Pappa, "and consequently you need to keep four cubits from me before reciting your morning prayers."

What is uncontrollable nocturnal emissions? said the Sages in unison.

Alright! Exclaimed Rav Pappa. That's it for me, goodnight everybody.

Well we appear to be out of Sages, Master, said Yontl the Librarian.

I know, and we've only scratched the surface of Jewish ailments, lamented Rav Huna.

Hey if you release us, shouted Zutra the Mohel from the window ledge, I can give Abba the Surgeon Gonorrhea with my deli slicer. I learned how in mohel school.

Did you hear what he said, asked Rav Huna.

Something about "purging diarrhea" over the window ledge, speculated Yontl the Librarian, straining to hear.

Been there, done that, replied Rav Huna. Meeting adjourned.

The Bookstore

GEMARAH:

Friends, said Rav Huna convening the meeting, I think the Halakhah for "The Bookstore" is pretty straightforward.

Indeed it is, said Bar Kappara. There is one question before us: who is the biggest sinner from among Leo the book thief, Kramer & Newman the slave drivers, or George, better labeled as "he who defecates within four cubits of Impressionist art"?

Who is Leo? asked Shimon ben Pazi.

Jerry's Uncle Leo, you dimwit, replied Resh Lakish.

Oh, right, "Uncle" Leo. I forgot his first name, conceded Shimon ben Pazi.

Clearly George is the biggest sinner and there is no debating the Halakhah here, said Rabbah with an air of finality.

If one defecates within 4 cubits of Impressionist art, both the art and the defecator are rendered impure, agreed Rav Kahana.

But what if the book was more than 4 cubits from George while he was sitting on the can? asked Rav Sheshet.

Impossible, replied Bar Kappara. George insisted that he found the soothing pastoral images conducive to relieving himself. He must have been holding the book.

He could have opened and stood the volume on the counter and then retreated 5 cubits to the toilet, countered Rav Pappa. So it is in theory possible the book's purity was preserved during the act of defecation.

The book is rendered impure by the very act of it being brought into the bathroom, insisted Resh Lakish.

No the book is rendered impure by the very act of George touching it, insisted Rabbah. George was already impure from urinating publicly in the health club shower.

So? He may have subsequently purified himself, countered Rav Pappa.

Yeah, right, George doesn't care about purification, said Bar Kappara. This is the same yold who admitted to "going through the motions" of washing his hands for show, after visiting the bathroom. So even if he had purified himself in the past, there is no doubt he picked up that book when he was done with his business without soaping up and washing his hands.

Are we certain George went number 2 and not number 1, asked Rav Pappa, because the Halakhah is also clear on this matter: one can urinate within 4 cubits of an object without rendering it impure, so long as there is no splash.

But one doesn't need soothing pastoral Impressionist art to urinate, countered Rabbah.

I find it helps me, admitted Rav Pappa. I learned from the cultured Europeans how to urinate with a little grace.

You can't urinate with a "little grace," countered Bar Kappara. You either gracefully urinate or urinate like someone – and again let me quote Costanza himself – who goes to the bathroom in front of a lot of people and doesn't care ("The Nose Job," s3e9). Costanza is an ungraceful urinator.

Moreover, added Rav Sheshet, you're forgetting that George may have gone to the bathroom to break wind. What is the Halakhah on ritual purity and farting?

The Sages sat in silence.

Breaking wind is somewhere between a number 1 and number 2, mused Bar Kappara. Let's call it a number 1.5. So would making a number 1.5 render a book impure?

That depends on whether the book was downwind or not, suggested Yontl the Librarian. There's plenty of Halakhah on this as well.

All signs from this episode and previous ones, concluded Rav Huna, point to George's guilt. The book is contaminated, he is contaminated, and he rendered Monk's contaminated by bringing the book into the coffee shop and placing it near food.

Yes, agreed Resh Lakish. That book should have been consigned to the fires of Gehenna. It should have been destroyed. George probably should have been destroyed too.

Isn't that a bit harsh? asked Rav Pappa. It is a sin to burn books. People too.

So what would have been the most suitable punishment for George? asked Rabbah.

He should have been forced to transport homeless people in Kramer and Newman's rickshaw, suggested Bar Kappara.

Why should George be punished for the crime against the homeless committed by Kramer and Newman? asked Rav Sheshet.

Kramer and Newman should be pulling the homeless in the rickshaw, insisted Rav Kahana. And the homeless should be given that book on Impressionist art a gift to ease their tribulation.

What could they possibly need that book for? asked Bar Kappara.

Just because they are homeless, Kappara, doesn't mean they do not yearn for soothing pastoral images to induce a number 2, countered Rav Pappa.

Where exactly do the homeless do their private business if they haven't got a home? asked Shimon ben Pazi.

The Sages sat in silence puzzling over Pazi's question.

If they were smart they would do it in the rickshaw while they have the chance, suggested Rav Sheshet.

Yes! agreed Rav Pappa. While absorbed in their book on Impressionist art.

But the book is impure, countered Bar Kappara. They can't even bring the book on the rickshaw with them.

OK, so they don't need the book, surmised Rabbah. Why? Because they will be eating those muffin stumps anyway. The bran muffin stumps are equally conducive for making number 2.

So then what do we do with this book? asked Rav Kahana.

Maybe they should just burn it, suggested Shimon ben Pazi.

And what about George? The Romans burn people all the time, pointed out Resh Lakish.

And let's not forget George did offer to burn himself – and his parents I'll add – in "The English Patient," said Rav Sheshet.

That was in order to out-Neil Mr. Peanut, said Rav Pappa. That doesn't apply here.

I think it does, concluded Rav Huna. Let us rule that George should be burned in the manner of Mr. Peanut, whose skills George so admires.

The Frogger

GEMARAH:

Fellow Sages, said Rav Huna convening the meeting, what shall we discuss from "The Frogger"?

How about whether George looks like a frog or not? suggested Shimon ben Pazi. Next! said Bar Kappara.

No Pazi has a point, said Rav Pappa. First off, it is in the script, so it is Torah. Second, our shiurs have been graced with pig men, horse faces, monkeys and apes, gigantic whales, all sorts of mutilated birds, not to mention two of every animal that was sheltered on Noah's Ark, when the boat catastrophically rammed into the Andrea Doria, causing the worst nautical catastrophe aside from Rose sinking the Titanic.

Sorry Pappa, countered Bar Kappara, Slippery Pete is the one who said George looked like a frog, and the word of Slippery Pete isn't Torah, even if he like you, once acquired a mail order bride. And, I will add, Rose didn't sink the Titanic, even if she deliberately drowned her lover.

Actually, Shlomo said he looked like a frog, not Slippery Pete, interjected Rav Huna.

OK fine, then let's discuss The Lopper, suggested Rav Pappa.

Please proceed, Pappa, said Rav Huna.

If The Lopper decapitated someone who looks like Jerry, does it not follow that The Lopper is targeting horsed-faced people, since Jerry's yichus is the Horse-Faced House of Seinfeld?

So the question is, asked Shimon ben Pazi, is Jerry a homicide target because he looks like the Lopper's previous victim or because he looks like a horse? And if the latter, doesn't Cousin Jeffrey have far more to worry about?

Seriously, said Rabbah, Cousin Jeffrey works for the Parks Department. It can't be safe for him to spend his time in the wooded areas of New York where such serial killers tend to roam. He's making himself an easy target.

I disagree, said Resh Lakish. It is far safer in the woods because that is where the actual horses of New York tend to be. Think of Ruthie Cone on horseback. There is safety in numbers, Cousin Jeffrey gets a measure of protection among the equine.

You're assuming the killer can't distinguish between a horse and a horse-faced man, countered Rav Sheshet.

Has nobody ever mistaken you for an actual pig, Sheshet? provocatively asked Resh Lakish.

Despite the occasional "wee wee wee all the way home" joke from my so-called rabbinic friends, I am pleased to say that nobody has attempted to turn me into bacon, said Rav Sheshet who finally accepted his humanoid divergent countenance and moniker. So surely a prolific murderer like The Lopper can distinguish the horse from the horse-faced?

A good point Sheshet, said Rabbah, but you assume that he's not also targeting horses. If he's targeting both the equine and the equine adjacent, then among the horses is where Cousin Jeffrey would be safest.

If George were smart he would have gotten a horse and buggy to transport the Frogger, said Shimon ben Pazi.

What's wrong with Shlomo? asked Rav Pappa. He is one of the best truck drivers.

No, he's just a good truck driver, countered Bar Kappara. And he's a "Shlomo." Jews can't drive trucks. That Frogger wouldn't have lasted five minutes.

Well Jews can't ride horses either, said Rav Sheshet. Shlomo would have smashed up that horse and the Frogger would have likewise perished.

The best solution would have been to transport the Frogger by rickshaw, suggested Rav Pappa. Shlomo could have driven the rickshaw without any problems.

Agreed, said Rami bar Hama. When we were slaves in Egypt we conducted our taskmasters on rickshaws every day, with great toil and suffering.

So then making Shlomo drive a rickshaw would have been antisemitic, countered Bar Kappara.

And poor Shlomo was worried about how much jail time they were looking at, noted Shimon ben Pazi.

It appears that Shlomo is the true victim of this episode, concluded Rav Huna. The Jews just can't get a break in New York City.

The Maid

GEMARAH:

So Chevreh, said Rav Huna convening the meeting, the question from "The Maid" is pretty straightforward: Is Jerry paying for sex?

No, insisted Rav Pappa, he's merely shtupping a woman who happens to be his maid.

Hey Pappa, would you sleep with your maid? asked Bar Kappara.

Yes, in fact I do so regularly! Thank you for asking, replied a beaming Rav Pappa. But she compensates me in shekels for the privilege of getting a juicy piece of Pappa.

First of all, gross. And second of all, you're admitting to being a prostitute? asked an alarmed Rav Huna. Yontl please stop taking minutes for a second.

Not in the least, countered Rav Pappa. I help her out with most of the cleaning; she pays me for my domestic labor. The sex is purely incidental.

I don't understand, said Bar Kappara. Your maid pays you to clean your own house?

Yes, and I can assure you our arrangement is kosher. So please stop harassing me, said Rav Pappa in anger. You're all obsessing over my carnal activities and, yet again, you are missing the bigger picture: this episode is replete with antisemitic tropes.

And, here we go again, grumbled Rav Huna. Where's the antisemitism? She didn't overcook Jerry's hamburger, she didn't convert to Judaism for the jokes, and near as I can tell there was no "Bird Libel" in this episode, an antisemitic charge I am all but certain Bar Kappara invented because of his unfortunate name and the recurrent chicken feces on his melon-shaped head.

No Pappa is correct, said Rabbah. There is a tenacious antisemitic stereotype of the perfidious Jewish employer who shtupps the Christian maid and proselytizes her; he draws her through housework out of the arms of Jesus and sucks her into the arms of Judas. She's vacuumed out of the Kingdom of Christ, in a manner of speaking. This is why the Roman Empire banned Jews from hiring Christian domestic workers.

I see no evidence that Jerry proselytized his maid, countered Rav Huna. Jerry did not convert her to Judaism.

And what about George? asked Bar Kappara. He admitted to shtupping his maid as well. Is he guilty? Did he convert her? And if so, then to what? To Latvian Orthodoxy?

There was no antisemitism here, concluded Rav Huna, this is an absurd discussion. And at the risk of sounding like Abba the Surgeon, there was far more anti-simianism in this episode.

Agreed, said Bar Kappara. George somehow got ensnared into the bosom of monkeydom and was baptized Koko the Monkey. And everyone acted as if that was some sort of humiliating joke.

Agreed, said Rav Kahana. This was an affront to our brilliant Sage Baruch, proud chimp and accomplished Rabbi. What did he ever do to deserve such disrespect?

Perhaps Baruch slept with his made and tried to convert her? suggested Rav Sheshet.

Oh no Baruch, you didn't!? said Rav Huna.

Baruch lowered his head in shame.

If the goys get wind of this they are going to launch a pogrom, said Bar Kappara.

Against whom? asked Rav Sheshet. Against Jews or against monkeys? Or does it depend on whether Baruch converted her to Judaism or monkeydom?

I think it could go either way, concluded Rav Huna. Yontl: you need to bury this. This discussion never took place. If the authorities ever inquire, we've seen nothing, heard nothing, know nothing. Baruch – I assume we can count on you to keep your mouth shut?

The Puerto Rican Day

GEMARAH:

It's a good thing Abba isn't here, said Rav Huna convening the meeting. He would endlessly kvetch about the racism in this episode.

I can hear you from the window ledge, shouted Abba the Surgeon from his Babylonian rabbinic captivity.

Did anyone hear that? asked Bar Kappara.

We heard nothing, said the Sages in unison.

So was this episode racist? asked Shimon ben Pazi.

It's hard to say, replied Rav Huna. Some have accused us Jews of being oversensitive to alleged discrimination.

That's absurd, said Bar Kappara. We Jews are targeted wherever we go, it's well documented we can't even order a hamburger without it being overcooked. I walk around with chicken sh*t, rooster sh*t, and hen sh*t on my cranium, which is a testament to our centuries of humiliation and tribulation.

Yontl, let the record show that Bar Kappara continues to blame the enemies of Israel for his unfortunate name and the normal bodily functions of the chicken, said Rav Huna.

Perhaps we should change his name to "Koko the Monkey," signed Baruch the Chimp.

"Bar Kokoppara," has a nice ring to it. Now back to the Puerto Ricans, continued Rav Huna. Apparently the Puerto Ricans resented Kramer burning their flag, even if it was accidental.

According to the American constitution it is legal to burn the American flag in the United States, said Yontl the Librarian.

But what about burning the Puerto Rican flag? asked Rav Sheshet.

That act would fall under the same protection, noted Yontl the Librarian.

But what about burning the Puerto Rican Flag IN Puerto Rico, asked Rav Sheshet.

The Sages sat in Silence.

No idea, but according to SIRI, cock fighting is deeply ingrained in Puerto Rican culture, said Yontl the Librarian, who, despite his PhD, had resigned himself to being replaced by an Apple device.

But this episode didn't take place in Puerto Rico, countered Rav Huna, so it's immaterial.

Yet the entire episode implied the inundation of New York with Puerto Ricans, said Resh Lakish.

Yes, the Seinfeld Four, the epitome of New York City, were literally imprisoned in a claustrophobic congested parade of Puerto Ricans, added Rabbah.

That's racist, shouted Abba the Surgeon from the windowsill.

I am merely offering my interpretation of this episode, countered Rabbah. Not stating a fact.

And helping Donald Trump get elected, noted Yontl the Librarian.

Look, near as I can tell this episode was entirely devoid of a plot other than the Seinfeld Four being trapped in a Puerto Rican parade, insisted Rabbah. Nothing happened.

Yes, said Rav Sheshet, this episode marked *Seinfeld*'s return to being a show about nothing.

A show about nothing with implied racism, said Bar Kappara.

A show about nothing with the implied incarceration of the Seinfeld Four, said Rav Pappa.

Agreed, shouted Zutra the Mohel from the windowsill. Imprisoning innocent Jews without cause is cruel and unusual punishment.

Did anyone hear that? asked Bar Kappara.

We heard nothing, said the Sages in unison.

Let's call it a day, concluded Rav Huna. It's Sunday night and watching 60 minutes is part of my weekend wind-down.

The Chronicle

PREAMBLE:

And on the 170th day of the most rigorous of schedules, relentlessly debating

Seinfeld, the Sages learned they were required to discuss yet another clip episode.

GEMARAH:

Yet another one-hour clip episode? said Resh Lakish yawning. Haven't we done this already?

That was way back in Season 6, replied Bar Kappara. Think of all the great debates and monumental changes that have come to the Academy since then.

He has a point, said Rav Pappa. Who could have predicted that we would get our chests waxed and acquire a monkey?

And we are better rabbis for both, said Rabbah.

Maybe some of us are, retorted Bar Kappara. But then there's Rav Pappa, who not only deflowered all four of my daughters, but shares these escapades of his with envious admirers in the marketplace every day.

Fair enough, Kappara, said Rav Huna, but our Yeshivah has nevertheless become more enlightened in so many other ways.

Yes, someone already mentioned the monkey, grumbled Bar Kappara. Some achievement.

We've become far more open to the neurodivergent, the gender queer, and the humanoid and hominid adjacent, countered Rav Huna. We have even experimented with female rabbis, which was admittedly less successful than ordaining a monkey. This is the most progressive Yeshivah in Babylon. We are in full compliance with HR's DEI guidelines. You poo-poo, Kappara, but we say, "Go Team!"

Go Team! said the Sages in unison.

I object! shouted Abba the Surgeon from the window ledge.

Did anyone hear that? asked Rabbah.

We heard nothing, said the Sages in unison.

You are all missing the point, said Rav Yehudah. We are supposed to be debating *Seinfeld*'s greatest moments, not patting ourselves on the back for having ordained a monkey and a pig man.

Such a discussion seems rather unnecessary, said Rabbah. Lord knows we rabbis have occasionally been accused of being redundant and repetitive, of saying the same things over and over again, of dissecting the minutiae of every excruciating bit of Halakhah. And now we are supposed to do that for 169 Seinfeld episodes we have already analyzed?

Rabbah has a point, said Rav Sheshet. We've covered this stuff ad nauseam, while some of the weightier issues have slipped through the cracks.

Like what? asked Rav Huna.

For instance, said Rav Sheshet, what was Kramer going to wear home after he slipped in mud in Bob Sacamano's pants, ruining the very pants he was returning?

Or what would have happened had Darren not gone away for a long, long time and instead attempted to put ketchup and mustard in the same container? suggested Rabbah.

And we never figured out if the dough becomes a pizza before or after it comes out of the oven, added Rav Kahana.

Those are important halakhic questions! admitted Rav Huna. Why have we never dissected them?

Because, began Yontl the Librarian, we decided instead to obsess over the following topics:

-Manya eating her horse-faced relative to fight off an assault by the Gazpacho Police before fleeing on the Titanic
-Zutra's uncanny ability to repeatedly overdo a circumcision as if he were trimming some sideburns
-Horse manure
-Pappa's impressive ability to shtupp every Kappara from Pumbedita to Palestine and live to tell the tale
-The proper culinary preparation and order of consumption of our flock of Rabbis should we suffer a famine after a plane crash in the Andes
-Sheshet's porcine deformity and whether he is a humanoid or hominid adjacent
-Discussing whether a pig man is lower or higher on the evolutionary scale than a monkey with a rabbinical degree who can sign in biblical Hebrew
-Discussing whether Ukraine had been part of the Netherlands, until it sank in conjunction with Holland after Abba got his medical license in Anne Frank's attic
-Horse manure
-The number of pigeons that perished at sea after Captain James Polk piloted the Andrea Doria into Noah's Ark
-Discussing the Moby Dick that swallowed George who swallowed the fly yet didn't die
-Petzls, shmekls, beytzim, dingdongs, and shlongs
-Horse manure

Gee Yontl, you make it sound as if we've accomplished nothing through our halakhic debates, lamented Rav Huna.

Not at all, said Yontl the Librarian. I am merely suggesting that our sacred Seinfeld Talmud consists of 100,000 words spoken by a gaggle of sweaty rabbis whose greatest achievement was the acquisition of an oversized chest of drawers that may or may not contain horse manure.

Well I think it's a fine document, said Rav Pappa. Future generations will marvel at the breadth of The Seinfeld Talmud's erudition and the beauty of our finely waxed chests.

And the accomplishments of our monkey, added Rami bar Hama, patting a beaming Baruch on the back.

Agreed, said Rav Huna. We are accomplished humanistic Jews who have made the world a better place, An inclusive Garden of Eden. Me so happy. Me want to cry. Group hug everyone!

Objection! shouted Zutra the Mohel from the windowsill.

Did anyone hear that? asked Bar Kappara.

We heard nothing, said the Sages in unison.

The Finale

MISHNAH:

Rabban Gamliel: What an ending to the series.

Yohanan ben Zakkai: Agreed. Those four belong in jail.

Jose the Galilean: Yet I can't help but wonder if there is an antisemitic undercurrent to this episode.

Yohanan ben Zakkai: OK Uncle Leo, please elaborate.

Jose the Galilean: They were four New Yorkers of "Jewish sensibility" marooned in as goyish a milieu as one can imagine, just minding their own business doing what tourists do, having a good time. And then they were arrested for violating a "Good Samaritan Law"?

Rabbi Tarfon: He has a point. they're literally being charged with a crime invented in that sequel to our sacred text inspired by the Hanged One, whose name we shall not mention.

Shimon bar Yochai: Yes one may argue the entire episode is a metaphor for the Jews as a persecuted people in Christian exile.

Rabban Gamliel: But they filmed someone getting robbed and laughed at him for being fat. They were literally Bad Samaritans.

Rabbi Tarfon: Yes, Gamliel has a point. Even the goys don't accuse Judas of laughing at fat people for thirty pieces of silver. And look at our own Akivah, who faced severe punishment for violating a Good Samaritan.

Rabban Gamliel: It is difficult for us to tell what is antisemitic when we have such a small sample.

Yohanan ben Zakkai: Akivah was most certainly guilty, and a Bad Samaritan. The worst. He defiled my wagon by depositing his small sample inside a Good Samaritan.

Rabbi Tarfon: A bit graphic, Zakkai?

Yohanan ben Zakkai: I'm still bitter. Akivah belongs in jail with the Seinfeld Four. Fortunately, the rest of our rabbinate is so well behaved. We will be a model community in exile, studying Torah and quietly awaiting our Messiah.

GEMARAH:

Friends, said Rav Huna convening the meeting, let's discuss –
[Banging on the door]
Open up in the name of the Sassanid authorities, came a voice from outside.
May we help you? asked Rav Huna.
You are all under arrest for violating the fundamental laws of the land, said the Persian soldier.
For what? asked an incredulous Rav Huna. What exactly are the charges?
You are being charged with the following, continued the soldier:

-Taking pleasure in the misfortune of Gentiles
-Taking pleasure in the misfortune of Jews
-Taking pleasure in the misfortune of animals
-Exploiting a monkey

Objection! said Bar Kappara. We reject the first three charges on the grounds of freedom of speech. And we demand an accounting of how exactly we have exploited a monkey.

Well, continued the soldier, you forcibly converted him to another religion, mutilated his body with a deli slicer, and compelled him to take a rabbinic exam in a language he barely speaks.

That's not fair, said Bar Kappara. Baruch's biblical Hebrew is impeccable and we're working on his Aramaic.

What else have you got? asked an alarmed Rav Huna.

You are charged with employing a physician who performed surgery with a license from a country of questionable existence, read the soldier.

Yontl, didn't you find Ukraine on the map? asked Rav Huna. Please show the soldier the map.

The problem is that it depends on the map, replied Yontl. Ukraine may or may not exist.

This surgeon is also charged with performing unauthorized upper body gender reassignment surgery without a license, read the soldier.

We will have to challenge that one, said Bar Kappara. You should have seen how bosomy Resh Lakish and his family members were before the operation.

Objection, said Resh Lakish. I would have been far happier in a mansier.

The authorities would like to question this surgeon, demanded the soldier. Where is he?

Uh … he's shackled to the windowsill, replied Rav Huna.

And you are also charged with the illegal confinement of an unlawful surgeon, continued the soldier. We are also charging you with having employed a second-rate tailor to cover up the sloppy work of a third-rate mohel.

Objection! said Motl the Tailor. I was healing the shabby handiwork of a butcher who got his mohel license out of a Cracker Jack box.

Well then the authorities would also like to question this mohel, said the soldier. Where is he?

Uh … he's shackled to the windowsill, replied Rav Huna.

And you are also charged with the unlawful confinement of a third-rate mohel, continued the soldier.

What else you got? asked Rav Huna.

You, continued the soldier, are also charged with:

-Keeping horse manure in some oversized Farbman chests of drawers and then forcing rabbis to sleep in them.

-Making fun of the disabled, the neurodivergent, the gender queer, Polish people, Helen Keller, and Jesus.

-Sinking the Titanic and accusing poor Rose of being a liar and a tramp.

You will never get the Titanic charge to stick, countered Bar Kappara. I'm calling my lawyer.

Is your lawyer also shackled to the windowsill? asked the soldier. Because we can always amend the charges.

How did you find us out? asked Rav Huna.

So you are admitting your guilt? asked the soldier.

Nope, replied Rav Huna. We are pleading the Fifth!

The fifth of what? replied the Soldier. Please speak in plain Aramaic.

I still don't understand how you got wind of us, repeated Rav Huna.

Well for starters, we smelled the oversized manure-laden Farbman drawers and followed the stench of your sweaty Sages. Here's a tip: don't build a Yeshivah upwind of a police station. Second, it was the Monkey, continued the soldier. He came in and pressed charges. He told us everything. We agreed to drop the charges we had laid against him: having shtupped, proselytized, and converted his Persian maid.

Out of curiosity, did Baruch convert her to Judaism or Simianism? asked Rav Huna.

That remains unclear, admitted the soldier. Finally, your beloved Rav Pappa corroborated everything.

You ratted us out Pappa? asked an angry Bar Kappara. How could you?

I felt it was time to be on the right side of the law, replied Rav Pappa evasively.

Actually, he agreed to testify in return for us letting him serve out his sentence in a women's facility.

That's caged heat, said Rav Pappa. Pappa's ready to be cuffed and taken away. Pappa will tell all the gals he's new on the cell block. Pappa will take in a shower fight. Pappa's not threatened by their sexuality. On the contrary, Pappa's pretty sweet on the Persian prison system.

Afterword

Jewish Luck and the
Persian Prison System

It is told that the Babylonian Sages lived out their days in the Sassanid Persian prison system, except for: Abba the Surgeon and Zutra the Mohel, whom the authorities left shackled to the windowsill out of convenience; Rav Sheshet, who was incarcerated in the "Oversized Farbman Drawers for Wildlife and the Hominid Divergent;" and Baruch, who finally – like any good Jewish primate – enrolled in law school to make his mother happy.

As for Rav Pappa, rumor has it that he perished in the shower after instigating a tickle fight. He was unaware that prison orgies were more likely to degenerate into gang warfare than a ménage à trois. But it is said that Pappa died with a smile on his face while the scent of his weirdo orgy lotions wafted down the prison corridor.

Fortunately, Yontl served his time as jailhouse librarian and devoted his days and nights to compiling The Seinfeld Talmud for future generations. "May the wretchedness of our exile be comforted by The Seinfeld Talmud," he wrote in his afterword. "This is the script. This is our Torah. And these Persian prison pretzels are making me thirsty."

Glossary

Note: if a Jewish word is missing from this list, it is safe to assume it means "penis."

Apikores – A Jew who is lax in his observance, an atheist.

Avraham Avinu – Hebrew for Abraham our Forefather.

Adon Olam – A Jewish liturgical hymn that's part of daily services.

Amoraim (sing: Amora) – The Sages who compiled the Gemarah, commentary on the Mishnah, that forms the bulk of the Talmud; they were located in Palestine (Israel) and in Babylon (Persia).

Bar Kochbah – A false messiah who led a massive rebellion against the Roman Empire between 132-135 CE.

Bogdan Khmelnitsky – a Ukrainian Cossack who conducted a massacre of thousands of Jews between 1648-1649.

Beytzim (sing: beytzah) – Eggs, testicles. Most of our rabbis had two of them.

Boruch HaShem – Thank God, literally "Blessed is the Name."

Chazer – The Jewish word for pig in Hebrew and Yiddish.

Chevreh – Friends.

Chevrutah – Traditional rabbinic approach to studying the Talmud in pairs or small groups.

Chutzpah – Audacity.

Cubit – An ancient unit of measurement, app. 17.5 inches.

Daven – Pray.

Dina d'malkhuta dina – "The law of the land is the law" – A central tenet of the Jews of the talmudic era, proclaiming them a people in exile bound to the laws of the land in which they lived.

Gemarah – The commentary on the Mishnah that forms the bulk of the Talmud, compiled in Babylon c. 500 CE.

Gonef – Thief.

Goyishe kop – Literally "the head of a Gentile," used to describe a stupid person.

Haggadah – The text ritually read by participants during the Passover Seder.

Halakhah – The entire body of Jewish law.

HaShem – Literally, "The Name," the respectful way Jews refer to God in everyday conversation.

Hanged One – A Jewish euphemism for Jesus.

Kapparot – An atonement ritual Jews practice on the eve of Yom Kippur in which a chicken is waved over an individual's head.

Keinehora – A Yiddish expression to ward off the evil eye or bad luck.

Kehilla – A pre-modern Jewish community or the council that governed it.

Kreplach – Small dumplings filled with ground meat, mashed potatoes, or another filling.

Kvetch – To complain, whine.

Lahshon harah – The wicked tongue, i.e. to speak ill of someone.

Lemechke – See Shmegegge.

Lomed Vovnik – A "36er," coming from the mystical belief that 36 righteous Jews walk the earth at any given moment.

Luftmensh – A man who lives on air, i.e. an impoverished person who must eek out a living through any scheme he can concoct.

Lulav – The palm branch waved during the ritual for the Jewish festival Sukkot.

Makher – Someone who gets things done, a wheeler-dealer, a big shot.

Mamzer – A bastard.

Mar – Mister.

Mashgiach – A Jewish person empowered to supervise and determine whether a food distribution site is kosher or not.

Meshpuchah – Family.

Menshlichkeit – Manliness, in the sense of a good wholesome, caring person.

Meshugeneh – Crazy, a crazy person.

Mikvah – A pool of water in which Jews immerse themselves to become ritually pure according to Jewish law.

Milchig or Fleishig Dishes – Milk or meat dishes. Jewish law mandates the use of separate dishes and utensils for milk and meat products.

Mishnah – A compilation of rabbinic discussions surrounding the Torah; compiled in Palestine C. 200 CE. In many talmudic texts a passage from the Mishnah precedes a passage from the Gemarah.

Mitzvah – Good deed.

Mohel – The person who performs the Jewish ritual of circumcision.

Narishkeit – Yiddish term for foolishness.

Nazarene – A person from Nazareth, or a follower of Jesus, the alleged messiah from Nazareth.

Nephilim – Giant beings who inhabited the earth before the Flood according to the Bible.

Nitl Nakht and Nitl Tog – Christmas Eve and Christmas Day.

Oral Torah – A companion to the written Torah (Pentateuch) also allegedly given to Moses on Mount Sinai. It the foundation upon which the Talmud was written.

Parthians, the Parthian Empire – The Parthians preceded the Sassanids as the rulers of ancient Persia. As a professional historian I felt it necessary to give them a moment in the spotlight. That said, I know nothing of their attire, or the role nudity played in their downfall.

Pesachdick – Appropriate for or kosher for Passover (Pesach).

Petzl – A small penis.

Peyos – Sidelocks or sideburns commonly worn by traditional and orthodox Jews, as stipulated in Jewish law.

Pirkei Avot – The section of the Mishnah that recounts the transmission of the Oral Torah from Moses to the early Sages.

Potz – A regular sized penis.

Pumbedita – A city in Babylon where the talmudic sages built Yeshivahs and had their talmudic debates.

Rabbeinu – Our Rabbi.

Rakhmones – Pity, empathy.

Sassanids – The rulers of the Persian Empire between the 224-651 CE, during which time the Babylonian Sages compiled the Talmud.

Shabbosdick – Appropriate for or in the spirit of the Jewish Sabbath (Shabbos).

Shicker – A drunk.

Seychel – Wit, intelligence.

Shema – "Shema Israel," one of the most important prayers in Judaism, recited daily.

Sheyneh meydl – A pretty young woman.

Sheyneh ponim – A pretty face, pretty woman.

Shiksa – A non-Jewish woman.

Shiur – Lesson.

Shlepp – To carry heavy things, a burden, see Shlepper

Shlepper – One who carries things, a servant; also, an incompetent stupid person.

Shlong – See Potz.

Shmegegge – A moron, dolt, etc.

Shmekl – See Petzl.

Shmendrik – See Shmegegge.

Shmuck – See Potz.

Shmutz – Dirt, filth, garbage.

Shnorrer – A mooch, beggar, who professes a moral right to other people's things.

Shnoz – Nose.

Shnook – See Shmegegge.

Shtreymel – A fur hat worn by devout Jewish men of certain sects.

Shtupp – Sexual intercourse.

Shvitz – Sweat, or a sweat lodge, as in a sauna.

Sufganiyah – A Jelly donut that Jews commonly eat during Hanukkah

Talmud – The compendium of Jewish law including the numerous debates conducted by the Rabbis collected in the Mishnah and Gemarah; compiled in Palestine (Israel) and in Babylon (Persia) between 400-500 CE.

Tefillin – Phylacteries worn by Jews during prayer.

Tohu Vavohu – Chaos, Disorder. The term used to describe the earth in Genesis 1, before God created light.

Torah – The Pentateuch, but more broadly, Jewish law as received by Moses on Mt. Sinai and later interpreted by the rabbis.

Treyf – Not kosher.

Tzaddik – A righteous person.

Tzedakah – Charity.

Tzimmes – Ruckus. Literally a casserole in Jewish cooking.

Tzitzit – The fringes or tassels worn by devout Jews to remind them of the Commandments.

Vilna Gaon – Elijah ben Solomon Zalman, an eminent Jewish sage who lived in Lithuania, 1720-1797.

Wise Men of Chelm – a mythical village of Jewish fools, located in Poland.

Yavneh – The principal center of Rabbinic life in Palestine (Israel) after the destruction of the Second Temple, where the Mishnah and the Jerusalem Talmud were redacted.

Yeshivah – An academy of rabbinic learning and Torah study.

Yeshivah bokher – A praiseworthy student of the Talmud at the yeshivah.

Yeshu, Yoizl, Yoshke Pandrek – Various Jewish terms for Jesus Christ, some derogatory.

Yichus – Pedigree, one's ancestors.

Yiddishe kop – Literally "Jewish head," used to describe an intelligent person.

Yold – See Shmegegge.

Yontef – A Jewish holiday on which work is prohibited

Z"L – Of blessed memory, may they rest in peace, used after a reference to people who have died.

Zaftig – Having a full rounded figure; plump.

Zohar – An important work of Jewish mysticism (Kabbalah) allegedly written by Shimon bar Yochai, but in reality composed many centuries later.